BASIC ORGANIZATIONAL BEHAVIOR

John R. Schermerhorn, Jr.
Ohio University

James G. Hunt
Texas Tech University

Richard N. Osborn
Wayne State University

John Wiley & Sons, Inc.
New York • Chichester • Brisbane • Toronto • Singapore

For MiMi with love.
—Bob

To my mother for her love, wisdom, and support.
—Dick

For Arja and Eero who have helped me
more than they know.
—Jerry

ACQUISITIONS EDITOR   Tim Kent
ASSISTANT EDITOR   Ellen Ford
MARKETING MANAGER   Debra Riegert
SENIOR PRODUCTION EDITOR   John Rousselle
DESIGNER   Harry Nolan
MANUFACTURING OPERATIONS DIRECTOR   Susan Stetzer
FREELANCE ILLUSTRATION COORDINATOR, SR.   Edward Starr
ILLUSTRATOR   Scott Dougald
COVER PHOTO   Westlight/M. Angelo

This book was set in 10/12 Century Old Style by Achorn Graphics and
printed and bound by Donnelley (Crawfordsville). The cover was printed by Phoenix Color Corp.

Library of Congress Cataloging-in-Publication Data

Schermerhorn, John R.
    Basic organizational behavior / John R. Schermerhorn, Jr., James
G. Hunt, Richard N. Osborn.
        p.   cm.
    Includes index.
    ISBN 0-471-10768-9 (pbk.)
    1. Organizational behavior.   2. Management.   I. Hunt, James G.,
1932–   . II. Osborn, Richard.   III. Title.
HD58.7.S338   1995
658—dc20
                                                                        94-41702
                                                                        CIP

Printed in the United States of America

10 9 8 7 6 5 4 3 2 1

PREFACE

Basic Organizational Behavior brings to its readers the essentials of organizational behavior in a compact format and with a strong managerial theme. As the authors, we recognize many important changes taking place in the manager's environment, and we respect their implications for new organizational forms and management practices. Workforce diversity, the global economy, quality and competitive advantage, and managerial ethics are integrating themes in our teaching and in our writing. With a firm anchor in this dynamic action context and in the discipline of organizational behavior, *BOB* stresses a theory-into-practice view that helps its readers understand how core organizational behavior concepts and theories can be utilized in today's dynamic work settings.

This edition of *Basic Organizational Behavior* is presented in the format of a professional book, with open page layouts and clear text. Study questions begin each chapter to provide direction for the reader; they also help to organize a chapter-ending summary. Occasional figures within each chapter clarify concepts, while Effective Manager boxes highlight special applications. The list of suggested readings at the end of the book can also help readers further explore selected topics for research projects or personal interest.

Importantly, *BOB* is an efficient and practical paperback book that tries to make the essentials of organizational behavior accessible to the reader. We believe it can meet the needs of instructors who want their students to gain a basic introduction to organizational behavior without bearing the cost of using a larger textbook. Thus, we are pleased to offer to you this edition of *Basic Organizational Behavior.*

Acknowledgments

Basic Organizational Behavior has benefitted from the insights of several management educators whose reviews of draft versions greatly improved the quality of the finished manuscript. We express our appreciation to: Joseph Garcia, Western Washington University; John Stengrevics, Babson College; Richard Litherland, Friends University; Vernon Buck, University of Washington; and Gail Hankins, North Carolina State University.

Thanks also go to Petri Olin for his assistance with the manuscript. In addition, we are indebted to Tim Kent, our editor at John Wiley & Sons, and his excellent supporting staff for making this book possible. Tim's devotion to the basic book concept, and the Wiley team's commitment to product quality and timeliness were motivating and indispensable to us. John, Jerry, and Dick thank profusely the following Wiley professionals for putting their imprints on *Basic Organizational Behavior:*

John Rousselle, Senior Production Editor; Ellen Ford, Assistant Editor; Harry Nolan, Designer; Debra Riegert, Marketing Manager; Susan Stetzer, Manufacturing Operations Director; and Edward Starr, Senior Freelance Illustration Coordinator.

John Schermerhorn
Jerry Hunt
Dick Osborn

BRIEF CONTENTS

C O N T E N T S

PART I
THE NEW WORK ENVIRONMENT

PART II
INDIVIDUALS IN ORGANIZATIONS

CHAPTER **5**   **MOTIVATION AND REWARDS**   67

CHAPTER **6**   **REINFORCEMENT, PAY PRACTICES, AND SELF-MANAGEMENT**   81

CHAPTER 7   JOB DESIGN, GOAL SETTING, AND PERFORMANCE APPRAISAL   94

PART III
GROUPS IN ORGANIZATIONS

PART IV
PROCESSES IN ORGANIZATIONS

CHAPTER **12**   **COMMUNICATION AND DECISION MAKING**   176

PART V
ORGANIZATIONS

CHAPTER **15**   **ORGANIZATIONAL DESIGN**   235

CHAPTER **16**   **ORGANIZATIONAL CULTURE**   252

CHAPTER **17**   ORGANIZATIONAL CHANGE AND DEVELOPMENT   269

ORGANIZATIONAL

BEHAVIOR AND

MANAGEMENT

As you read Chapter 1, keep in mind these study questions:

- What is organizational behavior?

- Why is organizational behavior useful for managers?

- What are organizations?

- Who are the managers in organizations?

- What is the management process?

- What is the day-to-day nature of managerial work?

This book is about people at work in organizations. It pays special attention to their performance accomplishments and job satisfaction. It is also about **managers,** those individuals in an organization who are responsible for work that is accomplished through the performance contributions of one or more other persons. Being a manager is a unique challenge that carries distinct responsibilities. People are key and irreplaceable resources of organizations. They deserve to be treated well, and they deserve every opportunity to use their full capabilities to achieve the highest possible performance results. A manager's job is to make sure that these opportunities exist. Simply put, a manager's job is to help other people get important things done in a timely and high-quality fashion.

What Is Organizational Behavior?

Formally defined, **organizational behavior** (OB) is the study of individuals and groups in organizations. It is a body of knowledge that has special implications. Tomorrow's world of work will be different from the one in which past managers achieved their great success. Frankly, the challenges for you and other managers of the future may actually be greater. The workplace is changing, and it will continue to do so. A *Fortune* magazine article entitled "Managing in the Midst of Chaos" describes the situation this way: "Call it whatever you like—reengineering, restructuring, transformation, flattening, downsizing, rightsizing, a quest for global competitiveness—it's real, it's radical, and it's arriving every day at a company near you."[1] The same article poses the following challenge to you and other managers whose careers must unfold in such a setting: "the revolution feels something like this: scary, guilty, painful, liberating, disorienting, exhilarating, empowering, frustrating, fulfilling, confusing, challenging. In other words, it feels very much like chaos."[2]

Your study of organizational behavior must be grounded in full awareness of the complex and shifting demands that this dynamic environment will make of you. The successful twenty-first century manager will understand these and other "realities" of the new workplace:

1. **The workforce is changing.** The watchwords of the day include *workforce diversity, workforce skills,* and *workforce values.*[3] Managers must be prepared to deal well with people of different ethnic and racial backgrounds, of different genders and ages, of different life-style preferences, and of different personal values. They must also be prepared to deal with workers whose skills, whether gained through formal education or on the job, may not be consistent with the demands of new technologies and changing workplace tasks. And

they must be prepared to deal with workers whose values reflect a dynamic society in which family values, environmental concerns, and the very concept of a career are changing. The successful twenty-first-century manager will value diversity and will always find ways to meet the needs of a multicultural workforce.

2. **Customer expectations are changing.** In today's marketplace, only organizations that are able to deliver what customers want in terms of *quality, service,* and *cost* will prosper. This is the age of **total quality management,** that is, management dedicated to ensuring that an organization and all of its members operate with commitments to continuous improvement and totally meeting customer needs.[4] The successful twenty-first-century manager will value quality and customers, and will personally do things that add value to the organization's ability to meet customers' needs.

3. **Organizations are changing.** They are changing now, and they will continue to change in order to survive and prosper in a complex environment. We see organizations downsizing, forming alliances, creating new structures, going global, and employing ever more sophisticated technologies as they attempt to deal with competitive pressures. We see organizations pursuing productivity gains, pressing for innovation, and trying to adapt themselves to best fit changing times. Some of the terms heard now in the executive suites include "reengineering," "network organizations," "virtual corporations," and more. By all indications, the successful twenty-first-century manager must be comfortable working in and with organizations operating in new and different ways.

4. **Managers must change too.** There is no doubt about it; the directions are clear; the future is there. But in order to succeed, managers must be willing to step forward and make the personal and organizational changes necessary to secure it. Indeed, some consultants and authors are questioning the very term *manager.*[5] They believe that the changing nature of organizations in the new workplace may make the term *coordinator,* or perhaps *coach* or *facilitator,* a more apt description of the role. Regardless of the term used, however, the message is clear. The successful twenty-first-century manager must make the behavioral and attitudinal adjustments necessary to succeed in very dynamic times.

Usefulness of Organizational Behavior

The field of organizational behavior helps managers both deal with and learn from their workplace experiences. A manager who understands OB is better prepared to know what to look for in work situations, to understand what they find, and to take or help others to take the required action. This is a process for which physicians are carefully trained. When giving a physical exam, a doctor systematically asks questions and is quick to note where one condition (such as a recurrent facial sore) may be symptomatic of a problem that requires further medical attention (treatment for a small skin cancer). Instead of sores and headaches, the manager's action indicators typically deal with the performance accomplishments of people at work, their attitudes and behaviors, and events that occur in the work unit, in the organization as a whole, and even in the external environment. Good managers are able both to recognize the significance of these indicators (for example, an increase in turnover among employees) and to take constructive action to improve things as a result of this insight (such as updating benefits and incentive pay schemes).

Basic Organizational Behavior offers a meaningful introduction to OB and its managerial implications in the new workplace. Our goal as authors, as suggested in the accompanying Memorandum to the Reader, is to help you become a successful and respected manager of individuals and groups in any work setting—small or large, public or private. The book is organized into five major parts, with each one covering basic concepts, important theories, and practical applications relating to a core OB topic. The parts are organized in a logical building-block fashion: Part 1 deals with the *environment;* Part 2 with *individuals;* Part 3 with *groups;* Part 4 with *processes;* and Part 5 with *organization.* As you read and study the material, remember that OB provides managers with at least three important capabilities: (1) a way of systematically thinking about the behavior of people at work; (2) a vocabulary of terms and concepts that allow work experiences to be analyzed, shared, and discussed clearly; and (3) a set of techniques for dealing with the problems and opportunities that commonly occur in work settings.[6]

A Brief History of Organizational Behavior

Organizational behavior first emerged as an academic discipline during the late 1940s. It is an interdisciplinary body of knowledge that draws on a variety of scholarly vantage points to build concepts, theories, and understandings about human behavior in organizations. OB has strong ties to the behavioral sciences, such as psychology, sociology, and anthropology, as well as to allied social sciences, such as economics and political science. OB is also unique in its devotion to applying and integrating these diverse insights to promote a better understanding of human behavior in organizations.

Among the special characteristics of OB are its applied focus, its contingency orientation, and its emphasis on scientific inquiry. OB is an *applied* scientific discipline that tries to answer practical questions; "relevancy" is an important criterion for OB-related research. The ultimate goal of the field is to help people and organizations achieve high performance levels and to help ensure that all organization members achieve satisfaction from their work.

Rather than assume that there is "one best" or universal way to manage people and organizations, OB adopts a *contingency approach.*[7] That is, OB researchers try to identify how different situations can be understood and best be dealt with. They will not endorse any advice that suggests that there is "one best way" to manage in all circumstances. Today, for example, OB scholars recognize that "cultural differences" among people may affect the way theories and concepts of management apply

MEMORANDUM

To: The Student
From: John Schermerhorn, Jerry Hunt, Dick Osborn
Subject: Basic Organizational Behavior

This book has been designed with you—the student—in mind. By content and design it is intended for serious students who want to understand the essentials of organizational behavior and their value for managers today. From a practical standpoint, we wanted to make the material accessible for you. In order to accomplish this, we designed the book in the following manner:

- Study Questions These open every chapter and provide not only an overview of the chapter, but show you the framework of the chapter and directly tie in to the chapter summaries.
- Section Headings These are the major points in each chapter. You will see that they match the chapter objectives. If you understand the objectives of each chapter beforehand, it will be easier to study the material.
- Effective Manager Boxes These boxes are used to identify ways to immediately apply a concept or theory in the text.
- In Summary The summaries are organized in a question and answer format and refer back to the study questions at the beginning of each chapter.
- Glossary This list of key terms and definitions at the end of the book serves as a resource for review purposes.

In addition, as you read and study this book, keep in mind the following points:

1. The issues, concepts, theories, and insights it presents are relevant to managers working in organizations of all types and sizes.
2. The best learning about OB is active learning; you should actively experiment with and apply the book's ideas in your personal experiences.
3. The book is designed to help you become quickly familiar with the core content of OB while still recognizing theory-into-practice applications.

Finally, remember that we believe Basic Organizational Behavior is more than a textbook. It is an introduction to a very useful body of knowledge—one that can help you succeed as a manager in any career setting.

in different countries.[8] What works well in one cultural setting—such as individual incentive schemes in the highly individualistic American culture—may not work as well somewhere else where different cultural influences predominate—such as in the more collectivist cultures of Asia.

OB uses *scientific methods* to develop and empirically test generalizations about behavior in organizations.[9] The scientific foundations of OB emphasize the use of solid research methods and designs, in which (1) the process of data collection is controlled and systematic; (2) proposed explanations are carefully tested; and (3) only explanations that can be scientifically verified are accepted.

Learning about Organizational Behavior

We believe that an understanding of organizational behavior can help you master the challenges of change. Your learning about OB may begin with this book and an OB course. But it can, and should, continue in the future as you benefit from actual work experiences. Indeed, your most significant learning about OB may well come with the passage of time and as your career progresses. But it will do so only *if* you prepare well and *if* you are diligent in taking maximum advantage of each learning opportunity that arises. As management consultant Tom Peters says, "Students: Remember that (1) education is the *only* ticket to success and (2) it doesn't stop with the last certificate you pick up. Education is the 'big game' in the globally interdependent economy."[10]

The process of continuous learning from the full variety of your actual work and life experiences is called life-long learning. It is both a personal responsibility and a prerequisite to your long-term career success. Day-to-day work experiences, conversations with colleagues and friends, counseling and advice from mentors, training seminars and workshops, professional reading and videotapes, and the information available in the popular press and mass media all provide frequent opportunities for continuous learning about OB. In progressive organizations, supportive policies and a commitment to extensive training and development are among the criteria of organizational excellence. The opportunities for life-long learning are there. You must make the commitment to take full advantage of them at all times.

The Nature of Organizations

The study of OB must begin with the nature of organizations themselves. Formally defined, an **organization** is a collection of people working together in a division of labor to achieve a common purpose. Organizations are social instruments through which many people combine their efforts and work together to accomplish more than any one person could do alone. This logic has brought us the automobile, the personal computer, the space shuttle, and an infinite number of other products and services that are part of our daily lives. This same logic applies in any work setting. In all cases, the goal is to utilize everyone's talents to the fullest and to achieve outcomes that are beyond individual capabilities alone.

The purpose of any organization is to produce a good or service. Nonprofit organizations produce services with public benefits, such as health care, education, judicial processing, and highway maintenance. Large and small businesses produce consumer goods and services such as automobiles, appliances, gourmet dining, and accommodations. A clear statement of purpose is important to guide the activities of an organization and its members. For example, the corporate purpose of Ben & Jerry's Homemade, Inc., is formally stated as follows: To make, distribute, and sell the finest quality, all-natural ice cream and related products in a wide variety of innovative flavors made from Vermont dairy products.

To achieve its purpose, any organization depends on human effort. The division of labor is a process of breaking the required work into tasks that can be performed by individuals or groups. It is a way of allocating work among many people and, hopefully, to everyone's best advantage.

A well-functioning organization with a clear purpose and appropriate division of labor achieves **synergy,** the creation of a whole that is greater than the sum of its parts. You might think of synergy as the potential to make a simple sum, such as "2 + 2," equal to something greater than "4." Synergy in organizations occurs when people work well together while using available resources to pursue a common purpose.

Organizations depend on the activities and collective efforts of many people for their success. In this sense, people are the essential **human resources** of organizations—the individuals and groups whose performance contributions make it possible for the organization to serve a particular purpose. But organizations need more than people if they are to survive and prosper. They also need material resources including technology, information, physical equipment and facilities, raw materials, and money. All of these resources, and more, are necessary in order for an organization to ultimately produce some useful good or service.

Many OB scholars believe that organizations can be best understood as **open systems** that obtain human and material resource "inputs" from their environments and transform them into product "outputs" in the form of finished goods and/or services. The outputs are then offered to the environment for consumption. If everything works right, the environment accepts these outputs and allows the organization to obtain the resource inputs it needs to continue operating in the future. Of course, things can go wrong; an organization's survival depends on satisfying environmental demands. When the organization's goods and/or services are not well received by the environment, it will sooner or later have difficulty obtaining the resource inputs it needs to operate. In the extreme case, the organization will be forced to go out of existence.

Managers in Organizations

Now, we can speak more precisely about what it means to be a manager. Earlier, we identified a manager as a person in an organization who is responsible for work that is accomplished through the performance contributions of one or more other persons. These other persons have traditionally been identified as a manager's immediate "subordinates" or "direct reports." In the new workplace, it is increasingly common to refer to them as a manager's team members or associates, and the like. The managers, in turn, are identified by a wide variety of possible job titles, including supervisor, department head, team leader, coordinator, administrator, general manager, and president.

A **work unit** or **work team** is a task-oriented group that includes a manager and his or her direct reports. Such groups are found in organizations of all types, and they can be small or large. Examples include departments in a retail store, divisions of a corporation, branches of a bank, wards in a hospital, and teams in a manufacturing plant. Even the college classroom can be considered a work team; the instructor is its manager and students are team members.

What Is an Effective Manager?

Any manager should seek two key results for a work unit or work team. The first is **task performance,** the quality and quantity of the work produced or the services provided by the work unit as a whole. The second is **human resource maintenance,** the attraction and continuation of a capable workforce over time. High performance and good human resource maintenance are the key criteria of an **effective manager**—that is, a manager whose work unit or team achieves high levels of task accomplishment and maintains itself as a capable workforce over time.

An effective manager achieves long-term or sustainable success. It is just not enough for a work unit to achieve high performance on any given day; the unit must be able to achieve this high performance every day, both now and in the future. This need to ensure long-term and sustainable high performance focuses a manager's attention on the need to "maintain" all of a work unit's resources properly—human and material resources alike. Just as the manager should not allow a valuable machine to break down for lack of proper maintenance, he or she should never allow a valuable human contribution to be lost for lack of proper care.

Good human resource maintenance is a major concern of OB. It directs a manager's attention to such matters as job satisfaction, job involvement, organizational commitment, absenteeism, and turnover, as well as performance. One potential sign of poor human resource maintenance is job burnout, a term used to describe the mental exhaustion sometimes experienced by people facing too many demands and pressures in their work. Progressive organizations and their managers recognize the danger of this phenomenon and take special steps to prevent its occurrence.

This concept of the effective manager is important for understanding the insights of OB and for developing your personal managerial skills. In this and future chapters, a special text feature called *The Effective Manager* will be used to help remind you of these applications. To begin, The Effective Manager 1.1 identifies selected skills and personal characteristics identified by the American Assembly of Collegiate Schools of Business (AACSB) as foundations of managerial success.[11] You can use it as a "checklist" to quickly assess your skills and to identify possible areas for further personal development.

THE EFFECTIVE MANAGER 1.1

Selected Skills and Personal Characteristics of an Effective Manager

Analytic thinking—Ability to understand, integrate, interpret, and explain patterns in complex situations.

Behavioral flexibility—Ability to modify personal behavior to reach a goal or respond to situational changes.

Decision making—Ability to use logic and information to choose among alternatives in complex situations.

Leadership—Ability to stimulate and guide individuals or groups toward goal or task accomplishment.

Oral communication—Ability to clearly and persuasively express ideas orally to individuals and groups.

Personal impact—Ability to create a good early impression; to command the attention and respect of others.

Planning and organizing—Ability to set and keep a course of action, and allocate resources to reach goals.

Resistance to stress—Ability to maintain work performance while experiencing significant personal stress.

Self-objectivity—Ability to realistically assess personal strengths and weaknesses as applied to a job.

Tolerance for uncertainty—Ability to maintain work performance under uncertain or unstructured conditions.

Written communication—Ability to clearly and persuasively express ideas in various written forms.

Productivity and Managerial Performance

An effective manager must be concerned with the "productivity" of work units and their members. Formally defined, **productivity** is a summary measure of the quantity and quality of work performance achieved, which also takes resource utilization into account. Good managers establish and support the conditions needed to ensure high productivity—for themselves, for individual contributors, for their work units, and for the organization as a whole. This involves a commitment to the accomplishment of two different, but complementary, performance outcomes for any individual, work unit, or total organization.

> **Performance effectiveness** Measures whether or not important task goals are being attained.

> **Performance efficiency** Measures how well resources are being utilized.

At Inland Fisher Guide, for example, the company once manufactured 15 styles of steering wheels for the auto industry.[12] But it used to take seven weeks to make just one style. Parts were made in batches and were stored until needed, and unfinished wheels were stored between production steps. When the company shifted to a new system that allowed a single model to be made in a work shift by groups of workers doing multiple tasks, productivity increased. The amount of scrap, product reworking, labor cost per unit, lead time, and use of floor space were greatly reduced. Just as before, the workers got the job done. But this time they did it both effectively and efficiently.

Productivity is a primary measure of work accomplishment in and by organizations today, and it is likely to remain a benchmark of managerial and organizational success in the years ahead. In today's complex and demanding times, it is not acceptable simply to "get a job done." Any job must also be done with the best use of available resources—human and material.

Value-Added Managers

The best organizations want value-added managers, managers whose efforts clearly enable their work units to achieve high productivity and improve "bottom-line" performance. Value-added managers create high-performance systems in which individuals and groups work well together, to the benefit of the entire organization and its clients or customers. Value-added managers are also the most likely to reap the rewards of satisfying careers. In an age of organizational restructuring and downsizing, often designed to reduce the number of management levels, value-added managers will have little trouble justifying their jobs.

The Manager's Challenge

In many ways, this book is about you becoming a value-added manager. As you think more about building your personal managerial skills and capabilities in this regard, remember that most managers simultaneously serve in at least two capacities: as the head of one work unit and as a subordinate in another. This creates what we refer to as the *manager's challenge:* At the same time that a manager is held "accountable" by higher level superiors for work unit results, the manager is "dependent" on the efforts of others to make these results possible. Of course, in the new workplace, this performance is defined as that meeting customer expectations for high-quality and service standards. Much of any manager's time is spent dealing in one way or another with the stresses and strains of simultaneously meeting the demands of upward accountability and downward dependency.

The Management Process

Effective managers create opportunities for individuals and groups to make high-performance contributions in organizations and to experience job satisfaction. They do this, in part, through the **management process** of planning, organizing, leading, and controlling the use of organizational resources to achieve high-performance re-

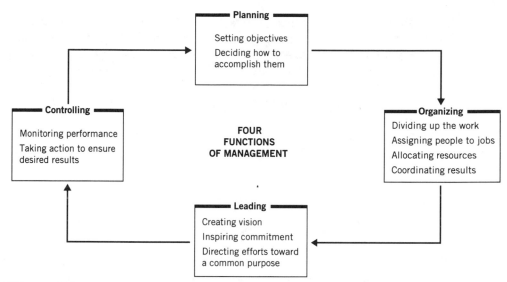

Figure 1.1 The four functions of management.

sults. These four functions of management, as shown in Figure 1.1, are defined as follows.

1. **Planning** The process of setting performance objectives and identifying the actions needed to accomplish these objectives.

2. **Organizing** The process of dividing up the work to be done and then coordinating the results to achieve a desired purpose.

3. **Leading** The process of directing the work efforts of other people to enable them to accomplish their assigned tasks successfully.

4. **Controlling** The process of monitoring performance, comparing the actual results to the objectives, and taking corrective action as necessary.

The management process applies in any occupational setting. The action framework provided by the four management functions can help any manager answer the following question: "What are my basic responsibilities in this job?" Consider, for example, the case of a computer maker hoping to compete successfully with its larger rivals.

In respect to *planning,* the president of the firm senses the need for a new product line in order to stay competitive with the industry leaders. Once the top management team has discussed the issue, a decision is made to field test a new model within six months.

In respect to *organizing,* the president convenes a special task force to create the new product. People with various skills are selected and assigned to the task force. A budget, clerical support, facilities, and equipment are made available. One person is appointed to "head" the task force and is assigned to report directly to the president.

In respect to *leading,* the president states the performance objective at the first task force meeting, answers questions that arise, and explains why the new product is so important to the firm. The task force head is introduced as someone in whom the president has complete confidence. Before leaving, the president encourages everyone to be enthusiastic and to work hard to accomplish the set objective.

In respect to *controlling,* the president had frequent conversations with the head of the task force and stays informed about efforts to create the new product. Sometimes she attends task force meetings to ask and answer questions with the group as a whole. When it appears that the timetable is slipping, additional personnel are assigned, and the budget is increased slightly. At last, all task force members are present when the new model is unveiled for market testing.

The Nature of Managerial Work

In his classic book, *The Nature of Managerial Work,* Henry Mintzberg offers an in-depth examination of the daily activities of corporate chief executives. The following is an insightful excerpt from Mintzberg's observations regarding an executive's typical workday.

> There was no break in the pace of activity during office hours. The mail (average of 36 pieces per day), telephone calls (average of 10–15 per day), and meetings (average of eight) accounting for almost every minute from the moment these executives entered their offices in the morning until they departed in the evenings. A true break seldom occurred. Coffee was taken during meetings, and lunchtime was almost always devoted to formal or informal meetings. When free time appeared, ever-present subordinates quickly usurped it. If these managers wished to have a change of pace, they had two means at their disposal—the observational tour and the light discussions that generally preceded scheduled meetings. But these were not regularly scheduled breaks, and they were seldom totally unrelated to the issue at hand: managing the organization . . .[13]

Mintzberg continues:

> Why do managers adopt this pace and workload? One major reason is the inherently open-ended nature of the job. The manager is responsible for the success of the organization. There are really no tangible mileposts where one can stop and say, "Now my job is finished." The engineer finishes the design of a casting on a certain day; the lawyer wins or loses a case at some moment in time. The manager must always keep going, never sure when he or she has succeeded, never sure when the whole organization may come down because of some miscalculation. As a result, the manager is a person with a perpetual preoccupation. The manager can never be free to forget the job, and never has the pleasure of knowing, even temporarily, that there is nothing else to do.

This example points out clearly that a manager's job in any organization is busy and demanding. The results of continuing research on managerial work can be summarized as follows:[14]

Managers work long hours. A workweek of at least 50 hours is typical; up to 90 hours is not unheard of. Furthermore, the length of the workweek tends to increase as one advances to higher managerial levels. Heads of organizations often work the longest hours.

Managers are busy people. Their work is intense and involves doing many different things on any given workday. The busy day of a manager includes at least 20 to 30 separate incidents or episodes during an 8-hour period for chief executives, and up to 200 at supervisory levels.

Managers are often interrupted. Their work is fragmented and variable. Interruptions are frequent, and many tasks must be completed quickly.

Managers work mostly with other people. In fact, they spend little time working alone. Time spent with others includes working with bosses, peers, subordinates, subordinates of their subordinates, as well as outsiders, such as customers, suppliers, and the like.

Managers are communicators. Much of their work is face-to-face verbal communication that takes place during formal and informal meetings. Higher level managers spend more time in scheduled meetings than do lower level managers. In general, managers spend a lot of time getting, giving, and processing information.

Managerial Activities and Roles

From his research, Mintzberg identified three sets of activities in which managers engage, often on a daily basis. In *interpersonal activities* managers work directly with other people. In *informational activities* managers exchange information with other people. In *decisional activities* managers make decisions that affect other people.[15] As described in The Effective Manager 1.2, these three sets of activities involve ten action roles that managers must be prepared to perform.[16]

Other research suggests that managers working at different levels may emphasize somewhat different tasks.[17] First-level managers serving as department heads, supervisors, or team leaders tend to emphasize one-on-one activities with their subordinates or team members. Middle-level managers may deal more with group and intergroup issues. Their attention is on planning and allocating resources, coordinating interdependent groups, and managing group performance. Top-level managers or senior executives keep "an eye on the outside." They are concerned with monitoring the organization's environment so that they stay informed about important trends and developments.

Managerial Networks

At all levels of responsibility, managers are concerned about representing their work units or teams to others—something the researchers identify as an ambassadorial

---

THE EFFECTIVE MANAGER 1.2

Ten Roles of an Effective Manager

INTERPERSONAL ROLES

Figurehead—Hosting and attending official ceremonies.
Leader—Creating enthusiasm and serving people's needs.
Liaison—Maintaining contacts with important people and groups.

INFORMATIONAL ROLES

Monitor—Seeking out relevant information.
Disseminator—Sharing relevant information with insiders.
Spokesperson—Sharing relevant information with outsiders.

DECISIONAL ROLES

Entrepreneur—Seeking problems to solve and opportunities to explore.
Disturbance handler—Helping to resolve conflicts.
Resource allocator—Allocating resources to various uses.
Negotiator—Negotiating with other parties.

---

task. All managers must establish and maintain good working relationships, or networks, with a multitude of people in order to get their work done. The ability to do so is indispensable to managerial success. Consider this description in John Kotter's book *The General Managers.*

> B. J. Sparksman had a good working relationship with his four bosses and a close mentor-protege relationship with one of them. He had cordial-to-good relations with his peers, some of whom were friends and all of whom were aware of his track record. . . . He also had a good working relationship with many of the subordinates of his peers (hundreds of people) based mostly on his reputation. B. J. had a close and strong working relationship with all but one of his main direct reports because they respected him, because he was the boss, and the fact that he tried to treat them fairly and with respect. Outside the firm, B. J. maintained fairly strong relationships with dozens of top people in firms that were important clients for his organization. . . . He also had relationships with dozens of other important people in the local community.[18]

This case describes a manager who uses a complex set of interpersonal networks, many falling outside the formal chain of command, in order to help get the job done. Inside the organization, Sparksman's networks included both vertical relationships with a variety of superiors and subordinates, and lateral relationships with peers. His networks also included relationships with many outsiders, such as customers and suppliers. The ability to develop, maintain, and work well within such networks is increasingly recognized as an important aspect of managerial work.

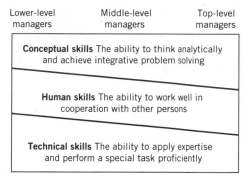

| Lower-level managers | Middle-level managers | Top-level managers |

Conceptual skills The ability to think analytically and achieve integrative problem solving

Human skills The ability to work well in cooperation with other persons

Technical skills The ability to apply expertise and perform a special task proficiently

Figure 1.2   How essential skills vary among levels of managerial responsibility.

Managerial Skills and Competencies

The prior look at managerial activities, roles, and networking responsibilities of managerial work raises an important question, both for you personally as well as for the field of organizational behavior. That question is: What "skills" are required to achieve managerial success in such a dynamic and demanding work setting?

A skill is an ability to translate knowledge into action that results in desired performance. It is a competency that allows a person to achieve superior performance in one or more aspects of his or her work. Robert Katz divides the essential managerial skills into three categories—technical, human, and conceptual skills.[19]

A **technical skill** is an ability to apply specialized knowledge or expertise to perform a job. This skill involves being highly proficient at using select methods, processes, and procedures to accomplish tasks. Examples include the work of accountants, engineers, and attorneys, whose technical skills are acquired through formal education. Most jobs have some technical skill components. Some require preparatory education, whereas others allow skills to be learned through appropriate work training and on-the-job experience.

Human skill is the ability to work well in cooperation with others. It emerges as a spirit of trust, enthusiasm, and genuine involvement in interpersonal relationships. A person with good human skills will have a high degree of self-awareness and a capacity for understanding or empathizing with the feelings of others. This skill is clearly essential to the manager's "networking" responsibilities we described earlier.

The ability to analyze and solve complex problems is a **conceptual skill.** All good managers ultimately have the ability to view the organization or situation as a whole and to solve problems to the benefit of everyone concerned. Conceptual or analytical ability draws heavily on one's mental capacities to identify problems and opportunities, to gather and interpret relevant information, and to make good problem-solving decisions that serve the organization's purpose.

According to Katz, the relative importance of these essential skills varies across levels of management. In Figure 1.2, technical skills are shown as being more important at lower management levels, where supervisors must deal with concrete problems. Broader, more ambiguous, and longer term decisions dominate the manager's concerns at higher levels, where conceptual skills are more important. Human skills are consistently important across all managerial levels. The basics of organizational behavior, as discussed in the following chapters, are useful foundations for the continued development of your managerial skills.

In Summary

What is organizational behavior?

- Organizational behavior (OB) is formally defined as the study of individuals and groups in organizations.
- OB is an academic discipline that can help managers make good decisions while working with people in complex and dynamic environments.

Why is organizational behavior useful for managers?

- Learning about organizational behavior helps managers better deal with their workplace experiences.
- Probably the best learning about OB is learning from experience; one of the best sources of experiential learning is in the workplace and on the job.
- A commitment to life-long learning may be a distinguishing characteristic of managers who achieve career success.
- With roots in the behavioral sciences, OB is an applied discipline, taking a contingency approach, and emphasizing scientific methods.

What are organizations?

- Organizations are collections of people working together in a division of labor for a common purpose.
- As open systems, organizations interact with their external environments in the process of transforming human and material resource inputs into goods and/ or services as product outputs.
- A successful organization provides outputs of value to the external environment and is always able to obtain needed resource inputs.

Who are the managers in organizations?

- A "manager" is anyone in an organization to whom one or more others directly report.
- An effective manager is one whose work unit accomplishes high levels of task performance and good human resource maintenance.
- Productivity involves performance effectiveness in goal accomplishment and performance efficiency in resource utilization.

- Every manager's challenge is to fulfill a higher-level performance accountability while being dependent upon others to do the required work.

What is the management process?

- The management process involves the four functions of planning, organizing, leading, and controlling.
- Planning sets the directions.
- Organizing brings together people and other resources to do the needed work.
- Leading creates the enthusiasm need to fulfill work requirements.
- Controlling makes sure things turn out as desired.

What is the day-to-day nature of managerial work?

- Managerial work involves long hours, intense activity, and frequent interruptions.
- Managerial work involves a variety of interpersonal, informational, and decisional roles.
- Managerial work involves pursuit of action agendas through a variety of complex interpersonal networks.
- The essential managerial skills include human skills, technical skills, and conceptual skills.

ORGANIZATIONAL

BEHAVIOR AND

THE NEW WORKPLACE

As you read Chapter 2, keep in mind these study questions:

- How is the manager's external environment changing?

- What is total quality management?

- Why is workforce diversity so important today?

- Why are managerial ethics and social responsibility so important today?

- What creates job satisfaction and a high quality of work life?

A n effective manager is one whose work unit achieves high levels of performance and maintains itself as a capable workforce over time. This manager is consistently able to help other people get important tasks accomplished in a timely and productive fashion. But any manager's job today is complicated by unprecedented environmental changes. Global competition, new technologies, shifting demographics, and changing social values are just a few of the significant trends that challenge a manager's effectiveness. The following quotations are further reminders of just how challenging managerial work in the new workplace can be.

> My day always ends when I'm tired, not when I am done. A manager's work is never done: There is always more to be done, more that should be done, always more that can be done.—Andrew Grove, president of Intel Corporation and author of *High Output Management*.

> No matter what kind of managerial job, managers always carry the nagging suspicion that they might be able to contribute just a little bit more. Hence they assume an unrelenting pace in their work.—Henry Mintzberg, management scholar and author of *The Nature of Managerial Work*.[1]

The Manager's Changing Environment

The term *future shock* indicates the discomfort that is experienced in times of continual and uncertain change. It is an undeniable characteristic of the modern workplace.[2] Managers of the twenty-first century must be able to achieve productivity with satisfaction, and be able to do so while performing under the pressures of rapid, and even unprecedented, change. They must be willing and able to anticipate and deal with changing environmental circumstances, and they must be willing and able to help others do the same. Among the forces in this dynamic environment of management are the global economy, human rights in the workplace, organizational transitions, developments in information technologies, and new ways of organizing.[3] These, of course, are in addition to total quality management, workforce diversity, and quality of work life, themes that are ever present in the modern manager's workplace.

The Global Economy

The many nations and cultures of the world are increasingly interdependent. The emergence of regional trade groupings such as NAFTA (North American Free Trade

Agreement), EC (European Community), and APEC (Asia-Pacific Economic Cooperation) are everyday reminders that the global economy is real. It will only continue to grow in complexity and power. More businesses around the world are cooperating in strategic alliances and joint ventures. More and more wage earners find themselves working at home for foreign employers. More and more senior executives are arriving at their positions with the benefit of "overseas experience." And more and more junior executives are being asked and encouraged to take such assignments. As a consequence, today's managers must "think globally" in pursuing their opportunities.[4] Chapter 3 examines at greater length some of the key international dimensions of organizational behavior.

Organizational Transitions

Over the last two decades, the global economy has not only materialized, but it has also demonstrated a tremendous power. One outcome is quite new in its demands on organizations and their members: the reality of economic decline instead of continuous growth. No longer can the scholar or manager be content to view the management of growth as a predominant concern. Learning to live with, cope with, and manage in situations of decline are now equally significant challenges and concerns. The realities of corporate downsizing, restructuring, demassing, and the like are likely to be with us for some time to come.

Managers in progressive organizations recognize that effectively managing organizational transitions involves more than simply cutting employees and reducing the levels of management. A popular development, for example, is **process reengineering,** or process redesign, formally defined as "the fundamental rethinking and radical redesign of business processes to achieve dramatic improvements in critical contemporary measures of performance such as cost, quality, service, and speed."[5] Managers adopting this approach are asked to "start over," to forget how things were done in the past, and to ask only how things should be done to best meet the critical performance measures. Answers to these questions are used to redesign activities and workflows in order to give better value to customers, be they inside or outside of the organization. The result involves a substantial shift in values, as shown in The Effective Manager 2.1.

Human Rights in the Workplace

Human rights and social justice are increasingly revered in the new workplace, just as they are in the world at large. All managers must deal with growing *pressures for self-determination* by people at work. They want more freedom to determine how to do their jobs and when to do them. They want the benefits of increased participation found in such workplace initiatives as job enrichment, autonomous work groups, flexible working hours, and compressed workweeks. All of this is changing the nature of day-to-day human resource management. Indeed, the informed manager today is well prepared to deal with not only these pressures, but also those in the following list.

> ### THE EFFECTIVE MANAGER 2.1
>
> #### Moving from Traditional to Reengineered Values
>
> ##### TRADITIONAL VALUES TOWARD WORK
>
> - The boss pays our salaries; keep the boss happy.
> - To keep your job, stay quiet and don't make waves.
> - When things go wrong, pass problems on to others.
> - The more direct reports the better; a good manager builds an empire.
> - The future is predictable; past success means future success.
>
> ##### REENGINEERED VALUES TOWARD WORK
>
> - Customers pay our salaries; help keep them happy.
> - All of our jobs depend on the value we create.
> - Accept ownership for problems; help solve them.
> - We are all part of a team; a good manager builds teams.
> - The future is uncertain; constant learning is the key to future success.

Pressures for employee rights People expect their rights to be respected on the job as well as outside of work. These include the rights of individual privacy, due process, free speech, free consent, freedom of conscience, and freedom from sexual harassment.

Pressures for job security People expect their security to be protected. This includes security of their physical well-being—in terms of occupational safety and health matters, as well as security of their economic livelihood—in terms of guaranteed protection against layoffs and provisions for cost-of-living wage increases.

Pressures for equal employment opportunity People expect—and increasingly demand—the right to employment without discrimination on the basis of age, sex, ethnic background, or disabilities. Among these demands will remain a concern for furthering the modest but dramatic gains made in recent years by women and other minorities in the workplace. "Progress" will be applauded, but it will not be accepted as a substitute for true equality of opportunity.

Pressures for equity of earnings People expect to be compensated for the "comparable worth" of their work contributions. They will require answers other than the fact that certain occupations (such as nursing) have traditionally been dominated by women, whereas others (such as carpentry) have been traditionally dominated by men.

Developments in Information Technologies

We live at a time when expert systems and artificial intelligence are increasingly being used in organizational decision making; we live at a time when new top management jobs with the title of chief information officer are being created; and we live at a time when personal computers and their electronic networks are integral to managerial workstations. Yet, most of the technological revolution probably lies ahead of us.[6] As the pace of change in information and computer technology quickens, the results will be revolutionary—for workers, managers, and organizations alike.

At the present time, high technology allows machines to do many routine chores more cheaply and accurately than people can do; high technology makes available more information for planning and control to more people at all levels of organizational responsibility; and high technology is causing both people and organizational structures to change old habits and adopt new ways of doing things. Although computers and information technology have their limits, they offer indispensable advantages in highly competitive environments. That is, they offer these advantages to those who plan well for high-technology applications and then carefully implement them with full respect for the people involved.

New Values and New Ways of Organizing

Along with technological changes, the contemporary environment has also seen the advent of new values and new ways of organizing in the workplace. In the more progressive work settings, this means more emphasis on allowing workers the freedoms to use their talents to best advantage and to supplement individual work with more "teamwork."[7] Managers in these settings share the common goal of bringing people and technology together to create "high-performance" systems. They are experimenting with production and service operations that emphasize teamwork and group-based tasks, performance-based incentives and reward systems, intense training and development of employees, continuous learning and improvement for the organization as a whole, reduced external supervision and increased individual responsibilities, fewer levels of management, smaller numbers of staff personnel, and greater emphasis on organizational adaptation, innovation, and performance.

British management consultant Charles Handy uses the shamrock, with its three leaves per stem, to symbolize how some organizations are evolving as they adapt to changing environments.[8] In the **shamrock organization,** shown in Figure 2.1, Handy identifies each leaf with a different group of people. *Leaf 1* represents a core group of workers who are permanent, full-time employees with critical skills and who follow standard career paths. It is here that the most essential work of the organization gets done, while the remaining work is accomplished by contracted or part-time workers. *Leaf 2* represents outside contractors engaged by the core to perform a variety of essential and specific day-to-day jobs. Many of these jobs, such as maintenance and mail services, would be performed by full-time employees in a more traditional organization. *Leaf 3* represents part-time employees who are hired temporarily by the core as the needs of the business grow and who can just as easily be let go when business falls. Handy believes that many workers of tomorrow must be prepared to participate mainly in leafs 2 and 3.

A second, perhaps futuristic description of new ways of organizing is the **virtual corporation.**[9] This organization exists only as a temporary network or alliance of otherwise independent companies who are jointly pursuing a particular business interest. The network is a cooperative alliance that makes it possible for members to pursue good ideas by pooling their resources and quickly adapting to shifting

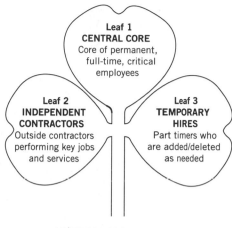

SHAMROCK ORGANIZATION

Figure 2.1   Charles Handy's shamrock organization.

business conditions. A network might consist of independent suppliers, customers, and even competitors, who are linked by the latest electronic information technologies and who share such things as information skills, costs, and access to global markets.

Importantly, it may be that the 1990s will be remembered as the decade that fundamentally changed the way people work.[10] Consider the **"upside-down" pyramid** shown in Figure 2.2. This figure rejects the traditional view of the organization as a top-down work setting where managers are the bosses and all others simply follow their orders. Instead, it reflects an emerging and more progressive view of managers who act as helpers, coaches, and supporters. It emphasizes a customer orientation and recognizes the potential of every employee to serve both the customer's and the organization's interests. It is into this view of organizations that twenty-first-century managers will step.

Total Quality Management

The customer reigns supreme in today's demanding society. In the new workplace, customer service and product quality always get attention. Indeed, the concept of total quality management (TQM) is now popular and commonplace in the vocabulary of managers.[11] You should recall from Chapter 1 that TQM refers to management with a total commitment to high quality results and continuous improvement in all aspects of one's work or an organization's operations. **Quality,** in this sense, means that the customers' needs are being met and that all task requirements are completed correctly the first time. A benchmark of TQM is the notion of **continuous improvement**—that is, the belief that anything and everything should be continually evaluated by asking two questions: (1) Is this necessary? and (2) if so, can it be done better?

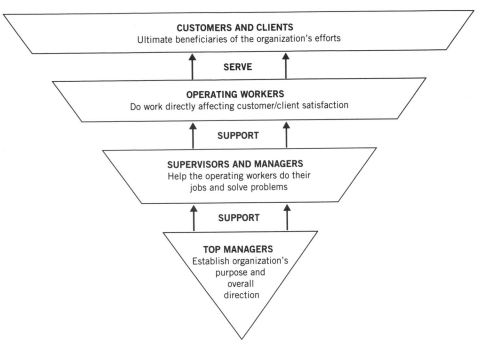

Figure 2.2 The upside-down pyramid in the new workplace. *Source:* John R. Schermerhorn, Jr., *Management for Productivity, 4th ed.* (New York: John Wiley & Sons, 1993), p. 698. Used by permission.

Employee involvement is an important element in successful TQM programs.[12] The TQM concept expects employees to be constantly on the alert for quality problems and to bring these problems to management's attention. They are also expected to remain on the alert for ways to do their jobs better and to help improve other aspects of organizational operations. A popular mechanism for gaining employee participation in these processes of continuous improvement is the **quality circle.** Formally defined, this is a small group of 6 to 12 employees that meets regularly to review work operations and discuss ways of ensuring total quality. One member of a quality circle at AT&T sums up the benefits of the approach in this way:

> Before I got involved with the circle, if I noticed a problem I'd think: "That's wrong, why don't they fix it?" But now I know there's nothing as simple as 1–2–3 and it's fixed. . . . I also like the fact that, through the circle, management is saying that when it comes to doing my job, I'm the expert and my ideas are valuable.[13]

Total quality management is also a major force in the global economy. The term ISO 9000 stands for quality standards set by the International Standards Organization in Geneva, Switzerland. Along with other related standards of this office, it sets a universal framework for quality assurance within the European Community. ISO 9000 certification is a requirement for European companies. In addition, its quality standards have been endorsed by more than 50 countries, including the United States,

Canada, and Mexico. ISO certification is rapidly becoming a must-have criterion for companies everywhere who want reputations as total quality, world-class manufacturers.

In any work setting, quality counts for the goods produced and the services rendered. Any good manager understands the TQM concept and helps the organization perform in ways that fulfill the commitment evident in these eight rules of total quality management.[14]

Rule 1 Quality is everyone's job.

Rule 2 Quality comes from prevention, not inspection.

Rule 3 Quality means meeting the needs of customers.

Rule 4 Quality demands teamwork.

Rule 5 Quality requires continuous improvement.

Rule 6 Quality involves strategic planning.

Rule 7 Quality means results.

Rule 8 Quality requires clear measures of success.

Management and Workforce Diversity

The term **workforce diversity** refers to the presence of demographic differences among members of a given workforce.[15] These differences include gender, race and ethnicity, age, and ablebodiness. The term itself gained popularity with the publication in the United States of the influential report, *Workforce 2000* (1987).[16] Significantly, population demographics are known to be shifting and workforce diversity to be increasing in the world at large. U.S. managers are being reminded about the following trends:[17]

- The size of the workforce is growing more slowly than in the past.
- The pool of younger workers is a smaller percentage of the workforce.
- The average age of the workforce is rising.
- More women are entering the workforce.
- The proportion of ethnic minorities in the workforce is increasing.
- The proportion of immigrants in the workforce is increasing.

Among the many environmental challenges to be faced by twenty-first-century managers, workforce diversity clearly has special prominence. These managers must be skilled in managing a workforce consisting of a broad mix of workers from different racial and ethnic backgrounds, of different ages and genders, and of different domestic and national cultures. Trends such as those highlighted above increase the importance of **multiculturalism,** the presence in the same work setting of people from more than one cultural background.[18] Multiculturalism, in turn, brings to the new workplace new demands for interpersonal sensitivity and understanding. It also creates demands for responsive employment practices. Some organizations are responding by appointing people to serve in a new job category—diversity manager or something similar. The responsibility of this job holder is to lead efforts to make the workplace truly open to the talents of persons of all cultures and demographic backgrounds. More and more employers are also training managers to handle diversity in the new workplace. Many are also offering special employee assistance programs to help workers, often from dual-career or single-parent households, as they try to balance work and family responsibilities for child care and elder care.

Reports such as *Workplace 2000* note that jobs are becoming more complex and, consequently, require workers with higher levels of skills. At the same time, they express concern over the current and projected availabilities of skilled workers, and the quality of the educational systems responsible for creating the skilled workforce of the future.[19] As today's employers search for employees to fill high-skill jobs in scarce labor markets, for example, some are starting their own in-house education programs to ensure the future availability of qualified job candidates.

Fair and progressive employment practices help address diversity in the workplace. Also at issue, however, are the attitudes and behaviors of the managers and others who work in today's organizations. Tendencies toward *prejudice*—the display of negative attitudes toward others of different ethnic or minority group identities—and *discrimination*—action that seeks to disadvantage such persons from their full rights of organizational membership—must become relics of the past. There are no ethnic or demographic borders to talent and ability. Good managers act every day with this principle in mind, and by "valuing diversity" they help to create a high-performance edge for their organizations.[20]

Managerial Ethics and Social Responsibility

Formally defined, **ethical behavior** is behavior that is morally accepted as good and right, as opposed to bad or wrong, in a particular setting. Today a trend is clear. The public at large is demanding that government officials, managers, workers in general, and the organizations they represent, all act in accordance with high ethical and moral standards. Ethical managerial behavior is behavior that conforms not only to the dictates of law but also to a broader moral code that is common to society as a whole. Just exactly what moral code governs a person's choices, however, is a subject of debate. Over the years, philosophers such as John Stuart Mill, John Locke, and Thomas Jefferson have identified these four ways of thinking about ethical behavior:

1. **Utilitarian view** Ethical behavior is that which delivers the greatest good to the greatest number of people.
2. **Individualism view** Ethical behavior is that which is best for one's long-term self-interests.
3. **Moral rights view** Ethical behavior is that which respects fundamental rights shared by all human beings.

4. **Justice view** Ethical behavior is that which is fair and impartial in its treatment of people.

In OB, two aspects of the justice view are considered especially important for managers.[21] The first is **procedural justice,** the degree to which the rules and procedures specified by policies are properly followed in all cases under which the policy is applied. In sexual harassment cases, for example, this may mean that all required hearings are held for every case submitted for administrative review. The second is **distributive justice,** the degree to which all people are treated the same under a policy, regardless of race, ethnicity, gender, age, or any other demographic characteristic. Again in a sexual harassment case, for example, this might mean that a case filed by a man against a woman would get the same hearing as one filed by a woman against a man. Obviously, both procedural justice and distributive justice are important elements in the new workplace.

Ethical Dilemmas

An **ethical dilemma** is a situation in which a person must decide whether or not to do something that, although benefiting oneself or the organization or both, may be considered unethical. Is it ethical, for example, to pay a bribe to obtain a business contract in a foreign country? Is it ethical to allow your company to dispose of hazardous waste in an unsafe fashion? Is it ethical to withhold information that might discourage a good worker from taking another job? Is it ethical to conduct personal business on company time?

Ethical dilemmas are common in life and at work. Research suggests that managers encounter such dilemmas in their working relationships not only with superiors and subordinates but also with customers, competitors, suppliers, and regulators. Common issues underlying the dilemmas involve honesty in communications and contracts, gifts and entertainment, kickbacks, pricing practices, and employee terminations.[22] And although some organizations publish formal codes of conduct to help guide the ethical conduct of their members, the ultimate test is always the strength of an individual's personal ethical framework. Consequently, more and more organizations are offering ethics training programs to help managers clarify their ethical frameworks and practice self-discipline when making decisions in difficult circumstances. The Effective Manager 2.2 offers a useful seven-step checklist that can help you deal with ethical dilemmas.[23]

One more point must be considered on this subject of ethical managerial behavior. It is unfortunately the case that each of us can easily use rationalizations to help justify actual or potential misconduct. That is, we have ways of making ourselves believe that such acts are acceptable. The best way to prevent such thinking from leading us astray is to recognize it for what it is—flawed and self-serving logic. It is helpful to be on guard against these four common rationalizations for unethical behavior:[24]

1. Pretending the behavior is not really unethical or illegal.
2. Excusing the behavior by saying it's really in the organization's or your best interest.

THE EFFECTIVE MANAGER 2.2

How to Deal With an Ethical Dilemma

Step 1. Recognize and clarify the dilemma.
Step 2. Get all the possible facts.
Step 3. List all of your options.
Step 4. Test each option by asking three questions:

"Is it legal?"
"Is it right?"
"Is it beneficial?

Step 5. Make your decision.
Step 6. Double check your decision by asking two questions:

"How would I feel if my family found out about my decision?"
"How would I feel if my decision were printed in the local newspaper?"

Step 7. Take action.

---

3. Assuming the behavior is okay because no one else would ever be expected to find out about it.
4. Expecting your superiors to support and protect you if anything should go wrong.

Corporate Social Responsibility

The term **corporate social responsibility** refers to the obligation of organizations to behave in ethical and moral ways as institutions of the broader society. This concept suggests that managers—the people who make the decisions that guide the behavior of organizations—must ensure that their ethical frameworks extend to the organization as a whole. Managers must be the role models for other organizational members and must take the lead in committing the organization to act in ways that are consistent with both the quest for high productivity and the objective of corporate social responsibility. It doesn't always turn out this way; we are occasionally made aware of notorious cases of organizational wrongdoing. Some time ago, for example, two Beech-nut senior executives were sentenced to jail for their roles in covering up the fact that Beech-nut was selling adulterated apple juice for infants. Although the juice was labeled "100% fruit juice," it turned out to be a blend of chemical ingredients.[25]

One internal guardian of corporate social responsibility is the **whistleblower,** someone who exposes organizational wrongdoing in order to preserve ethical standards and to protect against wasteful, harmful, or illegal acts. In fact, it was a whistleblower, the firm's former director of research and development, who brought the Beech-nut case to public attention. The danger for whistleblowers is the threat of potential retaliatory action by disgruntled employers. Even though some state and federal laws offer protection, whistleblowers are still at personal risk in many organizational settings.

The external guardian of corporate social responsibility is the public at large, together with the government agencies, media, and advocates who act in its behalf. Today's organizations and their managers face clear and increased social accountability for their decisions. We expect socially responsible organizations to deliver safe and quality products and services to their customers and clients; we expect socially responsible organizations to avoid harming the environment; we expect socially responsible organizations to provide safe working conditions that do not harm the health of employees; and we expect socially responsible organizations to contribute positively to the general well-being of their host communities.

Job Satisfaction and the Quality of Work Life

Work is formally defined as any activity that produces value for other people. It is something people do in exchange for things, such as money and retirement security, that they cannot directly provide for themselves. Work is also something that can— and should—be accomplished in settings that meet high ethical and social responsibility standards.

What Is Job Satisfaction?

One measure of a person's relationship with his or her employer is **job satisfaction,** that is, the degree to which an individual feels positively or negatively about his or her job.[26] Two closely related concepts are organizational commitment and job involvement. *Organizational commitment* refers to the degree to which a person strongly identifies with and feels a part of the organization. *Job involvement* refers to the willingness of a person to work hard and apply effort beyond normal job expectations. An individual who has high organizational commitment is considered very loyal; an individual who is highly involved in a job is considered a good corporate or organizational citizen.

Job satisfaction is an emotional response to one's tasks, as well as to the physical and social conditions of the workplace. It is discussed further in Chapter 4 as among the important attitudes that can and do influence human behavior at work. Thus, OB researchers are interested in accurately measuring job satisfaction and understanding its consequences for people at work. Good managers are able to gauge the job satisfaction of others by carefully observing and interpreting what they say and do while going about their daily tasks. It can be useful at times to formally assess or "benchmark" the levels of job satisfaction among groups of workers. Some common survey measures assess satisfaction with

1. **The work itself** Responsibility, interest, and growth.
2. **Quality of supervision** Technical help and social support.
3. **Relationships with co-workers** Social harmony and respect.

4. **Promotion opportunities** Chances for further advancement.

5. **Pay** Adequacy of pay and perceived equity vis-à-vis others.[27]

Management and the Quality of Work Life

One way organizations can create job satisfaction for their members is to provide them with positive work environments. The term **quality of work life** (QWL) has gained prominence in OB as an indicator of the overall quality of human experiences in the workplace. This concept expresses a special way of thinking about people, their work, and the organizations in which their careers are fulfilled. QWL establishes a clear objective that high productivity can—and should—be achieved, along with satisfaction of the human resources—the people who do the required work.

QWL activities represent special applications of the many OB concepts and theories we will discuss throughout this book. In particular, true commitments to QWL are highlighted by the following benchmarks of managerial excellence:[28]

- **Participation** Involving people from all levels of responsibility in decision making.
- **Trust** Redesigning jobs, systems, and structures to give people more freedom at work.
- **Reinforcement** Creating reward systems that are fair, relevant, and contingent on work performance.
- **Responsiveness** Making the work setting more pleasant and capable of serving individual needs.

The QWL concept involves an important aspect of social responsibility. Because what happens to people at work may "spill over" to affect their nonworking lives as well, a manager's job is a socially important one. Poor management of people at work can decrease the quality of their lives overall, not just the quality of their work lives. Fortunately, good management can increase both. The remaining chapters in this book will help you to develop your abilities to accomplish just that.

In Summary

How is the manager's environment changing?

- Today's dynamic environment is creating pressures for a new workplace where systems, structures, and practices are consistent with emerging social values and expectations.
- Significant issues facing managers of the 1990s include: a focus on total quality, the global economy, workforce diversity and shifting population demographics, concerns for human rights in the workplace, organizational transitions, developments in information technologies, and new ways of organizing.

- The ability to deal with a complex and changing environment will be a benchmark of effective management in the twenty-first century.

What is total quality management?

- Total quality management (TQM) is management with a total commitment to high-quality results in all aspects of one's work or an organization's operations.
- TQM is an important concept in the new workplace, and it directs organization-wide attention to the importance of customers.
- TQM focuses on quality in the sense that customers' needs should be met and all tasks should be done right the first time.
- TQM involves continuous improvement, the belief that anything and everything should be continually evaluated and improved as a normal course of the work process.

Why is workforce diversity so important today?

- Workforce diversity is defined on the basis of such differences as gender, age, race, ethnicity, and ablebodiedness.
- Managers are being asked to develop the skills and sensitivities needed to work well with diverse employee populations and to help others do the same.
- Demographic indications are that the future workforce will grow older on the average, and including proportionately more women and minorities.
- More employers are helping their employees to fulfill nonwork responsibilities for child care and elder care.
- More employers have formal diversity management programs designed to help ensure that women, African-Americans, and other minorities get the employment opportunities they deserve.

Why are managerial ethics and social responsibility so important today?

- Managerial ethics and social responsibility are topics of utmost importance to managers and to society at large.
- Ethical managerial behavior involves making decisions based on moral concepts of what is right and wrong from the societal perspective.
- Managers must develop strong ethical frameworks to help them resolve the ethical dilemmas common to the workplace.
- Managers must support the development of corporate social responsibility—the obligation of organizations as a whole to act in ethical ways.
- Managers must lead by example to help insure that others with whom they work behave in ethical and socially responsible ways.

What creates job satisfaction and a high quality of work life?

- Job satisfaction is a measure of people's attitudes toward their work, workplace, and coworkers.
- The insights of OB can help managers build and maintain work environments that offer people a high quality of work life (QWL).
- *Participation, independence, equity,* and *responsiveness* are some of the words that describe a high QWL work setting.

3

ORGANIZATIONAL

BEHAVIOR AND THE

GLOBAL ECONOMY

As you read Chapter 3, keep in mind these study questions:

- What is the global imperative of management?

- What is culture?

- How does the global economy affect people at work?

- How do management practices compare around the world?

- What is a "global" view on learning about organizational behavior?

In his book, *The Competitive Advantage of Nations,* Harvard's Michael Porter examines the factors that make nations as well as their industries truly competitive in the global marketplace.[1] After a four-year study of ten countries, Porter concludes that sustainable economic advantage is possible only with the right combination of industries, support institutions, people . . . and competition. Yes, competition at home—the more the better—tends to create the foundations for industries to achieve their full potential internationally. The pressures of the market and a commitment to total quality management are helping organizations around the world stay competitive in a demanding environment.

Management and the Global Imperative

Competitive success in the global economy is increasingly dependent on the contributions of a new breed of manager—the global manager. This is someone who knows how to do business across borders.[2] Often multilingual, this manager "thinks" with a worldview and is able to map strategy accordingly. If you fit this description of the global manager, or soon will, get ready. Corporate recruiters are scrambling to find people with these types of global skills and interests. But in order to take full advantage of these opportunities, you must understand the *global imperative* of today's work environment:

- We all live in an increasingly global economy.
- International work opportunities are becoming part of more and more careers.
- Domestic organizations are feeling the impact of international competition.
- More and more people are now working at home for foreign employers.
- Many local jobs are lost as employers shift them to "lower cost" foreign labor markets.

When you travel—for leisure or for business—you expect to encounter international differences. What may not be so obvious is how two dimensions of globalization, the geographical dispersion of business and the multiculturalism of the workforce, are influencing our everyday lives.[3] The term *geographical dispersion* refers to the conduct of business affairs over large global distances. Perhaps its most immediate impact is felt through foreign direct investment or purchase of local assets. For example, foreigners now own all or parts of such classic American symbols as Howard Johnson's, Baskin-Robbins, Saks Fifth Avenue, Alka-Seltzer, and Rockefeller Center. The transnational movement of products, trends, values, and innovations is further changing life-styles at a rapid pace. We purchase more and more foreign products, and international suppliers play increasingly key roles in the operations of many industries. Even the U.S. automobile industry imports Japanese, Mexican, and Brazilian engines, uses German instruments and British electronics, and employs Italian designers in its external sourcing networks.

The movement of people from one country to another is also having a profound impact on management. Cultural diversity among populations is increasing, and multiculturalism of the workforce, where people from different cultures work and interact together, is a timely management challenge. International businesses come face to face with multiculturalism as they employ workers and try to sell their products in foreign environments. With advances in computer and communication technology, today it is even possible for a firm to employ foreigners who work for the home office by "telecommuting" from sites in their own home countries.

Yet, the global imperative of multiculturalism extends even further into the realm of management. It applies equally well to the underlying character of the local workforces with whom most managers must deal. As pointed out in reports such as *Workforce 2000,* discussed in the last chapter, the U.S. employment pool is and will continue to be a multicultural one.[4] More than ever before, employers in the United States draw their workers from nontraditional labor sources and from ethnic backgrounds representing all corners of the globe. U.S. managers, in turn, must respond by being sensitive and comfortable in dealing with the cultural differences represented by such workforce diversity. Success for them and for other global managers of the twenty-first century will be a function of cultural sensitivity as well as technical managerial skills.

What Is Culture?

Specialists tend to agree that **culture** is the learned, shared way of doing things in a particular society.[5] This includes how its members eat, dress, greet one another, teach their offspring, and so on. It is a constellation of factors that makes, for example, the "cultures" of the United States and India distinguishable from those of Spain and Tanzania.

We are not born with a culture; rather, we are born into a society that *teaches* us its culture. We learn culture from others around us in the environment. Furthermore, culture consists of many interrelated facets. If it is modified in one place, everything else is affected. Because culture is shared by people, it also defines the "boundaries" between them. For someone born into an Islamic culture, for example, the cultural expectations include eating only food that is *halal,* prepared according to religious guidelines. The boundaries set by this expectation would make it awkward for a Muslim visitor to the United States to comfortably accept an invitation to a traditional backyard barbecue hosted by an American business associate. Without ever knowing the real reason, the American may simply be thanked for the invitation and told by his Muslim friend that he already has another commitment.

Popular Dimensions of Culture

The popular dimensions of culture are found in the differences that are most apparent to the traveler. They include language, time orientation, use of space, and religion.

Language is perhaps the most conspicuous aspect of culture; at least it is one the traveler most often notices first. The structure of language can influence the manner in which one understands the environment.[6] Similarly, the vocabulary of a language can reveal the history of a society and the things that are or were important to it. For example, Arabic supposedly has more than six thousand different words for the camel, its parts, and related "equipment." As you might expect, English is very poor in its ability to describe camels.

The fact that people apparently speak the same language should be taken with caution; it doesn't mean that they share the same culture or that words necessarily carry the same meanings. Consider how the English language is used around the world. An American can be quite puzzled by the English term "lorry" (truck) or the Canadian reference to "hydro" (electric power). And within the United States, grocery shoppers in the Midwest might carry "pop" in their "sacks," while their East Coast counterparts carry "soda" in their "bags." Even organizations develop their own languages, or jargons, which become important mainstays of the organizational cultures, as discussed in Chapter 15. The same happens as groups, like a marketing department, form subcultures within organizations.

Time orientation and attitudes toward time vary in different cultures. In some cultures, the traditional concept of time is a "circle," which suggests repetition and another chance to pass the same way again. If an opportunity is lost today—no problem, it is likely to return again tomorrow. The emphasis in such cultures is on the present rather than the future. Time may also be measured by recurring natural events, such as the phases of the moon. For Muslims this determines the fasting month of Ramadan, and for the Chinese it determines the New Year. In other cultures, time is perceived more like a straight line. The past is gone; the present is with us only briefly; and the future is almost upon us. Time is viewed and measured with the precise movement of a clock, and it is something to be "saved" and "wasted." Long-range goals become important to this time orientation, and planning is a way of managing the future.

The anthropologist Edward T. Hall distinguishes between **monochronic cultures,** in which people tend to do one thing at a time, and **polychronic cultures,** in which people tend to do more than one thing at a time.[7] Monochronic cultures distinguish clearly between different activities, such as work and rest; polychronic cultures do not. For example, a North American or Northern European manager might allow a half hour to deal with a visitor. The visitor receives her undivided attention during this time. When the meeting ends, the manager moves to the next task or visitor. In contrast to this monochronic behavior, a cabinet minister in a Mediterranean country may have a large reception area outside of his office. People wait in this area and transact business in public. Government officials may move around the room conferring with first one person, then another, then perhaps going back to speak with the first, and so on. This behavior is more representative of a polychronic culture.

The *use of space* varies among cultures. Personal space is the "bubble" that surrounds us, and the preferred size of this bubble differs from one culture to another.[8] We feel uncomfortable when others invade or "close in" on our personal space. But then again, we also feel uncomfortable if people are too far away and communication with them becomes difficult. When a Saudi moves close enough to feel comfortable with a visiting Canadian executive, the visitor may back away in discomfort and try to keep more distance between them.

In some cultures, space is organized in such a way that many activities can be carried out simultaneously, consistent with the polychronic view of time. Spanish and Italian towns are organized around central squares (plazas or piazzas), whereas U.S. towns are structured linearly along a "main" street. Cultural influences are also seen in the way in which work space is organized. North Americans prefer individual offices with doors, whereas open floor plans are common in Japan.

Religion can be one of the more visible manifestations of a culture. The influence of religion often prescribes day-to-day dress, greetings, rituals, holy days, and foods that can or cannot be eaten. Codes of ethics and moral behavior tend to have roots in religious beliefs, and the influence of religion on economic matters can also be significant.[9] In Iran one finds "Islamic" banks that operate on religious principles set forth in the holy Koran; and in Malaysia a business dinner should be scheduled after 8:00 P.M. so that any Muslim guests can first have their evening or *Maghrib* prayer.

Values and National Cultures

Dutch scholar Geert Hofstede offers a useful approach to understanding value differences across national cultures.[10] In a study of some 116,000 employees of a U.S.-based multinational corporations operating in more than 40 countries, he identified four dimensions of national culture—power distance, uncertainty avoidance, individualism–collectivism, and masculinity–femininity. His more recent work with Michael Bond has added a fifth value dimension called long-term–short-term orientation.[11] These five dimensions of national culture can be described as follows.[12]

1. **Power distance** The degree to which people in a country accept a hierarchical or unequal distribution of power in organizations. Indonesia is a high power-distance culture; the Netherlands is a relatively low power-distance culture.

2. **Uncertainty avoidance** The degree to which people in a country feel uncomfortable with ambiguous and unstructured situations. France is a high uncertainty-avoidance culture; Singapore is a low uncertainty-avoidance culture.

3. **Individualism–collectivism** The degree to which people in a country focus more on working as individuals or on working together in groups. The United States is a highly individualistic culture; Sweden is a more collectivist culture.

4. **Masculinity–femininity** The degree to which people in a country emphasize so-called masculine traits, such as assertiveness, independence, and insensitivity to feelings, as dominant values.[13] Japan is a highly masculine culture; Norway is considered a more feminine culture.

5. **Long-term–short-term orientation** The degree to which people in a country emphasize values associated with the future—such as thrift and persistence versus values that focus on the past or present—such as social obliga-

---
THE EFFECTIVE MANAGER 3.1

How to Deal with Differences in National Cultures

POWER DISTANCE

Status is important in high power-distance cultures; therefore, respect the difference between superiors and subordinates, and expect "bosses" to be somewhat aloof and inaccessible. In low power-distance cultures, expect closer relationships between superiors and subordinates.

UNCERTAINTY AVOIDANCE

Because structure is important in high uncertainty-avoidance cultures, don't be surprised by tendencies to reduce or avoid risk. In low uncertainty-avoidance cultures, be prepared for less emphasis on structure and security and more tendency to let time "have its way."

INDIVIDUALISM–COLLECTIVISM

The individual comes first in high individualism cultures, so expect an emphasis on self-interest and individual decisions. In high collectivism cultures, be prepared for more emphasis on the "group" and a tendency to think and behave according to "we" terms.

MASCULINITY–FEMININITY

Independence is valued in high masculinity cultures; expect differentiated gender roles and an emphasis on assertiveness, competition, and success. In high femininity cultures, be prepared for more emphasis on interdependence, gender equality, quality of life, interpersonal relations, and respect for "beautiful" things.

LONG-TERM–SHORT-TERM ORIENTATION

Tradition, age, and relationships are respected in high long-term orientation cultures; therefore, expect an emphasis on the Confucian values of thrift, persistence, and saving "face." In high short-term cultures, be prepared for less respect for age, greater willingness to express direct criticism, and more emphasis on formal written contracts.

---

tions and tradition. China, with its strong Confucian traditions, is high on long-term orientation; the United States is high on short-term orientation.

The Effective Manager 3.1 lends more insight into the managerial implications of all five dimensions of national culture.[14] OB research continues to examine them and others in order to establish how countries can be grouped into those sharing generally similar dominant values. Such "cluster maps" are helpful in determining if and how various management practices can be transferred across cultures. It is common, for example, to compare "Anglo" countries such as the United States, Canada, and Great Britain with the "Asian Dragons" of Hong Kong, Singapore, Japan, and South Korea. The Anglos tend to be individualistic, moderate power-distance, and rather short-term cultures; the Asian Dragons are more collectivist, high power-distance, and long-term cultures. Just in these differences alone, one can see the potential for conflict and misunderstanding as managers and others from these countries try to work together in the vast commercial ties linking the Anglo and Asian Dragon countries in the global economy.

Developing Cultural Awareness and Sensitivity

The starting point for dealing better with people from different cultures is to understand your own culture. This helps guard against two problems that arise frequently in international dealings. One is the danger of **parochialism**—the assumption that the ways of your culture are the *only* ways of doing things. The other is the danger of **ethnocentrism**—the assumption that the ways of your culture are the *best* ways of doing things.[15] It is parochial for a traveling British businesswoman to assume that all of her foreign business contacts will speak English; it is ethnocentric for her to think that anyone who doesn't speak English can't be very sophisticated in business dealings.

In order to become more aware of other cultures, we must also be able to see ourselves as others see us. We need to recognize and understand how we may be viewed through the eyes of "foreigners." This recognition requires good communication skills, especially the ability to learn through listening. The following comments illustrate how American culture may appear in the eyes of others.[16]

"Americans seem to be in a perpetual hurry." (India)

"Americans appear to us rather distant." (Kenya)

"[To Americans] work seems to be the one type of motivation." (Colombia)

"[For Americans] even the littlest thing has to be 'why, why, why?'" (Indonesia)

"The American is very explicit; [he or she] wants a 'yes' or 'no'." (Ethiopia)

A Global Perspective on People at Work

The term **international management** is used to describe management that involves the conduct of business activities in more than one country of the globe. **International organizational behavior** involves the study of individuals and groups in organizations in this global setting.[17] International OB scholars try to learn how the principles and concepts of management and organizational behavior apply across cultural and national boundaries.

Multinational Employers

There are many different ways of conducting international business, including direct import and export arrangements, portfolio investment, contract and other foreign manufacturing, foreign licensing, and turnkey projects. Of particular interest is the **multinational corporation** (MNC). As business firms with extensive international operations in more than one foreign country, MNCs are more than just companies that "do business abroad." They are global concerns whose missions and strategies are both geographically dispersed and multicultural in scope. Of growing importance, too, are the roles of other multinational organizations (MNOs) in our complicated world. Their nonprofit missions and operations also span the globe and involve a variety of social and economic development missions. Examples are the World Wildlife Fund, Amnesty International, the International Red Cross, the International Labor Organization, the United Nations, and the World Bank.

MNCs are complex organizations in which a diverse network of wholly or partially owned production and marketing operations located in different countries have to be coordinated. The complexity of multinational operations creates many management problems and provides a rich field of study for the OB scholar. Alvin Toffler calls the MNC a *transnational corporation* and describes it as one that

> may do research in one country, manufacture components in another, assemble them in a third, sell the manufactured goods in a a fourth, deposit its surplus funds in a fifth, and so on. It may have operating affiliates in dozens of countries. The size, importance, and political power of this new player in the global game has skyrocketed.[18]

Multicultural Work Forces

The ways in which the management process of planning, organizing, leading, and controlling is implemented varies across cultures.[19] This is an obvious problem for managers who must work transnationally. It is to be expected, for example, that problems may arise for an Australian contractor managing a construction project in Saudi Arabia and employing workers from Asia, the Middle East, Europe, and North America. The sheer multiculturalism of the workforce presents challenges, let alone the further complexities of the setting. It must also be expected that a great deal of patience will be needed, as many businesspeople are finding, to successfully establish a joint venture in the Ukraine, Kazakhstan, or another country from the former Soviet Union. In these and other settings, political instabilities and bureaucratic difficulties further complicate the already complex process of creating transnational business partnerships.

Managing across cultures can also be a key problem in one's home environment, where more and more organizations are experiencing domestic multiculturalism— cultural diversity within a given national population.[20] What has happened over the past three decades in Los Angeles is one case in point. With the second largest Mexican population after Mexico City, the city is a popular home to many immigrant groups. It must constantly adjust to the shifting rhythms of ethnic diversity from subcultures. It is said, in fact, that some 20 percent of the city's school-children speak other languages more fluently than they speak English.

Formally defined, an **expatriate** is someone who works and lives in a foreign country. Expatriates often face problems when moving into a foreign culture to work; they also can face problems of reentering their home culture after an assignment abroad. Many progressive MNCs try to minimize the problems of expatriate assignments by[21]

- Recruiting and selecting employees with skills and motivation to live abroad.

- Training and orienting them to best prepare for life in the foreign culture.

THE EFFECTIVE MANAGER 3.2

Attributes of the Global Manager

- Able to apply high technical expertise to a job.
- Able to adapt skillfully to different business environments.
- Able to negotiate effectively in different business environments.
- Able to solve problems quickly and under different circumstances.
- Able to motivate and communicate well with people from different cultures.
- Able to speak more than one major language.
- Able to understand different government and political systems.
- Able to understand business partners' backgrounds and their mentality.
- Able to convey a positive attitude and enthusiasm when dealing with others.

- Actively supporting them while on assignment abroad, especially in the early stages.
- Paying careful attention to the needs of their spouses and families.

Comparative Management and Organizational Practices

A global manager, even with the skills and personal characteristics shown in The Effective Manager 3.2, must be well informed on the many international dimensions of organizational behavior.[22] The following discussion illustrates how these dimensions can be applied to the concepts and issues found in the following parts of this book—individuals, groups, processes, and organizations.

Individuals across Cultures

Individual *motivation* to work is an important and popular topic in most parts of the world. Several key theories of motivation are discussed in Chapter 5, but they have largely been developed in the United States. We run the risk of being parochial or ethnocentric by assuming that people in other cultures will be motivated by the same things, and in the same ways, as we are. Although these theories may help explain the behavior of Americans, serious questions must be raised about their generalizability to other cultures, Western and non-Western alike.[23] Consider Hofstede's framework again and its application to the management of reward systems. The American preference for individual rewards reflects their high individualism; the Japanese preference for group rewards reflects their high collectivism. When an American expatriate attempts to use individual incentives in Japan, problems are likely to occur. By the same token, Japanese managers in the United States may find American workers somewhat reluctant in their responses to group-based incentive systems.

Groups across Cultures

The management of *group process,* or the way in which members of a group work together, is a key topic in Chapters 8 and 9. It, too, has a cultural aspect that must be understood. Consider the following perspective: Actual group performance = Potential performance − Group process losses.[24] To the extent that multiculturalism adds to the difficulty of managing the group process, it may also be a factor in determining the level of performance success in a group. Theoretically at least, we like to believe that diversity is an asset and not a liability in the work setting.[25] But even though diversity brings many potential benefits to a work group or team, including the creative and problem-solving advantages of more ideas and information, it also increases the complexity of various group processes. Consider this description of a multicultural project team in Europe:

> The British representative appeared unable to accept any systematic approach; he wanted to discuss all potential problems before reaching a decision. The French and Swiss representatives agreed to examine everything before making a decision, but then disagreed on the sequence and scheduling of operations . . . As a result . . . we never started the project. . . . If the project had been discussed by three Frenchmen, three Swiss, or three Britons, a decision, good or bad, would have been made. The project would not have been stalled for lack of agreement.[26]

Some of the specific problems that must be mastered in multicultural groups if they are to achieve high performance results are:[27]

- **Attitude problems** Group members from different cultures may tend to distrust one another and be drawn more closely to members of their own cultures.
- **Stereotyping problems** Group members may be prone to ethnic, gender, age, or national stereotypes that interfere with understandings between individuals.
- **Communication problems** Language differences, both verbal and nonverbal, may make it difficult for group members from different cultures to communicate well.
- **Stress problems** Unfamiliar habits, styles of behavior, and related difficulties may create stress as group members from different cultures try to work together.
- **Efficiency problems** Members of multicultural groups must spend more time working on their relationships and group processes, detracting from direct task accomplishment.

Processes across Cultures

Important cross-cultural differences exist in the area of *leadership,* the subject of Chapter 11. By way of example, Figure 3.1 summarizes research on how the expectations of the manager's leadership and supervision roles vary among selected national

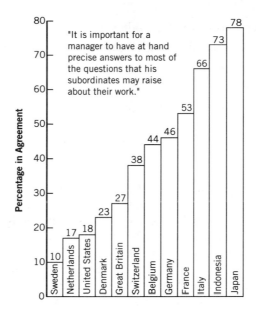

Figure 3.1 How expectations regarding the manager's role vary across cultures. *Source:* Developed from Andrè Laurent, "The Cultural Diversity of Western Conceptions of Management," *International Studies of Management and Organization,* 13 (Spring–Summer 1983), pp. 75–96. Reprinted by permission of publisher, M. E. Sharpe, Inc., Armonk, New York.

cultures. Workers in some cultures want their superiors to act as experts and be directive in dealing with them. Indonesian workers, for example, may feel uncomfortable with a boss who delegates too much authority to them; Danish workers would more likely want their managers to involve them in more participative and problem-solving approaches.

Global managers should also expect the process of *decision making,* discussed in Chapter 12, to be affected by cultural differences. Employees from high power-distance cultures will most likely want their supervisors to make most decisions; employees from more collectivist cultures are likely to prefer making decisions in teams or groups. In collectivist Japan, many companies use the *ringi* system for making decisions. This is a group decision approach whereby all affected company members affix their sign of approval to widely circulated written proposals. In more individualistic France, decisions tend to be made at the top of companies and passed down the hierarchy for implementation.[28]

The process of *communication,* discussed in Chapter 13, is certainly a critical managerial activity. And language, as previously discussed, must be of special concern when communicating across cultures. But while English is fast becoming the global language of business, relatively few English speakers are learning other languages. In business dealings, say in Hong Kong, Tunis, or Santiago, it is common to find the visiting American depending on others to communicate in English, even though it is their second, or even third, language. This approach carries many risks, including:

- Learning only what the other party wants you to know and tells you in English.
- Misunderstandings because the other party's English isn't as good as you think.
- Losing opportunities by being limited to dealing only with people who speak English.

When dealing with someone who speaks an unfamiliar language, translation becomes necessary. Here too, however, problems can easily occur. Translating is difficult and often imprecise, especially in fast-paced conversations and discussions. Even in the written word, translation may fail to deal accurately with local idioms and other features of language. General Motors' well-known "Body by Fisher" label was translated into Flemish as "Corpse by Fisher." When Ford introduced its low-cost truck, the "Fiera," into some developing countries, it belatedly discovered that the name means "ugly woman" in colloquial Spanish.[29]

The "silent language" of body postures and gestures also varies across cultures.[30] It is quite easy to move or behave in a familiar way, only to offend someone unintentionally. Westerners tend to be quick to indicate support or pleasure with the "thumbs up" sign. But while this signal means "go ahead" or "jolly good" to them, it may be considered vulgar and insulting in other places like Ghana and Iran. To point at someone or something with an extended index finger is common in the United States. In Malaysia, pointing with an extended finger is rude; the culturally sensitive Westerner points with the fist closed and thumb indicating the object or person in question.

Organizations across Cultures

As we will see in Chapter 15, the *structures* adopted by an organization will depend on a variety of factors, including the industry, technology, and environment. Cultural preferences regarding communication, the role of leaders in decision making, and so on, can all affect the structure of the organization in a number of ways. These

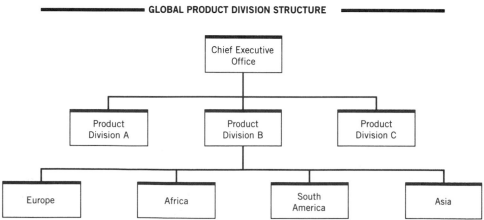

Figure 3.2 A global product division structure for a multinational business.

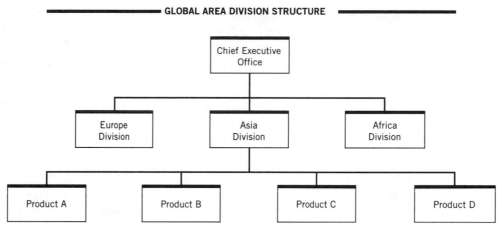

Figure 3.3 A global geographic or area division structure for a multinational business.

include the number of subordinates reporting to a manager, the number of levels in the chain of command, and the degree of centralization, among other possibilities. Japanese auto manufacturers operate with fewer levels of management than their U.S. counterparts. Even though recent restructurings by Ford, GM, and Chrysler have closed the gap, differences—perhaps tied to cultural roots—still remain.

Structural issues arise when organizations first enter into or expand their global operations. A firm typically enters the international marketplace on a small scale, such as by exporting products. As the international side of the business grows, the firm may eventually find that it must establish subsidiaries in foreign countries. As the number of foreign subsidiaries grows, a headquarters group, or *international division,* is often formed to oversee all of the firm's global operations. As international operations continue to grow and prosper, top management may change its view of the firm to that of a truly multinational enterprise. At this point, a global structure of one of the following types may be implemented. **Global product structures** have separate divisions responsible for a line of products sold around the world (see Figure 3.2). **Global geographic structures** have separate divisions responsible for all operations in specific geographical areas of the world (see Figure 3.3).

A "Global" View on Learning about Organizational Behavior

It wasn't too long ago that the importance of global learning about organizational behavior and management was thrust upon the world stage with great fanfare.[31] But along with envy of Japan's economic success at the time came a premature rush by many Western managers to copy what the Japanese were doing. Since then, the Japanese economy has had problems of its own, and the rest of the world has become a more informed and sophisticated consumer of so-called Japanese management practices. The emphasis is now on the "lessons" to be learned from Japanese management—given proper thought and cultural awareness.

On Hofstede's scale of national cultures, Japan ranks as a highly collectivist society. This contrasts markedly with the highly individualistic cultures of the United States and other Western nations. Therefore, one would expect to find differences in Japanese and Western approaches to management and organization. In general, the Japanese approach has been described as involving

- Lifetime employment practices, emphasizing employee–employer loyalty.
- Slow promotion and career advancement, emphasizing broad career paths.
- Group decision making (the *ringi* system), emphasizing census-building.

Although this pattern remains generally characteristic of Japanese management and organization practices, it isn't uniformly true. Developments in Japanese society are creating their own pressures for change. In particular, the emerging values and attitudes of younger workers contrast with those of the past.[32] Some observers note that employees tend to be less loyal to employers, to display greater concerns for their own self-interests, to focus more on monetary gain and tangible rewards, and to show more respect for equal work opportunities for women, who have suffered job discrimination in the past.

Still, Japanese approaches to management are a great source of insight and constructive change around the world. There are good lessons to be learned, if they are applied with due sensitivity to cultural differences. The lessons are particularly evident in a number of the new workplace themes with which you are already becoming familiar. These include the value of teams and work groups, consensus decision making, employee involvement, "flatter" structures, and strong corporate cultures.[33]

The special and popular case of Japan is just one example of how a careful study of "foreign" management and organizational practices can have important implications at home. Today there is genuine interest in how management is practiced around the globe. This interest extends to learning more about management practices in various countries or geographical regions, such as Korea and Russia. It also extends to learning more about how dominant values such as the legacies of Confucian dynamism in Asia and Islamic principles in the Muslim world influence management practices. We must be alert to what managers are doing around the world, wherever they may be—Africa, Asia, Europe, the Middle East, North or South America. And we must carefully examine what they are accomplishing in each setting, and why.

The international dimensions of OB are obviously important in today's world. Managers from different cultures have a lot to learn from one another. It is no longer sufficient to accept local practices and beliefs as the most, or only, correct ones. The truly informed and progressive managers of the twenty-first century will be those who become the "global managers" first described in the chapter introduction.

In Summary

What is the international imperative of management?

- Management and the international imperative are at the forefront of current interest in the global economy.

- "Global managers" with a strong worldview are needed to help organizations achieve a competitive edge in the global economy.

- Many nations, including those in Europe, North America, and Asia, are forming cooperative unions to gain economic strength.

- Wherever you live and work, more and more major businesses are "foreign" owned, in whole or in part.

- A managerial career in today's work environment will sooner or later bring contact with international issues and considerations.

What is culture?

- In its popular dimensions, culture represents observable differences between people on such things as language, time, space orientation, and religion.

- In its subjective dimensions, culture represents deeply ingrained influences on the way people from different societies think and behave.

- National cultures may vary on Hofstede's dimensions of power distance, individualism–collectivism, uncertainty avoidance, masculinity–femininity, and long-term–short-term orientation.

- Managers must overcome the limits of parochialism and ethnocentrism, and must develop cultural empathy—an ability to understand things from another culture's point of view.

How does the global economy affect people at work?

- Multinational corporations (MNCs) are major employers in the global economy.

- Expansion of international business dealings is strategically viewed as the route to continued growth and prosperity for many large and small companies.

- Expatriate employees who work abroad for extended periods of time face special challenges, including both adjustment problems abroad and reentry problems upon returning home.

How do management and organizational practices compare around the world?

- Communication in an international environment, where language—spoken and unspoken—is often a source of misunderstandings and unintentional mistakes.

- Motivation to work may vary across cultures where different values and attitudes predominate.

- The global product division and global geographic division are two popular organization structures used by firms emphasizing international operations.

- Cross-cultural differences in leadership and supervision may be traced to such value differences as power-distance and individualism.

What is a "global" view on learning about organizational behavior?

- Management innovations around the world include an emphasis on work teams, enriched job designs, employee involvement, alternative organization structures, and the like.

- An understanding of Japanese management has shown how long-term employment, cohesive work groups, and employee services can have a positive impact on performance.

- Any management concept or technique must be transferred selectively and with cultural sensitivity; neither American nor Japanese practices apply universally to other cultures.

I N D I V I D U A L
D I F F E R E N C E S
A N D   D I V E R S I T Y

As you read Chapter 4, keep in mind these study questions:

- What are demographic characteristics of individuals?

- What are competency characteristics of individuals?

- What are personality characteristics of individuals?

- What are values?

- What are attitudes?

- What is perception, and what are some common perceptual distortions?

- What are some key strategy areas for capitalizing on workplace diversity and dealing with individual differences?

I n this chapter we examine some key individual difference factors of employees and how these differences can be matched with an organization's current and future job requirements. First, we look at three broad categories of factors important in our study of OB: demographic or biographic characteristics (e.g., gender, age, ethnicity); competency characteristics (aptitude/ability, or what a person can do); and personality characteristics (a number of traits reflecting what a person is like). We then look at values, attitudes, and perception—three more ways in which individuals differ. Finally, we show the importance of individual differences in planning strategies you can use to deal with the increasing diversity in the new workforce and to help obtain the all-important match with job requirements.

Demographic Differences among Individuals

Demographic characteristics are the background variables that help shape what a person has become. They are sometimes called *biographic characteristics.* Usually, demographic characteristics are easy to determine by appearance or from a person's personnel file. Some key demographic characteristics are gender, age, race and ethnicity, and disability. In addition, it's useful to think of these characteristics both in current terms (e.g., a worker's current income) and historical terms (e.g., where and in how many places a person has lived growing up).

Demographic characteristics are important for at least three reasons.

1. **Workplace legislation** A series of federal, state, and local laws has outlawed workplace discrimination on the basis of gender, age, ethnicity or race, or disability.[1]

2. **Performance and human resources maintenance** An approach known as biodata is sometimes used to establish a link between demographic characteristics and performance and human resource maintenance. Information is obtained on a wide range of such variables. For example, parents' socioeconomic background and the number of places in which a person lived while growing up might be considered. The biodata approach would then compare such characteristics for high-performing and low-performing workers to provide a profile against which to compare new job applicants.

3. **Stereotypes** Stereotypes occur when an individual is assigned to a group or category (e.g., old person), and the attributes commonly associated with the group or category are assigned to the person in question (e.g., older people aren't creative). Demographic characteristics may serve as the basis of stereo-

---

THE EFFECTIVE MANAGER 4.1

Tips in Dealing with Male and Female Managers

A manager should emphasize the following points when dealing with female and male managers.

- Do not assume that male and female managers differ in personal qualities.
- Make sure that his or her own and the organization's policies, practices, and programs minimize creation of sex differences in managers' job experiences.
- Do assume that managers of either sex are no more superior than those of the other sex.
- Do not assume that women and men are different types of managers.
- Do assume that there will be excellent, good, and poor managers within each sex.
- Do assume that success requires the best use of talent, which calls for identifying and developing the best managers regardless of sex.

---

types that obscure individual differences and can prevent people from getting to know others as individuals and from accurately assessing their performance potential. Someone who believes that older people aren't creative, for example, may mistakenly decide not to assign a very inventive 60-year-old person to an important task force.

To help dispel some of these stereotypes, let's look briefly at what the research data tell us.

Gender

The research on working women in general tells us that there are very few differences between men and women that would affect job performance. Thus, there are no consistent differences in the problem-solving abilities, analytical skills, competitive drive, motivation, learning ability, or sociability of a man versus a woman.[2] However, women do tend to be more conforming and to have lower expectations of success than do men. Finally, absenteeism rates tend to be higher among women than among men. This finding may change as we see men starting to play a more active role in raising children.

Regardless of these general findings, a recent large-sample survey of workers and managers showed that nearly 40 percent of respondents believed that increasing employment of women has led to a breakdown of the family; 36 percent believed that women obtained their current position only because they were women.[3] The Effective Manager 4.1 emphasizes some important points concerning female and male managers.[4]

Age

The research findings concerning age are particularly important given the fact that the workforce is aging. From 1985 to the year 2000, the number of workers between

45 and 65 years of age is expected to increase by more than 40 percent[5] and shortages of younger workers are expected to continue.[6] Even today, most workers no longer have to retire even at age 70.

A common stereotype concerns age and learning and flexibility. Many people associate the elderly with a sense of inertia. However, the truth is that it depends on the individual. Furthermore, age and performance have been found to be unrelated. That is, older people are no more likely than younger people to be unproductive. In terms of absenteeism, although older workers have higher rates of unavoidable absences than do younger workers, their *avoidable* absences are less frequent. Older workers are also less likely to quit a job than are younger workers, so there is a managerial advantage if they are performing well. Overall, contrary to many stereotypes, the data suggest that most older workers are likely to be good workers.[7]

Disability

A recent survey of managers at all levels in small companies reported that disabled workers did their jobs as well as did nondisabled employees. The study further indicated that the costs of accommodating disabled workers are generally not very high and were not an important barrier to hiring these workers. Indeed, some firms are hiring both the physically and mentally disabled.[8]

Racioethnicity

Consistent with some current literature, we use the term *racioethnicity* to reflect the broad spectrum of employees of differing ethnicities or races who are providing an ever-increasing portion of the new workforce.[9] For each of the previous demographic variables, we reported some research evidence concerning their linkage with productivity and other work-related aspects. Here, there are so many racioethnic groups to be considered that we don't try to summarize the kind of research evidence above. Rather, we simply make the point that besides white Americans, four broad racioethnic groups receiving increasing attention are the Native Americans, Asian Americans, African Americans, and Hispanic Americans. Once again, stereotypes exist for these as well as other racioethnic groups.

Other Demographic Characteristics

Some other general demographic characteristics[10] that are frequently considered are marital status, number of children, and experience. In general, the research shows that married individuals have fewer absences, lower turnover rates, and greater job satisfaction than do unmarried individuals. There is typically a positive relationship between number of children and absences and job satisfaction, while data for turnover are mixed.

Finally, a look at experience and performance shows only a weak relationship between the two variables. More experienced workers tend to have low absence rates and relatively low turnover, however. In addition, turnover on a worker's previous job is strongly related to future turnover.

Overall, we conclude the following: If carefully validated, demographic variables can be used to assist in the selection process. For demographics concerned with gender, age, racioethnicity, or disability, such validation is absolutely critical in terms of various governmental discrimination laws. Too often, demographics are used stereotypically, and people are not given a fair chance to demonstrate their true underlying capabilities in a work setting. Stereotypes can create special problems in the new workplace because of the diverse demographic characteristics of the workers.

Competency Differences among Individuals

Competency is the central issue concerning the aptitudes and abilities of people at work. **Aptitude** represents a person's capability to learn something. **Ability** reflects a person's existing capacity to perform the various tasks needed for a given job and includes both relevant knowledge and skills.[11] Aptitudes, in fact, are potential abilities, whereas abilities are the knowledge and skills that an individual already possesses.

Competency is an important consideration for a manager when initially hiring or selecting candidates for a job. Once people with the appropriate aptitudes or abilities have been selected, on-the-job and continuing education or training activities can be used to develop or enhance the required job skills.

We are all acquainted with various tests used to measure mental aptitudes and abilities. Some of these provide an overall "IQ" score (e.g., the Stanford–Binet IQ test). Others provide measures of more specific competencies that are required of people entering various educational programs or career fields. All such tests seek to measure mental aptitude or ability and thus facilitate the screening and selection of applicants.

Personality Differences among Individuals

We use the term **personality** to represent the overall profile or combination of characteristics that capture the unique nature of a person as that person reacts and interacts with others.

Personality combines a set of physical and mental characteristics that reflect how a person looks, thinks, acts, and feels. Understanding personality contributes to an understanding of organizational behavior by adding a consideration of what individuals are like to that of what they *can* do (competency) and what they *will* do (motivation). That is, we expect there to be a predictable interplay between an individual's personality and his or her tendency to behave in certain ways. A common expectation, for example, is that introverts don't tend to be sociable.

Personality Determinants and Development

The issue of just what determines personality has given rise to the nature/nurture controversy. That is, is personality determined by heredity, or genetic endowment, or by one's environment? Heredity consists of those factors that are determined at conception and includes physical characteristics and gender, in addition to personality factors. Environment consists of cultural, social, and situational factors.

Cultural values and norms play a substantial role in the development of an individual's personality and behaviors. Contrast the individualism of U.S. culture with the collectivism of Mexican culture, for example.[12] Social factors reflect such things as family life, religion, and the many kinds of formal and informal groups in which people participate throughout their lives. Finally, situational factors can influence personality. Such situational factors as the opportunity to assume increasingly challenging goals and the opportunity to come back from failure can help build a person's feeling of self-worth.

There is considerable debate concerning the impact of heredity on personality. The most general conclusion is that heredity sets the limits on just how much personality characteristics can be developed. Environment determines development within these limits. These limits appear to vary from one characteristic to the next. However, across all the characteristics studied, the average proportion is about a 50–50 split between heredity and environment.[13]

Developmental Approaches   The developmental approaches of Chris Argyris and Daniel Levinson systematically examine the ways in which personality develops across time. Argyris is a management expert who is especially concerned with conflicts between individuals and organizations.[14] Argyris notes that people develop along a continuum of dimensions from immaturity to maturity.

From Immaturity	To Maturity
Passivity	Activity
Dependence	Independence
Limited behavior	Diverse behavior
Shallow interests	Deep interests
Short-time perspective	Long-time perspective
Subordinate position	Superordinate position
Little self-awareness	Much self-awareness

Argyris believes that the nature of the mature adult personality can sometimes be inconsistent with work opportunities. Organizations and their managers may neglect the "adult" sides of people. They may use close supervision and control that is more typically needed by "infants" whose personalities are still immature.

Others, such as Daniel Levinson, see an individual's personality as developing in a series of stages over time. For Levinson, there are four key transitions: age 30, mid-life, age 50, and late adult. He sees these stages as having a crucial impact on a worker's job and career and on the employing organization.[15]

The point of both Argyris's and Levinson's work is that (1) personalities develop

THE EFFECTIVE MANAGER 4.2

Four Problem-solving Styles and Their Occupational Match-ups

SENSATION-THINKING:
Decisive, Dependable, Applied Thinker, Sensitive to Details

Accounting	Market research
Production	Engineering
Computer programming	

INTUITIVE-THINKING:
Creative, Progressive, Perceptive Thinker, with Many Ideas

Systems design	Middle/top management
Systems analysis	Teaching business, economics
Law	

SENSATION-FEELING:
Pragmatic, Analytical, Methodical, and Conscientious

Direct supervision	Selling
Counseling	Interviewing
Negotiating	

INTUITIVE-FEELING:
Charismatic, Participative, People Oriented, and Helpful

Public relations	Politics
Advertising	Customer services
Personnel	

in predictable ways over time, and (2) these developments require quite different managerial responses.

Important Personality Traits

Numerous personality traits are described in the literature. Six that are especially important for OB are: (1) problem-solving style; (2) locus of control, (3) authoritarianism/dogmatism; (4) Machiavellianism; (5) self-monitoring; and (6) type A and type B orientation.

The problem-solving style reflects the way a person goes about gathering and evaluating information in solving problems and making decisions. In terms of information gathering, there are sensation-type and intuitive-type individuals. The former prefer routine and order and emphasize well-defined details in gathering information. The latter prefer the big picture and like solving new problems.

In terms of evaluation, or making judgments about how to deal with information once it has been collected, there are feeling-type and thinking-type persons. The former are oriented toward conformity and accommodating themselves to others; they try to avoid problems that could lead to disagreements. The latter use reason and intellect to deal with problems and downplay emotional aspects.

When these two dimensions of information gathering and evaluation are combined, the matrix of problem-solving styles shown in The Effective Manager 4.2

results.[16] The four basic problem-solving styles are sensation-feeling (SF), intuitive-feeling (IF), sensation-thinking (ST), and intuitive-thinking (IT), together with various occupational pairings. Research suggests a number of basic differences between different problem-solving styles, emphasizing the importance of fitting such styles with a task's information processing and evaluation requirements.[17]

A second important personality trait is Rotter's **locus of control,** which measures the internal–external orientation of a person—that is, the extent to which a person feels able to affect his or her life.[18] People have general conceptions about whether events are controlled primarily by themselves, which indicates an internal orientation, or by outside forces or their social and physical environment, which indicates an external orientation. **Internals,** or persons with an internal locus of control, believe that they control their own fate or destiny. In contrast, **externals,** or persons with an external locus of control, believe that much of what happens to them is beyond their control and is determined by environmental forces.

In general, externals are more extroverted in their interpersonal relationships and are more oriented toward the world of people and things around them. Internals tend to be more introverted and are more oriented toward their inner world of feelings and ideas.

Authoritarianism/dogmatism represents a third important personality trait. Both deal with the rigidity of a person's beliefs. A person high in **authoritarianism** tends to adhere rigidly to conventional values and to obey recognized authority. This person is concerned with toughness and power and opposes the use of subjective feelings. A person high in **dogmatism** sees the world as a threatening place. This person often regards legitimate authority as absolute and accepts or rejects others according to how much they agree with accepted authority. Superiors possessing these latter traits tend to be rigid and closed. Dogmatic subordinates tend to want certainty imposed on them.[19]

Machiavellianism is the fourth trait to be considered. It owes its origins to Niccolo Machiavelli, the sixteenth-century author whose very name evokes visions of a master of guile, deceit, and opportunism in interpersonal relations. Machiavelli earned his place in history by writing *The Prince,* a nobleman's guide to the acquisition and use of power.[20] From its pages emerges the personality profile of a **Machiavellian**—someone who views and manipulates others purely for personal gain.

Psychologists have developed a series of instruments called Mach scales to measure a person's Machiavellian orientation.[21] A *high-Mach* personality is someone

- with tendencies to behave in ways consistent with Machiavelli's basic principles.
- with tendencies to approach situations logically and thoughtfully, with the capability of lying to achieve personal goals.
- with a reluctance to be swayed by loyalty, friendships, past promises, or the opinions of others.
- who is skilled at influencing others.

Research using the Mach scales has led to a number of predictions regarding the way high and low Machs behave in various situations. A person with a "cool" and "detached" high-Mach personality can be expected to take control and try to exploit loosely structured environmental situations but will perform in a perfunctory, even detached, manner in highly structured situations. Low Machs tend to accept direction imposed by others in loosely structured situations; they work hard to do well in highly structured ones.

Self-monitoring is a fifth important trait. **Self-monitoring** reflects a person's ability to adjust his or her behavior to external, situational (environmental) factors.[22]

High self-monitoring individuals are very sensitive to external cues and tend to behave differently in different situations. Like high Machs, high self-monitors can present a very different appearance from their true self. In contrast, low self-monitors, like their low-Mach counterparts, aren't able to disguise their behaviors. With them, as with low Machs, "what you see is what you get."

There is also evidence that high self-monitors are closely attuned to the behavior of others and can conform more readily than can low-monitors.[23] Thus, they appear flexible and, for example, may be especially good at changing their leadership behavior to fit subordinates with high or low experience, tasks with high or low structure, and so on.

The final trait which we consider is Type A and Type B orientation. Individuals with a **Type A orientation** are characterized by impatience, desire for achievement, and perfectionism. In contrast, those with **Type B orientations** are characterized as more easygoing and as less competitive in relation to daily events.[24] There is some evidence suggesting that Type A people tend to be obsessive and to suffer from heart disease more than their Type B counterparts.

Value Differences among Individuals

Values can be defined as broad preferences concerning appropriate courses of action or outcomes. As such, values reflect a person's sense of right and wrong or what "ought" to be.[25] "Equal rights for all" and "people should be treated with respect and dignity" are representative of values. Values tend to influence attitudes and behavior. For example, if you value equal rights for all and you go to work for an organization that treats its managers much better than it does its workers, you may form the attitude that the company is an unfair place to work, and, consequently, you will not produce well or perhaps quit.

Sources and Types of Values

Parents, friends, teachers, and external reference groups can all influence individual values. Indeed, peoples' values develop as a product of the learning and experience they encounter in the cultural setting in which they live. As learning and experiences differ from one person to another, value differences result. Such differences are likely to be deep-seated and difficult (though not impossible) to change; many have their roots in early childhood and the way a person was raised.[26]

The noted psychologist Milton Rokeach has developed a well-known set of values classified into two broad categories.[27] **Terminal values** reflect a person's preferences concerning the "ends" to be achieved: they are the goals individuals would like to achieve during their lifetime. Rokeach has a complete set of 18 terminal values. Let's consider three of these: pleasure, sense of accomplishment, and salvation. Think how differently you might behave and feel depending on the relative importance you placed on these and other end states as lifetime goals.

Instrumental values reflect the "means" for achieving desired ends. Now think how differently you might go about achieving your important end states depending on the relative importance you attached to, say, the instrumental values of helpfulness, independence, and imagination (from Rokeach's complete set of 18 instrumental values).

Another classification of human values was developed in the early 1930s by psychologist Gordon Allport and his associates. These values fall into six major types:[28]

1. **Theoretical** Interest in the discovery of truth through reasoning and systematic thinking.
2. **Economic** Interest in usefulness and practicality, including the accumulation of wealth.
3. **Aesthetic** Interest in beauty, form, and artistic harmony.
4. **Social** Interest in people and love as a human relationship.
5. **Political** Interest in gaining power and influencing other people.
6. **Religious** Interest in unity and in understanding the cosmos as a whole.

These value classifications have had a major impact on the values literature, but they were not specifically designed for people in a work setting. However, a more recent values schema has been developed by Meglino and associates, which is aimed at people in the workplace.[29]

1. **Achievement** Getting things done and working hard to accomplish difficult things in life.
2. **Helping and concern for others** Being concerned with other people and helping others.
3. **Honesty** Telling the truth and doing what you feel is right.
4. **Fairness** Being impartial and doing what is fair for all concerned.

The Meglino framework was developed specifically from information obtained in the workplace; the four values listed above were shown to be especially important. Thus, the framework should be particularly relevant for studying values in OB.

Patterns and Trends in Values

Values are important to managers and to the field of OB because of their potential to influence workplace attitudes, behaviors, and outputs. In addition, values can be influential through *value congruence*. **Value congruence** occurs when individuals express positive feelings upon encountering others who exhibit values similar to their own. When values differ, or are *incongruent,* conflicts over such things as goals and the means to achieve them may result. The Meglino et al. value schema was used to examine value congruence between leaders and followers. The researchers found greater follower satisfaction with the leader when there was such congruence in terms of the earlier mentioned achievement, helping, honesty, and fairness values.

We should also be aware of applied research on values trends over time. Daniel Yankelovich notes a movement away from valuing economic incentives, organizational loyalty, and work-related identity and toward valuing meaningful work, pursuit of leisure, and personal identity and self-fulfillment. He believes that the modern manager must be able to recognize value differences and trends among people at work. For example, he reports finding higher productivity among younger workers who are employed in jobs that match their values and/or who are supervised by managers who share their values. These findings, of course, reinforce the above-mentioned discussion of value congruence.

Before moving on to attitudes, we should reinforce our point that values are individual preferences, but, as we have shown, many tend to be shared within cultures. Our examples thus far have emphasized values within a national or societal culture, but you should be aware that there is also a narrower set of shared values within organizations.

Attitude Differences among Individuals

Like values, attitudes are an important OB component. Attitudes are influenced by values, but they focus on specific people or objects, while values have a more general focus. "Employees should be allowed to participate" is a value; your positive or negative feeling about your job because of the participation it allows is an attitude. Formally defined, an **attitude** is a predisposition to respond in a positive or negative way to someone or something in one's environment. For example, when you say that you "like" or "dislike" someone or something, you are expressing an attitude. One important work-related attitude is job satisfaction. This attitude expresses a person's positive or negative feelings about various aspects of his or her job and work environment.

Regardless of the specific attitude considered, it's important to remember that an attitude, like a value, is *inferred* from the things people say (informally or in formal opinion polls) or do (their behavior).

Components of Attitudes[30]

Figure 4.1 shows attitudes as accompanied by antecedents and results. The beliefs and values antecedents in the figure form the **cognitive component** of an attitude: the beliefs, opinions, knowledge, or information a person possesses. Beliefs represent ideas about someone or something and the conclusions people draw about them; they convey a sense of "what is" to an individual. "My job lacks responsibility" is a belief shown in the figure. Note that the beliefs may or may not be accurate. "Responsibility is important" is a corresponding aspect of the cognitive component that reflects an underlying value.

Figure 4.1   A work-related example of the three components of attitudes.

The **affective component** of an attitude is a specific *feeling* regarding the personal impact of the antecedents. This is the actual attitude itself, such as "I don't like my job." The **behavioral component** is an intention to behave in a certain way based on your specific feelings or attitude. This intended behavior is a result of an attitude and is a predisposition to act in a specific way, such as "I'm going to quit my job."

Attitudes and Behavior

Look again at Figure 4.1. It is essential to recognize that the link between attitudes and behavior is tentative. An attitude results in *intended* behavior. This intention may or may not be carried out in a given circumstance. When are attitudes most likely to be substantially related to behavior? First, the more specific are attitudes and behaviors, the stronger the relationship. Second, it is important that there is a good deal of freedom available to carry out the intent. Finally, the attitude and behavior linkage tends to be stronger when the person in question has had experience with the stated attitude.

Attitudes and Cognitive Dissonance

One additional avenue of research on attitudes involves cognitive dissonance that Leon Festinger, a noted social psychologist, describes as a state of inconsistency between an individual's attitudes and his or her behavior.[31] Assume that you have the attitude that recycling is good for the economy but you don't recycle. Festinger predicts that such an inconsistency results in discomfort and a desire to reduce or eliminate it. Three ways of achieving this reduction or elimination are by

- **Changing the underlying attitude** You decide that recycling really isn't very good after all.
- **Changing future behavior** You start recycling.
- **Developing new ways of explaining or rationalizing the inconsistency** Recycling is good for the economy, but you don't recycle because the plastic recycling bags and procedures require more resources than are saved through recycling.

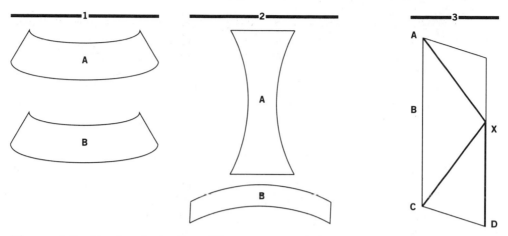

Figure 4.2 Line lengths in three different perceptual objects.

Festinger's cognitive dissonance theory offers yet another perspective on attitudes as special attributes of people at work. Among the work-related implications of the theory are:[32]

1. A recognition that behavior may influence attitudes and that attitudes may influence behavior.
2. A recognition that attitudes may develop consistent with a person's initial emotional response to a new person or object.

Perceptual Differences among Individuals

Look at Figure 4.2 and compare parts 1 A and B, 2 A and B, and 3 AX, XD, and XC. Objectively, the lines in each of these diagrams are the same length, but if you are like most people they do not look that way.

The example of the figure illustrates the notion of perception. Through perception, people process information inputs into decisions and actions. Perception is a way of forming impressions about oneself, other people, and daily life experiences. It is also a screen or filter through which information passes before having an effect on people. The quality or accuracy of a person's perceptions, therefore, has a major impact on the quality of the decisions made or actions taken in a given situation.

Common Perceptual Distortions

There are several common kinds of distortions that can make perceptions inaccurate. These are stereotypes, halo effects, selective perception, projection, and expectancy.

Stereotypes   Stereotypes obscure individual differences. They can prevent managers from getting to know people as individuals and from accurately assessing their needs, preferences, and abilities. Some common sources of negative stereotypes were discussed earlier concerning age, gender, and racioethnicity. We reiterate our previous message: Both managers and employees need to be sensitive to stereotypes and attempt to overcome them and recognize that an increasingly diverse workforce can be a true competitive advantage.

Halo Effects   A **halo effect** occurs when one attribute of a person or situation is used to develop an overall impression of the individual or situation. Halo effects are common in our everyday lives. When meeting a new person, for example, a trait such as a pleasant smile can lead to a positive first impression of an overall "warm" and "honest" person. The result of a halo effect, however, is the same as that associated with a stereotype: Individual differences are obscured.

Selective Perception   **Selective perception** is the tendency to single out those aspects of a situation, person, or object that are consistent with one's needs, values, or attitudes. This perceptual distortion is identified in a classic research study involving executives in a manufacturing company.[33] When asked to identify the key problem in a comprehensive business policy case, each executive selected problems consistent with his or her functional area work assignments.

Managers should test whether or not situations and individuals are being selectively perceived. The easiest way to do this is to gather additional opinions from other people. When these opinions are contradictory with their own, an effort should be made to check the original impression.

Projection   **Projection** is the assignment of one's personal attributes to other individuals. A classic projection error is exemplified by the manager who assumes that the needs of his or her subordinates are the same as his or her own. By projecting your needs on your subordinates, individual differences are lost.

Expectancy   A final perceptual distortion that we consider is **expectancy**—the tendency to create or find in another situation or individual that which you expected to find in the first place. Expectancy is sometimes referred to as a self-fulfilling prophecy or the "Pygmalion effect."[34] Pygmalion was a mythical Greek sculptor who created a statue of his ideal mate and then made her come to life. His expectations came true! Through expectancy, you may also create in the work situation that which you expect to find.

Attribution Theory

Attribution theory is the study of how people attempt to (1) understand the causes of a certain event, (2) assess responsibility for the outcomes of the event, and (3) evaluate the personal qualities of the people involved in the event.[35] Essentially, in applying attribution theory, we try to determine whether one's behavior was internally or externally caused. Internal causes are believed to be under an individual's control (you believe Bill's performance is poor because he is lazy). External causes are seen as outside a person (you believe Sally's performance is poor because her machine is old).

There are two errors that have an impact on causal attribution. These are the *fundamental attribution error* and the *self-serving bias.*[36] In a health care study supervisors were asked to identify, or *attribute,* causes of poor performance on the part of subordinates. They more often chose internal deficiencies of the individual—ability and effort—rather than external deficiencies in the situation—support. This demonstrates the **fundamental attribution error**—the tendency to underestimate the influence of situational factors and to overestimate the influence of personal factors in evaluating someone else's behavior. When asked to identify causes of their own poor performance, however, the supervisors overwhelmingly cited lack of support— an external or situational deficiency. This indicates the **self-serving bias**—the tendency to deny personal responsibility for performance problems but to accept personal responsibility for performance success.[37]

The managerial implications of attribution theory and the earlier discussion can be traced back to the fact that perceptions influence behavior. For example, a manager who feels that subordinates are *not* performing well and perceives the reason to be an internal lack of effort is likely to respond with attempts to "motivate" the subordinates to work harder; the possibility of changing external, situational factors to remove job constraints and to provide better organizational support may be largely ignored. This oversight could sacrifice major performance gains.

Individual Differences and Workplace Diversity Strategies

The previous discussion of individual differences has implications for workplace strategies that may be employed to deal with these differences and capitalize on the increasing diversity of the new workforce. These strategies fall into four areas:

1. **Hiring and employment conditions** Essentially, the organization needs to make sure everyone in the organization is sensitive to individual differences; seek innovative ways to match increasingly diverse workers with job requirements; develop innovative recruiting strategies to attract new sources of labor; and develop flexible employment conditions to better utilize the increasingly diverse workers.

2. **Education, training and development, and followup** The organization needs to emphasize a broad range of programs ranging from basic skills to workshops designed to encourage managers and employees to value those with very different demographic factors.

3. **Rewards and promotions** The organization needs to develop and promote a merit and promotion system that rewards people for recognizing and dealing with diversity issues.

4. **Team-based job designs** Where possible, the organization needs to use group-based work teams to take advantage of diversity in individual differences and to encourage cross-fertilization of ideas.

Notice that strategies are tailored to link rewards and promotions with performance on the various aspects of diversity (diversity emphases), further reinforcing the importance of diversity actions.

The fourth strategy area is also extremely important. Emphasizing team-based job designs is the most far-reaching of all the strategies mentioned. It calls for designing (or redesigning) jobs to take advantage of the potential creativity brought about through diversity. Part 3 on managing groups provides important insights.

The strategies call for a mix of management and employee actions and are ongoing. That is, they are not a state to be reached but a continual process that involves moving toward acquiring and utilizing competitive-edge diversity. The hiring and employment conditions strategies assume a labor shortage, following the predictions discussed in Chapter 2.

In general, organizations must stress flexible employment conditions, in contrast to the "one-size-fits-all" philosophy of the past. Family care, including that for elders and other family members, will need to go beyond simple child care availability for the new workforce.

The second group of strategies—education, training and development, and followup—offers important training in basic skills. Such training will be required if there are deficiencies in a given local public school system or because a number of these workers can be expected to be foreigners or disadvantaged. This group of strategies also emphasizes various aspects of education and training in working with diverse employees for both managers and workers. Such training is ongoing, and some firms involve managers in conducting the training needed to help provide them with a feeling of responsibility for making diversity successful.

In Summary

What are demographic characteristics of individuals?

- Demographic characteristics among individuals are background variables that help shape what a person has become.

- Some demographic characteristics are current (e.g., a worker's current income); others are historical (e.g., how many places a person lived while growing up).

- Gender, age, racioethnicity, and disability are particularly important demographic characteristics for at least three reasons: (1) there is workplace legislation concerning them; (2) there are links between demographics and performance and human resource maintenance; and (3) they serve as the basis of stereotypes.

What are competency characteristics of individuals?

- Competency characteristics among individuals consist of aptitude (the capability to learn something) and ability (the existing capacity to do something).
- Aptitudes are potential abilities.
- Both physical and mental competencies are used in employee selection and training. The assessments should be valid and job related.
- Individual competency characteristics are important in matching individuals to jobs.

What are personality characteristics of individuals?

- *Personality* captures the overall profile or combination of characteristics that represent the unique nature of a person as that person reacts and interacts with others. We expect there to be a predictable interplay between an individual's personality and his or her tendency to behave in certain ways.
- Personality traits important in OB are: problem-solving style; locus of control; authoritarianism/dogmatism; Machiavellianism; self-monitoring; and type A and type B orientation.
- It is important that personality, in combination with demographics and competency characteristics, be matched with job requirements.

What are values?

- Values are global concepts that guide actions and judgments across a variety of situations.
- Values are especially important in OB because they can directly influence outcomes, such as performance or human resource maintenance; they can also have an indirect influence on behavior by means of attitudes and perceptions.
- Though treated as characteristics of individuals in this chapter, values also can reflect differences among various societal and organizational cultures.

What are attitudes?

- Attitudes are influenced by values but focus on specific people or objects; in contrast, values have a more global focus.
- Attitudes are predispositions to respond in a positive or negative way to someone or something in one's environment.
- Attitudes operate through intended behavior to influence actual behavior or other variables.

What is perception, and what are some common perceptual distortions?

- Individuals use perception to form impressions about themselves, other people, and daily life experiences.

- Causal attributions are particularly important in perception. People use perception to deal with information for decision and action responses.
- Perceptual distortions, including stereotypes, halo effects, projection, selective perception, projection, and expectancy, can affect perceptual responses.

What are some key strategy areas for capitalizing on workplace diversity and dealing with individual differences?

- There are four key strategy areas for capitalizing on workforce diversity and dealing with individual attributes. These are (1) hiring and employment conditions; (2) education, training and development, and followup; (3) rewards and promotions; and (4) team-based job designs.
- These strategies closely tie into most of the remaining chapters of the book, especially those covering reinforcement and rewards, alternative work arrangements, managing pay, and groups and team-based job designs.
- The fit between job requirements and the previously mentioned individual characteristics categories assumes increasing importance in light of an increasingly diverse workforce.
- Education and a wide range of training in particular become more and more important.

MOTIVATION

AND REWARDS

As you read Chapter 5, keep in mind these study questions:

- What is Maslow's hierarchy of needs theory, and how does it compare to Alderfer's ERG theory?

- Which needs are emphasized in McClelland's acquired needs theory?

- What is Herzberg's two-factor theory?

- What are equity theory and expectancy theory?

- What is an integrated model of motivation?

I n this chapter, we examine a number of current motivation theories that are an important foundation for later ideas. *Motivation to work* refers to forces within an individual that account for the level, direction, and persistence of effort expended at work. Level refers to the amount of effort a person puts forth (e.g., a lot or a little); direction refers to what the person chooses when presented with a number of possible alternatives (e.g., exert effort toward product quality or product quantity); and persistence refers to how long a person sticks with a given action (e.g., to try for product quantity and give up when you find it difficult to attain).

Content and Process Theories

We divide motivation approaches into content and process theories. **Content theories** are concerned primarily with what it is within an individual or an individual's environment that energizes or sustains his or her behavior. These theories are useful because they lend insight into people's needs and help managers understand what people will or will not value as work rewards or need satisfiers. However, they are sometimes criticized as being static and descriptive..

Process theories offer a more dynamic alternative; they strive to provide an understanding of the thought or cognitive processes that take place within the minds of people to influence their behavior.[1]

Maslow's Hierarchy of Needs Theory

Abraham Maslow's hierarchy of needs theory, as shown in Figure 5.1, is the first content theory we consider. It identifies **higher order needs**—self-actualization and esteem—and **lower order needs**—social, safety, and physiological requirements. Maslow's formulation suggests a prepotency of these needs; that is, some needs are assumed to be more important (potent) than others and must be satisfied before the other needs can serve as motivators. Thus, according to the figure, the physiological needs must be satisfied before the safety needs are activated, and the safety needs must be satisfied before the social needs are activated, and so on.

Let's briefly elaborate on each of the needs listed in Figure 5.1. As indicated, the physiological needs are considered the most basic; they consist of needs for such things as food, water, and the like. Individuals try to satisfy these needs before turn-

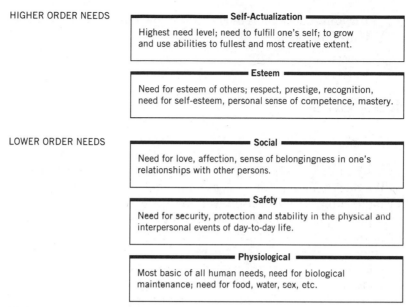

HIGHER ORDER NEEDS

Self-Actualization

Highest need level; need to fulfill one's self; to grow and use abilities to fullest and most creative extent.

Esteem

Need for esteem of others; respect, prestige, recognition, need for self-esteem, personal sense of competence, mastery.

LOWER ORDER NEEDS

Social

Need for love, affection, sense of belongingness in one's relationships with other persons.

Safety

Need for security, protection and stability in the physical and interpersonal events of day-to-day life.

Physiological

Most basic of all human needs, need for biological maintenance; need for food, water, sex, etc.

Figure 5.1   Maslow's hierarchy of needs.

ing to needs at the safety level, which involve security, protection, stability, and the like. When these needs are active, people will look at their jobs in terms of how well they satisfy these needs.

The social needs consist of a sense of belonging and a need for affiliation. Once the physiological and safety needs are satisfied, relationships and belonging are activated. The kinds of work teams emphasized in total quality management and other high-performance systems are one means of satisfying these needs.

The higher order needs depicted in Figure 5.1 consist of the esteem, recognition, and self-actualization needs—being all that one can be. Here, challenging work and recognition for good performance assume center stage. Some research suggests that there is a tendency for higher order needs to increase in importance over lower order needs as individuals move up the managerial hierarchy.[2] Other studies report that needs vary according to a person's career stage,[3] the size of the organization,[4] and even geographical location.[5] However, there is no consistent evidence that the satisfaction of a need at one level will decrease its importance and increase the importance of the next higher need.

To what extent does Maslow's theory appear to operate outside the United States? Basic cultural values, such as those discussed in Chapter 3, appear to play a role. For example, in those countries high in Hofstede's uncertainty avoidance, such as Japan or Greece, security tends to motivate most employees more strongly than does self-actualization. Similarly, social needs tend to dominate in countries that emhasize Hofstede's femininity value (e.g., Sweden, Norway, and Denmark). In general, a person's frame of reference will determine the order of importance of his or her needs, and that frame of reference is influenced by societal culture.[6]

Clayton Alderfer has modified Maslow's theory to make it more flexible in terms of individual behavior.

Alderfer's ERG Theory

ERG theory differs from Maslow's theory in three basic respects.[7] First, the theory collapses Maslow's five need categories into three: **existence needs** relate to a person's desire for physiological and material well-being; **relatedness needs** represent the desire for satisfying interpersonal relationships; and **growth needs** are desires for continued personal growth and development. Second, while Maslow's theory argues that individuals progress up the hierarchy as a result of the satisfaction of lower order needs (a satisfaction–progression process), ERG theory includes a "frustration–regression" principle, whereby an already satisfied lower level need can become activated when a higher level need cannot be satisfied. Thus, if a person is continually frustrated in his or her attempts to satisfy growth needs, relatedness needs will again surface as key motivators. Third, according to Maslow, a person focuses on one need at a time. In contrast, ERG theory contends that more than one need may be activated at the same time.

Even though additional research is needed to shed more light on its validity, the supporting evidence on ERG theory is stronger than that for Maslow's theory. For now, the combined satisfaction–progression and frustration–regression principles provide the manager with a more flexible approach to understanding human needs than does Maslow's strict hierarchy.

McClelland's Acquired Needs Theory

A third content theory was developed in the late 1940s by the psychologist David I. McClelland and his coworkers. They began experimenting with the Thematic Apperception Test (TAT) as a way of measuring human needs.[8] The TAT is a projective technique that asks people to view pictures and write stories about what they see.

Three Types of Acquired Needs

In one case, McClelland tested three executives on what they saw in a photograph of a man sitting down and looking at family photos arranged on his work desk. One executive wrote of an engineer who was daydreaming about a family outing scheduled for the next day. Another described a designer who had picked up an idea for a new gadget from remarks made by his family. The third was an engineer who was intently working on a bridge-stress problem that he seemed sure to solve because of his confident look.

McClelland distinguished three themes that can appear in such TAT stories. Each theme corresponds to an underlying need that he feels is important for understanding individual behavior. These needs are:

- **Need for Achievement (nAcH)** The desire to do something better or more efficiently, to solve problems, or to master complex tasks.
- **Need for Affiliation (nAff)** The desire to establish and maintain friendly and warm relations with others.
- **Need for Power (nPower)** The desire to control others, to influence their behavior, or to be responsible for others.

McClelland's basic theory is that these three needs are acquired over time, as a result of life experiences. People are motivated by these needs, each of which can be associated with individual work preferences. The theory encourages managers to learn how to identify the presence of nAch, nAff, and nPower in themselves and in others and to be able to create work environments that are responsive to the respective need profiles.

One interesting direction of McClelland's research seeks to identify the need profiles typical of successful managers. Working with what he calls the "leadership motive pattern," McClelland has found that the combination of a moderate to high need for power and a lower need for affiliation enables people to be effective managers at higher levels in organizations. High nPower creates the willingness to have influence or impact on others; lower nAff allows the manager to make difficult decisions without undue worry of being disliked.[9]

The power need is particularly interesting. A management consultant, Charles M. Kleey, uses the term *destructive achiever* to describe executives who are high in nPower but who misuse that power. These people usually have the charisma and other characteristics needed to move up to high-level positions, but because they misuse their power, they usually don't make it to the top; they tend to get sabotaged by those they stepped on earlier.[10] This example reinforces McClelland's point that nPower is most useful for managers when it is used to accomplish group and organization goals rather than selfishly motivated goals. This focus is sometimes termed *socialized power,* and some consider it an important factor in understanding charismatic leadership, as we show in Chapter 11.

Herzberg's Two-factor Theory

Some time ago, Frederick Herzberg began his research on motivation by asking workers to comment on two statements:[11]

1. "Tell me about a time when you felt exceptionally good about your job."
2. "Tell me about a time when you felt exceptionally bad about your job."

After analyzing nearly 4000 responses to these statements, Herzberg and his associates developed the *two-factor theory,* also known as the **motivator–hygiene theory** (again a content theory). They noticed that respondents identified different things as sources of work dissatisfaction—subsequently called "dissatisfiers" or 'hygiene factors"—than they did as sources of satisfaction—subsequently called "satisfiers" or "motivator factors."

Satisfiers or Motivator Factors

To improve *satisfaction,* a manager must use **motivator factors** as shown below.

- Achievement
- Recognition
- The work itself
- Responsibility
- Advancement
- Growth

These factors are related to job content—what people actually do in their work. Adding these satisfiers or motivators to people's jobs is Herzberg's link to performance. According to Herzberg, when these opportunities are absent, workers will not be satisfied, nor will they perform well.

Dissatisfiers or Hygiene Factors

Hygiene factors are associated with the **job context**—those aspects related to a person's work setting; that is, job dissatisfaction is linked more to the environment in which people work than to the nature of the work itself. Hygiene factors are:

- Company and policy administration
- Supervision
- Relationship with supervisor
- Work conditions
- Salary
- Relationship with peers
- Personal life
- Relationship with subordinates
- Status
- Security

Perhaps the most surprising of these factors is salary. Herzberg found that low salary makes people dissatisfied, but that paying them more does not satisfy or motivate them. Improved working conditions (e.g., special offices, air conditioning) act in the same way. The reason for these conclusions is that in the two-factor theory, job satisfaction and job dissatisfaction are totally separate dimensions; that is, improving a hygiene factor, such as working conditions, will not make people satisfied with their work; it will only prevent them from being *dis*satisfied.

Research and Practical Implications

There is debate about the merits of Herzberg's theory.[12] The most serious criticism is that it is method bound: that is, it is supportable only by applying Herzberg's original methodology. Such a criticism is very serious because the scientific approach requires that theories be verifiable when different methods are used.

In spite of this and other criticisms, we think Herzberg's theory is useful first because it causes management to be cautious about expecting high base salaries and such hygiene factors as piped-in music to motivate employees to work hard. Second, it is useful because its satisfiers can be used to increase the content level of jobs and thus contribute to job enrichment (see Chapter 7).

Equity Theory

Equity theory is the first of the process motivation theories we consider. It is based on the phenomenon of social comparison and is best known through the writing of J. Stacy Adams.[13] Adams argues that when people gauge the fairness of their work outcomes in comparison with others, felt inequity is a motivating state of mind. That is when people perceive inequity in their work, they will be aroused to remove the discomfort and to restore a sense of felt equity to the situation. Inequities exist whenever people feel that the rewards or inducements they receive for their work inputs or contributions are unequal to the rewards other people appear to have received for their inputs. For the individual, the equity comparison or thought process that determines such feeling is

$$\frac{\text{Individual rewards}}{\text{Individual inputs}} \quad \xleftrightarrow{\text{compared}} \quad \frac{\text{Others' rewards}}{\text{Others' inputs}}$$

Resolving Felt Inequities

A **felt negative inequity** exists when an individual feels that he or she has received relatively less than others have in proportion to work inputs. **Felt positive inequity** exists when an individual feels that he or she has received relatively more than others have. Both felt negative and felt positive inequity are motivating states. When either exists, the individual will likely engage in one or more of the following behaviors to restore a sense of equity.

1. Change work inputs (e.g., reduce performance efforts).
2. Change the outcomes (rewards) received (e.g., ask for a raise).
3. Leave the situation (e.g., quit).

4. Change the comparison points (e.g., compare self to a different coworker).

5. Psychologically distort the comparisons (e.g., rationalize that the inequity is only temporary and will be resolved in the future).

6. Take actions to change the inputs or outputs of the comparison person (e.g., get a coworker to accept more work).

Equity theory predicts that people who feel either underrewarded or overrewarded for their work will act to restore a sense of equity. The research of Adams and others, largely accomplished in laboratory settings, lends tentative support to this prediction. The research indicates that people who feel overpaid (feel positive inequity) have been found to increase the quantity or quality of their work, while those who are underpaid (feel negative inequity) decrease the quantity or quality of their work. The research is most conclusive in respect to felt negative inequity. It appears that people are less comfortable when they are underrewarded than when they are overrewarded.

Managing the Equity Dynamic

The equity comparison intervenes between a manager's allocation of rewards and his or her impact on the work behavior of subordinates. Feelings of inequity are determined solely by the individual's interpretation of the situation. Thus, the assumption that all employees in a work unit will view their annual pay raise as fair is incorrect. It is not how a *manager* feels about the allocation of rewards that counts; it is how the *individuals* receiving the rewards feel or perceive the rewards that will determine the motivational outcomes of the equity dynamic. Managing the equity dynamic therefore becomes quite important to the manager who strives to maintain healthy psychological contracts—that is, fairly balanced inducements and contributions—among subordinates.

Rewards that are received with feelings of equity can foster job satisfaction and performance. In contrast, rewards that are received with feelings of negative inequity can damage these key work results. Managers need to take control of the situation and make sure that any negative consequences of the equity comparisons are avoided, or at least minimized, when rewards are allocated.[14] The Effective Manager 5.1 shows how you can deal with these concerns.

THE EFFECTIVE MANAGER 5.1

Steps for Managing the Equity Process

Three steps for managing the equity process:

- Recognize that an equity comparison will likely be made by each subordinate whenever especially visible rewards, such as pay, promotions, and so on, are being allocated.
- Anticipate felt negative inequities.
- Communicate to each individual your evaluation of the reward, an appraisal of the performance on which it is based, and the comparison points you consider to be appropriate.

Expectancy Theory

In 1964, a book entitled *Work and Motivation* by Victor Vroom, covering the expectancy theory of work motivation, made an important contribution to the OB literature.[15] Vroom's theory (a second process motivation theory) seeks to predict or explain the task-related effort expended by a person. The theory's central question is "What determines the willingness of an individual to exert personal effort to work at tasks that contribute to the performance of the work unit and the organization?" To answer this question, Vroom argues that managers must know three things:

1. The person's belief that working hard will enable various levels of task performance to be achieved.
2. The person's belief that various work outcomes or rewards will result from the achievement of the various levels of work performance.
3. The value the individual assigns to these work outcomes.

The Theory

Expectancy Theory argues that work motivation is determined by individual beliefs regarding effort–performance relationships and the desirabilities of various work outcomes that are associated with different performance levels. Simply put, the theory is based on the logic "People *will do* what they *can do* when they *want to.* For example, if I want a promotion and see that high performance can lead to that promotion and that if I work hard I can achieve high performance, I will be motivated to work hard.

Figure 5.2 illustrates the managerial foundations of expectancy theory. Individuals are viewed as making conscious decisions to allocate their behavior toward work efforts and to serve self-interests. The three key terms in the theory are:

1. **Expectancy** The probability assigned by an individual that work effort will be followed by a given level of achieved task performance. Expectancy would equal "0" if the person felt it were impossible to achieve the given performance level; it would equal "1" if a person were 100 percent certain that the performance could be achieved.
2. **Instrumentality** The probability assigned by the individual that a given level

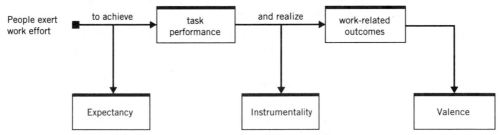

Figure 5.2 Expectancy theory terms in a managerial perspective.

of achieved task performance will lead to various work outcomes. Instrumentality also varies from "1," meaning the reward is 100 percent certain to follow performance, to "0," indicating that there is no chance that performance will lead to the reward.*

3. **Valence** The value attached by the individual to various work outcomes. Valences form a scale from −1 (very undesirable outcome) to +1 (very desirable outcome).

Multiplier Effects and Multiple Outcomes

Vroom posits that motivation (*M*), expectancy (*E*), instrumentality (*I*), and valence (*V*) are related to one another by the equation

$$M = E \times I \times V$$

The equation states that motivation to work results from expectancy times instrumentality times valence. This multiplicative relationship means that the motivational appeal of a given work path is sharply reduced whenever any one or more of these factors approaches the value of zero. Conversely, for a given reward to have a high and positive motivational impact as a work outcome, the expectancy, instrumentality, and valence associated with the reward all must be high and positive.

Suppose that a manager is wondering whether or not the prospect of earning a merit pay raise will be motivational to a subordinate. Expectancy theory predicts that motivation to work hard to earn the merit pay will be *low* if

1. **Expectancy is low.** A person feels that he or she cannot achieve the necessary performance level.

2. **Instrumentality is low.** The person is not confident a high level of task performance will result in a high merit pay raise.

3. **Valence is low.** The person places little value on a merit pay increase.

4. Any combination of these exists.

The multiplier effect requires managers to act to maximize expectancy, instrumentality, and valence when seeking to create high levels of work motivation among subordinates through the allocation of certain work rewards. A "zero" at any location on the right side of the expectancy equation will result in "zero" motivation.

Basically, expectancy logic argues that a manager must try to understand individual thought processes and then actively intervene in the work situation to influence them. This includes trying to maximize work expectancies, instrumentalities, and valences that support the organization's production purposes. In other words, a manager should strive to create a work setting in which work contributions serving the organization's needs will also be valued by the individual as paths toward desired personal outcomes or rewards.

---

*Strictly speaking, Vroom's treatment of instrumentality would allow it to vary from −1 to +1. We use the probability definition here and the 0 to +1 range for pedagogical purposes; it is consistent with the basic instrumentality notion.

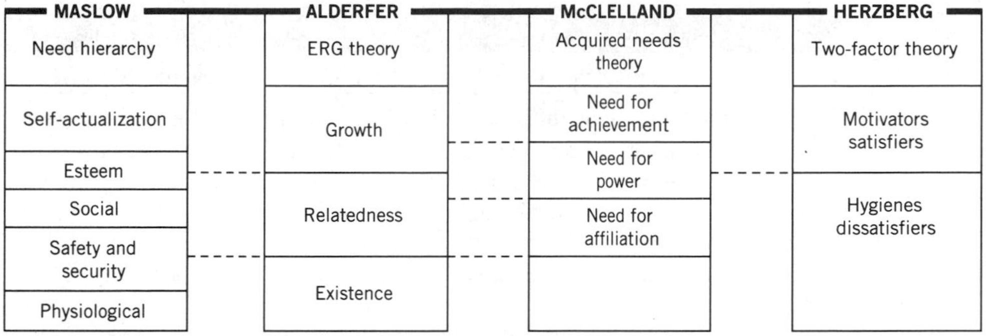

MASLOW	ALDERFER	McCLELLAND	HERZBERG
Need hierarchy	ERG theory	Acquired needs theory	Two-factor theory
Self-actualization	Growth	Need for achievement	Motivators satisfiers
Esteem	Growth	Need for power	Motivators satisfiers
Social	Relatedness	Need for affiliation	Hygienes dissatisfiers
Safety and security	Relatedness	Need for affiliation	Hygienes dissatisfiers
Physiological	Existence		Hygienes dissatisfiers

Figure 5.3 Comparison of content motivation theories.

One of the more popular modifications of Vroom's original version of the theory distinguishes between extrinsic and intrinsic rewards as two separate types of possible work outcomes. **Extrinsic rewards** are positively valued work outcomes that are given to the individual by some other source in the work setting. An example is pay. Workers typically do not pay themselves directly; some representative of the organization administers the reward. In contrast, **intrinsic rewards** are positively valued work outcomes that are received by the individual directly as a result of task performance; they do not require the participation of another person. A feeling of achievement after accomplishing a particularly challenging task is one example of an intrinsic reward. The distinction between extrinsic and intrinsic rewards is important because each type of reward demands separate attention from a manager seeking to use rewards to increase motivation. We discuss these differences more thoroughly in Chapters 6 and 7.

It is important to remember that expectancy theory is universal to the extent that it does not specify the types of rewards that motivate particular groups of workers.[16] Expectancy theory allows for the fact that the rewards and their link with performance may be seen as quite different in various groups and societal cultures.

An Integrated Model of Motivation

Each of the theories presented in this chapter is potentially useful for the manager and can be used in an integrative approach. We start with a comparison of the content theories as shown in Figure 5.3. The similarity of these theories suggests that the manager's job is to create a work environment that responds positively to individual needs. Poor performance, undesirable behaviors, and/or decreased satisfaction can be partially explained in terms of "blocked" needs or needs that are not satisfied on the job. The motivational value of rewards can also be analyzed in terms of "activated" needs to which a given reward either does or does not respond. Ultimately,

> ### THE EFFECTIVE MANAGER 5.2
>
> Guidelines to Follow in Using Content Motivation Theories
>
> - Understand how individuals differ in what they need from their work.
> - Know what can be offered to these individuals in response to their needs.
> - Know how to create work settings that give people the opportunity to satisfy their needs by contributing to the task performance of the work unit and the organization.

content theorists argue that managers should follow the guidelines in The Effective Manager 5.2.

In addition, the equity and expectancy theories have special strengths. The logic of expectancy theory is used in Figure 5.4 to integrate the insights of the various motivational theories to create a model of individual performance and satisfaction. In the figure, performance is determined by individual differences, work effort, and work-setting support. Individual motivation directly determines work effort, and the key to motivation is the manager's ability to create a work setting that positively responds to individual needs and goals. Whether or not a work setting provides motivation depends on the availability of rewards. When the individual experiences intrinsic rewards for work performance, motivation will be directly and positively affected. Motivation can also occur when job satisfactions result from either extrinsic or intrinsic rewards that are felt to be equitably allocated. When felt negative inequity results, satisfaction will be low and motivation will be reduced.

Figure 5.4 is an extension of Vroom's original expectancy theory and an expanded model proposed by Lyman W. Porter and Edward E. Lawler.[17] It includes a key role for equity theory and recognizes job performance and satisfaction as separate, but potentially interdependent, work results. The content theories enter the model as the manager's guide to understanding individual differences and identifying the needs that give motivational value to the various work rewards allocated by the managers.[18]

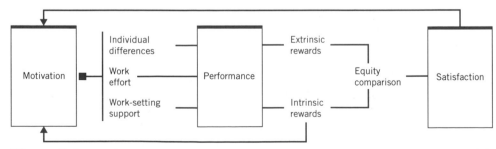

Figure 5.4 Predicting individual work performance and satisfaction: an integrated model.

In Summary

What is Maslow's hierarchy of needs theory, and how does it compare to Alderfer's ERG theory?

- Maslow's hierarchy of needs theory arranges human needs into the following five-step hierarchy: physiological, safety, social (the three lower order needs), esteem, and self-actualization (the two higher order needs).

- Satisfaction of any need activates the need at the next higher level, and people are presumed to move step by step up the hierarchy.

- Alderfer's ERG theory has modified this theory by collapsing the five needs into three: existence, relatedness, and growth. Alderfer also allows for more than one need to be activated at a time.

Which needs are emphasized in McClelland's acquired needs theory?

- McClelland's acquired needs theory focuses on the need for achievement (nAch), affiliation (nAff), and power (nPower).

- The theory argues that these needs can be developed through experience and training.

- Persons high in nAch prefer jobs with individual responsibility, performance feedback, and moderately challenging goals.

- Successful executives typically have a high nPower that is greater than their nAff.

What is Hertzberg's two-factor theory?

- Herzberg's two-factor theory treats job satisfaction and job dissatisfaction as two separate issues. Satisfiers, or motivator factors, are associated with job content and include such factors as achievement, responsibility, and recognition.

- An improvement in job content is expected to increase satisfaction and motivation to perform well.

- In contrast, dissatisfiers, or hygiene factors, are associated with the job context and consist of such factors as working conditions, relations with coworkers, and salary.

- Improving job context does not lead to more satisfaction but is expected to reduce dissatisfaction.

What are equity theory and expectancy theory?

- Equity theory is a process theory of motivation that points out that people compare their rewards (and inputs) with those of others. The individual is then motivated to engage in behavior to correct any perceived inequity. At the extreme, feelings of inequity may lead to reduced performance or job turnover.

- Expectancy theory is also a process theory of motivation that argues that work motivation is determined by an individual's beliefs concerning effort–performance relationships (expectancy), work–outcome relationships (instrumentality), and the desirability of various work outcomes (valence).

- Based on Vroom's classic work, the theory states the Motivation = Expectancy × Instrumentality × Valence. Managers, therefore, must build positive expectancies, demonstrate performance–reward instrumentalities, and use rewards with high positive valences in their motivational strategies.

What is an integrated model of motivation?

- An integrated model of motivation integrates the content and process motivation theories, recognizes individual differences, and shows how a supportive work setting and well-managed rewards can lead to high levels of both individual performance and satisfaction.

REINFORCEMENT,

PAY PRACTICES, AND

SELF-MANAGEMENT

As you read Chapter 6, keep in mind these study questions:

- What is learning, and what are four general approaches to learning?

- What are reinforcement, its foundation, and its linkage to rewards?

- What is organizational behavior modification (OB Mod), and how do you use the four reinforcement strategies involved in it?

- What are social learning theory and behavioral self-management?

- As a manager, how can you deal with pay as an extrinsic reward?

I n this chapter, we address the subject of learning and the management of various forms of reinforcement and rewards.

Learning

Learning is a relatively permanent change in behavior resulting from experience. Managers with an understanding of basic learning principles are well positioned to help others "learn" the behaviors necessary to achieve maximum positive outcomes from their work. There are four general approaches to learning: classical conditioning, operant conditioning, cognitive learning, and social learning.

Classical Conditioning

Classical conditioning is a form of learning through association. As shown in Figure 6.1, this type of learning involves the manipulation of a *stimulus* or *stimuli* to influence behavior. We define a **stimulus** as something that incites action. Classical conditioning associates a previously neutral stimulus—one that has no effect on behavior—with another stimulus that does affect behavior. The former thus becomes a *conditioned stimulus,* which, upon its occurrence, also draws forth the now *conditioned response.* Involuntary or reflexive behaviors of humans are susceptible to classical conditioning. Someone who is verbally reprimanded on several occasions after being "asked to step into the boss's office" may become conditioned to display apprehension and nervous reactions whenever asked to come into the office in the future.

Classical conditioning is quite common inside and outside the workplace. But it often is hard to know just when it is taking place. For example, it might take both the manager and the employee a long time to figure out the stimulus and response connection shown in Figure 6.1. Nevertheless, the classical conditioning approach alerts good managers to such possibilities. They may then gain a better understanding of their subordinates.

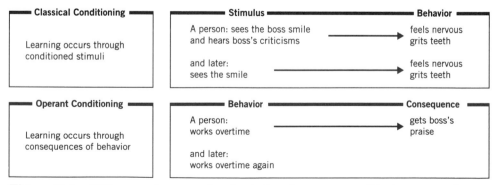

Figure 6.1 Differences between the classical and operant conditioning approaches to learning.

Operant Conditioning

Operant conditioning is learning that is achieved when the *consequences* of a behavior lead to changes in the probability of its occurrence, that is, learning through reinforcement. Figure 6.1 clarifies how this operant, or behaviorist, approach contrasts with classical conditioning. The former approach views behavior as "operating" on its environment to produce sequences that affect its future occurrence. It is a way of controlling behavior by manipulating its consequences.[1] The method consists of the three-component framework: Antecedents $\rightarrow$ Behavior $\rightarrow$ Consequences, sometimes called A,B,C contingencies or "if/then" relationships. Let's return to Figure 6.1. The antecedent (A)—the condition leading up to behavior— might be an agreement between the boss and the employee to work overtime as needed. If the employee engages in the overtime behavior (B)—the consequence (C)—the result of the behavior—is the boss's praise.

Classical conditioning works only on behaviors that are involuntary in nature. However, operant conditioning has a broader application to almost any human behavior.

Cognitive Learning

Cognitive learning is learning that is achieved by thinking about the perceived relationship between events and individual goals and expectations as in the process motivation theories of Chapter 5. Cognitive learning differs markedly from behaviorist explanations of operant conditioning. As an example, a hotel employee greets a hotel customer with a smile and receives a compliment from the boss. Thereafter, the employee spends more time smiling at hotel customers.

The Cognitive Learning Explanation The employee exhibits a friendly smile with the goal in mind of receiving compliments from his boss—something he highly values. The employee *reasons* that increased friendly greetings will please his boss and thus *decides* to seek out customers to greet.

The Operant Conditioning Explanation The *antecedent* was a hotel orientation session emphasizing the importance of greeting customers in a friendly manner. The *behavior* of greeting a customer with a friendly smile was positively reinforced by the consequence of the boss's compliment. Having been positively reinforced, the behavior is repeated whenever the employee sees a customer in the future. No cognitive explanation is needed.

Social Learning

Social learning is learning that is achieved through the reciprocal interactions among people, behavior, and environment. That is, environmental determinism and self-determinism are combined. Thus, behavior is seen not simply as a function of external antecedents and consequences or as being caused solely by internal needs, satisfaction, or expectations, but as a combination of the two.

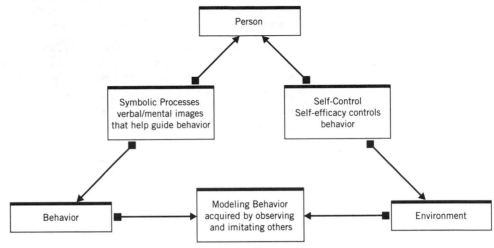

Figure 6.2   Social learning model. (Adapted from R. Kreitmer and F. Luthans, "A Social Learning Approach to Behavioral Management: Radical Behaviorists' Mellowing Out." *Organizational Dynamics,* Autumn 1984, p. 55)

In Figure 6.2 the individual uses modeling to acquire behavior by observing and imitating others and practicing the new behavior. The "models" could be the person's parents, friends, or even well-known celebrities. The model also might be a manager or coworker who demonstrates desired behaviors.

The symbolic processes depicted in Figure 6.2 are also important in social learning. Words and symbols used by managers and others in the workplace can help communicate values, beliefs, and goals and thus serve as guides to the person's behavior.

At the same time, the person's self-control is important in influencing his or her own behavior. Self-efficacy is a very important part of such self-control. *Self-efficacy* refers to the person's belief that he or she can perform adequately in a given situation.[2] In other words, high self-efficacy people believe that they can manage their environmental cues and consequences and their cognitive processes to control their own behavior.

Of course, even persons who are high in self-efficacy do not control their environment entirely. As a manager, you can have an impact on the environment and other factors listed in Figure 6.2 (even though the impact is less than in the operant approach). This is especially the case in influencing a person's self-efficacy. A manager's expectations and peer support can go far in increasing a worker's self-efficacy and feelings of control.

Reinforcement

Reinforcement plays a key role in the learning process. The foundation for this relationship is the **law of effect,** as stated by E. L. Thorndike.[3]

Law of Effect   Behavior that results in a pleasant outcome is likely to be repeated: behavior that results in an unpleasant outcome is not likely to be repeated.

The implications of the law of effect are rather straightforward. Rewards are outcomes or environmental consequences that are considered by the reinforcement perspective to determine individual behavior. Recall that **extrinsic rewards** are positively valued work outcomes that are given to the individual by some other person. They are important external reinforcers or environmental consequences that can substantially influence people's work behaviors through the law of effect. Some of these are *contrived,* or *planned,* rewards that have direct costs and budgetary implications; examples are pay increases and cash bonuses which we cover later in the chapter. A second category includes natural rewards, such as verbal praise, that have no cost other than the manager's personal time and efforts.

We now use an approach called **organizational behavior modification** or **OB Mod** to bring together the application of the previously mentioned operant conditioning, reinforcement, and extrinsic reward notions. You can think of OB Mod as the systematic reinforcement of desirable work behavior and the nonreinforcement or punishment of unwanted work behavior. OB Mod includes four basic reinforcement strategies: positive reinforcement, negative reinforcement (or avoidance), punishment, and extinction.

Positive Reinforcement

B. F. Skinner and his followers advocate **positive reinforcement:** the administration of positive consequences, which tends to increase the likelihood of repeating the desirable behavior in similar settings.

To use positive reinforcement well in the work setting, you must first be aware of the wide variety of contrived and natural rewards that have potential reward value. In using these for reinforcement purposes, several things must be kept in mind.

To begin, we need to be aware that positive reinforcers and rewards are not necessarily the same. Recognition is both a reward and a positive reinforcer *if* a person's performance later improves. Sometimes, however, apparent rewards turn out not to be positive reinforcers.

In order to have maximum reinforcement value, a reward must be delivered only if the desired behavior is exhibited. That is, the reward must be *contingent* on the desired behavior, as in the contingent if/then ABC model. This principle is known as the **law of contingent reinforcement**. Finally, the reward must be given as soon as possible after the desired behavior. This is known as the **law of immediate reinforcement.**[4]

Sometimes, desired behavior is more complex than that above, and so another form of positive reinforcement, called shaping, will be used. **Shaping** is the creation of a new behavior by the positive reinforcement of successive approximations to the desired behavior.

Negative Reinforcement (Avoidance)

A second reinforcement strategy is **negative reinforcement,** or *avoidance*—the withdrawal of negative consequences, which tends to increase the likelihood of re-

THE EFFECTIVE MANAGER 6.1

Guidelines for Using Punishment

1. Tell the individual what is being done wrong.
2. Tell the individual what is right.
3. Punish in private.
4. Punish in accord with the laws of contingent and immediate reinforcement.
5. Make sure the punishment matches the behavior.

peating the desirable behavior in similar settings. Note that there are two aspects here: *first,* the negative consequences, *then* the withdrawal of these consequences when desirable behavior occurs. The term *negative reinforcement* comes from this withdrawal of the negative consequences. This strategy is also sometimes called "avoidance" because its intent is for the person to avoid the negative consequence by performing the desired behavior.

Both positive and negative reinforcement seek to encourage desirable behavior. The first type of reinforcement provides pleasant consequences; the second provides unpleasant consequences, followed by their withdrawal when the desired behavior occurs.

Punishment

A third strategy is punishment. Unlike, positive reinforcement and negative reinforcement, punishment is not intended to encourage positive behavior but to discourage negative behavior. **Punishment** is the administration of negative consequences or the withdrawal of positive consequences that tend to reduce the likelihood of repeating the behavior in similar settings.

Problems with the Punishment Strategy   Problems such as resentment and sabotage may accompany a manager's use of punishment. It also is wise to remember that

- Although a behavior may be suppressed as a result of punishment, it may not be permanently abolished.
- The person who administers punishment may end up being viewed negatively by others.
- Punishment may be offset by positive reinforcement received from another source.

Does all of this mean you should never punish? No. The important things to remember are to administer punishment selectively and then to do it right.

Some Final Points to Keep in Mind   If you are going to administer punishment, The Effective Manager 6.1 provides some useful guidelines.[5] Don't forget that sometimes negative reinforcement and punishment are confused, however. A major difference lies in their effects on behavior. Negative reinforcement *increases* the likelihood of repeating the behavior, whereas punishment *decreases* that likelihood: negative reinforcement *removes* negative consequences following behavior (I stop yelling at you for being late when you start coming to work on time), while punishment *presents* negative consequences or the withdrawal of positive consequences following behavior (you are late to work for the third time in two weeks and I dock your pay).

Extinction

The final OB Mod reinforcement strategy is **extinction:** the withdrawal of the reinforcing consequences for a given behavior. For example, Jack is often late for work, and his coworkers cover for him (positive reinforcement). The manager instructs Jack's coworkers to stop covering for him, withdrawing the reinforcing consequences. Here, extinction is used to get rid of an undesirable behavior. This strategy decreases the frequency of the behavior. The behavior is not "unlearned"; it simply is not exhibited. Since the behavior is no longer reinforced, it will reappear if reinforced again. Whereas positive reinforcement seeks to establish and maintain desirable work behavior, the goal of extinction is to weaken and eliminate undesirable behavior.

Extinction and Positive Reinforcement   Extinction can be especially powerful when combined with positive reinforcement. In the previous example, extinction caused Jack to stop coming to work late. If the manager now provides praise whenever Jack shows up on time, she has combined positive reinforcement with extinction. These extrinsic rewards should have a positive reinforcing effect on desirable behavior. The combined strategy of extinction and positive reinforcement should be more effective than extinction alone.

Figure 6.3 summarizes the use of each of the OB Mod strategies using the ABC framework.

Social Learning Theory and Behavioral Self-Management

Recently, some scholars have applied social learning theory in the workplace to encourage employees to help manage or lead themselves, either as individuals or as part of a team. The Effective Manager 6.2 shows self-management strategies recommended by one set of authors. Notice how these strategies build on social learning theory to emphasize both behavioral and cognitive foci. Their use is designed to enhance self-efficacy and the worker's feeling of self-control. For example, 3M is an organization that encourages behavioral self-management actions, such as those listed in The Effective Manager 6.2 among its employees, wherever possible. People are encouraged to "work outside the boxes" to facilitate new product innovations.[6]

Managing Pay as an Extrinsic Reward

The earlier part of this chapter focused on a number of different kinds of reinforcers and extrinsic rewards. Pay is an especially complex extrinsic reward. It can help

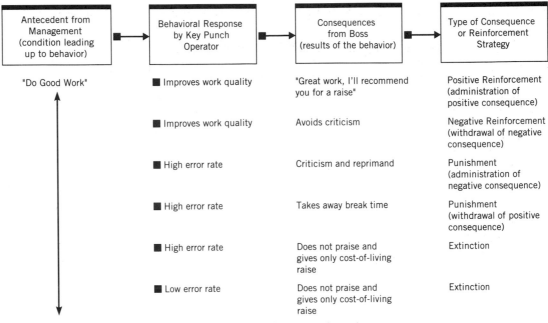

Figure 6.3 Applying the ABC framework in a work setting.

organizations attract and retain highly capable workers, and it can help satisfy and motivate these workers to work hard to achieve high performance. But, if there is dissatisfaction with the salary, pay can also lead to strikes, grievances, absenteeism, turnover, and sometimes even poor physical and mental health. The various aspects of pay make it especially important to deal with as an extrinsic reward.[7]

Multiple Meanings of Pay

Pay can serve as a good motivator of work effort, *when properly managed.* This phrase is the real key. For pay to prove successful as a reward that is truly motivational to the recipient, it must be given (1) contingent on the occurrence of specific and desirable work behaviors, and (2) equitably. Merit pay and a variety of emerging creative pay practices are applications that need to be dealt with in more detail.

Merit Pay

Recent research generally concludes that, for pay to serve as a source of work motivation, high levels of job performance must be viewed as the path through which high pay can be achieved.[8] **Merit pay** is defined as a compensation system that bases an individual's salary or wage increase on a measure of the person's performance accomplishments during a specified time period. That is, merit pay is an attempt to make pay contingent on performance.

THE EFFECTIVE MANAGER 6.2

Self-Management Strategies

BEHAVIORAL FOCUSED STRATEGIES

Behavior	Strategy
Self-set goals	Setting goals for your own work efforts.
Management of cues	Arranging and altering cues in the work environment to facilitate your desired personal behaviors.
Rehearsal	Physical or mental practice of work activities before you actually perform them.
Self-observation	Observing and gathering information about your own specific behaviors that you have targeted for change.
Self-reward	Providing yourself with personally valued rewards for completing desirable behaviors.
Self-punishment	Administering punishments to yourself for behaving in undesirable ways. (This strategy is generally *not* very effective.)

COGNITIVE FOCUSED STRATEGIES

Building natural rewards into tasks	Self-redesign of where and how you do your work to increase the level of natural rewards in your job. Natural rewards that are part of, rather than separate from, the work (i.e., the work, like a hobby, becomes the reward) result from activities that cause you to feel • a sense of competence • a sense of self-control • a sense of purpose
Focusing thinking on natural rewards	Purposely focusing your thinking on the naturally rewarding features of your work.
Establishing constructive thought patterns	Establishing constructive and effective habits or patterns in your thinking (e.g., a tendency to search for opportunities rather than obstacles embedded in challenges) by managing your • beliefs and assumptions • mental imagery • internal self-talk

To work well, a merit pay plan should

• Be based on realistic and accurate measures of individual work performance.

• Create a belief among employees that the way to achieve high pay is to perform at high levels.

• Clearly discriminate between high and low performers in the amount of pay reward received.

- Avoid confusing "merit" aspects of a pay increase with "cost-of-living" adjustments.

Note that these guidelines are consistent with the basic laws of reinforcement and the guidelines for positive reinforcement discussed earlier in the chapter.

Creative Pay Practices

Merit pay plans are but one attempt to enhance the positive value of pay as a work reward and to use it as a positive reinforcer. Indeed, some argue that merit pay plans are not consistent with the demands of today's organizations since they fail to recognize the high degree of task interdependence among employees as illustrated particularly in TQM programs. Still others contend that the nature of any incentive scheme should be tied to the overall organizational strategy and the nature of the desired behavior. For example, the pay system of a firm that needs highly skilled individuals in short supply should emphasize employee retention rather than performance.[9]

With these points in mind, let us look at a variety of creative pay practices.

Skill-Based Pay   Skill-based pay rewards people for acquiring and developing job-relevant skills. Pay systems of this sort pay people for the mix and depth of skills they possess, not for the particular job assignment they hold. In a typical manufacturing plant, for example, a worker may be paid for knowing how to perform several different jobs, each of which requires different skills.

Gain-Sharing Plans   Cash bonuses, or extra pay for performance above standards or expectations, have been common practice in the compensation of managers and executives for a long time. Top managers in some industries earn annual bonuses of 50 percent or more of their base salaries. Attempts to extend such opportunities to all employees are growing in number and significance today. One popular plan is **gain-sharing,** an approach that links pay and performance by giving workers the opportunity to share in productivity gains through enhanced earnings.

The Scanlon Plan is probably the oldest and best known gain-sharing plan. Some others are the Lincoln Electric Plan, the Rucker Plan™, or IMPROSHARE™. Gain-sharing plans possess some similarities to profit-sharing plans, but they are not the same. Typically, profit-sharing plans grant individuals or work groups a specified portion of any economic profits earned by an organization as a whole. In contrast, gain-sharing plans involve a specific measurement of productivity, combined with a calculation of a bonus designed to offer workers a mutual share of any increase in total organizational productivity. Usually, everyone responsible for the increase receives the bonus. Gain-sharing involves some kind of "hard productivity" measurement, while profit-sharing typically does not.

The intended benefits of gain-sharing plans include increased worker motivation owing to the pay-for-performance incentives, and a greater sense of personal responsibility for making performance contributions to the organization. Because they can be highly participative in nature, gain-sharing plans may also encourage cooperation and teamwork in the workplace. Although more remains to be learned about gain-sharing, it is being used by a growing number of large and small organizations.

An interesting alternative to a typical pay increase spread over weeks or months is the **lump-sum increase** program, by which people can elect to receive an increase in one or more lump-sum payments. The full increase may be taken at the beginning of the year and used for some valued purpose (e.g., a down payment on a car or a sizable deposit in a savings account). Or a person might elect to take one-half of the raise early and get the rest at the start of the winter holiday season. In either case, the motivational significance of the pay increase is presumably enhanced by allowing the individual to receive it in larger doses and to realize the most personal significance out of its expenditure as possible.

Another related but more controversial development in this area is the lump-sum *payment,* which differs from the lump-sum *increase.* The lump-sum payment is an attempt by employers to hold labor costs in line while still giving workers more money, if corporate earnings allow. It involves giving workers a one-time lump-sum payment, often based on a gain-sharing formula, instead of a yearly percentage wage or salary increase. In this way, a person's base pay remains fixed, while overall monetary compensation varies according to the bonus added to this figure by the annual lump-sum payment.

Flexible Benefit Plans   The total compensation package of an employee includes not only direct pay but also any fringe benefits that are paid by the organization. These fringe benefits often add an equivalent of 10 to 40 percent to a person's salary. It is argued that organizations need to allow for individual differences when developing such benefit programs. Otherwise, the motivational value of this indirect form of pay incentive is lost. One approach is to let individuals choose their total pay package by selecting benefits, up to a certain dollar amount, from a range of options made available by the organization. These **flexible benefit plans** allow workers to select benefits according to needs. A single worker, for example, may prefer quite a different combination of insurance and retirement contributions than would a married person. The predicted result is increased motivational benefit from pay as an extrinsic work reward.

In Summary

What is learning, and what are four general approaches to learning?

- Learning is a relatively permanent change in behavior resulting from experience. It is an important part of rewards management.
- The four general approaches to learning are classical conditioning, operant conditioning, cognitive learning, and social learning.

- Of special importance here are cognitive learning, which relates to the motivational theories discussed in Chapter 5; operant conditioning, which is achieved when the consequences of behavior lead to changes in the probability of its occurrence; and social learning.

What are reinforcement, its foundation, and its linkage to rewards?

- Reinforcement is the means through which operant conditioning takes place.

- Its foundation is the law of effect, which states that behavior will be repeated or extinguished, depending on whether the consequences are positive or negative.

- Reinforcement is related to extrinsic rewards (valued outcomes that are given to the individual by some other source) because these rewards serve as environmental consequences that can influence people's work behaviors through the law of effect.

What is organizational behavior modification (OB Mod), and how do you use its four reinforcement strategies?

- OB Mod utilizes four reinforcement strategies to change behavior: positive reinforcement, negative reinforcement (avoidance), punishment, and extinction.

- Positive reinforcement is used to encourage desirable behavior. It is the administration of positive consequences that tend to increase the likelihood that a person will repeat a behavior in similar settings. Positive reinforcement should be contingent (administered only if the desired behavior is exhibited) and immediate (as close in time to the desired behavior as possible).

- Negative reinforcement, or avoidance, is used to encourage desirable behavior. The withdrawal of negative consequences tends to increase the likelihood that a person will repeat a desirable behavior in similar settings.

- Punishment is the administration of negative consequences or the withdrawal of positive consequences, which tends to reduce the likelihood of repeating a given behavior in similar settings. Punishment is used to weaken or eliminate undesirable behavior. A number of problems can occur with punishment. Thus, one must be especially careful to follow appropriate reinforcement guidelines (including the laws of contingent and immediate reinforcement), when using it. Punishment is likely to be more effective if combined with positive reinforcement.

- Extinction is the withdrawal of the reinforcing consequences for a given behavior. It is often used to withhold reinforcement for a behavior that has previously been reinforced. This is done to weaken or eliminate the undesirable behavior. It is an especially powerful strategy when combined with positive reinforcement.

What are social learning theory and behavioral self-management?

- Social learning theory advocates learning through the reciprocal interactions among people, behavior, and environment. Thus, it combines operant and cognitive learning approaches.
- Behavioral self-management builds on social learning theory to emphasize both behavioral and cognitive foci, with a special emphasis on enhancing a worker's self-efficacy and feeling of self-control.
- Self-management is useful both in treating workers as individuals and as part of self-managed teams.

As a manager, how can you deal with pay as an extrinsic reward?

- Managing pay as an extrinsic reward is particularly important because pay has multiple meanings—some positive and some negative.
- As a major and highly visible extrinsic reward, pay plays a role in reinforcement and in the motivation theories discussed previously. Its reward implications are especially important in terms of merit pay.
- Other pay practices that are important and offer creative reward opportunities are skill-based pay, gain-sharing plans, lump-sum pay increases, and flexible benefit plans.

JOB DESIGN, GOAL
SETTING, AND
PERFORMANCE
APPRAISAL

As you read Chapter 7, keep in mind these study questions:

- What are some alternative job design strategies, and how are they related to intrinsic work rewards?

- What is a diagnostic approach to job enrichment?

- What are some alternative work arrangements, and why are they important?

- How is goal-setting theory linked to job design?

- What is the performance appraisal process and purpose?

- What are performance appraisal measurement errors?

- What are some performance appraisal methods?

J ob design involves the planning and specification of job tasks and the work setting designated for their accomplishment. How can we help make jobs meaningful, interesting, and challenging? Alternative work arrangements focus on different kinds of work schedules and telecommuting (employees working away from the workplace but linked to it electronically). Goal setting involves building challenging and specific goals into jobs and providing appropriate performance feedback. Performance appraisal entails the systematic evaluation of performance, including feedback so that adjustments can be made.

As mentioned in Chapter 5, **intrinsic work rewards**[1] are those rewards received by an individual directly as a result of task performance. You can think of these as rewards that people give to themselves in return for successful task completion. One example is the feeling of achievement that comes from completing a challenging project. Such feelings are individually determined and integral to the work itself. They are self-regulated in that a person is not dependent on an outsider, such as the manager, to provide them. This concept is in direct contrast to the nature of extrinsic rewards, such as pay, which are externally controlled.

When we discussed extrinsic rewards in the last chapter, we viewed the manager as responsible for allocating extrinsic rewards, such as pay, promotion, and verbal praise to employees. Thus, a manager must be good at evaluating performance, maintaining an inventory of valued work rewards, and giving these rewards to employees contingent on work performance. Managing intrinsic work rewards presents an additional challenge. The manager still acts as an agent of the organization. Now, however, he or she must design jobs for individual subordinates so that intrinsic rewards become available to them as a direct result of working on assigned tasks.

Job Design Approaches

A **job** is one or more tasks that an individual performs in direct support of an organization's production purpose. **Intrinsic motivation** is essentially task motivation; that is, it is a desire to work hard solely for the pleasant experience of task accomplishment. When a job is properly designed, both task performance and job satisfaction should be facilitated. Additional human resource maintenance aspects, such as absenteeism, commitment, and turnover, may also be influenced.

As mentioned earlier, **job design** is the planning and specification of job tasks and the designated work setting in which they are to be accomplished. This definition includes both the specification of task attributes and the creation of a work setting for these attributes. The manager's responsibility is to design jobs that will be motivational for the individual employee. The general approaches to job design include

Job simplification.

Job enlargement.

Job rotation.

Job enrichment.

Job Simplification

Job simplification involves standardizing work procedures and employing people in very clearly defined and specialized tasks. The machine-paced automobile assembly line is a classic example of this job design strategy.

Simplified jobs are highly specialized and usually require an individual to perform a narrow set of tasks repetitively. The potential advantages of this approach include increased operating efficiency. Indeed, that was the original intent of the job simplification approach: low-skill and low-cost labor; little training; and controlled production quantity. Some possible disadvantages of this "de-skilling" include loss of efficiency owing to low-quality work; high rates of absenteeism and turnover; and the need to pay high wages to get people to do unattractive jobs. For most people, simplified job designs tend to be low in intrinsic motivation. The jobs lack challenge and lead to boredom.

In today's high-technology age, a natural extension of job simplification is complete **automation**—allowing a machine to do the work previously accomplished through human effort. This approach increasingly involves the use of robots, which are becoming ever more versatile and reliable. For example, the Walgreen's drugstore chain has increased the rate of packing shipments from its distribution center to its stores by more than 800 percent with its use of robots.[2]

Job Enlargement and Job Rotation

The job enlargement and job rotation strategies seek to increase the breadth of a job by adding to the variety of tasks performed by a worker. Task variety is assumed to offset some of the disadvantages of job simplification, thereby increasing job performance and satisfaction for the individual.

Job enlargement increases task variety by combining two or more tasks that were previously assigned to separate workers into one job. The only change in the original job design is that a worker does more different tasks than previously. Often, job enlargement has not lived up to its promise. How different is it, really, if you used to screw two nuts on two bolts and now you screw four nuts on four bolts?

Job rotation increases task variety by periodically shifting workers among jobs involving different tasks. The tasks themselves stay the same. Job rotation can be arranged according to almost any time schedule, such as hourly, daily, or weekly schedules. As with job enlargement, the results have sometimes been disappointing. If a rotation cycle takes employees through a series of the same old jobs, the employees simply experience many boring jobs instead of just one. Job rotation may decrease efficiency, but it can add to flexibility since people can be moved from one job to another. Its current use often is primarily for the latter purpose.

Job Enrichment

Frederick Herzberg, whose two-factor theory is discussed in Chapter 5, feels that it is illogical to expect to get high levels of motivation from employees whose jobs are designed according to the rules of simplification, enlargement, or rotation. Rather than pursuing one of these job design strategies, therefore, Herzberg recommends that managers practice job enrichment.[3]

Job enrichment is the practice of building motivating factors into job content. This job design strategy differs from the previous ones in that it seeks to expand job content by adding some of the planning and evaluating duties normally performed by the manager to the subordinate's job. Herzberg refers to these changes that increase the "depth" of a job as a **vertical loading** of the job tasks, as opposed to the **horizontal loading** involved in enlargement and rotation.

In the job enlargement and rotation strategies, managers retain all responsibility for work planning and evaluating. In contrast, the job enrichment strategy involves vertical loading, which allows subordinates to share in these planning and evaluating responsibilities as well as to do the actual work.

A Diagnostic Approach to Job Enrichment

The diagnostic approach developed by Richard Hackman and Greg Oldham addresses job design in a contingency fashion.[4] The current version of this diagnostic approach or **Job Characteristics Theory** is shown in Figure 7.1. Five core job characteristics are identified as being task attributes of special importance to job designs. A job that is high in these core characteristics is said to be enriched. The core job characteristics are:

1. **Skill variety** The degree to which a job requires a variety of different activi-

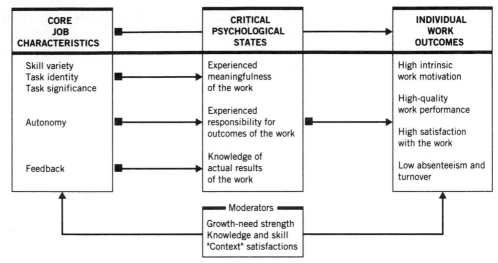

Figure 7.1 Core job characteristics and individual work outcomes. (Adapted from J. Richard Hackman and Greg R. Oldham, "Development of the Job Diagnostic Survey," *Journal of Applied Psychology,* vol. 60, 1975, p. 161. Used by permission.)

ties in carrying out the work and involves the use of a number of different skills and talents of the employee.

2. **Task identity** The degree to which the job requires completion of a "whole" and identifiable piece of work; that is, one that involves doing a job from beginning to end with a visible outcome.

3. **Task significance** The degree to which the job is important and involves a meaningful contribution to the organization or society in general.

4. **Autonomy** The degree to which the job gives the employee substantial freedom, independence, and discretion in scheduling the work and determining the procedures used in carrying it out.

5. **Job feedback** The degree to which carrying out the work activities results in the employee's obtaining direct and clear information regarding how well the job has been done.

Hackman and Oldham state further that three critical psychological states must be realized in order for people to develop intrinsic work motivation: (1) experienced meaningfulness in the work; (2) experienced responsibility for the outcomes of the work; and (3) knowledge of actual results of the work activities. These psychological states represent intrinsic rewards that are believed to occur and to influence later performance and satisfaction when the core job characteristics are present in the job design.

Individual Difference Moderators

Job Characteristics Theory recognizes that the five core job characteristics do not affect all people in the same way. Figure 7.1 shows three individual difference moderators:

Growth-need strength This is the degree to which a person desires the opportunity for self-direction, learning, and personal accomplishment at work. It is similar to Maslow's esteem and self-actualization and Alderfer's growth needs. The theory predicts that people with strong growth needs will respond positively to enriched jobs, whereas people low in growth-need strength will have negative reactions and will find enriched jobs a source of anxiety.

Knowledge and skill Those with the knowledge and skill needed for performance on an enriched job are predicted to feel good about the enrichment. In other words, they have a sense of self-efficacy.

Context satisfaction This is the extent to which an employee is satisfied with the kind of hygiene factors emphasized by Herzberg. For example, those satisfied with salary levels, supervision, and working conditions are more likely than their dissatisfied colleagues to support job enrichment.

In general, people whose capabilities match the requirements of an enriched job are likely to experience positive feelings and to perform well; people who are inadequate or who feel inadequate in this regard are likely to have difficulties.

Experts generally agree that the job diagnostic approach is quite useful, but it is not a universal panacea for job performance and satisfaction problems. The experts also recognize that job enrichment can fail when job requirements are increased beyond the level of individual capabilities and interests. In summary, remember that jobs high in core characteristics (especially as perceived by employees) tend to increase both satisfaction and performance, particularly among high growth-need employees. The Effective Manager 7.1 provides some useful guidelines.

Alternative Work Arrangements

In addition to job design, another important aspect of the work setting concerns alternative work arrangements. These arrangements essentially reshape the traditional 40-hour a week, 9 to 5 arrangements, where work is done on the premises. Virtually all such plans are designed to influence employee satisfaction and to serve as both extrinsic and intrinsic motivating devices by helping employees balance some of the demands of their working and nonworking lives. These arrangements are becoming more and more important in our fast-changing society in order to deal with our increasingly diverse workforce. Such arrangements include the compressed workweek, flexible working hours, job sharing, part-time work, and telecommuting, each of which is concerned with fitting work arrangements with individual needs.

The Compressed Workweek

A **compressed workweek** is any scheduling of work that allows a full-time job to be completed in fewer than the standard five days. The most common form of compressed workweek is the "4–40"; that is, 40 hours of work accomplished in four 10-

---

THE EFFECTIVE MANAGER 7.1

Guidelines for Implementing a Program of Job Enrichment

Consider a job to be a candidate for job enrichment only when evidence exists that job satisfaction and/or performance is either deteriorating or open for improvement. Use a diagnostic approach and proceed with actual job enrichment only when

- Employees view their jobs as deficient in one or more of the core job characteristics.
- Extrinsic rewards and job context are not causing dissatisfaction.
- Cost and other potential constraints do not prohibit job design changes necessary for enrichment.
- Employees view core job characteristics positively.
- Employees have needs and capabilities consistent with the new job designs.

Whenever possible, conduct a careful evaluation of the results of job enrichment to discontinue the job design strategy (if necessary) or to make constructive changes to increase its value.

Expect that enrichment will also affect the job of the supervising manager since duties will be delegated.

- Do not feel threatened or become anxious or frustrated.
- Get help if needed for required personal work adjustments.

---

hour days. It is currently the least used of all the alternative work arrangements. Added time off is a major feature for the worker. The organization can benefit, too, in terms of reduced energy consumption during three-day shutdowns, lower employee absenteeism, improved recruiting of new employees, and the extra time available for building and equipment maintenance.

The disadvantages of the compressed workweek may include increased fatigue from the extended workday and family adjustment problems for the individual, as well as increased work scheduling problems and possible customer complaints due to breaks in work coverage.

Research results are mixed on the compressed workweek.[5] This schedule sometimes has a positive effect on productivity, absenteeism, and the like, but it sometimes does not. What seems to happen is that positive effects occur when the compressed workweek is first implemented, and then these effects wear off.

Flexible Working Hours

Flexible working hours are defined as "any work schedule that gives employees daily choice in the timing between work and nonwork activities." More than 9 million workers are estimated to be on a flexible working schedule.[6] A sample flexible working hour schedule involves employees working 4 hours of "core" time. They are then free to choose their remaining 4 hours of work from among flexible time blocks.

Flexible working hours, or "flextime," increases individual autonomy in work scheduling and allows worker opportunities to attend to such personal affairs as dental appointments, home emergencies, visiting the bank, and so on. Research on this scheduling strategy supports the argument that the discretion it allows workers in scheduling their own hours of work encourages them to develop positive attitudes and to increase commitment to the organization.

Job Sharing

Another work-setting alternative is **job sharing,** whereby one full-time job is assigned to two or more persons, who then divide the work according to agreements made between or among themselves and with the employer.[7] Job sharing often occurs when each person works half a day, although it can also be done on such bases as weekly or monthly sharing arrangements. It is still used by only a relatively small percentage of employers, but human-resource experts say job-sharing arrangements are increasingly being allowed in major U.S. companies.[8]

Organizations can benefit from job sharing when they are able to attract talented people who would otherwise be unable to work. Through job sharing, two persons able to work half a day can be employed to handle one job.

Part-time Work

There are two kinds of part-time work: **temporary part-time work** (where an employee is classified as "temporary" and works less than the standard 40-hour workweek) and **permanent part-time work** (where a worker is considered "permanent" but works fewer hours than the standard workweek). Employees involved in job sharing typically fit this latter category. There are currently more than 20 million part-time employees working in the United States.[9]

Temporary part-timers are usually easy to release and hire as needs dictate. As a result, many organizations use part-time work to hold down labor costs and to help smooth out peaks and valleys in the business cycle. This alternative work schedule can be a benefit to people who also hold full-time jobs, or who want something less than a full workweek for a variety of personal reasons.

Telecommuting

Telecommuting is work done at home or in a remote location by using a computer and/or facsimile ("fax") machine linked to a central office or some other employment location. Sometimes this arrangement is called "flexiplace" or "the electronic cottage."[10] Telecommuting emphasizes place rather than scheduling, although working at home does allow flexible working hours.

Telecommuting is currently the most controversial of the alternative work arrangements. Even so, the number of telecommuters is estimated to have grown by nearly 40 percent since 1990.[11]

Not long ago, the Environmental Protection Agency approved a regulation requiring firms with more than 100 employees in four Southern California counties to present plans to cut commuter glut, thus encouraging telecommuting. Telecommuting also offers the potential advantages of flexibility, the comforts of home, and choice of locations consistent with one's lifestyle.

One organizational advantage is the cutting of overhead. There is resistance from some firms, however. Managerial considerations in dealing with remote employees seem to be a prime reason for this resistance. Other reasons are a sense of isolation from coworkers, decreased identification with the work team, and technical difficulties with computer linkages. Research is still needed to determine whether these disadvantages will overcome the advantages and appeal of telecommuting.

Goal-setting Theory

Goal-setting is the "process of developing, negotiating, and formalizing the targets or objectives that an employee is responsible for accomplishing." Expanding job design to include goal setting results in specific task goals for each individual. These task goals are important because of their linkage with task performance. Over a number of years, Edwin Locke has developed a set of arguments and predictions concerning this linkage. This set of predictions serves as the basis for goal-setting theory. Locke's research, and that of others, provides considerable support for his predictions that[12]

1. **Difficult goals are more likely to lead to higher performance than are less difficult ones.** However, if the goals are seen as too difficult or impossible, the relationship with performance no longer holds. For example, you are likely to sell more if you have a goal of six refrigerators a month than if you have a goal of three. However, if your goal is 60 refrigerators a month, you may see that as impossible, and your performance very likely will be lower than with a goal of six.

2. **Specific goals are more likely to lead to higher performance than are no goals or vague or very general ones (such as "do your best").** For example, setting a goal of selling six refrigerators a month is more specific and should lead to more performance than a simple "do your best" goal.

3. **Task feedback, or knowledge of results, is likely to motivate people toward higher performance by encouraging the setting of higher performance goals.** Feedback lets people know where they stand and if they are on- or off-course in their efforts. For example, think about how eager you are to find out how well you did on an examination.

4. **Goals are most likely to lead to higher performance when people have the abilities and the feelings of self-efficacy required to accomplish them.** The person must actually be able to accomplish the goals and feel confident in those abilities. For example, you may actually be able to do what's required to sell six refrigerators a month and feel confident that you can.

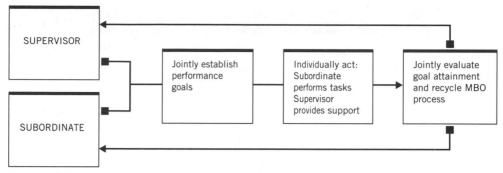

Figure 7.2 The management by objectives (MBO) process.

However, if your goal is 60 refrigerators a month, you may not have either the ability or the confidence to sell that many.

5. **Goals are most likely to motivate people toward higher performance when they are accepted and there is commitment to them.** One way of obtaining such acceptance or commitment is by participating in the goal-setting process. You then get "ownership" of the goals. However, Locke and Latham report that goals assigned by someone else can be equally effective. The assigners are likely to be authority figures, and that can have an impact. Also, the assignment implies that the subordinate can actually reach the goal. Third, assigned goals often are a challenge. Finally, assigned goals help define the standards people use to attain self-satisfaction with their performance.[13] According to Locke and Latham, assigned goals only lead to poor performance when they are curtly or inadequately explained.[14]

Goal Setting and MBO

When we speak of goal setting and its potential to influence individual performance at work, the concept of *management by objectives (MBO)* immediately comes to mind. This approach has been used by such firms as Purex, Tenneco, and Black & Decker. The essence of MBO is a process of *joint* goal setting between a supervisor and a subordinate.[15] It involves managers working with their subordinates to establish performance goals and plans that are consistent with higher level work unit and organizational objectives.

Figure 7.2 shows a comprehensive view of MBO. The concept is consistent with the notion of goal setting and its associated principles discussed above. Notice how joint supervisor–subordinate discussions are designed to extend participation from the point of initial goal establishment to the point of evaluating results in terms of goal attainment. Key issues for the mutual goal setting are summarized in The Effective Manager 7.2.[16] In addition to these goal-setting steps, a successful MBO system calls for careful implementation. This means that the previous steps are translated into the kinds of strategies or plans mentioned earlier that will lead to goal accom-

---

THE EFFECTIVE MANAGER 7.2

Key Issues for Mutual Goal Setting in an MBO Program

- *What must be done?* Start with higher level goals, job descriptions stating tasks to be performed, outcomes expected, necessary supplies and equipment, and so on.
- *How will performance be measured?* Time, money, or physical units may often be used to measure performance. If the job is more subjective, emphasize behaviors or actions believed to lead to success.
- *What is the performance standard?* Start with previous performance of others doing this job. Where these measures do not exist, use mutual supervisor–subordinate judgment and discussion.
- *What are the deadlines for the goals?* Discuss deadlines in terms of daily, weekly, or longer terms.
- *What is the relative importance of the goals?* Not all goals are equally important. The manager and subordinate should decide together on the goal ranking.
- *How difficult are the goals?* Watch especially for high task complexity and multiple goals. Come up with a clearly agreed upon decision.

---

plishment. Subordinates must have freedom to carry out the required tasks; managers may have to do considerable coaching and counseling.

Performance Appraisal: Process and Purpose

An important foundation for the managerial application of motivation theories is the process of performance appraisal, or evaluation.[17] Formally defined, **performance appraisal** is a process of systematically evaluating performance and providing feedback on which performance adjustments can be made. Essentially, performance appraisal works on the basis of the equation: desired performance − actual performance = need for action. To the extent that desired levels exceed actual levels, a performance variance requiring special attention exists. For example, if you have a sales quota of eight new cars per month (desired performance) and you only sell two cars per month (actual performance), there is a performance variance of six cars that will need the attention of the sales manager. Of course, only when actual performance is accurately measured is one well prepared to apply his or her knowledge of OB to analyzing the performance situation, identifying the problems and the opportunities involved, and taking appropriate action.

Any performance appraisal system is central to an organization's human resource management activities. The major functions of performance appraisal are to[18]

1. **Define the specific job criteria** against which performance will be measured.

2. **Measure past job performance** accurately.

3. **Justify the rewards** given to individuals or groups, thereby discriminating between high and low performance.
4. **Define the development experiences** the ratee needs both to enhance performance in the current job and to prepare for future responsibilities.

These four functions include two general purposes served by good performance–appraisal systems: evaluation and development. For the manager, this means that fulfilling both judgmental (evaluation) and counseling (developmental) roles are essential to the performance–appraisal process. From an evaluation perspective, performance appraisal lets people know where they stand relative to objectives and standards. As such, the performance appraisal is an input to decisions that allocate rewards and otherwise administer the personnel functions of the organization. From a counseling perspective, performance appraisal facilitates implementing decisions relating to planning for and gaining commitment to the continued training and personal development of subordinates.

Performance appraisals have traditionally been conducted by an individual's immediate superior.[19] However, other sources can provide useful appraisal information. For instance, the increasing emphasis on various kinds of creative work teams has increased the importance of coworker evaluations of one another.

Others are self-appraisals and subordinate appraisals of their supervisors. Self-appraisals are typically used in combination with other ratings, such as those of the superior, as a part of the appraisal feedback process.[20] Also, the growth of TQM programs and the like may even inspire performance evaluations by customers as well as by those in other cross-functional areas that work with given individuals or work groups.

Measurement Errors in Performance Appraisal

To be meaningful, an appraisal system must be both reliable (provide consistent results each time it is used) and valid (actually measure people on relevant job content). A number of measurement errors can threaten the reliability and validity of performance appraisals.[21]

Halo Errors

A **halo error** results when one person rates another person on several different dimensions and gives a similar rating for each dimension. For example, a sales representative considered to be a "go-getter" (and thus rated high on "dynamism") would also be rated high on dependability, tact, and whatever other performance dimensions were used. The rater fails to discriminate between the person's strong and weak points; a "halo" carries over from one dimension to the next. This effect can create a problem when each of the performance dimensions is considered an important and relatively independent aspect of the job.

Leniency/Strictness Errors

Just as some professors are known as "easy A's," some managers tend to give relatively high ratings to virtually everyone under their supervision. This is known as a **leniency error.** Sometimes the opposite occurs: Some raters tend to give everyone a low rating. This is called a **strictness error.** The problem in both instances is that there is very little discrimination between the good and poor performers.

Central Tendency Errors

In contrast to a tendency to rate all subordinates as very good or very bad, **central tendency errors** occur when managers lump everyone together around the "average," or middle, category. This tendency gives the impression that there are no very good or very poor performers on the dimensions being rated. No true performance discrimination is made.

Recency Errors

A **recency error** occurs when a rater allows recent events to influence a performance rating over earlier events. Take, for example, the case of an employee who is usually on time but shows up one hour late for work the day before his or her performance rating. The employee is rated low on "promptness" because the one incident of tardiness overshadows his or her usual promptness.

Personal Bias Errors

Raters sometimes allow specific biases to enter into performance evaluations. When this happens, **personal bias errors** occur. For example, a rater may intentionally give higher ratings to whites than to nonwhites. In this case, the performance appraisal reflects a racial bias. Bias toward members of other demographic categories can also occur.

Performance Appraisal Methods

A number of methods are commonly used in performance appraisal. Each method has its own strengths and weaknesses in terms of purpose, dimensions and standards, and rating errors.[22]

Ranking

Ranking is the simplest of all the comparative techniques. It consists of merely rank ordering each individual from best to worst on each performance dimension being considered. For example, in evaluating work quality, I compare Smith, Jones, and Brown. I then rank Brown number 1, Smith number 2, and Jones number 3. The ranking method is relatively simple to use, although it can become burdensome when there are many people to consider.

Paired Comparison

In a **paired comparison** method, each person is directly compared with every other person being rated. The frequency of endorsement across all pairs determines one's final ranking. Every possible paired comparison within a group of ratees is considered, as shown here (italics indicate the person rated better in each pair):

Bill vs. Mary	*Mary* vs. Leslie	*Leslie* vs. Tom
Bill vs. Leslie	*Mary* vs. Tom	
Bill vs. Tom		

Number of times Bill is better   = 3
Number of times Mary is better   = 2
Number of times Leslie is better = 1
Number of times Tom is better   = 0

Overall, the best performer in this example is Bill, followed by Mary, then Leslie, and, last of all, Tom. The paired comparison approach can be even more tedious than the ranking method when there are many people to compare.

Forced Distribution

In the case of **forced distribution,** a small number of performance categories are used, such as "very good," "good," "adequate," "poor," and "very poor." Each rater is instructed to rate a specific proportion of employees in each of these categories. For example, 10 percent of employees must be rated very good; 20 percent must be rated good; and so on. This method *forces* the rater to use all of the categories and to avoid rating everyone as outstanding, poor, average, or the like.

Graphic Rating Scales

Graphic rating scales list a variety of dimensions that are thought to be related to high-performance outcomes in a given job and that the individual is accordingly expected to exhibit, such as cooperation, initiative, and attendance. The scales allow the manager to assign the individual scores on each dimension. These ratings are sometimes given point values, culminating in a summary numerical rating of performance.

The primary appeal of graphic rating scales is that they are relatively easy to do; they are efficient in the use of time and other resources; and they can be applied to a wide range of jobs. Unfortunately, they are also subject to halo, leniency/strictness, central tendency, recency, and personal bias errors. Also, because of generality, they may not be linked to job analysis or to other specific aspects of a given job.

Critical Incident Diary

Supervisors may use **critical incident diaries** to record incidents of each subordinate's behavior that led either to unusual success or to failure in a given performance aspect. These incidents are typically recorded in a diary-type log that is kept daily or weekly under predesignated dimensions.

This approach is excellent for employee development and feedback. Since the method consists of qualitative statements rather than quantitative information, however, it is difficult to use for administrative decisions. To provide for such information, the critical incident technique is sometimes combined with one of the other methods.

Behaviorally Anchored Rating Scales (BARS)

The procedure for developing this type of scale starts with the careful collection of descriptions of observable job behaviors. These descriptions are typically provided by managers and personnel specialists and include both superior and inferior performance. Once a large sample of behavioral descriptions is collected, each behavior is evaluated to determine the extent to which it describes good versus bad performance. The final step is to develop a rating scale, in which the anchors are specific critical behaviors, each reflecting a different degree of performance effectiveness.

As you can see, the BARS approach is detailed and complex. It requires much time and effort to develop. But the BARS also provides specific behaviors that are useful for counseling and feedback combined with quantitative scales that are useful for administrative comparative purposes.

In Summary

What are some alternative job design strategies, and how are they related to intrinsic work rewards?

- Job design strategies include three broad alternatives: job simplification, job enlargement and job rotation, and job enrichment.
- Job simplification standardizes work procedures and employs people in very clearly defined and specialized tasks.
- Job enlargement increases task variety by combining two or more tasks previously assigned to separate workers.
- Job rotation increases task variety by periodically rotating work among jobs involving different tasks.
- Job enrichment builds motivating factors into job content by adding planning and evaluating duties.
- The intrinsic work rewards made available by these strategies range on a continuum from low (job simplification) to high (job enrichment).

What is the diagnostic approach to job enrichment?

- The diagnostic approach to job enrichment has been developed by Richard Hackman and his associates. It does not assume that everyone wants an enriched job. Rather, it considers those with high and low growth-needs and related aspects. It then looks at the effect of five core job characteristics (ranging from skill variety to feedback from the job itself) on intervening critical psychological states that influence motivation, performance, and satisfaction.

- There is quite a bit of research support for the job diagnostic approach.

- The job diagnosis approach needs to recognize cultural as well as individual difference characteristics; and it should not be applied to everyone's job. People high in growth-need strength and related aspects seem to respond best to the approach.

What are some alternative work arrangements, and why are they important?

- The compressed workweek allows full-time work to be completed in less than five days.

- Flexible working hours allow employees a daily choice in timing between work and nonwork activities.

- Job sharing occurs when two or more people divide one full-time job according to agreement among themselves and the employer.

- Part-time work is done on a schedule classifying the worker as temporary or permanent and requires less than a 40-hour workweek.

- Telecommuting involves doing work at home or at a remote location, using a computer or "fax" machine with linkage to the employment location.

- These alternative work arrangements are becoming more and more important as a way of obtaining the services of an increasingly diverse workforce in our rapidly changing society.

How is goal-setting theory linked to job design?

- Goal setting is the process of developing, negotiating, and formalizing the targets or objectives that an employee is responsible for accomplishing. It includes a number of predictions that link it to job design and that serve as the basis for goal-setting theory.

- These predictions emphasize challenging, specific goals, knowledge of results, ability and a feeling of self-efficacy to accomplish the goals, and goal commitment or acceptance.

- A managerial technique that applies goal-setting theory is management by objectives (MBO). A manager and subordinate mutually agree on individual goals that are consistent with higher level ones. A process is then implemented to monitor and assist the subordinate in task accomplishment, and the subordinate's performance is evaluated in terms of accomplished results.

- If implemented well, many positive aspects of goal-setting theory can be realized from MBO, but effective MBO systems are difficult to establish and maintain.

What is the performance appraisal process and purpose?

- Performance appraisal is a process of systematically evaluating performance and providing feedback.
- Evaluation and development are two broad purposes of performance appraisal. Evaluation lets people know where they stand relative to objectives and standards. The developmental aspect facilitates implementing decisions relating to planning for and gaining commitment to the continued training and development of subordinates.

What are performance appraisal measurement errors?

- Measurement errors are those that can threaten the reliability or validity of performance appraisals.
- Five common errors are: halo (a similar rating is given for separate performance dimensions); leniency/strictness (raters tend to give virtually everyone relatively high or relatively low ratings); central tendency (raters lump virtually everyone together around the middle category); recency (recent events influence a rating more than earlier events); and personal bias (specific biases against race, etc., influence one's ratings).

What are some performance appraisal methods?

- There are numerous performance appraisal methods, each with its own strengths and weaknesses.
- Six common performance appraisal methods are: ranking (each individual is ordered from best to worst on each dimension considered); paired comparison (each ratee is directly compared with every other person being rated); forced distribution (a small number of performance categories is used and a specific proportion of ratees is placed in each category); graphic (each ratee is assigned a score on each dimension believed to be an important aspect of performance); critical incident diary (incidents are recorded that led either to unusual success or failure during a given period); and behaviorally anchored rating scales (BARS) (critical behaviors are developed, each reflecting a different degree of performance effectiveness).

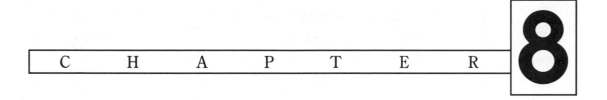

GROUPS AND WORK TEAMS

As you read Chapter 8, keep in mind the following study questions:

- What types of groups are found in organizations?

- How do groups help organizations?

- What is an effective group?

- What are employee involvement groups?

- What are self-managing teams?

- How can managers encourage teamwork?

The *new* workplace values change and adaptation. As organizations pursue higher productivity, total quality, customer satisfaction, and the like, they are finding new and creative ways to utilize "groups" as foundations for performance improvements.[1] One *Fortune* magazine article opens with the headline: "Who needs a boss?" The answer offered in the first paragraph is: "Not the employees who work in self-managed teams." Indeed, the concepts of *groups* and *teams,* as discussed in this chapter and the next, are major keys to productivity and quality of working-life improvements in the *new* workplace. Teams allowed General Mills in Lodi, California, to stop relying on the presence of managers on the night shift; teams at Saturn's Spring Hill, Tennessee, plant have shifted into workers' hands responsibility for decisions ranging from hiring new team members to setting operating budgets; if you stay abreast of new workplace developments, this list can go on and on.

Types of Groups in Organizations

Formally defined, a **group** is a collection of two or more people working with one another to achieve one or more common goals.[2] A group, in this sense, is more than just a collection of people. In a true group, members consider themselves mutually dependent on one another to achieve their goals, and they interact with one another regularly to pursue those goals over time. Managers, of course, must be comfortable participating in and leading the activities of many different types of groups in organizations.

Formal Groups

A *formal group* is an "official" group designated to serve a specific purpose within an organization. A good example is the work unit headed by a manager and consisting of one or more direct reports. It is expected to accomplish certain tasks for the organization, and the manager is held accountable for these performance results. Such work units and other *permanent work groups* often appear on organization charts as departments (e.g., market research department), divisions (e.g., consumer products division), or teams (e.g., product assembly team), among other possibilities. Permanent groups can vary in size from very small departments or teams of just a few people to large divisions employing a hundred or more people. In all cases, they share the common characteristics of having been officially created to perform certain tasks on an ongoing basis. They continue in existence until a decision is made to change or reconfigure the organization for some reason.

Temporary work groups are created for a specific purpose, and they disband once the purpose has been accomplished. Good examples are the many committees and task forces used in today's organizations to solve specific problems or perform special assignments.[3] The president of a company, for example, might ask a task force to study the feasibility of flexible work hours for nonmanagerial employees. Such temporary groups usually have appointed chairpersons or leaders who are held accountable for performance results, much as is the manager of a work unit. In the example, the president would expect the head of the task force to meet a deadline for submitting an action recommendation.

Work Teams

It is increasingly common today to use the word "team" when referring to various types of formal groups. In the workplace, a **team** is a small group of people with complementary skills who work together to achieve a common purpose for which they hold themselves collectively accountable.[4] Teams that should meet these criteria are of three broad types.[5]

1. **Teams that recommend things** In the form of task forces, ad hoc committees, project teams, and the like, teams study specific problems and recommend solutions, often working with a target completion date and disbanding once their purpose has been fulfilled.
2. **Teams that make or do things** As functional groups, such as marketing and advertising departments, they perform ongoing tasks for the organization and are relatively permanent.
3. **Teams that run things** Consisting of formal leaders, such as a "senior management group," they set purposes, goals, and values, and strategic directions, and help others to implement them.

Informal Groups

Organizations also consist of many **informal groups** that emerge unofficially and are not recognized as part of the organization's formal structure.[6] *Friendship groups* consist of persons with natural affinities for one another; they may tend to work together, sit together, take breaks together, and even do things together outside of work. *Interest groups* consist of persons who share common interests. They may be job-related interests, such as an intense desire to learn more about computers; they may also be nonwork interests, such as community service, sports, or religion.

How Groups Help Organizations

Groups are good for both organizations and their members. They help accomplish important and sometimes very complex tasks. And because they serve the interests of individual members, groups can also help maintain high-quality work environments. Harold J. Leavitt, scholar and management consultant, explains why managers must take groups seriously as valuable organizational resources.[7]

- Groups are good for people.
- Groups can stimulate innovation and creativity.
- Groups sometimes make better decisions than individuals do.
- Groups can speed the implementation of decisions.
- Groups can help control the behavior of members.
- Groups can help offset the negative side effects of large organization size.

Groups and Task Performance

Organizations and their managers have much to gain through the effective utilization of groups. They can help organizations gain synergy in the accomplishment of important tasks, especially under the following conditions.[8]

1. **Groups are better when no individual "expert" exists.** When there is no clear individual expert to handle a problem situation, groups tend to make better judgments than the average individual acting alone.

2. **Groups are better for complex tasks that can be subdivided.** When complex problem solving can be handled by a division of labor and the sharing of information, groups are typically more successful than are individuals.

3. **Groups are better when risk is desirable.** Because of their tendencies to make more extreme decisions, groups can sometimes be more creative and innovative in performing their tasks than individuals.

That is the positive side. But as we all know, groups can also have performance problems. The very word "group" produces both positive and negative reactions in the minds of most people. Although it is said that "two heads are better than one," we are also warned that "too many cooks spoil the broth." "A camel is a horse put together by a committee," admonishes the true group skeptic!

An important group performance issue centers on how well group members work together to accomplish a task. Far too often, some believe, group task performance is limited by social loafing or what may be more simply called "freeloading in groups."[9] Many students are acquainted with this phenomenon based on experiences in course study groups or in extracurricular groups to which they belong. A German psychologist by the name of Ringlemann formally identified this tendency in a simple experiment. He asked people to pull as hard as they could on a rope, first alone and then in a group. He found that the average effort dropped as more people joined the rope-pulling task. Today the term *Ringlemann effect* is used to describe the situation in which some people do not work as hard in groups as they do individually. The two main reasons for this effect relate to the lack of actual or perceived individual accountability. On the one hand, a social loafer may recognize

---

THE EFFECTIVE MANAGER 8.1

Why People Join Informal Groups

- *Needs for security*—Groups offer a sense of safety to people who are insecure or feel threatened.
- *Social needs*—Groups offer affiliation and interaction opportunities.
- *Esteem needs*—Groups offer opportunities to gain status and prestige.
- *Self-fulfillment needs*—Groups offer opportunities to gain a sense of self-worth.
- *Achievement needs*—Groups offer settings to pursue goals and accomplish difficult tasks.
- *Power needs*—Groups offer opportunities to assume leadership and influence others.

---

that his or her contributions are less noticeable in a group setting; on the other, a social loafer may simply prefer to let others carry all or most of the work load given the task at hand.

Groups and Individual Development

Groups have the ability to satisfy important needs for their members. They provide a framework or setting for social interaction and interpersonal fulfillment. A group can offer security in the form of direct work assistance and technical advice to a member, or it can offer emotional support to someone experiencing special crisis or pressure. Groups give their members something to identify with, and they offer many activities from which one can derive self-esteem and ego gratification. In sum, the opportunities of group involvements have the potential to help satisfy the full range of individual needs discussed in Chapter 5 on motivation in the workplace. Furthermore, the inability of someone's formal group affiliations to satisfy such needs may explain the appeal of informal groups. The Effective Manager 8.1 offers some tips on why people join groups of this type.

By working together and sharing task skills, members can help one another learn and perform at the desired levels of accomplishment. In a good work group, members are quick to give support, encouragement, and performance feedback to one another. In this way, group members acquire job competencies and may even make up for deficiencies in the organization's training programs. As is well known, newcomers often learn how to do their jobs from more "senior" members of their work groups. The pooling of skills and task knowledge can also help even experienced members solve unique problems.

Similarly, the attitudes group members display and the way they behave can serve as positive or negative "models" for the newcomer to follow; that is, they may encourage or discourage high levels of work effort. A new employee soon learns from coworkers, for example, who the "bad" supervisors are, or who you can and cannot "trust." These influences may even extend to how the individual should feel about his or her job and the organization. A coworker may positively indicate that "this is a good job to have and a great place to work" or may negatively suggest that "this is a lousy job and you are better off looking for something else." Naturally, managers would like all such influences of groups on individuals to be as positive and supportive of organizational goals as possible.

Foundations of Group Effectiveness

The best groups and teams contribute positively to organizations and their members in the ways just described. Formally stated, an **effective group** is one that achieves high levels of both task performance and human resource maintenance over time. In respect to *task performance,* an effective group achieves its performance goals relating to the quantity, quality, and timeliness of work results. For a permanent work group, such as a manufacturing unit, this might mean meeting daily work targets; for a temporary group, such as a new policy development team, this might involve submitting to the president the draft of a new organizational policy. In respect to *human resource maintenance,* an effective group is one whose members are sufficiently satisfied with their tasks, accomplishments, and interpersonal relationships to work well together on an ongoing basis. In other words, the social fabric of an effective group is pleasant and positive. For a permanent work group, this means the members work well together workday after workday; for a temporary work group, this means the members work well together for the duration of the assignment.

Practically speaking, an effective group gets its job done and takes good care of its members in the process. Although the concept is straightforward, achieving work group effectiveness is a major challenge to managers, group leaders, and group members alike. A classic listing of the characteristics of an effective group follows.[10]

- Members are loyal to one another and to the leader.
- Members and leaders have high confidence and trust in each other.
- Members are eager to help one another develop to their full potential.
- Members know when to conform and when not to, and for what purposes.
- Members communicate fully and frankly on all relevant matters.
- Members are secure in making decisions that seem appropriate to them.
- Members' values and needs match group values and goals.

Groups as Open Systems

One way you can better understand the foundations of group effectiveness is to view any group as an "open system" that interacts with its environment in the ongoing process of transforming resource inputs into product outputs. Consider the model

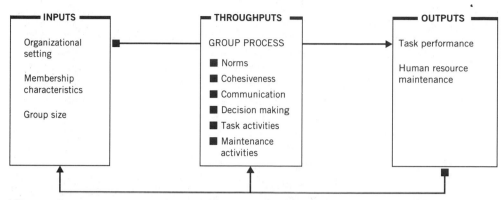

Figure 8.1 Understanding groups as open systems.

presented in Figure 8.1. The several elements in this model can be used to help explain, predict, and influence the behaviors of groups and their members.

The environment consists of other individuals and groups within the organization and with whom the group interacts. The group is dependent on these elements to provide the resources it needs to operate in the throughput process. In return for these resources, the group is expected to give something back to the environment— work results of real value. These outputs are described in the figure as task performance and human resource maintenance, the two key results of group effectiveness. And as just described, any group should be able both to accomplish its tasks and to satisfy its members in order to operate successfully for the long term.

This is a good time to recall that organizations are interlocking networks of groups, large and small, and operating at all different levels in the chain of command. These groups are highly interdependent, and their various activities are supposed to create synergy for the organization as a whole. The task outputs of one group, for example, become part of the inputs needed by other groups. In the words of total quality consultants, groups become the "internal customers" of one another. To be truly effective, therefore, a group must be able to achieve its task and human resource maintenance goals while also helping other groups in the organization to attain theirs.

Understanding Group Inputs

The effectiveness of any group is determined in part by the inputs with which it has to operate. A simple and straightforward principle generally applies: The better the group inputs, the better the chance for group effectiveness. Any manager is well advised when setting up a new group or working with an existing one always to make sure that the right inputs are available to accomplish the tasks at hand. Group inputs are the initial "givens" in a work situation; they set the stage for all subsequent group action. They also establish the initial performance ceiling with which the group will operate. A group with the right inputs has the foundations for achieving the highest levels of effectiveness; a group with insufficient inputs suffers, from the beginning, with many limitations.[11]

Among group input factors, the *organization setting* is important. This includes the goals, rewards, structure, technology, workflows, and culture of the organization as a whole. All of these factors help set the context within which a group must operate. Ideally, the organizational setting will support group performance by encouraging teamwork and providing the basic resources needed for goal accomplishment. The *group size* is also an important input variable, and managers, for example, must be very careful when choosing the size of a team or task force. One issue to be addressed is the absolute number of members. Most recommendations state that groups of five to seven members generally perform the best on problem-solving tasks. This size is large enough to allow diversity of inputs, but still small enough to avoid the disadvantages of limited participation, social loafing, subgroup domination, and the like. A second issue is whether there is an odd or even number of members. It is generally held that an odd number is preferable. This allows a clear majority when votes have to be taken, and it avoids the possibility of stalemates or "ties" in decision making.

The *membership* of any group is an essential and critical input variable. The skills and competencies of group members must be sufficient to perform the required tasks. In addition to this "ability" factor, the degree to which members are similar or dissimilar in terms of backgrounds, interests, and personal demographics can also affect outcomes. Generally speaking, members of more homogeneous groups may get along better and experience less conflict. But because of their diversity, members of heterogeneous groups are best prepared to handle more complex and challenging tasks. Finally, the mix of personalities must be considered. In any group there is a need for interpersonal compatibility among members. Although short-term task performance may be possible in situations where personalities clash, it is unlikely that long-term performance can be sustained under such conditions.

Understanding Group Throughputs

Even the best inputs do not guarantee the effectiveness of a group. Although they establish the capacity to perform, the inputs must be well utilized before high-performance results can be realized. This means that the group throughputs must be successful. Only if the internal operations function well can a group achieve its full potential. Even a team with the best inputs, for example, may fail if its members spend too much time in conflict with one another or are unable to make timely decisions.

This concern for throughputs directs a manager's attention toward **group dynamics**—the forces operating in groups that affect how the members work together for task performance and human resource maintenance.[12] If the group is an open system that transforms resource inputs into product outputs, group dynamics are the "processes" through which this transformation is accomplished. Thus, in OB and in management practice, it is common to use the term **group process** interchangeably with group dynamics. Both refer to the internal operations of groups as open systems. Among the most important group processes are norms and cohesiveness, task and maintenance activities, communication, and decision making. Each of these processes is covered in depth in Chapter 9.

Employee Involvement Groups

Managers in the new workplace are adopting many innovative ways of making better use of groups as human resources of organizations. The watchwords of these approaches are *participation* and *involvement*. Consider this short case from a manufacturing plant.[13]

In the past, when Mahmood Mohajer, a production supervisor at a Digital plant, realized that his work group was two weeks behind in an important production run, he would have put everyone on an overtime schedule. This time he first met with the production teams and outlined the problem. He then asked them to come up with a solution. "It was a real risk," he says of the approach, "I was so nervous I had to trust them." Everyone decided to work the entire weekend to catch up on the production schedule. It was still an overtime schedule but somewhat different from the one Mohajer might have set. Because it was their idea, team members were highly motivated to make their solution a real success. Mahmood says that his new approach to employee involvement requires a coaching rather than a policing role. One of his workers told him: "We wanted to tell you how to fix some problems before, but you wouldn't listen to us."

Many of the creative developments applied to the use of groups in organizations belong to the category of **employee involvement groups.** This term applies to a wide variety of settings in which groups of workers meet regularly for the purpose of collectively addressing important workplace issues. The goals of an employee involvement group often relate to *total quality concepts* and the quest for *continuous improvement* in all operations. Typically small in size, these groups spend time regularly discussing ways to enhance quality, better satisfy customers—internal and external—raise productivity, and improve the quality of work life. Employee involvement groups help bring the full advantages of group decision making to bear on everyday organizational affairs. These advantages include focusing worker know-how on real problems and gaining their commitments to implement fully any solutions that may be agreed upon.

Employee involvement groups are mechanisms for participation. They allow workers to gain influence over matters affecting them and their work. In order for these groups to succeed, however, traditional managers like Mahmood Mohajer must make sincere commitments to participation. The opportunities for the workers to influence what happens to them must be real. When accomplished, however, true employee involvement offers the potential for many positive contributions to the new workplace.

One special type of employee involvement group is the quality circle (QC).[14] As noted in Chapter 2, this is a small group of persons who meet regularly to discuss and develop solutions for problems relating to product or process quality. The use of QCs is a popular way to further the *total quality* and *continuous improvement* agendas so common in the new workplaces. In order for QCs to be successful, however, their members should receive special training in information-gathering and problem analysis techniques. QC leaders should also allow full participation in identifying and analyzing problems, and in choosing action alternatives. Once quality improvements are proposed, their implementation should be a joint effort between the QC and management.

THE EFFECTIVE MANAGER 8.2

Requirements for Quality Circle Success

- An informed and knowledgeable workforce.
- Managers willing to trust workers with necessary information.
- A team spirit in the quality circle group.
- Clear emphasis on quality in the organization's goals.
- An organization culture that encourages participation.

Originally developed in Japan to promote employee involvement, encourage innovation, and improve efficiency, QCs are now very popular around the world. But they should not be regarded as panaceas for all of an organization's ills. In fact, The Effective Manager 8.2 lists a number of conditions that must be met in order to keep the use of quality circles from becoming just another management "gimmick."

Self-managing Work Teams

Formally defined, **self-managing teams** are "small groups of people empowered to manage themselves and the work they do on a day-to-day basis."[15] Self-managing teams, which may also be called *self-directed teams* or *empowered teams,* are permanent work groups; they are part of the formal organizational structure. What differentiates them from more traditional work groups is their members' substantial responsibility for a wide variety of decisions involved in accomplishing assigned tasks. Indeed, the very concept of the self-managing work team is that it takes on some duties previously performed by traditional supervisors. These duties include quality control, work scheduling, and even performance evaluation. A true self-managing work team is one in which the group members themselves

- Make decisions on how to divide up tasks within the team.
- Make decisions on scheduling work within the team.
- Are able to perform more than one job for the team.
- Train one another to learn jobs performed by the team.
- Evaluate one another's job performance on the team.
- Are collectively held accountable for the team's performance results.

For example, at General Motors' Saturn plant, self-managing teams are an important part of the workplace organization. Employees who transfer to Saturn from GM's more traditional plants experience a major difference in the way things operate and in what is expected of them. Deborah Wikaryasz used to work in a Cadillac plant. At Saturn she became part of a team that is expected to do a lot more than she was used to before. Her Saturn team is actively involved in hiring workers, approving parts from suppliers, choosing equipment, and handling administrative matters including budgets. All this is done with an emphasis on product quality and customer

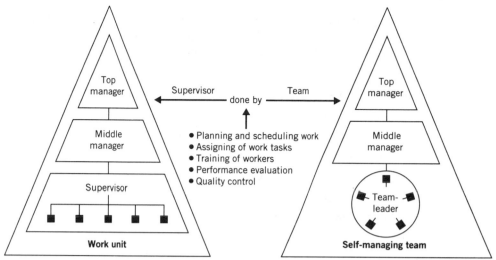

Figure 8.2 New workplace implications of self-managing work teams. *Source:* John R. Schermerhorn, Jr., *Mangement for Productivity,* 4th ed. (New York: John Wiley & Sons, 1993), p. 350. Used by permission.

satisfaction. She comments: "We can keep our costs down and pass the savings along to the customer."[16]

How Self-managing Teams Work

Self-managing teams, like Wikaryasz's Saturn team, are driven by *empowerment.* Through the process of empowerment (discussed in Chapter 10 on power and politics) individuals or groups are allowed to make decisions about important matters that affect them and their work. Members of self-managing work teams are given substantial discretion in determining work pace and in distributing tasks. This is made possible, in part, by multiskilling wherein team members are trained in and capable of performing more than one job on the team. In self-managing teams, members are expected to be able to perform many different jobs—even all of the team's jobs—as needed. The more "skills" a person masters, the higher the base pay. Typically, team members themselves conduct the training and certify one another in mastering the required job skills.[17]

Because a *self*-managing team really does manage itself in many ways, there is no real need for the former position of supervisor. Instead, a team leader usually represents the team in dealing with higher level management. The possible extent of this structural change is shown in Figure 8.2, where the first level of supervisory management has been eliminated and replaced by self-managing teams. The figure also shows that many traditional tasks of the supervisor are reallocated to the team. For persons learning to work in such teams for the first time and for those managers learning to deal with self-managing teams rather than individual workers, the implications of these changes can be quite substantial.

The potential benefits of using self-managing teams are also great, but they are not guaranteed. As just noted, implementing self-managing teams brings about structural changes. Many organizational and personal adjustments must be made if the teams are to succeed. The way these changes are handled can affect whether or not the benefits of the new team concepts are realized. When self-managing teams are successfully added to an organization, the potential advantages include[18]

- Improved productivity.
- Improved production quality.
- Greater production flexibility.
- Faster response to technological change.
- Fewer job classifications.
- Fewer management levels.
- Lower employee absenteeism.
- Lower employee turnover.
- Improved work attitudes.

Questions and Answers on Self-managing Teams

Before leaving this discussion, it may help to raise and tentatively answer some open questions on self-managing teams. These questions, in particular, may still be on your mind.

"What is the best size for a self-managing team?" Like any problem-solving group, a self-managing team should not be too large; the best teams probably have between 5 and 15 members. The team must be large enough to provide for sufficient membership resources, but also small enough to function efficiently. If team size gets too big, it will be as difficult for the members to successfully manage themselves as it would be for a traditional supervisor to manage them.

"How often should self-managing teams formally meet?" The team, simply put, must meet as often as necessary to get the job done. Probably the best teams have a quick meeting at the start of each workday to orient themselves; they are also likely to have longer and more formal meetings on a weekly basis to handle a variety of operating matters. Special planning and review sessions to share information, analyze performance accomplishments, and discuss potential improvements should also be regularly scheduled.

"Do self-managing teams have leaders?" The self-managing team should designate someone to serve in the leader role. At the Texas Instruments Malaysia plant, for example, this person is called a facilitator. Although the title doesn't matter, it is important that someone is always prepared to represent the team with upper management and convene the team as day-to-day events require. It is probably best if this person is not permanently assigned to the leader role. Ideally, it should be just another job that all team members are trained for and able to fill when asked.

"Should all work groups operate as self-managing teams?" No. Self-managing teams are probably not right for all organizations, work situations, and people. At a minimum, the essence of any self-managing team—participation and empowerment—must be consistent with the values and culture of the surrounding organization. If not, the presence of self-managing teams may create more problems than it resolves. Implementing self-managing teams also requires major changes in the structure of the organization and in the ways in which managers have traditionally approached their jobs. Unless everyone is willing to make the structural changes and personal adjustments, and has good training and other support from the organization in so doing, self-managing teams will have a difficult time living up to expectations.

Teamwork and Team Building for Group Effectiveness

Any group or work team—whether we are talking about a traditional work unit, an employee involvement group, or a self-managing team—must have members who feel responsible for accomplishing important tasks. That is, the members must feel "collectively accountable" for what they achieve through "teamwork." True **teamwork** occurs when members of a team work together in such a way that certain *core values,* all of which promote the utilization of skills to accomplish common goals, are represented. These values have been described as "listening and responding constructively to views expressed by others, giving others the benefit of the doubt, providing support, and recognizing the interests and achievements of others."[19]

We all know that teamwork doesn't always happen naturally; rather, team members and team leaders alike must work hard to achieve it. To take a sporting example, teams often run into problems as a season progresses. Members slack off or become disgruntled, and some get retired or are traded to other teams. Even world champion teams have losing streaks, and even the most talented players are prone to lose motivation at times, to quibble among themselves, and to go into slumps. When these downturns occur, the owners, managers, and players are apt to examine their problems and to take corrective action to rebuild the team. In short, they try to restore the teamwork that is needed to achieve high-performance results.

Workplace groups and teams have similar difficulties. When newly formed, they must master the many challenges of group formation. Even when long-lived and mature, most will encounter periodic problems as the level and quality of teamwork rise and fall over time. When difficulties occur, or as a means of preventing them from occurring, an action intervention called team building can help. **Team building** is a sequence of planned activities designed to gather and analyze data on the functioning of a group and to initiate changes designed to improve teamwork and increase group effectiveness.[20] Most team-building approaches proceed through the following action steps.

- Group members work together to identify existing or potential problems.
- Group members work together to gather data relating to the problem.
- Group members work together to analyze the data and plan for improvement.

- Group members work together to implement the action plans.
- Group members work together to monitor progress, evaluate results, and take further action.
- Group members work together to repeat the team-building process as often as needed.

The process just described is a collaborative one whose essence is, in itself, *team-work*—the very thing that team building is designed to improve in the first place. Notice that the "group members work together" to accomplish each team-building task. Throughout the process, everyone is expected to participate as outcomes and processes are evaluated and decisions are made on what, if anything, needs to be done to maintain or improve them in the future. Everyone then shares in the responsibility for implementing the agreed-upon action plans and in evaluating their action results. The entire process ideally results in at least four positive outcomes.[21]

1. Core values are clarified to guide and direct the behavior of members.
2. A broad purpose is transformed into specific performance objectives.
3. The right skills mix is acquired to achieve high-performance results.
4. Innovation and creativity are enhanced in task performance.

One way to summarize the implications of team building is in respect to the open systems framework presented earlier. Team building is a participative way for people to work together to assess a group's outputs and to take corrective action on its inputs and throughputs, with the goal of improving its effectiveness. On the input side, the targets for change might be aspects of the organization setting, group membership, and size. On the throughput side, the targets include any and all of the group process factors to be discussed in Chapter 9.

In Summary

What types of groups are found in organizations?

- A group is a collection of people who interact with one another regularly to attain common goals.
- Formal groups are "official" groups created by formal authority to achieve a specific purpose; they exist as work units, task forces, committees, and the like.
- Informal groups are "unofficial" and emerge outside of the formal structure of the organization.

How do groups help organizations?

- Groups are important contributors to organizational task accomplishment.
- Organizations are interlocking networks of groups; results accomplished by all groups should build upon one another to accomplish organizational goals.

- Social loafing occurs in groups when some members do not work as hard as they otherwise might individually.
- Groups can help to satisfy members' needs for social interaction, security, and the like.
- Groups can also assist members in such areas as job training and task accomplishment.

What is an "effective" group?

- An effective group is one that achieves *both* high levels of task accomplishment *and* good human resource maintenance.
- The members of an effective group accomplish their task goals.
- The members of an effective group do a good job of maintaining positive working relationships with one another.

What is an employee involvement group?

- An employee involvement group is any group whose members meet regularly to address important work-related problems and concerns.
- Typically, employee involvement groups deal with issues involving total quality management and the quest for continuous improvement of all operations.
- A quality circle is an employee involvement group that meets regularly to deal with "quality" issues in the work process.
- Because employee involvement groups are designed to facilitate group problem solving and take full advantage of group decision making, "participation" is a key to their success.

What is a self-managing team?

- A self-managing team is a formal work group whose members collectively take responsibility for task performance.
- Members of a self-managing team make many of the "supervisory" decisions relating to day-to-day operations and, in these ways, they "manage" themselves.
- Members of a self-managing team will typically plan, complete, and evaluate their own work; they will train and evaluate one another in task performance; they will share tasks and responsibilities; and they may even determine one another's pay grades.
- Self-managing teams can contribute to improved performance for organizations and improved quality of working life for their members.

How can managers encourage teamwork?

- Teamwork occurs when members of a group work together in such a way that core values promote the full utilization of individual skills to accomplish common goals.

- Team building is a way of building the capacity for teamwork and high performance in a group.
- Team building is a collaborative approach to analyzing the performance of a group and taking steps to improve its functioning in the future.
- The team-building process is highly participatory; it involves all group members in identifying problems and opportunities, as well as planning and taking appropriate actions.

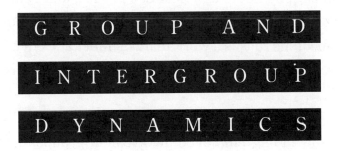
GROUP AND INTERGROUP DYNAMICS

As you read Chapter 9, keep in mind these study questions:

- What are the stages of group development?

- How do norms and cohesiveness affect groups?

- How do groups meet their task and maintenance needs?

- How do groups handle communications?

- How do groups make decisions?

- What should managers know about intergroup relations?

L ike many changes in the new workplace, the increased emphasis on teams and teamwork is a major challenge for people used to more traditional ways of working. As more and more jobs are turned over to teams, special problems relating to group and intergroup dynamics may occur. Team leaders and members alike must be prepared to deal positively with such problems as disagreements on goals, delays and disputes when making decisions, friction and conflicts among members and between groups, and concerns for increased work responsibilities on the parts of some members. Says Donald Owen about his role as a work team member at General Mills's Lodi plant: "I work a lot harder than I used to. You have to worry about the numbers."[1]

It is not enough for visionary managers to implement creative work group designs—including employee involvement groups, quality circles, and self-managing teams. They must also be able to help members properly develop and maintain their groups over time as "high-performance teams." This challenge brings us back once again to the issues of group process that were first introduced in the last chapter. Now, it is time to look in depth at the process foundations for long-term group effectiveness.

Stages of Group Development

One way to improve the internal operations of groups and to facilitate group effectiveness is to recognize different stages of development. Group effectiveness may be influenced by how well group members and leaders deal with the problems typical of each stage of development. An understanding of group development can help you better manage both newly formed groups and existing groups. It can also help you perform better as a member of such groups. The five stages of group development are the forming, storming, norming, performing, and adjourning stages.[2]

Forming Stage

In the forming stage of group development, a primary concern is the initial entry of members to a group. At this point, individuals ask a number of questions as they begin to identify with other group members and with the group itself. Among their concerns are: "What can the group offer me?" "What will I be asked to contribute?" "Can my needs be met at the same time that I contribute to the group?" People are interested in discovering what is considered acceptable behavior, determining the real task of the group, and defining group rules. All this is likely to be more complicated in the workplace than in other settings. Members of a new task force, for example, may have been in the organization for substantial time periods. Such things as multiple group memberships and identifications, prior experience with group members in other contexts, and impressions or organization philosophies, goals, and policies may all affect how these members initially behave in the newly formed task force. Similar considerations apply to other types of newly formed groups.

Storming Stage

The *storming stage* of group development is a period of high emotionality and tension among the members. Hostility and infighting between members may occur, and the group typically experiences many changes. Membership expectations tend to be clarified and further elaborated. Attention begins to shift toward obstacles standing in the way of group goals. Individuals begin to understand one another's interpersonal styles, and efforts are made to find ways to accomplish group goals while also satisfying individual needs. Outside demands, perhaps including premature expectations for performance results, may create pressures at this time. Depending on group size and membership composition, coalitions or cliques may appear in the form of emergent and informal subgroups. Conflict may develop over leadership and authority, as individuals compete to impose their preferences on the group and to achieve their desired status position.

Norming Stage

The *norming stage,* sometimes called the *initial integration stage,* is the point at which the group begins to come together as a coordinated unit. The interpersonal probes and jockeying behaviors of the storming phase give way here to a precarious balancing of forces. Group members, in their pleasure at the new sense of harmony, will most likely strive to maintain this balance. The group as a whole will try to regulate individual behavior toward this end; minority viewpoints and tendencies to deviate from or question group directions will be discouraged. With initial integration, members develop a preliminary sense of closeness and will want to protect the group from disintegration. Indeed, holding the group together may become more important to some than successfully working on the group's tasks. Thus, some group members may misperceive this stage as one of ultimate maturity. In fact, the sense of premature accomplishment needs to be carefully managed as a stepping stone to a higher level of group development, and not treated as an end in itself.

Performing Stage

The *performing stage* of group development, sometimes referred to as the *total integration* stage, sees the emergence of a mature, organized, and well-functioning group. The integration begun in the previous stage is completed during this period. The group is now able to deal with complex tasks and to handle membership disagreements in creative ways. Group structure is stable, and members are motivated by group goals and are generally satisfied. The primary challenges of this stage relate largely to continued work on human resource maintenance and task performance, but with a strong commitment to continuing improvement and self-renewal. An effective group at this stage of development is made up of members who (1) continue to work well together, (2) understand their individual and collective responsibilities to other groups and the larger organization, and (3) are able to adapt successfully as opportunities and demands change over time. A group that has achieved the level of total integration typically scores high on the criterion of group maturity shown in Figure 9.1.

Adjourning Stage

It is sometimes appropriate to address a fifth stage, the *adjourning stage,* of group development. A well-integrated group is able to disband, if required, when its work is accomplished. Adjourning is an especially important stage for the many temporary groups that are increasingly common in the new workplace, including task forces and committees. Members of these groups must be able to convene quickly, do their jobs on a tight schedule, and then adjourn—often to work together again in the future on other assignments. The willingness of members to disband when the job is done *and* to work well together in future responsibilities, group or otherwise, is an important long-run test of group success.

Group Norms and Cohesiveness

A group **norm** is an idea or belief about behavior that group members are expected to display. Norms are often referred to as rules or standards of behavior that apply to group members.[3] They help to clarify membership expectations in a group. Norms allow members to structure their own behavior and to predict what others will do; they help members gain a common sense of direction; and they reinforce a desired group or organizational culture. When someone violates a group norm, other members typically respond in ways that attempt to enforce the norm. These responses may include direct criticisms, reprimands, expulsion, and social ostracism.

Types of Group Norms

Groups operate with many types of norms. A key norm in any group is the *performance norm,* the rule or standard conveyed as to how hard group members should work. Work groups with more positive performance norms tend to be more successful in accomplishing their tasks than are groups with more negative norms. But other norms count too. Consider what it takes for a task force or a committee to operate effectively. Such groups will be affected by the norms that develop regarding

━━━━━━━━━━━━━ **A MATURE GROUP POSSESSES:** ━━━━━━━━━━━━━

1. Adequate mechanisms for getting feedback:

Poor feedback mechanisms	1	2	3	4	5	Excellent feedback mechanisms
			Average			

2. Adequate decision-making procedure:

Poor decision-making procedure	1	2	3	4	5	Very adequate decision-making procedure
			Average			

3. Optimal cohesion:

Low cohesion	1	2	3	4	5	Optimal cohesion
			Average			

4. Flexible organization and procedures:

Very inflexible	1	2	3	4	5	Very flexible
			Average			

5. Maximum use of member resources:

Poor use of resources	1	2	3	4	5	Excellent use of resources
			Average			

6. Clear communication:

Poor communication	1	2	3	4	5	Excellent communication
			Average			

7. Clear goals accepted by members:

Unclear goals— not accepted	1	2	3	4	5	Very clear goals— accepted
			Average			

8. Feelings of interdependence with authority persons:

No interdependence	1	2	3	4	5	High interdependence
			Average			

9. Shared participation in leadership functions:

No shared participation	1	2	3	4	5	High shared participation
			Average			

10. Acceptance of minority views and persons:

No acceptance	1	2	3	4	5	High acceptance
			Average			

Figure 9.1 Ten criteria for measuring the "maturity" of a group. *Source:* Edgar H. Schein, *Process Consultation,* Vol. 1. Copyright © 1988. Addison-Wesley Publishing Company, Inc., Chapter 6, p. 81. Figure 6.1, "A Mature Group Process." Reprinted with permission.

attendance at meetings, punctuality, preparedness, criticism, social etiquette, and so on. Other common norms in work groups deal with relationships with supervisors, colleagues, and customers, as well as honesty, security, personal development, and change. The following list gives examples of how such group norms may have both positive and negative implications for organizations and their managers.[4]

Norms of organizational and personal pride
Positive norm: Around here, it's a tradition for people to stand up for the company when others criticize it unfairly. *Negative norm:* In our company, they are always trying to take advantage of us.

Norms of performance excellence
Positive norm: In our company, people always try to improve, even when they are doing well. *Negative norm:* Around here, there's no point in trying harder —nobody else does.

Norms of teamwork
Positive norm: Around here, people are good listeners and actively seek out the ideas and opinions of others. *Negative norm:* In our company, it's dog-eat-dog and save your own skin.

Norms of leadership
Positive norm: Around here, managers and supervisors really care about the people they supervise. *Negative norm:* In our company, it's best to hide your problems and avoid your supervisor.

Norms of productivity
Positive norm: In our company, people are continually on the lookout for better ways of doing things. *Negative norm:* Around here, people tend to hang on to old ways of doing things even after they have outlived their usefulness.

Building Positive Group Norms

Because group norms are essentially determined by the collective will of group members, it is very difficult for organizations and their managers to dictate which norms a given work group will possess. Yet, the concerned manager must use a knowledge of group dynamics to help group members adopt norms supportive of organizational goals. A manager or group leader can do a number of things to encourage the development of positive group norms. Many of these can be incorporated into the team-building process reviewed in Chapter 8. Seven ways to create positive group norms are:[5]

1. Act as a positive role model.
2. Hold group meetings to gain agreement on desired behaviors.
3. Recruit and select new members who can and will perform as desired.
4. Train and orient new members in the desired behaviors.
5. Reinforce and reward the desired behaviors.

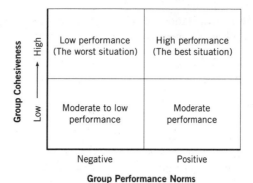

Figure 9.2 How group cohesiveness and performance norms can influence group performance.

6. Hold group meetings to discuss feedback and review performance.

7. Hold group meetings to plan ways to increase effectiveness.

Group Cohesiveness

The extent to which members of a group actually conform to its norms is strongly influenced by the level of **cohesiveness** in the group. This is the degree to which members are attracted to and motivated to remain part of a group.[6] Persons in a highly cohesive group value their membership and strive to maintain positive relationships with other group members. They derive a sense of loyalty, security, and high self-esteem from the group, and the group fulfills a full range of individual needs. Accordingly, cohesive groups are good for their members.

Members of highly cohesive groups tend to be concerned about their group's activities and achievements. In contrast to persons working in less cohesive groups, they tend to be more energetic, less likely to be absent, happier about group successes, and more upset about failures. However, as strange as it may seem, cohesive groups do not always serve the best interests of the organization. The critical question is whether or not the cohesiveness supports high-performance task outcomes.

Figure 9.2 helps to answer the question: "How does cohesiveness influence performance?"[7] It also demonstrates an important basic rule of group dynamics: The more cohesive the group, the greater the conformity of members to group norms; the less cohesive the group, the less the conformity to group norms. This rule is especially critical when it is applied to the relationship between cohesiveness and performance norms. After all, these are the norms that most directly influence individual attitudes toward such things as effort, quality, cooperation, and diligence in work tasks.

When the performance norms are positive and the group is cohesive, the figure shows this to be the best case or high-performance situation. The organization benefits from the high conformity of members to positive performance norms. But when negative performance norms are present in a highly cohesive group, the forces of group dynamics work against the organization's interests. This creates the worst case or low-performance situation in the figure. Members will behave in ways that conform to shared low-performance expectations.

How to Influence Group Cohesiveness

Look again at Figure 9.2. How would you deal with groups that fall into cells other than the high-performance one? A manager must recognize that sometimes steps should be taken to build cohesiveness in a work group, such as in a group with positive norms but low cohesiveness. Listed below are a number of actions a manager can take to increase group cohesiveness.

- Get agreement on group goals.
- Increase the homogeneity of membership.
- Reduce the group size.
- Focus attention on competition with outside groups.
- Reward members for group results.
- Isolate the group; reduce contacts with other groups.
- Create a sense of performance "crisis."

The opposite steps may be taken to *reduce* the cohesiveness of a group. Such actions may become necessary when members of a highly cohesive group are operating with negative performance norms *and* efforts to change these norms have failed.

Task and Maintenance Needs of Groups

The distinctions leader/manager or member/subordinate are often used to differentiate formal work assignments within a group. But the concept of *distributed leadership* in group dynamics suggests that *all* members of effective groups serve in leadership roles. They do this by making relevant and useful contributions to the group process, particularly those that help meet the group's task and maintenance needs.[8]

Group Task Activities

All groups need members who are able and willing to perform a variety of **task activities**—activities that directly contribute to the performance of important group tasks. If task activities are not adequate, group process will suffer, and the group will have difficulty accomplishing its objectives. In an effective group, the members enhance the group process by contributing these and other types of task activities as needed:[9]

- **Initiating** Offering new ideas or ways of defining problems; suggesting solutions to group difficulties.

- **Seeking information** Attempting to clarify suggestions in terms of factual accuracy; asking for ideas of others.
- **Giving information** Offering authoritative and relevant information and facts.
- **Clarifying** Clarifying relations among various suggestions or ideas; attempting to coordinate member activities.
- **Summarizing** Assessing group results; questioning the logic and practicality of member suggestions.

Group Maintenance Activities

The social and interpersonal relationships of a group are supported by members who contribute **maintenance activities** to the group process. These activities do just what the term suggests; they help *maintain* the group as an ongoing social system. If maintenance activities are not done well, group development will suffer as members become dissatisfied with one another and with their group membership. Emotional antagonisms and conflicts drain energies that could otherwise help advance group task agendas. In an effective group, each member helps to build good interpersonal relationships and enhance his or her ability to work together over time. Examples of important group maintenance activities include[10]

- **Encouraging** Praising, accepting, or agreeing with other members' ideas, indicating solidarity and warmth.
- **Harmonizing** Mediating squabbles within the group; reconciling differences; seeking opportunities for compromise.
- **Setting standards** Expressing standards for the group to achieve or use in evaluating group process.
- **Following** Going along with the group; agreeing to try out the ideas of others.
- **Gatekeeping** Encouraging the participation of group members; trying to keep some members from dominating.

Disruptive Activities in Groups

In addition, many different **disruptive activities** take place in groups. These activities serve no task or maintenance purpose; rather, they are *self-serving behaviors* that have negative implications for group process and outcomes. Everyone is well advised to guard against personal displays of such disruptive behaviors as showing extreme aggressiveness, acting in an overly competitive manner, withdrawing and refusing to participate, "horsing around" when there is work to be done, making irrelevant statements, and using the group as a forum for self-confession.

Communication in Groups

The topic of communication in the workplace is so important in OB that we devote much of Chapter 12 to it. Defined as an interpersonal process of sending and receiv-

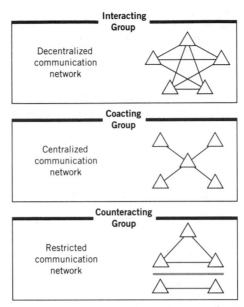

Figure 9.3 Interaction patterns and communication networks in groups.

ing symbols with meanings attached to them, communication enables group members to interact with one another, and to obtain and share information needed to accomplish necessary tasks.

Figure 9.3 depicts three interaction patterns that are commonly found in groups: interacting, coacting, and counteracting.[11] In interacting groups, members are very interdependent as they work on group tasks. Interacting groups are most effective for complex tasks that require intense information exchange and collaborative problem solving. Everyone in an interacting group must work in close coordination. This results in a **decentralized communication network,** which is sometimes also referred to as the *all-channel* or *star* communication network.[12] The "all-channel" nature of communication linkages gives everyone opportunities to be involved. Information is well distributed among group members, and with this comes the many advantages of participation and involvement.

Members of coacting groups work independently on group tasks. The required work is divided up and then largely completed by individuals working alone. Individual efforts are coordinated by a central control point. The person serving in this capacity usually collects or combines the various individual contributions to create a final "group" product. Coacting groups work best at simple tasks with well-identified components. Because most communication flows back and forth between individual members and a person serving as a control point, this creates a **centralized communication network.**[13] As shown in this figure, this network is sometimes referred to as a *wheel* or *chain* communication network. In this network, it is usually the central or "hub" person who experiences the most satisfaction.

The presence of subgroups that disagree on some aspect of overall group operations characterizes counteracting groups. These may be issue-specific disagreements, such as temporary debate over the best means to achieve a goal. They may also be of longer term duration, such as labor management disputes. In either case, the interaction pattern involves a *restricted communication network* in which polarized subgroups contest one another's positions and maintain sometimes antagonistic relations. As would be expected, communication between counteracting groups is often limited and biased. This is sometimes seen in labor–management relations, where disruptive strikes and extended contract bargaining can disrupt normal labor and management work routines.

Decision Making in Groups

The fundamentals of decision making, the process of choosing among alternative courses of action, are thoroughly discussed in Chapter 12. Obviously, the decisions made can have an important impact on group effectiveness. Our present interest is with the alternative ways in which groups make decisions as their members communicate and work together on various tasks.

How Groups Make Decisions

Edgar Schein, a noted scholar and consultant, has worked extensively with groups to analyze and improve their decision-making processes.[14] He observes that groups may make decisions through any of the six following methods.

1. **Decision by lack of response** A course of action is chosen by default or lack of interest.
2. **Decision by authority rule** One person dominates and determines the course of action.
3. **Decision by minority rule** A small subgroup dominates and determines the course of action.
4. **Decision by majority rule** A vote is taken to choose among alternative courses of action.
5. **Decision by consensus** Not everyone wants the same course of action, but everyone agrees to give it a try.
6. **Decision by unanimity** Everyone in the group wants to pursue the same course of action.

As you read more about these alternative decision methods, think about how often you encounter them in your own group activities. Think, too, about the consequences of each. In *decision by lack of response,* one idea after another is suggested without any discussion taking place. When the group finally accepts an idea, all others have been bypassed and discarded by simple lack of response rather than by critical evaluation. In *decision by authority rule,* the chairperson, manager, or some other authority figure makes a decision for the group. This can be done with or without discussion and is very time-efficient. Whether the decision is a good or bad one, however, depends on whether or not the authority figure has the necessary information and on how well this approach is accepted by other group members. In *decision by minority*, two or three people are able to dominate or "railroad" the group into making a decision. This is often done by providing a suggestion and then forcing quick agreement by challenging the group with statements like "Does anyone object? . . . Let's go ahead then."

One of the most common ways groups make decisions, especially when early signs of disagreement set in, is the *decision by majority rule*. Here, formal voting may take place, or members may be polled to find the majority viewpoint. This method is often used without awareness of its potential problems. The very process of voting can create coalitions; that is, some people will be "winners" and others will be "losers" when the final vote is tallied. Those in the minority—the "losers"—may feel left out or discarded without having had a fair say. As a result, they may be less committed to implementing the decision of the majority and may carry lingering antagonisms that will impair group effectiveness in the future.

Another alternative is *decision by consensus*. Formally defined, consensus is a state of affairs whereby discussion leads to one alternative being favored by most members, with the other members being willing to support it. When a consensus is reached, even those who may have opposed the chosen course of action know that they have been listened to and have had a fair chance to influence the decision outcome. Consensus, therefore, does not require unanimity. What it *does* require is for any dissenting member to be able to confidently say the following:

> I understand what most of you would like to do. I personally would not do that, but I feel that you understand what my alternative would be. I have had sufficient opportunity to sway you to my point of view but clearly have not been able to do so. Therefore, I will gladly go along with what most of you wish to do.[15]

A *decision by unanimity* may be the ideal state of affairs. Here, all group members agree totally on the course of action to be taken. This is a "logically perfect" group decision method that is extremely difficult to attain in actual practice. One reason why groups sometimes turn to authority decisions, majority voting, or even minority decisions is the difficulty of managing the group process to get consensus or unanimity. The Effective Manager 9.1 lists guidelines for consensus seeking in groups.

Assets and Liabilities of Group Decision Making

The decision methods just discussed can be arrayed on a continuum ranging from the more individual-oriented decisions at one extreme anchored by authority rule to more group-oriented decisions at the other extreme anchored by consensus. The different decision methods have their assets and liabilities, and the best groups and work teams are not limited to using just one method all of the time. Rather, they utilize a variety of methods, but always being sure to use the one that best fits the problem or task at hand. The potential benefits of more group-oriented decision making include:[16]

THE EFFECTIVE MANAGER 9.1

Ten Steps to Group Consensus

1. Involve everyone in the decision process.
2. Avoid blindly arguing your case.
3. Present clear and logical points.
4. Seek out and respect differences of opinion.
5. Listen carefully to the points of others.
6. Discuss assumptions underlying different positions.
7. Yield to positions with merit and sound foundations.
8. Do not change your mind just to avoid conflict.
9. Do not assume the situation is a win–lose contest.
10. Avoid majority votes, coin tossing, averaging, bargaining.

Source: Developed from guidelines presented in the classic article by Jay Hall, "Decisions, Decisions, Decisions," *Psychology Today* (November 1971), pp. 55–56.

- More knowledge and information are applied to solve the problem.
- A greater number of alternatives are examined, and "tunnel vision" is avoided.
- The final decision is better understood by all group members.
- The final decision is better accepted by all group members.
- There is greater commitment among all group members to make the final decision work.

Unfortunately, the time and interaction requirements of group-oriented decision making often create a number of potential liabilities. These include at least three common situations that you are probably quite familiar with. Sometimes group members encounter *social pressures to conform*. The desire to be a good member and to go along with the group can lead people to conform prematurely to poor decisions. Groups may also fall prey to *individual domination*. A dominant individual may emerge and control the group's decisions. This may be particularly true of the leader whose viewpoints may dominate group discussion. Groups can also suffer from *time constraints*. Decision making in groups almost always takes longer than decision making by individuals. Group decisions may also be delayed while members engage in extensive discussions or in conflicts. The result can be a quick decision made by members rushing to finish just as the group meeting time is running out.

Groupthink

Another, very subtle side to group process can work to a group's disadvantage in decision-making situations. The risk is that members of a group strive so hard to maintain harmony that they end up avoiding the discomforts of disagreement. But in so doing, they also make "poor" decisions.[17] Social psychologist Irving Janis calls this **groupthink**—the tendency of members in highly cohesive groups to lose their critical evaluative capabilities.[18] He believes that pressures to conform in highly cohe-

---

THE EFFECTIVE MANAGER 9.2

How to Deal with Groupthink

- Ask each member to be a critical evaluator.
- Encourage a sharing of objections.
- Don't let the leader seem partial to one course of action.
- Create subgroups with different leaders to work on the same problem.
- Have members discuss issues with outsiders and report back.
- Invite outside experts to observe and react to group discussions.
- Have a different member act as "devil's advocate" at each meeting.
- Write alternative scenarios for the intentions of competing groups.
- Hold "second-chance" meetings once an initial decision is made.

Source: Developed from Irving Janis, *Victims of Groupthink,* 2nd ed. (Boston: Houghton Mifflin, 1982).

sive groups cause their members to self-censor personal views and become unwilling to criticize views offered by others. Desires to hold the group together become more important than the quality of the decision under consideration. To avoid unpleasant disagreements, there is an overemphasis on concurrence and an underemphasis on realistic appraisals of alternatives. Poor decisions can result in such situations. When you are in a group experiencing groupthink, or supervising one that shows the symptoms, Janis suggests the action guidelines listed in The Effective Manager 9.2.

Intergroup Dynamics

Any organization ideally operates as a cooperative system whose component groups are willing and able to help one another as needed. In fact, a very important managerial role is to help ensure that groups work together to accomplish their goals in ways that benefit the organization as a whole. Yet whenever there is more than one group in a situation, intergroup dynamics influence what takes place. When these dynamics include rivalries and competition that detract from cooperation, the impact can be felt not only in what happens between groups, but also in what happens within them.

Between competing groups, the members of one group are likely to view the other group as an enemy. They tend to see it as weak and negative while viewing their own group as strong and positive. Competing groups are likely to restrict communication with each other. *Within competing groups,* by contrast, the members are likely to become more cohesive and loyal to their groups, as well as to act more dedicated and task-oriented. They may be more willing to accept their leader's directives, and to become more structured and organized in their group activities.

The above action tendencies contain both negatives and positives. On the negative side, intergroup competition may divert energies away from the performance of important tasks; group members may focus more on their relations with the other group than on dealing with the tasks at hand. Too much competition contributes to "grudges," animosities, or biased and selective viewpoints. All of this adds up to poor intergroup coordination. On the positive side, groups facing outside competition may work harder, become more focused on key tasks, develop more internal cohesion and satisfaction, and achieve greater creativity in problem solving.

Thus, managers walk a thin line as they try to deal with intergroup dynamics. Sometimes a bit of competition can help groups maintain their creative edge; at other times too much competition can harm the larger system. What is a person to do? How can the dynamics of intergroup competition be managed to advantage? Broadly stated, you have two alternatives in response to these questions. The first is to deal with unhealthy competition *after* it occurs. Among the recommendations for controlling the level of existing competition are:[19]

- Identifying a common enemy that can unite the groups
- Appealing to a common goal that can unite the groups.
- Getting direct negotiations started between the groups.
- Training members of the groups to work cooperatively.

The second alternative is to take action *before* it reaches a destructive level—that is, to keep it under control from the beginning. Recommended ways to prevent the emergence of unhealthy intergroup competition include:[20]

- Rewarding groups for making further contributions to the total organization.
- Avoiding win–lose competitions for important rewards.
- Rewarding groups for giving help to one another.
- Stimulating frequent interactions between members of different groups.
- Preventing groups from withdrawing and becoming isolated from one another.
- Rotating members among different groups.

In Summary

What are the stages of group development?

- Five stages of group development pose somewhat distinct management problems.
- The forming stage poses problems of managing individual entry.
- The storming stage poses problems of managing expectations and status.
- The norming stage poses problems of managing member relations and task efforts.
- The performing stage poses problems of managing continuous improvement and self-renewal.

- The adjourning stage poses problems of managing task completion and the process of disbanding.

What are group norms and cohesiveness?

- Norms are rules or standards regarding appropriate behavior for group members; they identify the way "loyal" members are supposed to behave.
- Positive norms in respect to standards, diligence, quality of work, and so on, can enhance performance; negative norms can cause poor performance.
- Cohesiveness is a measure of the attractiveness of a group for its members.
- In a highly cohesive group members tend to conform to group norms.
- The most favorable situation is a highly cohesive group with positive performance norms.

How do groups meet their task and maintenance needs?

- Groups must satisfy both task and maintenance needs if they are to successfully operate over time.
- Group members should engage in a variety of task activities—including initiating and summarizing—that make direct contributions to the group's task agenda.
- Group members should engage in a variety of maintenance activities—including encouraging and gatekeeping—that help to maintain the social fabric of the group over time.
- Group members should avoid disruptive behaviors that interfere with group functioning.

How do groups structure themselves for communication?

- Interacting groups display a high degree of member interdependency and adopt more decentralized communication networks.
- Decentralized communication networks, like the "all-channel" or "star," work best at more complex tasks.
- Coacting groups show more independence and adopt more centralized communication networks.
- Centralized communication networks, like "the wheel," work best at more simple tasks.
- Counteracting groups involve subgroups and utilize more restricted communication networks.

How do groups make decisions?

- Groups can make decisions by lack of response, authority rule, minority, majority, consensus, and unanimity.

- These group decision methods vary from the more individual-oriented at the former extreme to the more group-oriented at the latter.
- The benefits of more group-oriented decisions include the availability of information as well as better member understanding and commitment.
- The liabilities of more group-oriented decisions include social pressures to conform and greater time requirements.
- Managers should guard against "groupthink," the tendency of highly cohesive groups to lose their critical evaluative capabilities.

What should managers know about intergroup relations?

- Intergroup dynamics are the forces that operate between two or more groups.
- Groups are supposed to cooperate with one another in organizations, but they often become involved in dysfunctional conflicts and competition.
- The disadvantages of competition can be reduced through management strategies to direct, train, and reinforce groups to pursue cooperative actions.

C H A P T E R | **10**

P O W E R   A N D

P O L I T I C S

As you read Chapter 10, keep in mind these study questions:

- What is power and why do managers have power?

- How does the manager get the power needed to get the job done?

- What is empowerment and how can management empower others?

- Are organizational politics inevitable and must the manager live in a political world?

- How does organizational politics differ for the individual supervisor, the middle manager, and the chief executive officer?

- Can power and politics in an organization be considered ethical?

P ower and politics have dual faces. On the one hand, they represent the seamy side of management. Rather than being democracies composed of individuals with equal influence, some organizations are more akin to feudal states, where managers believe they can rule because of some divine right. Any attempt to separate politics from the organization strips away the heart of the firm's real action. Although people are admittedly political animals, some firms have become so political that organizational interests have become completely subordinate to individual interests. At the same time, power and politics are important organizational tools that managers must use to get the job done. Just because the organization is not a democracy does not mean that individuals should be ignored. In effective organizations, power is delicately developed, nurtured, and managed by astute individuals. Although politics is always infused into the organization, in many instances individual and organizational interests are compatible. The astute manager knows how to find these opportunities. Power and politics may be dirty words to some, but when used with care, they can bring together individual desires for joint accomplishment.[1]

Power

In organizational behavior, **power** is defined as the ability to get someone to do something you want done or the ability to make things happen in the way you want them to. The essence of power is control over the behavior of others.[2] Power is the force that makes things happen in an intended way, whereas **influence** is a behavioral response to the exercise of power. Managers use power to achieve influence over other people in the work setting, deriving power from both organizational and individual sources as shown in Figure 10.1. We call these sources *position power* and *personal power,* respectively.[3]

Position Power

Three bases of power are available to a manager solely as a result of his or her position in the organization: reward, coercive, and legitimate power.

Reward power is the extent to which a manager can use extrinsic and intrinsic

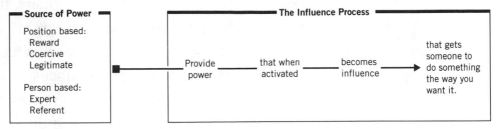

Figure 10.1   Power sources and the influence process.

rewards to control other people. Examples of such rewards include money, promotions, compliments, or enriched jobs. Although all managers have some access to rewards, success in accessing and utilizing rewards to achieve influence varies according to the skills of the manager.

Power can be founded on punishment as well as on reward. For example, a manager may threaten to withhold a pay raise, or to transfer, demote or even recommend the firing of a subordinate who does not act as desired. Such **coercive power** is the extent to which a manager can deny desired rewards or administer punishments to control other people. The availability of coercive power also varies from one organization and manager to another. The presence of unions and organizational policies on employee treatment can weaken this power base considerably.

The third base of position power is **legitimate power.** It stems from the extent to which a manager can use subordinates' internalized values or beliefs that the "boss" has a "right of command" to control their behavior.

Formal authority and legitimate power are synonymous. The two terms represent a special kind of power a manager has because subordinates believe it is legitimate for a person occupying the managerial position to have the right to command. In practice, it is often hard to separate authority, or legitimate power, from the use of reward and coercive power. This is because persons with authority usually have special access to rewards and punishments and can thereby alter their availability to subordinates.

Personal Power

Personal power resides in the individual and is independent of the position the individual holds. Two bases of personal power are expertise and reference. **Expert power** is the ability to control another person's behavior through the possession of knowledge, experience, or judgment that the other person does not have but needs. For example, a patient would typically listen to his or her doctor's recommendation because the doctor is more knowledgeable about medicine than is the patient. Access to or control over information is an important element in this particular power base, and access to key organizational decision makers is another. A person's ability to contact key persons informally can allow for special participation in the definition of a problem or issue, alteration in the flow of information to decision makers, and lobbying for use of special criteria in decision making.

Referent power is the ability to control another's behavior because the person wants to identify with the power source. In this case, a subordinate would obey the boss because he or she wants to behave, perceive, or believe as the boss does. This may occur, for example, because the subordinate likes the boss personally and therefore tries to do things the way the boss wants them done. In a sense, the subordinate behaves in order to avoid doing anything that would interfere with the pleasing boss–subordinate relationship.

The Milgram Experiments: Power, Formal Authority, and Obedience

Although managers may possess these different sources of power, they do not always get their way. Why do some people obey directives while others do not? Furthermore, why should subordinates respond to a manager's authority in the first place? These last questions point directly to Stanley Milgram's seminal research on obedience.[4] Milgram designed an experiment to determine the extent to which a group of 40 subjects would obey the commands of an authority figure, even if they believed that they were endangering the life of another person. The subjects were falsely told that the purpose of the study was to determine the effects of punishment on "learners." The subjects were to be the "teachers," the "learner" was a confederate of Milgram's who was strapped to a chair in an adjoining room with an electrode attached to his wrist. The "teachers" were instructed to administer a shock to the "learner" each time the learner gave a wrong answer to a question. The shock was to be increased one level of intensity each time the learner made a mistake. The "teachers" controlled the switches that ostensibly administered shocks ranging from 15 to 450 volts. In reality, there was no electric current in the apparatus but the learners "erred" often and responded to each level of "shock" in progressively distressing ways. Twenty-six subjects (65 percent) continued to the end of the experiment and shocked the "learners" at the highest level (435–450 volts) when the "learner" supposedly slumped into silence! None stopped prior to the "intense" (300 volt) level, the point at which the learner pounds on the wall. Only 14 subjects refused to obey the experimenter at various intermediate points.

Most people are surprised by these results, as was Milgram. The question it raised is why do some people tend to accept or comply with authoritative commands under such extreme conditions? Milgram conducted further experiments in an attempt to answer this question. The subjects' tendencies toward compliance were somewhat reduced when (1) experimentation took place in a rundown office (rather than a university lab), (2) the victim was closer, (3) the experimenter was farther away, and (4) the subject could observe other subjects. However, the level of compliance was still much higher than most of us would expect.

Obedience and the Acceptance of Authority

As the Milgram experiments suggest, individuals have strong tendencies to follow the instructions of the boss. Direct defiance within organizational settings is quite rare. If the tendency to follow instructions is great and defiance is rare, then why do so many organizations appear to drift into apparent chaos? The answer to this question lies at the heart of the contribution made by the famous management writer, Chester Barnard.[5] Essentially, Barnard's argument focused on the "consent of the governed" rather than on the rights derived from ownership. He argued that subordinates will accept or follow a directive from the boss only under special circumstances, all four of which must be met:

1. The subordinate can and must understand the directive.
2. The subordinate must feel mentally and physically capable of carrying out the directive.
3. The subordinate must believe that the directive is not inconsistent with the purpose of the organization.
4. The subordinate must believe that the directive is not inconsistent with his or her personal interests.

These four conditions are very carefully stated. For instance, to accept and follow an order, the subordinate does not need to understand how the proposed action will help the organization. He or she only needs to believe that the requested action is not inconsistent with the purpose of the firm. The astute manager will not take these guidelines for granted. In giving directives, the astute manager recognizes that the acceptance of the request is not assured. If the directive is routine, it is not surprising that the subordinate may merely comply without enthusiasm. Of course, the manager will need to understand what subordinates consider acceptable or unacceptable actions.

Obedience and the Zone of Indifference

Most people seek to achieve a balance between what they put into an organization (*contributions*) and what they get from an organization in return (*inducements*). Within the boundaries of the psychological contract, therefore, employees will agree to do many things in and for the organization because they think they should. That is, in exchange for certain inducements, subordinates recognize the authority of the organization and its managers to direct their behavior in certain ways. Based on his acceptance view of authority, Chester Barnard calls this area in which directions are obeyed the zone of indifference.[6]

A **zone of indifference** is the range of authoritative requests to which a subordinate is willing to respond without subjecting the directives to critical evaluation or judgment—that is, to which he or she is indifferent. Directives that fall within the zone are obeyed. Requests or orders falling outside the zone of indifference, however, are not considered legitimate under terms of the psychological contract, and so such "extraordinary" directives may or may not be obeyed.

Managerial Perspectives on Power and Influence

A considerable portion of any manager's time is directed toward what is called **power-oriented behavior**—behavior directed primarily at developing or using relationships in which other people are to some degree willing to defer to one's wishes.[7] When trying to influence persons in higher-level positions, managers must rely on the use of personal power to achieve influence over higher level superiors. In contrast, when facing downward, both position and personal power can be mobilized in dealing with subordinates. In lateral relations with peers and outsiders, the manager must again emphasize personal power to achieve the desired influence.

Acquiring Managerial Power

The effective manager is one who succeeds in building and maintaining high levels of both position and personal power over time. Only then will the manager have sufficient power of the right types available when he or she needs to exercise influence on downward, lateral, and upward dimensions.

As we mentioned earlier, position power is based on formal authority and on the legitimacy of a manager's location in the organization's hierarchy of authority. Managers can enhance position power when they learn to demonstrate to others that their work units are highly relevant to organizational goals and when they are able to respond to urgent organizational needs. In addition, these five general guidelines for enhancing one's position power should be followed.[8] As a manager, you should

1. **Increase your centrality and criticality in the organization** by acquiring a more central role in the workflow, having information filtered through you, making at least part of your job responsibilities unique, expanding your network of communication contacts, and occupying an office convenient to main traffic flows.

2. **Increase the personal discretion and flexibility of your job** by getting rid of routine activities, expanding task variety and novelty, initiating new ideas, getting involved in new projects, participating in the early stages of the decision-making process, and avoiding "reliable performance criteria" for judging your success on the job.

3. **Build tasks that are difficult to evaluate into your job** by creating an ambiguous job description, developing a unique language or set of labels in your work, obtaining advanced training, becoming more involved in professional associations, and exercising your own judgment.

4. **Increase the visibility of your job performance** by expanding the number of contacts you have with senior people, making oral presentations of written work, participating in problem-solving task forces, sending out notices of accomplishment that are of interest to the organization, and seeking additional opportunities to increase personal name recognition.

5. **Increase the relevance of your tasks to the organization** by becoming an internal coordinator or external representative, providing services and information to other units, monitoring and evaluating activities within your own unit, and expanding the domain of your work activities.

Personal power arises from the manager's personal characteristics rather than from the location and other characteristics of his or her position in the organization's hierarchy of authority. As we have already noted, two primary bases of personal power rest in expertise and reference. In addition, three personal characteristics have special potential for enhancing personal power in an organization.[9] Consistent with the earlier discussion these are (1) *knowledge and information,* (2) *personal attractiveness and "likability,"* and (3) *effort.* The demonstration of sincere hard work in behalf of task performance can also increase personal power by enhancing both expertise and reference.

Turning Power into Influence

The acquisition of power is an important task for any manager. Using this power well to achieve the desired influence over other people is yet another challenge. Practically speaking, there are many useful ways of exercising influence. The most common strategies involve[10]

- **Reason** Using facts and data to support a logical argument.
- **Friendliness** Using flattery, goodwill, and favorable impressions.
- **Coalition** Using relationships with other people for support.
- **Bargaining** Using the exchange of benefits as a basis for negotiation.
- **Assertiveness** Using a direct and forceful personal approach.
- **Higher authority** Gaining higher level support for one's requests.
- **Sanctions** Using organizationally derived rewards and punishments.

Actual research on these strategies for achieving managerial influence suggests that reason is the most popular strategy overall.[11] In addition, friendliness, assertiveness, bargaining, and higher authority are used more frequently to influence subordinates than supervisors. This pattern of influence attempts is consistent with our earlier contention that downward influence will generally include mobilization of both position and personal power sources, while upward influence will more likely draw on personal power.

Little research is available on the specific subject of upward influence in organizations. This is unfortunate inasmuch as a truly effective manager is one who is able to influence his or her boss as well as subordinates. One study reports that both supervisors and subordinates view reason, or the logical presentation of ideas, as the most frequently used strategy of upward influence.[12] When queried on reasons for success and failure, however, the two groups are shown to have both similarities and differences. The perceived causes of success in upward influence are similar for both supervisors and subordinates and involve the favorable content of the influence attempt, a favorable manner of its presentation, and the competence of the subordinate.[13] The two groups disagree on the causes of failure, however. Subordinates attribute failure in upward influence to the closemindedness of the supervisor, the unfavorable content of the influence attempt, and unfavorable interpersonal relationships with the supervisor. In contrast, supervisors attribute failure to the unfavorable content of the attempt, the unfavorable manner in which it was presented, and the subordinates' lack of competence.

THE EFFECTIVE MANAGER 10.1

Guidelines for Implementing Empowerment

1. *Delegation of authority to lower levels should be clear and unambiguous*—people must know what they are empowered to do and what they are being held accountable for.
2. *Planning must be integrated and participative at all levels*—people must be involved in planning if they are to understand plans and goals, and they must have the commitment needed to implement them effectively.
3. *Managers at all levels, but especially the top, should exercise strong communication skills*—information is the key to understanding goals and responsibilities as well as for understanding the "big picture" within which they become meaningful.

Empowerment

Empowerment is the process by which managers help others acquire and use the power needed to make decisions affecting themselves and their work. More than ever before, managers in progressive organizations are expected to be good at—and highly comfortable with—empowering the people with whom they work. Rather than considering power to be something to be held only at higher levels in the traditional "pyramid" of organizations, this view considers power to be something that can be shared by everyone working in flatter and more collegial structures.

The concept of empowerment is part of the sweeping changes that we are witnessing in today's industry. Corporate staff is being reduced; layers of management are being removed; and the number of employees is being cut back. What we see remaining is a leaner, trimmer organization staffed by fewer people who share more power as they go about their daily tasks.[14] While empowerment is so important, The Effective Manager 10.1 suggests that implementation can follow a few simple guidelines.

The Power Keys to Empowerment

One base for empowerment is a radically different view of power itself. Thus far, our discussion has focused on power that is exerted over other individuals. In contrast, the concept of empowerment emphasizes the ability to make things happen. Cutting through all the corporate rhetoric on empowerment is quite difficult because the term has become quite fashionable in management circles. However, each individual empowerment attempt needs to be examined in light of how power in the organization will be changed.

Changing Position Power   When an organization attempts to move power down the hierarchy, it must also alter the existing pattern of position power. Changing this pattern raises some important questions. For example, can "empowered" individuals give rewards and sanctions? Has their new right to act been legitimized with formal authority? All too often, attempts at empowerment disrupt well-established patterns of position power and threaten middle- and lower level managers. As one supervisor said, "All this empowerment stuff sounds great for top management. They don't have to run around trying to get the necessary clearances to implement the suggestions from my group. They never gave me the authority to make the changes, only the new job of asking for permission."

Expanding the Zone of Indifference   When embarking on an empowerment program, management needs to recognize the current zone of indifference and systematically move to expand it. All too often, management assumes that its directive for empowerment will be followed; they fail to show precisely how empowerment will benefit the individuals involved, however.

Power as an Expanding Pie   Along with empowerment, employees need to be trained to expand their power and their new influence potential. This is the most difficult task for managers and a difficult challenge for employees, for it often changes the dynamic between supervisors and subordinates. The key is to change the concept of power within the organization from a view that stresses power over others to one that emphasizes the use of power to get things done. Under the new definition of power, all employees can be more powerful.

Organizational Politics

Any study of power and influence inevitably leads us back to the subject of *politics*. This word often conjures up thoughts of illicit deals, favors, and special personal relationships. This image of shrewd, often dishonest practices of obtaining one's way is reinforced by Machiavelli's classic fifteenth-century work *The Prince,* which outlines how to obtain and hold power through political action. It is important, however, to adopt a perspective that allows politics in organizations to function in a much broader capacity.[15]

The Two Traditions of Organizational Politics

We encounter two quite different traditions in any analysis of organizational politics. One tradition builds on Machiavelli's philosophy and defines politics in terms of self-interest and the use of nonsanctioned means. In this tradition, *organizational politics* may be formally defined as the management of influence to obtain ends not sanctioned by the organization or to obtain sanctioned ends through nonsanctioned influence means.[16] Managers are often considered political when they seek their own goals or use means that the organization does not currently authorize. It is also important to recognize that where uncertainty or ambiguity exists, it is often extremely difficult to tell whether a manager is being political in this self-serving sense.[17]

The second tradition treats politics as a necessary function resulting from differences in the self-interests of individuals. Here, organizational politics is viewed as the art of creative compromise among competing interests. In a heterogeneous society, individuals will disagree as to whose self-interests are most valuable and whose concerns should therefore be bounded by collective interests. Politics arise because individuals need to develop compromises, avoid confrontation, and live together. The same holds true in organizations, where individuals join, work, and stay together because their self-interests are served. Furthermore, it is important to remember that organizationally powerful individuals establish the goals of the organization and the acceptable means in negotiation with others. Thus, *organizational politics* is also defined as the use of power to develop socially acceptable ends and means that balance individual and collective interests.

The Double-Edged Sword of Organizational Politics

These two different traditions of organizational politics are reflected in the ways in which executives describe their effects on managers and their organizations. In one survey, some 53 percent of those interviewed indicated that organizational politics enhanced the achievement of organizational goals and survival.[18] Yet, some 44 percent suggested that it distracted individuals from organizational goals. In this same survey, 60 percent of respondents suggested that organizational politics was good for career advancement, whereas 39 percent reported that it led to a loss of power, position, and credibility.

The truth is that organizational politics is not automatically good or bad. It can serve a number of important functions, including helping managers to overcome personnel inadequacies, cope with change, and act as a substitute for formal authority.

Self-Protection as Organizational Politics

Although organizational politics may be helpful to the organization as a whole, it is probably more commonly known and better understood in terms of *self-protection*.[19] Whether or not managers like it, all employees recognize that in an organization they must watch out for themselves first. In too many organizations, if they don't protect themselves, no one else will. Individuals can employ essentially three common strategies to protect themselves. They can

1. Avoid action and risk taking.
2. Redirect accountability and responsibility.
3. Defend their turf.

Avoiding Action In controversial areas where the employee must risk being wrong or where actions might lead to a sanction, avoidance is quite common. Perhaps the most common reaction is to *work to the rules*. That is, employees are protected when they strictly adhere to all of the rules, policies, and procedures or do not allow deviations or exceptions.

Passing the buck is another common method employees and managers use to avoid taking action. The trick here is to define the task in such a way that it becomes someone else's formal responsibility. We are always amazed at the ingenious ways individuals can redefine an issue to avoid action and transfer responsibility. Perhaps one of the most frustrating but effective techniques is to *play dumb*. We all do this at some time or another. When was the last time you said, "Officer, I didn't know the speed limit was 35. I couldn't have been going 52!"

More subtle techniques of self-protection include *depersonalization* and *stalling*. Depersonalization involves treating individuals, such as customers, clients, or subordinates, as numbers, things, or objects. Senior managers don't fire long-term employees; the organization is merely "downsized." Routine stalling involves slowing down the pace of work to expand the task so that the individuals look as if they are working hard. With creative stalling, the employees may spend the time supporting the organization's ideology, position, or program and delaying implementation.

Avoiding Responsibility   Politically sensitive individuals employ a variety of well-worn techniques to protect themselves from accepting blame for the negative consequences of their actions. One is *rigorous documentation,* taking action only when all the paperwork is in place and making it clear they are merely following procedure. Closely related to rigorous documentation is the *blind memo* that explains an objection to an action implemented by the individual. Here, the required action is taken, but the blind memo is prepared should the action come into question. Another method is to rewrite history. If a program is successful, the manager claims to have been an early supporter; if a program fails, the manager was the one who expressed serious reservations in the first place. Finally, *scapegoating* can be used to blame the problem on someone or some group who has difficulty defending himself or herself, or the situation can be blamed on uncontrollable events.

Defending Turf   *Defending turf* is a time-honored tradition in most large organizations. As noted earlier in the chapter, managers who want to improve their power attempt to expand the jobs their groups perform. Defending turf also results from the coalitional nature of organizations. That is, the organization may be seen as a collection of competing interests that are held by various departments and groups. As each group attempts to expand its influence, it starts to encroach on the activities of other groups. This turf protection can be seen more easily in an analysis of political action and the manager.

Political Action in Organizations

Political action is part of organizational life. It is best to view organizational politics in terms of its potential to contribute to managerial and organizational effectiveness. Political action links managers more formally to one another as representatives of their work units. In earlier chapters, we examined the group dynamics associated with such intergroup relationships. Five of the more typical lateral and intergroup relations in which you might engage as a manager are *workflow, service, advisory, auditing,* and *approval.*[20] These lateral relationships further challenge the manager's political skills because each type of lateral relationship requires the manager to

---

THE EFFECTIVE MANAGER 10.2

Typical Lateral Relations Engaged in by Managers and Their Associated Influence Requirements

TYPE OF RELATIONSHIP

Workflow—contacts with units that precede or follow in a sequential production chain.

Service—contacts with units established to help with problems.

Advisory—contacts with formal staff units having special expertise.

Auditing—contacts with units having the right to evaluate the actions of others.

Approval—contacts with units whose approval must be obtained before action may be taken.

---

achieve influence through some means other than formal authority (see The Effective Manager 10.2).

To be effective in political action, managers should understand the politics of subunit relations. Line units are typically more powerful than are staff groups, and units toward the top of the hierarchy are often more powerful than are those toward the bottom. In general, units gain power as more of their relations with others are of the approval and auditing types. Workflow relations are more powerful than advisory associations, and both are more powerful than service relations. Units can also increase power by incorporating new actions that tackle and resolve difficult problems.

Certain strategic contingencies can often govern the relative power of subunits. For a subunit to gain power vis-à-vis others, it must increase its control over such strategic contingencies as (1) scarce resources, (2) ability to cope with uncertainty, and (3) centrality in the flow of work, yielding the perception that their work is unique and not easily replaced.[21]

Political Action and the Chief Executive

Executive behavior can sometimes be explained in terms of **resource dependencies**—the firm's need for resources that are controlled by others.[22] Essentially, the resource dependence of an organization increases as

1. Needed resources become more scarce.
2. Outsiders have more control over needed resources.
3. There are fewer substitutes for a particular type of resource controlled by a limited number of outsiders.

Thus, one political role of the chief executive is to develop workable compromises among the competing resource dependencies facing the organization—compromises that enhance his or her power. To create such compromises, executives need to diagnose the relative power of outsiders and to craft strategies that respond differently to various external resource suppliers.

For larger organizations, many strategies may center on altering the firm's degree of resource dependence. Through mergers and acquisitions, a firm may bring key resources within its control. For instance, once U.S. firms could go it alone without the assistance of foreign corporations. Now, chief executives are increasingly leading them in the direction of more joint ventures and strategic alliances with foreign partners from around the globe. Such "combinations" provide access to scarce resources and technologies among partners, as well as new markets and shared production costs. Resource dependencies can also be managed by changing the "rules of the game"; a firm may also find protection from particularly powerful outsiders. For instance, markets may be protected by trade barriers, or labor unions may be put in check by right to work laws.

Organizational governance refers to the pattern of authority, influence, and acceptable managerial behavior established at the top of the organization. This system establishes what is important, how issues will be defined, who should and should not be involved in key choices, and the boundaries for acceptable implementation. Students of organizational governance suggest that a *dominant coalition* comprised of powerful organizational actors is a key to its understanding.[23] Although we would expect many top officers within the organization to be members of this coalition, the dominant coalition occasionally includes outsiders with access to key resources. Thus, analysis of organizational governance builds on the resource dependence perspective by highlighting the effective control of key resources by members of a dominant coalition.

This view of the executive suite recognizes that the daily practice of organizational governance is the development and resolution of issues. Through the governance system, the dominant coalition attempts to define reality. By accepting or rejecting proposals from subordinates, by directing questions toward the interests of powerful outsiders, and by selecting individuals who appear to espouse particular values and qualities, the pattern of governance is slowly established within the organization. Furthermore, this pattern rests, at least in part, on very political foundations.

The Ethics of Power and Politics

No treatment of power and politics in organizations can be complete without a consideration of the related ethical issues. We can begin this task by clarifying the distinction between the *nonpolitical* and *political* uses of power.[24] Power is nonpolitical when it remains within the boundaries of usually formal authority, organizational policies and procedures, and job descriptions, and when it is directed toward ends sanctioned by the organization. When the use of power moves outside the realm of authority, policies, procedures, and job descriptions, or when it is directed toward ends that are not sanctioned by the organization, that use of power is said to be political.

It is when the use of power moves into the realm of political behavior that a manager must consider more than a pure "ends justify the means" logic. These issues are broader and involve distinctly ethical questions.[25] A person's behavior must satisfy these three criteria to be considered ethical.[26]

1. **Criterion of utilitarian outcomes** The behavior results in optimization of the satisfactions of people both inside and outside the organization; that is, it produces the greatest good for the greatest number of people.

2. **Criterion of individual rights** The behavior respects the rights of all affected parties; that is, it respects basic human rights of free consent, free speech, freedom of conscience, privacy, and due process.

3. **Criterion of distributive justice** The behavior respects the rules of justice; that is, it treats people equitably and fairly, as opposed to arbitrarily.

The only exception to the above criteria involves a special case that must satisfy the criterion of overwhelming factors, in which the special nature of the situation results in (1) conflicts among criteria (e.g., a behavior results in some good and some bad being done), (2) conflicts within criteria (e.g., a behavior uses questionable means to achieve a positive end), and/or (3) incapacity to employ the criteria (e.g., a person's behavior is based on inaccurate or incomplete information).

Choosing to be ethical often involves considerable personal sacrifice. Four rationalizations are often used to justify unethical choices:

1. Individuals feel that the behavior is not really illegal and thus could be moral.

2. The action appears to be in the firm's best interest.

3. It is unlikely the action will ever be detected.

4. It appears that the action demonstrates loyalty to the boss or the firm.

Although these rationalizations may appear compelling at the moment of action, each deserves close scrutiny. The individual must ask, How far is too far?, What are the long-term interests of the organization?, What will happen when (not if) the action is discovered?, and Do individuals, groups or organizations that ask for unethical behavior deserve my loyalty?[27]

In Summary

What is power within the context of the organization and why do managers have power?

• Power, an essential managerial resource, is the ability to get someone else to do what you want them to do.

• Power vested in managerial positions derives from rewards, punishments, and legitimacy.

How does the manager get the power needed to get the job done?

• Managers can pursue various ways of acquiring both position and personal power.

- They can become skilled at using various tactics, such as reason, friendliness, ingratiation, and bargaining.

What is empowerment and how can management empower others?

- Empowerment is the process through which managers help others acquire and use the power needed to make decisions.
- Management can provide a clear delegation of authority, integrated planning, and the involvement of senior management.
- A key to successful empowerment lies in redefining power so that everyone can gain.

Are organizational politics inevitable and must the manager live in a political world?

- Organizational politics are inevitable.
- Managers must become comfortable with political behavior in organizations and then use that behavior responsibly and to good advantage.
- While politics involves the use of power to obtain ends not officially sanctioned, it is also a use of power to find ways of balancing individual and collective interests.

How does organizational politics differ for the individual supervisor, the middle manager, and the chief executive officer?

- For the supervisor politics often occurs in decision situations where individual interests clash.
- With mutual trust, "win–win" outcomes can often be realized.
- For middle managers politics also involves subunits that jockey for power.
- For chief executives, politics also come into play as resource dependencies with external environmental elements.

Can power and politics in an organization be considered ethical?

- When political behavior is ethical, it will satisfy the criteria of utilitarian outcomes, individual rights, distributive justice, and/or overwhelming factors.

L E A D E R S H I P

As you read Chapter 11, keep in mind these study questions:

- How do traditional leadership and new leadership differ?

- What are great man/trait and leadership behavior approaches, and why are they important?

- What are leader situational contingency approaches, and why are they important?

- How does attribution theory relate to the new leadership?

- What are charismatic leadership approaches, and why are they important?

- What are transformational leadership approaches, and why are they important?

Even though they don't always view leadership in the same way, most people probably agree that leadership makes a difference. Some think of leadership as an almost mystical quality that some people have and others don't; they can't define it, but they know it when they see it. Others think of leadership as something more specific, such as consideration toward subordinates. However, there are some who argue just as strongly that leadership doesn't matter, that it isn't important. For them, leaders are so bound by constraints in what they can do that they just don't have much impact. Furthermore, people sometimes give credit to leaders for occurrences that were caused by something else. The president of the United States, for example, will receive and accept credit for turning around a recession when his actions actually made no difference. In this chapter, we cover all these views and more in our look at how leadership fits in the organization.

We will treat **leadership** as a special case of influence that gets an individual or group to do what the leader (or manager) wants done. Leadership theories can be divided into two categories: traditional leadership and new leadership.[1] As you will see, both are important for a leader. The traditional perspectives go back many years, and they vary in the emphasis they place on the role of leadership. They include the trait, behavior, and situational contingency approaches. The new leadership shows a range of theories emphasizing some combination of charisma (attribution of exceptional abilities to the leader), vision, or change.

Trait and Behavioral Theories

All the trait and behavioral approaches make the assumption that, in one way or another, selected personal traits or behaviors have a major impact on leadership outputs; that is, according to these theories, leadership is central, and other variables are relatively less important. Among the various approaches, however, there are differences in terms of the explanations offered for leadership results.

Great Man/Trait Theory

The great man/trait theory is the earliest approach used to study leadership and dates back to as early as the turn of the century. The early studies attempted to identify those traits that differentiated the "great person" in history from the masses (e.g., How did Peter the Great differ from his followers?).[2] This approach led to a research emphasis that tried to separate leaders from nonleaders or more effective leaders from less effective leaders. The argument was that certain traits are related to success and that, once identified, these traits could be used to select leaders. This argument is made in Chapter 4, concerning individual differences, except that this earlier research concentrated on workers and looked for general traits, cutting across groups and organizations. Thus, researchers looked at such traits as height, integrity, intelligence, and the like.

For various reasons, including inadequate theorizing, inadequate measurement of many traits, and failure to recognize possible differences in organizations and situations, the studies were not successful enough to provide a general trait theory.[3] But they laid the groundwork for consideration of certain traits, in combination with other leadership aspects, such as behaviors, that form the basis for some of the more current theories.

Behavioral Theories

Like the great man/trait approach, the behavioral theories approach assumes that leadership is central to performance and human resource maintenance. In this case, however, instead of dealing with underlying traits, behaviors or actions are considered. Two classic research programs at the University of Michigan and Ohio State University provide useful insights into leadership behaviors.

Michigan Studies   In the late 1940s, researchers at the University of Michigan introduced a program of research on leadership behavior. The researchers were concerned with identifying the leadership pattern that results in effective performance. From interviews of high- and low-performing groups in different organizations, the researchers derived two basic forms of leader behaviors: employee centered and production centered. *Employee-centered supervisors* are those who place strong emphasis on the welfare of their subordinates. In contrast, *production-centered supervisors* tend to place a stronger emphasis on getting the work done than on the welfare of the employees. In general, employee-centered supervisors were found to have more productive work groups than did the production-centered supervisors.[4]

These behaviors may be viewed on a continuum, with employee-centered supervisors at one end and production-centered supervisors at the other. Sometimes, the more general terms *human relations–oriented* and *task-oriented* are used to describe these alternative leader behaviors.

Ohio State Studies   An important leadership research program was started at Ohio State University at about the same time as the Michigan studies. A questionnaire was administered in both industrial and military settings to measure subordinates' perceptions of their superiors' leadership behavior. The researchers identified two dimensions similar to those found in the Michigan studies: *consideration* and *initiating structure*.[5] A highly considerate leader is sensitive to people's feelings and, much like the employee-centered leader, tries to make things pleasant for his or her followers. In contrast, a leader high in initiating structure is more concerned with spelling out task requirements and clarifying other aspects of the work agenda; he or she might be seen as similar to a production-centered supervisor. These dimensions are related to what people sometimes refer to as socioemotional and task leadership, respectively. They also encompass what we discussed in Chapter 9 as group maintenance and task activities.

At first, the Ohio State researchers believed that a leader high on consideration, or socioemotional warmth, would have more highly satisfied and/or better performing subordinates. Later results indicated that leaders should be high on both consideration and initiating structure behaviors, however. This dual emphasis is reflected in the leadership grid approach.

The Leadership Grid® The Leadership Grid perspective was developed by Robert Blake and Jane Mouton.[6] It measures a manager's *concern for people* and *concern for production* and then plots the results on a nine-position grid that places concern for people on the vertical axis and concern for production on the horizontal axis, as shown in Figure 11.1. As the figure shows, a person with a 9/1 score is a "country club manager" (9 on concern for people, 1 on concern for production). Some other positions are 1/1—impoverished management style—and 1/9—task management style. A 5/5 style, in the middle of the grid, is a middle-of-the-road management style. The ideal position is a 9/9 "team manager" (high on both dimensions).

The behavioral approaches discussed share a common emphasis on the importance of people-oriented and production- or task-oriented behaviors in determining outputs. A timely question is: How well do these behaviors transfer internationally? Recent work in the United States, Britain, Hong Kong, and Japan shows that although the behaviors seem to be generally important in all these countries, they must be carried out in different ways in alternative cultures. For instance, British leaders are seen as considerate if they show subordinates how to use equipment, whereas in Japan the highly considerate manager helps subordinates with personal problems.[7]

Reward and Punishment Theory

In contrast to the theories discussed above, leader reward and punishment theory is based on the reinforcement concepts discussed in Chapter 6. In this case, the leader is seen as someone who manages reinforcements for subordinates.[8]

Recent research examines the following four leader behavior dimensions in this context:

1. **Performance-contingent reward behavior** The degree to which a leader administers positive reinforcers, such as acknowledgments, recognition, and so on, contingent on high subordinate performance.

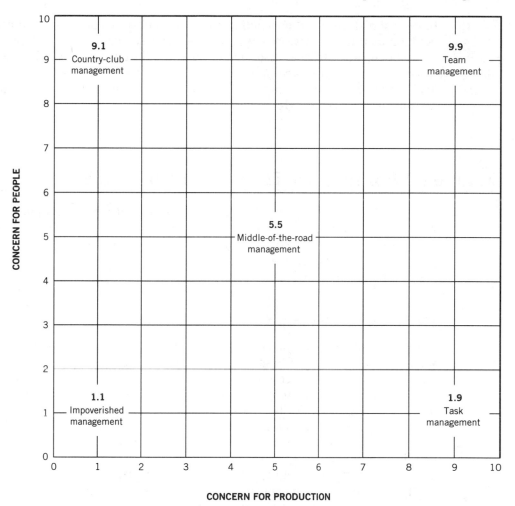

Figure 11.1   Concern for people/concern for production leadership grid. (From The Leadership Grid® Figure from *Leadership Dilemmas—Grid Solutions,* by Robert R. Blake and Anne Adams McCanse (formerly the Managerial Grid Figure by Robert R. Blake and Jane S. Mouton) Houston: Gulf Publishing Company, p. 29. Copyright © 1991, by Scientific Methods, Inc. Reproduced by permission of the owners.)

2. **Contingent punishment behavior** The extent to which a leader administers punitive measures, such as reprimands and disapproval, contingent on poor subordinate performance.

3. **Noncontingent reward behavior** The extent to which a leader rewards a subordinate, regardless of how well the subordinate performs.

4. **Noncontingent punishment behavior** The degree to which a leader uses punitive measures, regardless of how well a subordinate performs.

Results indicate that performance-contingent reward behavior is generally associated with higher levels of subordinate performance and satisfaction. Results for contingent punishment and noncontingent reward behavior are mixed, and noncontingent punishment behavior is often negatively associated with performance and satisfaction. Research has also found that subordinates strongly dislike seemingly discretionary or arbitrary punishment.[9] To summarize, performance-contingent leader rewards are most strongly related to performance and satisfaction; discretionary punishment is strongly disliked.

Situational Contingency Theories of Leadership

In the situational contingency theories, leader traits and behaviors act in conjunction with *situational contingencies* (other important aspects of the leadership situation) to determine outputs. The major contributions to this perspective include the work of Fred Fiedler, Robert House, Paul Hersey and Kenneth Blanchard, and Steven Kerr and John Jermier.

Fiedler's Leadership Contingency Theory

The first situational contingency approach we consider is Fred Fiedler's since his work essentially started the situational contingency era in the mid-1960s.[10] Fiedler's approach predicts work group effectiveness. His theory holds that group effectiveness depends on an appropriate match between a leader's style and the demands of the situation. Specifically, Fiedler considers the amount of control the situation allows the leader. **Situational control** is the extent to which a leader can determine what his or her group is going to do as well as the outcomes of the group's actions and decisions. For example, where control is high, leaders can predict with a good deal of certainty what will happen when they want something done.

Fiedler uses an instrument called the **least preferred coworker (LPC) scale** to measure a person's leadership style. Respondents are asked to describe the person with whom they have been able to work least well (their least preferred coworker, or LPC).

Fiedler argues that high LPC leaders (those describing their LPC very positively) have a relationship-motivated style, while low LPC leaders have a task-motivated style. In other words, relationship-motivated leaders describe more favorably the person with whom they were least able to work than do task-motivated leaders.

Figure 11.2 shows the task-motivated leader as having greater group effectiveness under high and low situational control, while the relationship-motivated leader has a more effective group under a moderate control situation. The figure also shows that Fiedler measures high, moderate, and low control with the following three variables arranged in the situational combinations indicated:

- **Leader-member relations (good/poor)** Member support for the leader.
- **Task-structure (high/low)** Spelling-out of the leader's task goals, procedures, and guidelines in the group.

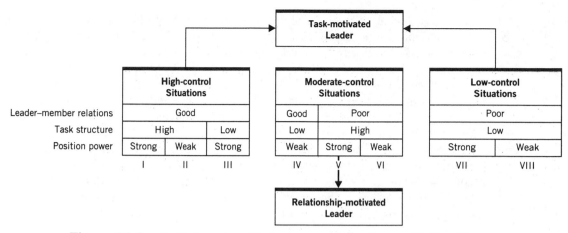

Figure 11.2 Predictions from Fiedler's contingency theory of leadership.

- **Position power (strong/weak)** The leader's task expertise and reward/punishment authority.

Fiedler's Cognitive Resource Theory[11] Fiedler recently moved beyond his contingency theory by developing the *cognitive resource theory*. Cognitive resources are abilities or competencies. According to this approach, whether a leader should use directive or nondirective behavior depends on the following situational contingencies: (1) the leader's or subordinate group members' ability/competency; (2) stress; (3) experience; and (4) group support of the leader. Basically, cognitive resource theory is most useful because it directs us to leader or subordinate group member ability, an aspect not typically considered in other leadership approaches.

The theory views directiveness as most helpful for performance when the leader is competent, relaxed, and supported. In this case, the group is ready, and directiveness is the clearest means of communication. When the leader feels stressed, he or she is diverted. In this case, experience is more important than is ability. If support is low, then the group is less receptive, and the leader has less impact. Group-member ability becomes most important when the leader is nondirective and there is strong support from group members. If support is weak, then task difficulty or other factors have more impact than do either the leader or the subordinates.

House's Path-Goal Theory of Leadership

Another well-known approach to situational contingencies is one developed by Robert House based on the earlier work of others.[12] This theory has its roots in the expectancy model of motivation discussed in Chapter 5. The term *path-goal* is used because of its emphasis on how a leader influences subordinates' perceptions of both work goals and personal goals and the links or paths found between these two sets of goals.

The theory assumes that a leader's key function is to adjust his or her behaviors to complement situational contingencies, such as those found in the work setting.

House argues that when the leader is able to compensate for things lacking in the setting, subordinates are likely to be satisfied with the leader. For example, the leader could help remove job ambiguity or show how good performance could lead to more pay. Performance should improve as the paths by which (1) effort leads to performance (expectancy) and (2) performance leads to valued rewards (instrumentality) become clarified. Redundant behavior by the leader will not help and may even hinder performance. People do not need a boss telling them how to do something that they already know how to do!

There are four types of leader behaviors—directive, supportive, achievement-oriented, and participative—and two categories of situational contingency variables—subordinate attributes and work-setting attributes. The leader behaviors are adjusted to complement the situational contingency variables in order to influence subordinate satisfaction, acceptance of the leader, and motivation for task performance.

- **Directive leadership** has to do with spelling out the what and how of subordinates' tasks and is much like the initiating structure mentioned earlier.
- **Supportive leadership** focuses on subordinate needs and well-being and promoting a friendly work climate; it is similar to consideration.
- **Achievement-oriented leadership** emphasizes setting challenging goals, stressing excellence in performance, and showing confidence in the group members' ability to achieve high standards of performance.
- **Participative leadership** focuses on consulting with subordinates and seeking and taking their suggestions into account before making decisions.

Directive leadership is predicted to have a positive impact on subordinates when the task is ambiguous; it is predicted to have just the opposite effect for clear tasks. That is, when task demands are ambiguous, leader directiveness is needed to compensate for the lack of structure. When task clarification is otherwise available, directiveness is seen as a hindrance by subordinates. In addition, the theory predicts that when ambiguous tasks are being performed by highly authoritarian and close-minded subordinates, even more directive leadership is called for.

Supportive leadership is predicted to increase the satisfaction of subordinates who work on highly repetitive tasks or on tasks considered to be unpleasant, stressful, or frustrating; the leader's supportive behavior helps compensate for these adverse conditions. For example, many would consider traditional assembly-line auto worker jobs to be highly repetitive, perhaps even unpleasant and frustrating. A supportive supervisor could help make these jobs more pleasant.

Achievement-oriented leadership is predicted to encourage subordinates to strive for higher performance standards and to have more confidence in their ability to meet challenging goals. For subordinates in ambiguous, nonrepetitive jobs, achievement-oriented leadership should increase their expectancies that effort will lead to desired performance.

Participative leadership is predicted to promote satisfaction on nonrepetitive tasks that allow for the ego involvement of subordinates. For example, on a challenging research project, participativeness allows employees to feel good about being able to deal with the challenge of the project on their own. On repetitive tasks, open-minded or nonauthoritarian subordinates will also be satisfied with a participative leader. On a task where employees screw nuts on bolts hour after hour, for example, those who are nonauthoritarian will appreciate having a leader who allows them to get involved in some ways to help break the monotony.

Hersey and Blanchard's Situational Leadership Theory

Like the approaches discussed earlier, situational leadership theory emphasizes situational contingencies. Hersey and Blanchard focus on the maturity, or "readiness," of followers, in particular. Readiness is the extent to which people have the ability and willingness to accomplish a specific task. Hersey and Blanchard argue that "situational" leadership requires adjusting the leader's emphasis on task behaviors (e.g., giving guidance and direction) and relationship behaviors (e.g., providing socioemotional support) according to the readiness of followers to perform their tasks.

Figure 11.3 displays the essence of this model of situational leadership. The figure identifies four leadership styles:

- Telling
- Selling
- Participating
- Delegating

Each emphasizes a different combination of task and relationship behaviors by the leader. As you can see, the figure also suggests the following situational matches as the best choice of leadership style for followers at each of four readiness levels.

A "telling" style is best for low follower readiness. The direction provided by this style defines roles for people who are unable and unwilling to take responsibility themselves; it eliminates any insecurity about the task that must be done.

A "selling" style is best for low to moderate follower readiness. This style offers both task direction and support for people who are unable but willing to take task responsibility; it involves combining a directive approach with explanation and reinforcement in order to maintain enthusiasm.

A "participating" style is best for moderate to high follower readiness. Able but unwilling followers require supportive behavior in order to increase their motivation; by allowing followers to share in decision making, this style helps enhance the desire to perform a task.

A "delegating" style is best for high readiness. This style provides little in terms of direction and support for the task at hand; it allows able and willing followers to take responsibility for what needs to be done.

This situational leadership approach requires the leader to develop the capability to diagnose the demands of situations and then to choose and implement the appropriate leadership response. The theory gives specific attention to followers and their feelings about the task at hand. It also suggests that an effective leader reassess

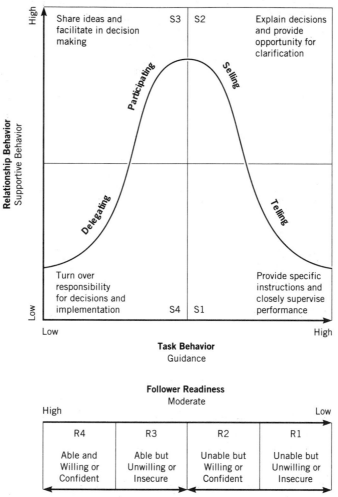

LEADER BEHAVIOR

Figure 11.3 Hersey and Blanchard model of situational leadership. (From Paul Hersey and Kenneth H. Blanchard, *Management of Organizational Behavior,* Prentice-Hall, Englewood Cliffs, N.J., 1988, p. 171. Used by permission.)

situations over time, giving special attention to emerging changes in the level of readiness of the people involved in the work. Again, Hersey and Blanchard advise that leadership style should be adjusted as necessary to remain consistent with actual levels of follower readiness. They further suggest that effectiveness should improve as a result.[13]

Substitutes for Leadership

The substitutes for leadership perspective argues that sometimes hierarchical leadership makes essentially no difference. John Jermier and others contend that there

are certain individual, job, and organizational variables that can either serve as substitutes for leadership or can neutralize a leader's impact on subordinates.[14] Some
examples of these variables include experience, ability, and training which can serve
as individual characteristics; a highly structured or routine job which can serve as
a job characteristic; and a cohesive work group which can serve as an organizational
characteristic.

Substitutes for leadership make a leader's influence both impossible and unnecessary. *Neutralizers* make a leader's influence impossible but not unnecessary.
Substitutes replace a leader's influence. For example, it will be difficult, if not impossible, for a leader to provide the kind of task-oriented direction already available
to a very experienced, talented, and well-trained subordinate. Furthermore, such
direction will be unnecessary because of the subordinate's characteristics. We can
make a similar argument for a highly structured task.

The substitutes for leadership perspective is a more generalized version of the
situational contingency approaches mentioned earlier, particularly House's path-goal
theory. However, the substitutes perspective goes further by making the assumption
that there are some cases where leadership has no impact on outputs because it is
replaced by other factors. The earlier situational approaches argued that both leadership and other factors are needed.

Attribution Theory and the New Leadership

The traditional leadership theories discussed above have all been based on the assumption that leadership and its substantive effects can be easily identified and measured. This is not always the case. Indeed, as you may recall from Chapter 4, attribution theory addresses this very point—that of individuals trying to understand
causes, to assess responsibilities, and to evaluate personal qualities, as all of these
are involved with certain events. As we will now show, attribution theory is particularly important in our understanding of leadership.

For openers, think about a work group or student group that you see as performing really well. Now assume that you are asked to describe the leader on one
of the leadership scales discussed earlier in the chapter. If you are like many others,
the group's high performance probably encouraged you to describe the leader favorably; in other words, you attributed good things to the leader based on the group's
performance. Similarly, leaders themselves make attributions about subordinate performance and react differently depending on these attributions. For example, if leaders attribute an employee's poor performance to lack of effort they may issue a
reprimand, whereas if they attribute the poor performance to an external factor,
such as work overload, they will probably try to fix the problem. There is currently
a great deal of evidence supporting these attributional views of subordinates and
leaders.[15]

Once again, considering subordinates' views of leadership, there is also evidence
that argues that people have in their minds implicit leadership theories.[16] In this
case, you picture in your mind what makes a "good leader" or ways in which "real

---

THE EFFECTIVE MANAGER 11.1

National Cultures and Leader Prototypes

The following are some predicted overall preferences for an effective leader prototype as a function of different national culture value clusterings:

- A high degree of directiveness, structuring, even manipulation (preferred in high-power distance cultures, such as those in Arabic, Far Eastern, and Latin clusterings)
- A strong emphasis on participation (preferred in low–power distance societies, such as Norway, Finland, Denmark, and Sweden)
- A strong emphasis on group facilitation (preferred in collectivist societies, such as those in the Near Eastern Countries, e.g., Greece, Turkey, and Pakistan; and the Far Eastern Countries, e.g., Thailand, Singapore).

---

leaders" would act in a given situation. Sometimes, this view is called a *leadership prototype,* whereby people have a picture in their minds of what the image of a model leader should look like.[17] These implicit theories or prototypes are usually made up of a mix of specific and more general characteristics. For example, a prototype of a bank president would differ in many ways from that of a high-ranking military officer. However, there would probably also be some core characteristics reflecting leaders in our society in general (e.g., integrity, self-efficacy, etc.). Given the importance of national culture, The Effective Manager 11.1 suggests that even these core characteristics are likely to be partly a function of preferences based on differences in cultural values.[18] The closer the behavior of a person in a leadership position is to the implicit theories of his or her followers, the more favorable the leader's relations and key outcomes tend to be.[19]

Both of the attributional treatments above emphasize leadership as something largely in the eye of the beholder. This idea has also carried over to a related set of research directions. The first of these argues that leadership makes little or no real difference in organizational effectiveness. The second tends to attribute greatly exaggerated importance to leadership and ultimately leads us into charisma and other aspects of the new leadership.

In terms of the first direction, Jeffrey Pfeffer is among those contending that even CEOs of large corporations have little leadership impact on profits and effectiveness, compared to environmental and industry forces. For example, the recent profit losses of defense contractors in response to cutbacks in the federal defense budget show the impact these forces can have on an organization.

Furthermore, these leaders are typically accountable to so many groups of people for the resources they use that their leadership impact is greatly constrained. Pfeffer argues that in light of such constraints, much of the impact a top leader does have is symbolic; leaders and others develop explanations to legitimize the actions they take.[20] This symbolic emphasis moves us into the second direction: the exaggeration of the importance of leadership.

This exaggeration or attribution occurs particularly when performance is either extremely high or extremely low or when the situation is such that many people could have been responsible for the performance. This phenomenon is called the "romance of leadership," whereby people attribute romantic, almost magical qualities to leadership.[21] A common example is the firing of a baseball manager whose team doesn't perform well. Neither the owner nor anyone else really knows why the team didn't do well. But the owner can't fire all the players, so a new team manager is brought in to symbolize "new leadership" that is intended to turn the team around. Similar actions also occur in large corporations.

Charismatic Approaches[22]

Robert House and his associates view **charismatic leaders** as those "who by force of their personalities are capable of having a profound and extraordinary effect on followers." Essentially, these leaders are high in need for power and have high feelings of self-efficacy and conviction in the moral rightness of their beliefs. That is, the need for power motivates these people to want to be leaders. This need is then reinforced by their conviction of the moral rightness of their beliefs. The feeling of self-efficacy, in turn, makes people feel that they are capable of being leaders. These traits then influence such charismatic behaviors as role modeling, image building, articulating goals (focusing on simple and dramatic goals), emphasizing high expectations, showing confidence, and arousing follower motives.

Some of the more interesting and important work based on aspects of House's charismatic theory involves a study of U.S. presidents. The research showed that behavioral charisma was indeed substantially related to presidential performance and that the kind of personality traits in House's theory, along with response to crisis, among other things, predicted behavioral charisma for the sample.

Jay Conger and Rabindra Kanungo have developed a four-stage charismatic leadership theory. In the first stage, the leader develops a vision of idealized change that moves beyond the status quo. For example, President Kennedy had a vision of putting a man on the moon by the end of the 1960s. In the second stage, the leader communicates the vision and motivates the followers to go beyond the status quo. In stage three, the leader builds trust by exhibiting qualities such as expertise, success, risk taking, and unconventional actions. Martin Luther King, Jr. displayed several of these qualities. In the final stage, the leader demonstrates ways to achieve the vision by means of empowerment, behavior modeling for followers, and so forth. Conger and Kanungo have argued that if leaders use behaviors such as vision and articulation, environmental sensitivity, and unconventional behavior, rather than maintaining the status quo, followers will attribute charismatic leadership to them. Such leaders are also seen as behaving quite differently from those labeled "noncharismatic."[23] Some ways to develop these behaviors are shown in The Effective Manager 11.2.

Transactional and Transformational Approaches

Transformational leadership has many similarities to charismatic leadership but is broader. Building on notions originated by James MacGregor Burns, as well as ideas

---

THE EFFECTIVE MANAGER 11.2

Ways to Develop Charismatic Skills Emphasized by Conger and Kanungo

- Sensitivity to most appropriate contexts for charisma
  —Emphasis on critical evaluation and problem detection
- Visioning
  —Courses in creative thinking to unlearn and think about profound change
  —Brainstorming concerning the environmental circumstances of the manager's organization and how to move beyond these
- Communication
  Working with oral and written linguistic aspects
- Impression management
  Emphasis on
  —Modeling
  —Appearance
  —Body language
  —Verbal skills
- Empowering
  Emphasis on
  —Communicating high-performance expectations
  —Improving participation in decision making
  —Loosening up bureaucratic constraints
  —Setting meaningful goals
  —Establishing appropriate reward systems

---

from House's work, Bernard Bass has developed an approach that focuses on both transactional and transformational leadership. The high points are summarized in Figure 11.4.[24]

Transactional leadership involves daily exchanges between leaders and subordinates and is necessary for achieving routine performance that is agreed upon between leaders and subordinates. These exchanges involve contingent rewards, active management by exception, passive management by exception, and laissez faire.

- **Contingent rewards** provide various kinds of rewards in exchange for mutually agreed upon goal accomplishment (e.g., your boss pays you a $500 bonus if you get an acceptable article completed by a certain date).

- **Active management by exception** involves watching for deviations from rules and standards and taking corrective action (e.g., your boss notices that you have an increasing number of defects in your work and helps you adjust your machine to correct these).

- **Passive management by exception** involves intervening only if standards are not met (e.g., your boss comes to see you after noticing your high percentage of rejects in the weekly production report).

- **Laissez faire** involves abdicating responsibilities and avoiding decisions (e.g., your boss is seldom around and does not follow through on decisions that need action).

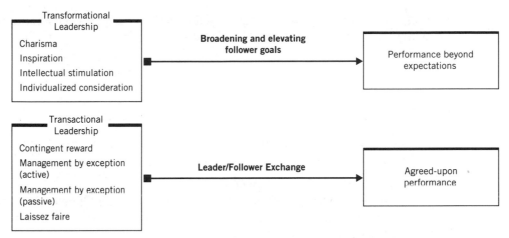

Figure 11.4 High points of Bass's transformational/transactional leadership approach.

Transformational leadership occurs when leaders broaden and elevate the interests of their followers, when they generate awareness and acceptance of the purposes and mission of the group, and when they stir their followers to look beyond their own self-interest for the good of others.

Figure 11.4 shows the four dimensions of transformational leadership.

- **Charisma** provides vision and a sense of mission and instills pride, along with follower respect and trust (e.g., Steve Jobs, former head of Apple Computer, showed charisma by emphasizing the importance of creating the Macintosh as a radical new computer).

- **Inspiration** communicates high expectations, uses symbols to focus efforts, and expresses important purposes in simple ways (e.g., in the movie *Patton,* George C. Scott stood on a stage in front of his troops with a wall-sized American flag in the background and pearl-handled revolvers in holsters at his side.)

- **Intellectual stimulation** promotes intelligence, rationality, and careful problem solving (e.g., your boss encourages you to look at a very difficult problem in a new way).

- **Individualized consideration** provides personal attention, treats each employee individually, and coaches and advises (e.g., your boss drops by and makes remarks reinforcing your worth as a person).

Together, charisma and inspiration transform follower expectations, but intellectual stimulation and individualized consideration are also needed to provide the necessary follow-through.

Transformational leadership is likely to be strongest at the top-management level, where there is the greatest opportunity for proposing and communicating a vision. It is by no means *restricted* to the top level, however; it is found throughout the organization. Furthermore, transformational leadership operates *in combination with* transactional leadership. Transactional leadership is similar to most of the traditional leadership approaches mentioned earlier, and leaders need both transformational and transactional leadership to be successful.

In Summary

How does leadership differ from management, and how do traditional leadership and new leadership differ?

- Traditional leadership approaches range from trait and behavior approaches that give leadership a central role in performance and human resource maintenance outputs to various approaches that combine leadership with situational contingencies to predict outputs.
- These various approaches culminate in the leadership substitutes approach, which argues that situational contingencies sometimes replace leadership in causing outputs.
- The new leadership differs from traditional leadership primarily in that it emphasizes vision and change and focuses on attribution, charisma, transformation, and related concepts.

What are great man/trait and leadership behavior approaches, and why are they important?

- Great man/trait and leadership behavior approaches argue that leader traits or behaviors have a major impact on leadership outcomes.
- Traits are considered more innate and harder to change than are behaviors.
- They are also often used in conjunction with behaviors in some situational contingency or even new leadership approaches.
- Leader traits can be used for selection, while leader behaviors are more suitable for leadership training.

What are leader situational contingency approaches, and why are they important?

- Leader situational contingency approaches argue that leadership, in combination with various situational variables, has a major impact on outcomes.
- Sometimes, as in the case of the substitutes for leadership approach, the role of the situational variables replaces that of leadership to the point where leadership has little or no impact in itself.
- Fiedler's contingency theory, House's path-goal theory, and Hersey and Blanchard's situational leadership theory are other approaches that consider the impact not just of leadership but of various situational contingencies.

How does attribution theory relate to the new leadership?

- Attribution theory overlaps traditional and new leadership by emphasizing the importance of the symbolic aspects of leadership.
- These aspects are an especially important part of the new leadership, charismatic, transformational, and related perspectives, according to which followers tend to attribute heroic or extraordinary leadership abilities to a leader when they observe certain behaviors from that leader.
- These attributions can then help transform followers to achieve goals that go beyond their own self-interest and, in turn, help transform the organization.

What are charismatic leadership approaches, and why are they important?

- Charismatic leadership approaches emphasize the kind of leader–follower social relationship summarized above.
- Two of these approaches emphasized earlier are House and associates' approach and the work of Conger and Kanungo.

What are transformational leadership approaches, and why are they important?

- Transformational leadership approaches are typically broader than are charismatic ones.
- Bass and associates' transformational approach is a particularly well-known theory that includes charisma as one of its dimensions. It separates vision-oriented transformational leadership from day-to-day transactional leadership and argues that the two work in combination.
- Transformational, charismatic, and the new leadership in general are important because of their facilitation of change in our increasingly fast-moving world.

12

COMMUNICATION

AND DECISION MAKING

As you read Chapter 12, keep in mind these study questions:

- What is the communication process?

- How are roles communicated effectively?

- What is decision making, and what types of decision making are common in organizations?

- What is the role of intuition, judgment, and creativity in managerial decision making?

- How do you manage participation in decision making?

- What is organizational learning, and how are organizational cycles helpful in understanding organizational behavior?

C ommunication is a word like "organization." Everyone knows what it means until asked to state its formal definition. It is useful to think of interpersonal communication as a process of sending and receiving symbols with attached meanings from one person to another. These interpersonal foundations form the basis for discussing the larger issue of communication within the organization. **Organizational communication** is the process by which entities exchange information and establish a common understanding.

The Communication Process

The key elements in the interpersonal communication process are illustrated in Figure 12.1. They include a source, who is responsible for encoding an intended meaning into a message, and a receiver, who decodes the message into a perceived meaning. The receiver may or may not give feedback to the source. Although this process may appear to be very elementary, it is not quite as simple as it looks.

The Intended Communication

The information source is a person or group of persons with a reason to communicate with someone else, the receiver. The reasons for the source to communicate include changing the attitudes, knowledge, or behavior of the receiver.

The next step in the process is **encoding**—the process of translating an idea or thought into meaningful symbols. This translation, or encoding, process results in the transmission of a message that may consist of verbal, written, or nonverbal (such

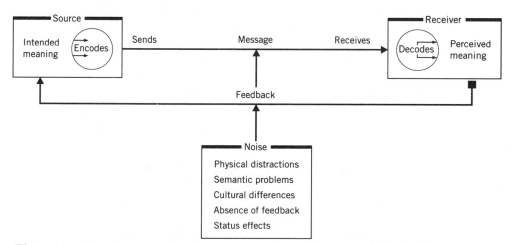

Figure 12.1　The communication process and possible sources of "noise."

as gestures) symbols, or some combination of all three. The message is what is communicated. As we will note later in greater detail, there are a variety of different channels. A **channel** is the median through which the message may be delivered in organizational communication. The choice of channels itself may alter the intended message. For many people, it is easier to communicate verbally and face to face, for example, than in a written letter or memo.

The Received Communication

The process does not stop with the sender. The **receiver** is the individual or group of individuals that hear the message. The receiver may or may not attempt to decode the message. **Decoding** involves interpreting the symbols sent. Although the knowledge and experience of the receiver are important, the message may be interpreted with the aid of authorities, peers, or others as well as by relying on manuals, books, or dictionaries. This process of translation may or may not result in the assignment of the same meaning intended by the source. In fact, the intended meaning of the source and the meaning perceived by the receiver frequently differ, or the receiver may have difficulty interpreting the message altogether.

Most receivers are well aware of the potential gap between an intended message that was sent and the message that is received. **Feedback** is the process whereby the receiver acknowledges the communication and returns a message concerning how he or she feels about the original message. Throughout the process, any number of disturbances may take place. **Noise** is the term used to indicate any disturbance within the communication process which disrupts the matching process between sender and receiver. It is a challenging task to communicate accurately. Managers and subordinates alike can make mistakes.

Nonverbal Communication

Nonverbal communication is communication that is provided through facial expressions, body position, eye contact, and other physical gestures rather than as written or oral expression. Although the nonverbal side of communication is widely recognized, we often underestimate its importance. Indirect nonverbal communication also affects the impressions we make on others. For instance, nonverbal communication can take place through the physical arrangement of space, such as that found in various office layouts. Placing a desk between the officeholder and the door suggests formality and distance.

Effective and Efficient Communication

Effective communication occurs when the intended meaning of the source and the perceived meaning of the receiver are one and the same. This should be the manager's goal in any interpersonal communication attempt, but it is not always achieved. Even now as we are writing, we are concerned about whether or not you are interpreting our words as we intended. Our confidence would be greater if we were face to face in class together and you could ask clarifying questions. This opportunity to offer feedback and ask questions is one way of increasing the effectiveness of communication.

Efficient communication occurs when the fewest resources are expended to send a message. Efficient communications are not always effective. For example, a low-cost communication, such as a computer memo, may save time for the sender, but it does not always achieve the desired results in terms of the receiver's perceived meaning. Similarly, an effective communication may not be efficient. For a manager to visit each employee and explain a new change in procedures may guarantee that everyone truly understands the change, but it may also be prohibitively expensive in terms of the required time expenditure.

Communication Channels

All communications move through one or a number of channels. In a very important sense, the firm is a network of information and communication channels. The new electronic age has added a third category to the well-known formal and informal communication channels. We will call these electronic networks **quasiformal channels.** Although comparatively few managers are in a position to establish organizationwide communication channels, each manager should understand and be able to use all the multiple channels for communication within his or her firm effectively.

Formal Channels

Formal communication channels follow the chain of command established by an organization's hierarchy of authority. For example, an organization chart indicates the proper routing for official messages passing from one level or part of the hierarchy to another. Because formal communication channels are recognized as official and authoritative, it is typical for written communication in the form of letters, memos, policy statements, and other announcements to adhere to these channels.

Informal Channels

Though necessary and important, formal channels constitute only one part of a manager's overall communication responsibilities. In Chapter 1, we identified interpersonal "networking" as an essential activity for effective managers. In the present context, such networks represent the use of the formal channels just described as well as a wide variety of **informal communication channels** that do not adhere to the organization's hierarchy of authority. These informal channels coexist with the formal channels, but they frequently diverge from them by skipping levels in the hierarchy or cutting across vertical chains of command. Much of the chapter on organizational cultures (Chapter 16) discusses the importance of informal channels.

Quasiformal Channels

While formal channels conform to the firm's chain of command and informal channels emerge from day-to-day activities, a whole set of quasiformal channels also exists in most corporations. Quasiformal channels are planned communications connections between holders of various positions within the organization. They are part of the firm's overall management information system.

Electronic networks that link employees together represent a new form of quasiformal channel. In some firms, the management information system is highly centralized through a central computer. In this situation, the firm protects information and doles it out only on an authorized basis. Conversely, some firms encourage the full development of electronic networks and open communication channels throughout the firm. Most corporations do not go to either extreme. Instead, they develop information systems with different levels of access and specified contact points linking individuals in specific positions.

Management must often plan quasiformal linkages to connect individuals and groups. With the aid of computers and electronic mail systems, it is now possible to connect workflow-related units across the globe. Yet, the implementation of a communication potential may be so important to the firm that an individual is assigned to increase the flow of communication between the members of interdependent and often conflicting groups.[1] These people are called "linking-pin individuals," and they have such titles as project managers and liaisons. Linking pins are expected to get to know each unit's operations, members, and social norms. With this knowledge, they work with unit members to develop creative solutions to the overall question of mutual adjustment. The diplomatic skills of such managers are often severely tested as they span the boundaries of the two groups. Though expensive, this technique is often used when different specialized groups, such as engineering and sales, must closely coordinate their efforts.

Barriers to Interpersonal Communication

In order to improve communications, it is important to understand the sources of noise common to most interpersonal exchanges. These sources can be considered barriers to effective communication; accordingly, they should be recognized and subjected to special managerial control.

Physical Distractions   Any number of physical distractions can interfere with the effectiveness of a communication attempt. In the United States some busy executives rudely allow phone calls, interruptions by staff, and the like to routinely disrupt interpersonal communications.

Semantic Problems   Semantic barriers to communication occur in the form of encoding and decoding errors and mixed messages. In this case, symbols are poorly selected by the source, and the message is subsequently misinterpreted by the receiver. Communication is effective only to the extent that the source makes good choices when creating messages.

THE EFFECTIVE MANAGER 12.1

Improving Your Cross-Cultural Communication Skills

Short of learning a foreign language, Nancy Adler, a well-known international management scholar, suggests that you can improve your international communication skills. Her tips for communicating with people from other cultures are:

1. Assume they are different until a similarity is demonstrated.
2. Delay judgment; emphasize description, not evaluation or interpretation.
3. Practice empathy and try to put yourself in the other person's shoes.
4. Treat interpretations as hypotheses for further testing.

One important semantic problem arises from the conflict between verbal and nonverbal communications. **Mixed messages** result when a person's words communicate one message, while his or her actions or "body language" communicate something else. For instance, a colleague points a finger in your face and says, "Thanks for sharing that with me."

Cultural Differences   Perhaps the most obvious difficulties associated with cross-cultural communication revolve around language differences. Yet an underlying, often unrecognized problem in cross-cultural communication is **ethnocentrism**—the tendency to consider one's culture and its values to be superior to those of others. Ethnocentric tendencies are accompanied by an unwillingness to understand alternative points of view and to take the values they represent seriously. This perspective can be highly disadvantageous when you are trying to conduct business and maintain effective working relationships with persons from different cultures. The Effective Manager 12.1 provides some tips for improving your cross-cultural communication skills.

Absence of Feedback   As in the case of a written memo or a voice recording on a message disk, there is no direct and immediate feedback from receiver to source in one-way communication. Two-way communications do include such feedback and are characterized by the normal interactive conversations that take place in our daily experiences. Research indicates that two-way communication is more accurate and effective than one-way communication; it is also more costly and time consuming.[2]

Status Effects   The hierarchy of authority in organizations can create yet another barrier to effective communication: Communication is frequently biased when flowing upward in organizational hierarchies.[3] Status differentials create special barriers between managers and their subordinates. On the one hand, given the authority of their positions, managers may be inclined to do a lot of "telling" but not much "listening." Subordinates, on the other hand, may *filter* information; that is, they tell their superiors only what they think the boss wants to hear. Whether the reason is a fear of retribution for bringing bad news, an unwillingness to identify personal mistakes, or just a general desire to please, the result is the same: The manager ends up making poor decisions because of a biased and inaccurate information base.

Active Listening

Effective communicators not only understand and deal with communication barriers, but they are also exceptionally good at active listening. They recognize that being a good receiver is just as important, and often even more important, than being an accurate sender.

As noted earlier, the ability to listen well is a distinct asset to managers who in the course of their jobs spend a large proportion of their time *communicating* with other people. After all, there are two sides to the communication process: (1) sending a message, or "telling," and (2) receiving a message, or "listening." As noted above, too many managers may emphasize telling and neglect the listening function, especially in their relationships with subordinates.[4] One solution is for managers to develop better **active listening skills**—the ability to help the source of a message say what he or she really means. This concept has evolved from the work of counselors and therapists, who are highly skilled at helping people express themselves and talk about things that are important to them. You should be familiar with active listening as a technique for improving the effectiveness of communications in organizations. Five guidelines are especially useful in this regard.[5]

1. **Listen for message content.** Try to hear exactly what is being said in the message.

2. **Listen for feelings.** Try to identify how the source feels in terms of the message content. Is the message pleasing or displeasing to the source? Why?

3. **Respond to feelings.** Let the source know that his or her feelings, as well as the message content, are recognized.

4. **Note all cues, both verbal and nonverbal.** Be sensitive to the nonverbal communication cues as well as the verbal ones; identify mixed messages that need to be clarified.

5. **Reflect back to the source, in your own words, what you think you are hearing.** Paraphrase and restate the verbal and nonverbal messages as feedback to which the source can respond with further information.

Giving Feedback

Managers frequently give feedback to others, often in the form of performance appraisals. You should learn that giving feedback in such a way that the receiver will accept and use it constructively is an art. Poorly given feedback can be threatening and may become a basis for resentment and alienation.

Feedback is so important in organizational settings that it is appropriate for us to define the term once again and to explore how to improve the process of giving feedback (see Figure 12.1). As we said earlier, feedback is the process whereby the receiver acknowledges the communication and returns a message concerning how he or she feels about the original message. In other words, **feedback** is the process of telling someone else how you feel about something that person did or said or about the situation in general.

The first requirement in giving feedback is to recognize when it is intended truly to benefit the receiver and when it is purely an attempt to satisfy a personal need. A manager who berates a secretary for typing errors, for example, may actually be angry about personally failing to give clear instructions in the first place.

Assuming that the sender's intent is to give helpful feedback to the receiver, a manager should recognize that constructive feedback is:[6]

- Given directly and with real feeling, ideally based on a foundation of trust.
- Specific rather than general, with good clear examples.
- Given at a time when the receiver appears most ready to accept it.
- Checked with others to support its validity.
- In respect to things that the receiver can really do something about.
- Not more than the receiver can handle at any particular time.

Giving criticism certainly presents one of the manager's most difficult communication situations. Communications designed to be polite and constructive can easily end up being unpleasant and even hostile.

Communication of Roles

One of the most important communications in which managers become involved is the sending and receiving of role expectations. A **role** is a set of activities expected of a person holding a particular office or position in a group or organization.[7] The various people who have these expectations regarding the behavior of someone in a role are considered to be members of the **role set.** For a subordinate, the role expectations communicated by the manager are likely to include instructions about desired behavior and unacceptable behavior, intentions regarding the allocation of rewards, and evaluations of past performance. At the organizational level, a key issue in establishing a unified sense of mission and culture is the communication of a shared role orientation for all the firm's members.

When the communication of role expectations is distorted by barriers such as those discussed earlier, role ambiguity and role conflict may occur. These role dynamics deserve your attention because they help explain why every manager should work hard at interpersonal communication skills.

Role Ambiguity

Role ambiguity occurs when the person in a specific role is uncertain about the role expectations of one or more members of the role set. In order to do their jobs well, people need to know what is expected of them. Sometimes these expectations may be unclear because the manager has not tried to communicate them to the subordinate or has done so inadequately. Or the failure of the subordinate to listen may create the lack of understanding. In either case, the resulting role ambiguity can be stressful for the individual. Research indicates that role ambiguity may cause a loss of confidence in the role sender, lowered self-confidence, and decreased job satisfaction.

Role Conflict

Role conflict occurs when the person in a particular role is unable to respond to the expectations of one or more members of the role set. The person understands the role expectations, but for some reason, he or she cannot comply with them. Role conflict is another source of potential tension that may result in a loss of job satisfaction, decreased confidence in one's boss, or a tendency to avoid the unpleasant work situation.

A common form of conflict is **role overload,** whereby too many role expectations are being communicated to a person at a given time. That is, there is too much to be done and too little time to do it. Managers may create role overload for their subordinates, especially when they rely on one-way communication. When cut off from valuable feedback, it is hard for managers to learn when or why a subordinate is experiencing stress.

Role conflict also occurs when the expectations of one or more members of the role set are incompatible. The four basic types of role conflict are intrasender, intersender, person–role, and inter-role conflicts:

1. **Intrasender role conflict** The same role-set member sends conflicting expectations.
2. **Intersender role conflict** Different role-set members send conflicting expectations.
3. **Person–role conflict** The values and needs of the individual conflict with the expectations of the members of the role set.
4. **Inter-role conflict** The expectations of two or more roles held by the same individual become incompatible.

Role ambiguities and conflicts such as these can create tensions that reflect adversely on individual work attitudes and behaviors. The informed manager will seek to minimize these negative consequences by opening and maintaining effective two-way communication with all members of his or her role sets. This same manager will use active listening to solicit feedback from others on their understandings of any reactions to role expectations.

Decision Making in Organizations

Although effective and efficient communications are vital in any organization, a key to success is action—and action should be guided by sound decision making. Formally defined, decision making is the process of choosing a course of action for dealing with a problem or opportunity.[8] The five basic steps involved in systematic decision making flow systematically from the definition of a problem or the opportunity. In brief, these steps are:

1. Recognize and define the problem or opportunity.
2. Identify and analyze alternative courses of action.
3. Choose a preferred course of action.
4. Implement the preferred course of action.
5. Evaluate the results and follow up as necessary.

Decision making in organizations takes place under various conditions and circumstances that make the process especially challenging. In this section we examine alternative environments for managerial decision making and the various types of decisions made by managers.

Decision Environments of Managers

Problem-solving decisions in organizations are typically made under three different conditions or environments: certain, risk, and uncertain.[9]

Certain environments exist when information is sufficient to predict the results of each alternative in advance of implementation. When a person invests money in a savings account, for example, absolute certainty exists about the interest that will be earned on that money in a given period of time. Certainty is an ideal condition for managerial problem solving and decision making. The challenge is simply to locate the alternative that offers a satisfactory or even ideal solution. Unfortunately, in managerial decision environments certainty is the exception instead of the rule.

Risk environments involve a lack of complete certainty regarding the outcomes of various courses of action but some awareness of the probabilities associated with their occurrence. A probability, in turn, is the degree of likelihood that an event will occur. Probabilities can be assigned through objective statistical procedures or through managerial intuition. Risk is a common decision environment faced by middle managers.

Uncertain environments exist when managers are unable to assign probabilities to the outcomes of various problem-solving alternatives. This is the most difficult of the three decision environments. Uncertainty forces managers to rely heavily on individual and group creativity to succeed in problem solving. It requires unique, novel, and often totally innovative alternatives to existing patterns of behavior. Responses to uncertainty are often heavily influenced by intuition, educated guesses, and hunches, all of which are in turn heavily influenced by perception.

Types of Decisions Made by Managers

Within these three conditions, two basic types of managerial decisions apply to the presence of routine and nonroutine problems. Thus, routine and nonroutine decisions may be considered basic types of decisions. *Routine problems* arise on a regular basis and can be addressed through standard responses called **programmed decisions.** These responses simply implement solutions that have already been determined by past experience as appropriate for the problem at hand. Examples of programmed decisions are reordering inventory automatically when stock falls below a predetermined level and issuing a written reprimand to someone who violates a certain personnel procedure.

Nonroutine problems are unique and new. Because standard responses are not available, these circumstances call for creative problem solving. These **crafted decisions** are specifically tailored to the situation at hand. Higher level managers generally spend a greater proportion of their decision-making time on nonroutine problems. As the discussion implies, nonroutine decisions are more likely to involve risky and uncertain circumstances.

Approaches to Decision Making

OB theorists recognize the two alternative approaches to decision making—classical and behavioral. A discussion of each will help you further understand the processes through which managers can and do make decisions.[10]

Classical Decision Theory   **Classical decision theory** views the manager as acting in a world of complete certainty. The manager faces a clearly defined problem, knows all possible action alternatives and their consequences, and then chooses the alternative that offers the best, or optimum, resolution of the problem. Clearly, this is an ideal way to make decisions. Classical theory is often used as a model for the manager's decision making. It is clearly applicable to examining program decisions in certain circumstances.

Behavioral scientists are cautious regarding classical decision theory. They recognize that the human mind is a wonderful creation, capable of infinite achievements, but they also recognize that human beings have cognitive limitations. The human mind is limited in its information-processing capabilities. Information deficiencies and overload compromise the ability of managers to make decisions according to the classical model. As a result, it is argued that behavioral decision theory gives a more accurate description of how people actually make decisions.

Behavioral Decision Theory   **Behavioral decision theory** states that people act only in terms of what they perceive about a given situation. Furthermore, such perceptions are frequently imperfect. Rather than facing a world of complete certainty, the behavioral decision maker is seen as acting under uncertainty and with limited information. Managers make decisions about problems that are often ambiguous; they have only partial knowledge of the available action alternatives and their consequences; and they choose the first alternative that appears to give a satisfactory resolution of the problem. Herbert Simon refers to this model as a **satisficing** style of decision making.[11]

A key difference between a manager's ability to make an optimum decision in the classical style and the tendency to make a satisfying decision in the behavioral style is the presence of cognitive limitations and their impact on our perceptions.

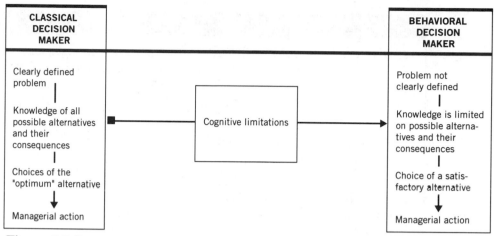

Figure 12.2 Managerial decision making viewed from the classical and behavioral perspectives.

(See Figure 12.2.) Cognitive limitations impair our abilities to define problems, to identify action alternatives, and to choose alternatives with ideal and predictable consequences. These cognitive limitations are so important in the day-to-day world of the manager that intuition and judgment become highly prized.

Intuition, Judgment, and Escalation of Commitment

A key element in successfully making nonprogrammed decisions in uncertain environments is intuition. *Intuition* is the ability to know or recognize quickly and readily the possibilities of a given situation.[12] Intuition adds an element of spontaneity to managerial decision making, and, as a result, it offers the potential for greater creativity and innovation. Especially in risk and uncertain environments, successful managers are probably using a good deal of intuition in problem solving. It is a way of dealing with situations where precedents are unclear, "facts" are limited or tenuous, and time is of the essence.

A debate among scholars regarding how managers really plan highlights the importance of intuition for the practicing manager. On one side of the issue are those who believe that planning can be taught and done in a systematic step-by-step fashion. On the other side are those who believe that the very nature of managerial work makes this systematic approach difficult to implement in actual practice. For instance, Mintzberg argues that managers must and do (1) favor verbal communications with feedback over more systematic and detailed written reports, (2) deal with impressions as they synthesize details in the search for the "big picture," and (3) work fast and do a variety of things while they are frequently interrupted.[13] Thus, they do not have a lot of quiet time alone to think, plan, or make decisions systematically.

THE EFFECTIVE MANAGER 12.2

Improving Your Intuition

Weston Agor, a well-known researcher of intuition, suggests a series of relaxation techniques, mental exercises, and analytical approaches to improve your intuition.

RELAXATION TECHNIQUES

- Drop the problem for a while.
- Take some quiet time by yourself.
- Try to clear your mind.

MENTAL EXERCISES

- Use images to guide your thinking.
- Let your ideas run without a specific goal in mind.
- Practice accepting ambiguity and a lack of total control.

ANALYTICAL TECHNIQUES

- Discuss problems with people with different viewpoints.
- Address problems at times of maximum personal alertness.
- Take creative pauses before making final decisions.

Source: Developed from Weston H. Agor, "How Top Executives Use Their Intuition to Make Important Decisions," *Business Horizons,* Vol. 29 (January–February, 1986, pp. 49–53; see also Weston H. Agor, *Intuition in Organizations* (Newbury Park, CA: Sage, 1989).

Although managers are limited, they do attempt to plan systematically in a step-by-step manner. Astute managers also recognize the job demands noted by Mintzberg, among others, and hone their intuitive skills accordingly. Effective managers are able to combine the analytical and intuitive approaches to create new and novel solutions. (See The Effective Manager 12.2 for some tips on improving your intuition.) To do so, they often use judgmental heuristics.

Judgmental Heuristics

Judgment, or the use of one's intellect, is important in all aspects of decision making. **Heuristics**—simplifying strategies or "rules of thumb" used to make decisions—can make it easier for managers to deal with uncertainty and limited information. But they can also lead to systematic errors that affect the quality of decisions made. Research shows that managers and others are prone to systematic errors and to display of biases that can interfere with the quality of any decisions made.[14]

Any decision maker should be aware of some common judgmental heuristic problems, including availability, representativeness, and anchoring and adjustment heuristics.[15]

Availability heuristic Assessing an event based on past occurrences that are easily available in one's memory. An example is the product manager who bases a decision not to fund a new product on her recollection of the recent failure of a similar product. In this case, the existence of a past product failure has negatively, and perhaps inappropriately, biased the manager's judgment of the new product.

Representativeness heuristic Assessing the likelihood of an event occurring based on the similarity of that event to one's stereotypes of similar occurrences. An example is the supervisor who hires a new employee not because of any special personal qualities but only because that individual has a degree from a university known to have produced high performers in the past. In this case, it is the individual's alma mater—and not his or her job qualifications—that is the basis for a hiring decision.

Anchoring and adjustment heuristic Assessing an event by taking an initial value from a historical precedent or other outside source and then incrementally adjusting it to make subsequent assessments. An example is the manager who arrives at salary increase recommendations for personnel by making adjustments to their base salary. In this case, the existing base salary becomes an "anchor" that affects subsequent salary increases.

In addition to using these judgmental heuristics, managers are prone to two more general biases in decision making. First is the confirmation trap, whereby the manager seeks confirmation for what is already thought to be true and neglects opportunities to look for disconfirming information. Second is the **hindsight trap,** whereby the manager overestimates the degree to which he or she really could have predicted an event that has already taken place.

Escalating Commitment

Social psychologists recognize another common and potentially dysfunctional tendency that hinders decision making and blocks creativity. Called **escalating commitment,** this is the tendency to continue with a previously chosen course of action, even though feedback indicates that it is not working.[16] Escalating commitment is encouraged by the popular adage, "If at first you don't succeed, try, try, again." Current wisdom in OB supports an alternative view, represented by this quote attributed to the late W. C. Fields: "If at first you don't succeed, try, try, again. Then quit. No use being a damn fool about it."

Good decision makers know when to call it quits. They are willing to reverse previous decisions and commitments, and thereby avoid further investments in unsuccessful courses of action. The self-discipline required to admit mistakes and change courses of action is sometimes difficult to achieve, however. Often, the tendency to escalate commitments to previously chosen courses of action outweighs the willingness to disengage from them. This occurs as decision makers[17]

- Rationalize negative feedback as simply a temporary condition.
- Protect their egos to avoid admitting that the original decision was a mistake.
- Use the decision as a way of managing the impressions of others, such as a boss or peers.

- View the negative results as a "learning experience" that can be overcome with added future effort.

Escalating commitments are a form of decision entrapment that leads people to do things that are not justified based on the facts of the situation. Managers should be proactive in spotting "failures" and open to reversing decisions or dropping plans that don't appear to be working.

Creativity

Now that we have discussed some limitations of heuristics and escalating commitment, let us balance the discussion by noting the importance of creativity. *Creativity* in decision making involves the development of unique and novel responses to problems and opportunities of the moment. In a complex and dynamic environment, creativity in making "crafted decisions" often determines how well organizations and their members respond to important challenges.

Earlier in the discussion of groups, we pointed out that the group is an important resource for improving creativity in decision making. Indeed, managers who make good use of such techniques as brainstorming, nominal groups, and the Delphi method can greatly expand their creative potential. Here, we look more specifically at the decision-making implications of these four stages of creative thinking.[18]

1. **Preparation and problem definition** Choosing good problems to solve and then framing them broadly to consider as many alternatives as possible.
2. **Incubation** Looking at problems in diverse ways that allow for the consideration of unusual alternatives; avoiding tendencies toward purely linear and systematic problem solving.
3. **Illumination** Responding to flashes of insight and recognizing when, "aha," all pieces of the puzzle suddenly fit into place.
4. **Verification** Avoiding the tendency to relax after illumination occurs and, instead, proceeding with logical analysis to confirm that good problem-solving decisions have really been made.

The creative process in managerial decision making can be limited by a number of factors. *Judgmental heuristics,* like those just reviewed, can limit the search for alternatives in decision making. When attractive alternatives are left unconsidered, creativity can be limited. *Cultural and environmental blocks* can also limit creativity. This occurs when people are discouraged from considering alternatives that might be viewed as inappropriate by cultural standards or inconsistent with prevailing norms.

Deciding to Decide

With regard to managing the decision-making process, we can say that an effective manager is one who is able to pick precisely which problems are amenable to managerial decision making.

Deciding to decide has two important aspects: selecting the problems and opportunities that deserve managerial attention, and picking a strategy for involvement.

Problem Selection

Managers are too busy and have too many valuable things to do with their time to personally make decisions on every problem or opportunity that comes their way. The effective manager knows when to delegate decisions to others, how to set priorities, and when to abstain from acting altogether. When confronted with a problem, therefore, managers should ask themselves the following questions.[19]

- **Is the problem easy to deal with?** Small, less significant problems should not get as much time and attention as bigger problems. Even if a mistake is made, the cost of a decision error on small problems is also small.
- **Might the problem resolve itself?** Putting problems in rank order leaves the less significant for last. Surprisingly, many of these less important problems will resolve themselves or will be solved by others before the manager gets to them. One less problem to solve leaves decision-making time and energy for other uses.
- **Is this my decision to make?** Persons at lower levels in the hierarchy can handle many problems. These decisions should be delegated. Other problems can and should be referred to higher levels. This is especially true for decisions that have consequences for a larger part of the organization than for those under a manager's immediate control.

To these three questions we add a fourth:

- **Is this a solvable problem within the context of the organization?** The astute manager recognizes the difference between problems that are amenable to solutions within the context of the organization and those that are simply not solvable on a practical level.

Involvement Strategy

One mistake many new managers make is presuming that they must solve the problem and make the decision themselves. In practice, managers end up making decisions in any or all of the following ways:

- **Individual decisions** The manager makes the final choice alone based on information that he or she possesses and without the participation of others. Sometimes called an *authority decision,* this choice often reflects the manager's position of formal authority in the organization.
- **Consultative decisions** The manager solicits inputs on the problem from other persons. Based on this information and its interpretation, the manager then makes a final choice.
- **Group decisions** The manager not only consults with others for information inputs but also asks them to participate in problem-solving discussions and in

making the actual choice. Though sometimes difficult, the group decision is the most participative of the three methods of final choice and the one that seeks true group consensus.

Good managers know when and how to use each of these methods. The basic goal, of course, is always to make a "good" decision—that is, one that is high in quality, timely, and both understandable and acceptable to those whose support is needed for implementation. Furthermore, good decisions can be made by each method—individual, consultative, or group—if the method fits the needs of the situation. Using these methods is part of managing participation in decision making.

Managing Participation in Decision Making

Victor Vroom, along with Phillip Yetton and Arthur Jago, has developed a framework for helping managers choose which of the three decision-making methods is most appropriate for the various problem situations encountered in their daily work efforts.[20] They expand the three basic decision-making methods discussed above into the five forms that follow:

1. **AI (first variant on the authority decision)** The manager solves the problem or makes the decision alone, using the information available at that time.

2. **AII (second variant on the authority decision)** The manager obtains the necessary information from subordinate(s) or other group members and then decides on the problem solution. The manager may or may not tell subordinates what the problem is before obtaining the information from them. The subordinates provide the necessary information but do not generate or evaluate alternatives.

3. **CI (first variant on the consultative decision)** The manager shares the problem with relevant subordinates or other group members individually, getting their ideas and suggestions without bringing them together as a group. The manager then makes a decision that may or may not reflect the subordinates' input.

4. **CII (second variant on the consultative decision)** The manager shares the problem with subordinates or other group members, collectively obtaining their ideas and suggestions. The manager then makes the decision that may or may not reflect the subordinates' input.

5. **G (the group or consensus decision)** The manager shares the problem with the subordinates as a total group and engages the group in consensus seeking to arrive at a final decision.

The central proposition in this model is that the decision-making method used should always be appropriate to the problem being solved. The challenge is to know when and how to implement each of the possible decision methods as the situation requires.

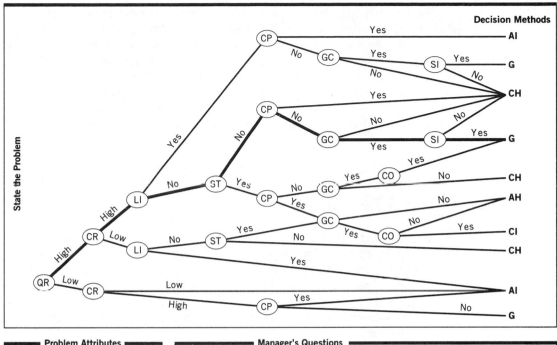

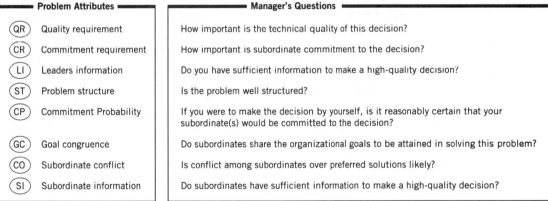

Problem Attributes		Manager's Questions
(QR)	Quality requirement	How important is the technical quality of this decision?
(CR)	Commitment requirement	How important is subordinate commitment to the decision?
(LI)	Leaders information	Do you have sufficient information to make a high-quality decision?
(ST)	Problem structure	Is the problem well structured?
(CP)	Commitment Probability	If you were to make the decision by yourself, is it reasonably certain that your subordinate(s) would be committed to the decision?
(GC)	Goal congruence	Do subordinates share the organizational goals to be attained in solving this problem?
(CO)	Subordinate conflict	Is conflict among subordinates over preferred solutions likely?
(SI)	Subordinate information	Do subordinates have sufficient information to make a high-quality decision?

Figure 12.3 Selecting alternative decision-making methods: The Vroom and Jago decision process flowchart. (*Source:* Reprinted from Victor H. Vroom and Arthur G. Jago, *The New Leadership* [Englewood Cliffs, NJ: Prentice-Hall, 1988], p. 184. Used by permission of the authors.)

Vroom and Jago use the flowchart depicted in Figure 12.3 to help managers analyze the unique attributes of a situation and choose a decision method most appropriate for the problem at hand. Key issues involve the quality requirements of a decision, the availability and location of the relevant information, the commitments needed for followthrough, and the amount of time available. For instance, note the heavy line in the figure indicating that the problem is best handled via a "G" or group-decision method.

The Vroom and Jago model shown in the figure seems complex and cumbersome. Although we certainly do not expect you to work through this figure for every problem faced, we want you to be aware that there is a very useful discipline in the model. Specifically, it helps you recognize how time, quality requirements, information availability, and subordinate acceptance issues can affect decision outcomes. It also helps you remember that all of the decision methods are important and useful. The key to managing participation in decision making effectively is evident: Know how to implement each decision method in situations for which it is most suited, and then do it well.

Organizational Learning

We realize that most discussions of decision making attempt to isolate decision making and implementing into separate events. This approach implies that managers can move through the classical or behavioral approaches separately and sequentially. Such is rarely the case in today's fast-paced, highly competitive firms, where elements of the decision-making process are being pushed down the chain of command. Today's environment calls for more than decision making; it calls on the organization to learn.

Organizational learning involves the adjustment of the organization's actions based on its experience and that of others. Formally defined, **organizational learning** is a process involving knowledge acquisition, information distribution, information interpretation, and organizational retention.[21] The challenge is doing to learn and learning to do. Although obtaining information and using it appropriately are important in both behavioral and classical decision making, the manipulation of usable information is the key to effective organizational learning. By discussing each aspect of the learning process, we hope to make the critical role of usable information apparent.

Knowledge Acquisition

All firms learn in a variety of ways and at different rates during their history by obtaining information. Perhaps the most important information is obtained from sources outside the firm at the time of its founding. During the firm's initial years, its managers copy, or mimic, what they believe are the successful practices of others.[22] As they mature, however, firms can also acquire knowledge through experience and systematic search.

Mimicry   *Mimicry* is important to the new firm because it (1) provides workable, if not ideal, solutions to many problems; (2) reduces the number of decisions that need to be analyzed separately, thus allowing managers to concentrate on more critical issues; and (3) establishes legitimacy or acceptance by employees, suppliers, and customers and narrows the choices for detailed explanation.

One of the key factors involved in examining mimicry is the extent to which managers attempt to isolate cause-effect relationships. Simply copying others without attempting to understand the issues involved often leads to failure.

Experience Of course, a primary way of acquiring knowledge is through *experience*. All organizations and managers can learn in this manner. Besides learning by doing, managers can also embark on structured programs systematically to capture the lessons to be learned from failure and success. For instance, a well-designed research and development program allows managers to learn as much through failure as through success.

Vicarious Learning Although mimicry and experience are important sources of information in all organizations, *vicarious learning* involves capturing the lessons of others' experiences. Some firms have learned that the process of searching for new information may not always be structured or planned in conjunction with an identified problem or opportunity. Managers may embark on learning in less systematic ways, including scanning, grafting, and contracting out.

Scanning involves looking outside the firm and bringing back useful solutions. At times, these solutions may be applied to recognized problems. More often, these solutions float around management until they are needed to solve a problem.[23] Astute managers can contribute to organizational learning by scanning external sources, such as competitors, suppliers, industry consultants, customers, and leading firms.

Grafting is the process of acquiring individuals, units, or firms in order to produce useful knowledge. Almost all firms seek to hire experienced individuals from other firms simply because experienced individuals may bring with them a whole new series of solutions. Of course, the critical problem in grafting is much the same as in scanning: Just obtaining the knowledge is not enough; it must be translated into action. A key problem with grafting one unit onto an existing organization is discussed in Chapter 16. That is, there may be a clash of cultures, and instead of getting new solutions, both units may experience substantial conflict.

Contracting out is the reverse of grafting and involves asking outsiders to perform a particular function. Astute managers recognize that close monitoring of external relationships is critical to the firm's learning when operations are contracted out. Although all organizations contract out, the key question for managers is often what to keep and what to buy. Generally, firms that contract out peripheral or staff functions can benefit from the expertise of others. If operations critical to the competitive success of the firm are contracted out, however, the firm may lose its long-term competitive advantage.

Information Distribution

Obtaining information is the first step in organizational learning, but managers must also establish mechanisms to distribute relevant information to the individuals who may need it. One of the primary challenges in larger firms is to locate quickly who has the appropriate information and who needs specific types of information. A partial solution is to develop computer and electronic networks that connect related organizational units. Just providing the data is not enough, however; the electronically sent messages must also be interpreted.

Information Interpretation

By data we do not mean information. Information within organizations is a collective understanding of the firm's goals and of the way the data relate to one of the firm's stated or unstated objectives within the current setting. Unfortunately, the process of developing multiple interpretations is often thwarted by a number of common problems.[24] Three factors that are particularly important in blocking interpretation are self-serving interpretations, managerial scripts, and common myths.

Self-Serving Interpretations A manager's ability to interpret events, conditions, and history to his or her own advantage is so common that we devote substantial parts of the discussion of power and politics as well as organizational change to aspects of this topic (see, for instance, Chapter 10).

Managerial Scripts A **managerial script** is a series of well-known routines for identifying problems and generating and analyzing alternatives common to managers within a firm.[25] Different organizations have different scripts, often based on what has worked in the past. In a way, the script is a ritual that reflects what the "memory banks" of the corporation hold. The organizational culture, existing transformation procedures, and the manager's current job responsibilities all help dictate the definition of the problem, acceptable alternatives, and the criteria for judging alternative courses of action. Managers become bound by what they have seen. The danger is that they are not open to what might actually be occurring.

The script may be elaborate enough to provide an apparently well-tested series of solutions based on the firm's experience. Larger, older firms are rarely structured for learning; rather, they are structured for efficiency. That is, the firm's formal and informal structures emphasize repetition, volume processing, and routine. In order to learn, the organization needs to be able to switch routines, to obtain information quickly, to provide various interpretations of events, and to tap into external archives.[26]

Few managers question a successful script. Consequently, they start solving today's problems with yesterday's solutions. Managers have been trained, both in the classroom and on the job, to initiate corrective action within the historically shared view of the world. That is, managers often initiate small, incremental improvements based on existing solutions rather than creating new approaches to identify the underlying problems.

Common Myths The world is far too complex for managers to have a well-tested and empirically demonstrated management approach that specifies all possible cause-effect relationships. Instead, all managers act on the shared meanings established within their organization. Interpretation is based on shared "social facts" or on views commonly held by organizational members. For instance, organizational members may believe that their industry is highly competitive, hostile, and dynamic. It might be—or it might not be.

An **organizational myth** is a commonly held cause-effect relationship or assertion that cannot be empirically supported. Even though myths cannot be substantiated, both managers and workers may base their interpretations of problems and opportunities on the potentially faulty views. Three common myths often block the development of multiple interpretations.

The first common myth is the presumption that a single organizational truth exists. This myth is often expressed as, "While others may be biased, I am able to define problems and develop solutions objectively." We are all subject to bias in varying degrees and in varying ways. The more complex the issue, the stronger the likelihood that there will be many different supportable interpretations.

A second common myth is the presumption of competence. This may be expressed as, "Most of the keys to effectiveness in my group [unit, or division] are known and just need to be perfected." Managers at all levels are subject to believing that their part of the firm is okay and just needs minor improvements. Other units are the ones needing major changes.

A third common myth is the denial of trade-offs. Most managers believe that their group, unit, or firm can avoid making undesirable trade-offs and simultaneously please nearly every constituency. The denial of trade-offs is common to politicians who claim that they can both cut taxes and the budget deficit and jump-start the short-term economy to build toward the long-term future.

Although the denial of trade-offs is common, it can be a very dangerous myth in some firms. For instance, when complex, dangerous technologies are involved, safe operations may come at some sacrifice to efficiency. Yet, some firms claim that "an efficient operation is a safe one" and aggressively move to improve efficiency. While managers are stressing efficiency, they may fail to work on improving safety. The results could be a serious accident.[27]

Organizational Retention

Organizations employ a variety of mechanisms for retaining useful information.[28] Six mechanisms deserve particular discussion here.

1. **Individuals** Individuals are the most important storehouses of information for organizations. Organizations that retain a large and comparatively stable group of experienced individuals are expected to have a greater capacity to acquire, retain, and retrieve information relevant to decision making. In keeping with the terms used earlier in this chapter, experienced individuals turn apparently unprogrammed decisions into programmed ones. Thus, with more experienced individuals, managers can move decision making farther down the organizational hierarchy.

2. **Culture** The shared experiences of individuals are an important repository. The culture often maintains the organizational memory via rich, vivid, and meaningful stories that outlive those who actually experienced the event.

3. **Transformation procedures** Documents, rule books, written procedures, and even standard but unwritten methods of operation are all mechanisms used to store accumulated information. In cases where operations are ex-

tremely complex but rarely needed, written sources of information are often invaluable.

4. **Structures** The organizational structure and the positions in an organization are less direct but equally important mechanisms for storing information. For example, when an aircraft lands on the deck of a U.S. Navy aircraft carrier, there are typically dozens of individuals on the deck, apparently watching the aircraft land. Actually, each person on the deck is there for a specific purpose. Each can often trace his or her position to a specific accident that would not have occurred had some individual originally been assigned that position.

5. **Ecology** Physical structures (or "ecology," in the jargon of learning theorists) are potentially important but often neglected mechanisms used to store information. For example, a very traditional way or ordering parts and subcomponents in a factory is known as the two-bin system. One bin is always kept in reserve. Once an individual opens the reserve bin, he or she automatically orders replacements. In this way, the plant never runs out of components.

6. **External archives** Finally, external archives can be tapped to provide valuable information on most larger organizations. Former employees, stock market analysts, suppliers, distributors, and the media can be important sources of valuable information. These external archives are important because they may provide a quite different view of events from the one contained in the organization.

Organizational Learning Cycles

Some recent work on learning cycles helps explain why many organizations apparently fail to learn while others appear to improve rapidly.[29]

Deficit Cycles

A **deficit cycle** is a pattern of deteriorating performance that is followed by even further deterioration. The same problems keep reoccurring, and the firm fails to develop adequate mechanisms for learning. The firm often encounters problems during one or more phases of the learning process. The past inability to adjust yields more problems and fewer resources available to solve the next wave of problems, and the firm continues to deteriorate.

Major factors associated with deficit cycles are still being uncovered. Three are obvious from the current work;[30] these are organizational inertia, hubris, and detachment.

Organizational Inertia As we discussed earlier, when an apparent problem is suspected, even the best managers may initiate a decision-making script based on the old prescribed manner. Unfortunately, scripted processes may fail to address the new opportunities and problems accurately.

Hubris and Excessive Power   Few senior managers in the largest U.S. corporations are willing to challenge their own success or the historical successes of their corporations. They are often overconfident in their own and the corporation's ability. In other words, they suffer from excessive pride, or hubris. Yet, most large organizations are filled with "maladaptive specializations." A **maladaptive specialization** is extensive experience with and knowledge of a competitively inferior process, procedure, technology, or business. For example, IBM is the master of the mainframe computer in an era when mainframe technology is less important. Mainframes are still important, but the new avenues for profitability in the 1990s call on computer firms to develop computer networks, workstations, and minicomputers.

Detachment from the Actual Business of the Firm   Understanding the problems facing the corporate giants of today requires managers to know too much. No senior manager or senior management group can be familiar with all of the businesses of the very large multi-industry firm. Senior management therefore can become detached and manage by the numbers rather than by a process of learning.

If information moved smoothly up, down, and across the organization, and if it could be accurately represented in balance sheets, income statements, and quarterly reports, senior managers could make small, incremental adjustments and help their various units learn. As we have seen, data and information are not synonymous. Organizational learning is dependent on a shared process. When this process breaks down, it may be replaced by an overreliance on scripts and myths. In order to break this cycle, astute executives must attempt to get directly involved.

Benefit Cycles

Though common, inertia, hubris, and detachment are not automatically the fate of all corporations. As we have repeatedly demonstrated, managers are trying to reinvent their firms each and every day. They hope to initiate a benefit cycle, a pattern of successful adjustment followed by further improvements. In this cycle, the same problems do not keep reoccurring as the firm develops adequate mechanisms for learning. The firm has a few major difficulties with the learning process, and managers continually attempt to improve knowledge acquisition, information distribution, information interpretation, and organizational memory.

Just as a prior inability to adjust yields more problems and fewer resources for solving the next wave of problems, organizations that successfully adapt can ride the benefit cycle. Inertia can work for managers if they do not become overconfident and if they can stay directly involved with the key operations of the firm.

In Summary

What is the communication process?

- In communication, information is encoded, sent, received, and decoded sometimes with and sometimes without feedback but is always affected by noise.
- Five special sources of noise include physical distractions, semantic problems, cultural differences, the absence of feedback, and status effects.

- Sources of noise should be recognized and subjected to special managerial control.
- The organization is a network of information and communication channels.
- Active listening is a "sender-oriented" approach to communication, that encourages a free and complete flow of communication.
- Feedback must be given directly and specifically at a time when the recipient may be most prepared to accept it.

How are formal, informal, and quasiformal communication channels different from one another?

- Formal communication channels follow the chain of command established by an organization's hierarchy of authority.
- Informal communication channels do not adhere to the organization's hierarchy of authority. While they coexist with formal channels, they frequently diverge from them by skipping levels of authority or cutting across vertical chains of command.
- Quasiformal channels are planned communications connections between holders of various positions within the organization.

What is decision making and what types of decision making are common in organizations?

- Decision making in organizations includes identifying problems and opportunities and choosing among alternative courses of action.
- Managers make many decisions in risky and uncertain environments where situations are ambiguous and the available information is limited.
- Some decisions can be programmed (used over again).
- Many others must be created as unique and "crafted" responses to nonroutine situations.
- In classical decision theory, managers seek an "optimum" while behavior decision theory sees managers as "satisficing."

What is the role of intuition, judgment, and creativity in managerial decision making?

- Intuition, judgment, and creativity are all critical.
- Intuition is the ability to recognize the possibilities of a situation quickly.
- Judgment is the use of cognitive skills to make choices among alternatives.
- Biases include the availability, representativeness, and anchoring and adjustment heuristics.
- Decision making can be improved through individual awareness and a good use of groups as problem-solving resources.

How do you manage participation in decision making?

- Managers must know how to involve others in decision making and how to choose among individual, consultative, and group decision methods.
- The Vroom–Yetton model identifies how decision methods can be varied to meet the unique needs of each problem.
- Key issues involve quality requirements, information availability, and time constraints.

What is organizational learning and how are organizational cycles helpful in understanding organizational behavior?

- Organizational learning is the process of knowledge acquisition, information distribution, information interpretation, and organizational memory to adapt successfully to changing circumstances.
- Organizational learning cycles help us understand how some organizations continually decline while others appear to be rising stars.

CONFLICT AND

NEGOTIATION

As you read Chapter 13, keep in mind these study questions:

- What is conflict?

- How can managers best deal with conflict?

- What is negotiation?

- What are the different approaches to negotiation?

- How do good managers deal with negotiation?

T he daily work of managers is intensely based on interpersonal relationships and the exchange of information.[1] Yet interpersonal relationships open the door for potential differences and disagreements to creep into the workplace. They may cause difficulties that affect not only what people may accomplish in their work, but also their satisfaction. A manager who understands the fundamentals of conflict and negotiation will be better prepared to deal successfully with these situations, inevitable as they are.

Conflict

If you listen in on some workplace conversations, you might hear the following:

"I don't care what you say, I don't have time to do it and that's that!"

"I can't stand working with him; he is such an antagonistic personality."

"We need the resources; why is it that the other departments are always getting special attention?"

At issue in each conversation is *conflict,* and the ability to deal successfully with such conflict is a key aspect of a manager's interpersonal skills.

What Is Conflict?

Conflict occurs whenever disagreements exist in a social situation over issues of substance or whenever emotional antagonisms create friction between individuals or groups.[2] Managers are known to spend up to 20 percent of their time dealing with conflict, including conflicts in which the manager is directly involved as one of the principal actors. In other situations, the manager may act as a mediator, or third party, whose job it is to try and resolve conflicts between other people.[3]

Two common examples of workplace conflict are (1) a disagreement with one's boss over a plan of action to be followed (e.g., a marketing strategy for a new product), and (2) a dislike for a coworker (e.g., someone who is always belittling the members of a minority group). The first example is one of *substantive conflict*—a conflict that usually occurs in the form of a fundamental disagreement over work goals and the means for their accomplishment.[4] When people work together day in and day out, it is only normal that different viewpoints on a variety of substantive workplace issues will arise. It is common for people to disagree at times over such things as group and organizational goals, the allocation of resources, the distribution of rewards, policies and procedures, and task assignments.

The second example is one of *emotional conflict*—a conflict that involves interpersonal difficulties that arise over feelings of anger, mistrust, dislike, fear, resentment, and the like. It is commonly known as a "clash of personalities." Emotional conflicts

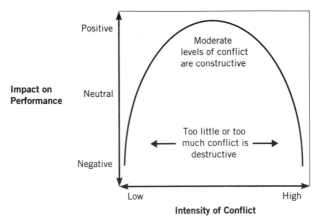

Figure 13.1 The two faces of conflict: constructive conflict and destructive conflict.

can drain the energies of people and distract them from important work priorities. They can emerge from a wide variety of settings and are common among coworkers as well as in superior–subordinate relationships. The latter is perhaps the most upsetting emotional conflict for any person to experience.

Figure 13.1 shows that any conflict can have two sides or faces, one constructive and the other destructive. **Constructive conflict** results in positive benefits to the group or organization. It offers the people involved a chance to identify otherwise neglected problems and opportunities; creativity and performance can improve as a result. Indeed, in some situations a good manager is able to stimulate constructive conflict to overcome satisfaction with the status quo and to encourage needed change and innovation.

Destructive conflict works to the group's or organization's disadvantage. It occurs, for example, when two employees are unable to work together owing to interpersonal hostilities or when the members of a committee fail to act because they cannot agree on group goals. Destructive conflicts of these and other types can decrease productivity and job satisfaction; they may also contribute to costly employee absenteeism and job turnover.

The very nature of the manager's position in an organization guarantees that conflict will be a part of his or her work experience. The manager may encounter conflict in supervisor–subordinate relationships, in peer or intergroup relationships, and in relationships with higher levels of management. The manager's ability to deal with such situations may in large part determine whether they have constructive or destructive impacts on the work situation. An effective manager is able to recognize and deal with each of the following conflict situations.

1. **Vertical conflict** Occurs between hierarchical levels; commonly involves supervisor–subordinate disagreements over resources, goals, deadlines, or performance results.

2. **Horizontal conflict** Occurs between persons or groups at the same hierarchical level; commonly involves goal incompatibilities, resource scarcities, or purely interpersonal factors.

3. **Line–staff conflict** Occurs between line and staff representatives; commonly involves disagreements over who has authority and control over certain matters, such as personnel selection and termination practices.

4. **Role conflict** Occurs when the communication of task expectations is unclear, incomplete, or upsetting; commonly involves uncertainties of expectations, overloads or underloads in expectations, or incompatibilities among expectations.

Conflict Management

The process of managing conflict to achieve constructive rather than destructive results can be pursued through both indirect and direct means. Even though it is an ideal state that is not always possible to accomplish, an important goal in conflict management is to achieve or set the stage for **conflict resolution,** a situation in which the underlying reasons for a given conflict are eliminated.

Indirect Conflict Management Approaches

Indirect conflict management actively deals with conflict but does so without involving the conflicting parties in direct interpersonal interactions. A number of useful indirect conflict management approaches are available. First, is the *appeal to common goals,* which is an attempt to focus the attention of actual or potentially conflicting parties on a higher level goal important to each. By elevating the potential dispute to a common framework within which the parties recognize a mutually desirable outcome, disputes can often be put in perspective.

A second alternative, *hierarchical referral,* makes use of the chain of command for conflict resolution. In this approach, problems are simply referred up the hierarchy for more senior managers to reconcile. These managers will typically be those to whom the conflicting parties mutually report. They will be managers who ultimately have the formal authority to resolve such disputes by directive if necessary. Although hierarchical referral can work in some instances, its continual use ties up valuable time for the senior managers. And because the conflicting parties are behaving in the desired fashion only because they have been told to do so, the same or similar conflicts may surface again in the future.

When the organizational design allows groups, units, and departments to operate in relative isolation from one another, conflict between them tends to be muted. But when tasks need to be coordinated, when resources must be shared, and when other workflow interdependencies exist, conflicts often arise. In this event, managers have a third option of trying to reduce conflicts by adjusting the organizational design at such friction points.[5] This can be done by *decoupling* the groups in conflict—separating them or reducing contact between them. In some cases, the tasks of the groups can be adjusted to reduce the number of required points of coordination. The conflicting groups can then be separated from one another, and each can be provided separate access to valued resources. *Buffering* is another organizational redesign approach that can be used when the inputs of one group are the outputs of another group. The classic buffering technique is to build an inventory between the two groups so that any output slowdown or excess is absorbed by the inventory and does not directly pressure the target group.

In organizations characterized by a great need for lateral coordination, it is often useful to formally assign certain people to serve as *linking pins* between groups that are prone to conflict.[6] Persons in linking-pin roles, such as project liaison, are expected to understand the operations, members, needs, and norms of their host group. Linking pins are supposed to use this knowledge to help their group work better with other groups to accomplish mutual tasks. A variation of the linking-pin concept is the *liaison group.*[7] The purpose of such a group, team, or department is to coordinate the activities of certain units and to prevent destructive clashes between them. Members of the department may be given formal authority to resolve disputes involving everything from technical matters to resource claims to work assignments.

Direct Conflict Management Approaches

The "conflict management grid" depicted in Figure 13.2 shows five alternative styles or ways of directly managing conflict.[8] The grid classifies each style as resulting from some combination of a person's action tendencies along two primary dimensions.[9]

- **Cooperativeness** A desire to satisfy the other party's concerns in a conflict situation.
- **Assertiveness** A desire to satisfy one's own concerns in a conflict situation.

Consultants and academics generally agree that true conflict occurs only in "win–win" conditions where everyone is ultimately satisfied with the outcomes and the underlying reasons for the conflict are eliminated.[10] Unfortunately, not all direct conflict management attempts result in this conclusion; win–lose and lose–lose outcomes are also very common in the workplace.

In **win–lose conflict,** one party achieves its desires at the expense of and to the exclusion of the other party's desires. This may result from outright *competition,* whereby a victory is achieved through force, superior skill, or domination. It may also occur as a result of *authoritative command,* whereby a formal authority simply dictates a solution and specifies what is gained and what is lost by whom. When the authority figure is a party to the conflict, it is easy to predict who will be the winner and who the loser. Win–lose strategies, as shown in the figure, are high in assertiveness and low in cooperation, They fail to address the root causes of the conflict and tend to suppress the desires of at least one of the conflicting parties. As a result, future conflicts over the same issues are likely to occur.

Lose–lose conflict occurs when nobody really gets what he or she wants. No one achieves his or her true desires, and the underlying reasons for the conflict remain unaffected. In this case, future conflict of a similar nature is likely to occur. Lose–lose conflicts often result from conflict management by avoidance, smoothing,

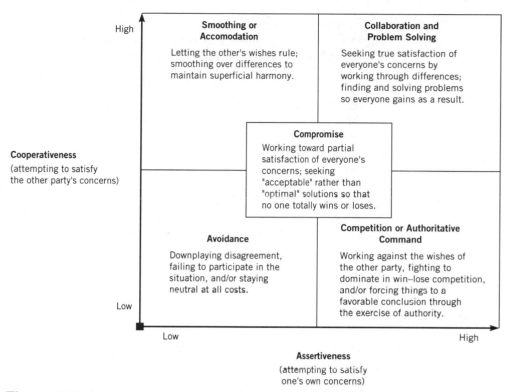

Figure 13.2 The conflict management grid with five conflict management styles.

or compromise. *Avoidance* is an extreme form of nonattention; everyone involved pretends that the conflict does not really exist and hopes that it will simply go away. *Accommodation,* or *smoothing,* involves playing down differences among the conflicting parties and highlighting similarities and areas of agreement. Peaceful coexistence through a recognition of common interests is the goal, but smoothing may ignore the true essence of a given conflict.

"Let's compromise" is a phrase frequently heard when conflicts emerge in a group setting. The classic example occurs whenever representatives of unions and management meet to prepare new labor contracts. *Compromise* in conflict management occurs when each party gives up something of value to the other. As a result, neither party gains its full desires, and the antecedent conditions for future conflicts are established. Although a conflict may appear to be settled for a while through compromise, it may well reappear at some future time.

Looking back at Figure 13.2, we see that the lose–lose style of avoidance is based on low cooperativeness and low assertiveness. The compromise style is based on moderate cooperativeness and moderate assertiveness. Accommodation is a conflict management style that is pursued through high cooperativeness and low assertiveness.

Win–win conflict is achieved when all conflicting parties are satisfied with the final result. It is gained through *collaboration* wherein everyone actively works together to address the real issues and use problem solving to reconcile differences. As shown in the figure, collaboration and *problem solving* is a direct and positive approach to conflict management utilizing both assertiveness and cooperation. It involves a recognition by all conflicting parties that something is wrong and needs to be corrected. When success is achieved through this style, true conflict resolution has occurred. Win–win conditions are established as all relevant issues are raised and openly discussed. The reasons for continuing or resurrecting the conflict are eliminated because nothing has been avoided or suppressed. A good test for a win–win solution is whether or not the conflicting parties are willing to say the following to each other:[11]

> "I want a solution that achieves your goals and my goals and is acceptable to both of us."

> "It is our collective responsibility to be open and honest about facts, opinions, and feelings."

Negotiation

Picture yourself at work trying to make decisions in the following situations. What would you decide to do?

Scenario 1 Your boss has told you that your merit salary increase for next year will be 5 percent of your base salary. You think you deserve more than that.

Scenario 2 You are part of a cross-functional corporate task force. There is some possibility that the task force may recommend a staff reduction in your department.

Scenario 3 You have ordered a new state-of-the art computer for your department. Another department has ordered a different brand of computer. Your boss indicates that only one brand will be ordered.

These scenarios are just a sampling of common negotiation situations that involve managers and other people in the workplace. **Negotiation** is the process of making joint decisions when the parties involved have different preferences. In other words, negotiation can be considered a way of getting what you want from others in the process of making decisions.[12] In particular, managers should be prepared to participate in at least four major action settings for negotiations:

1. **Two-party negotiation** The manager negotiates directly with one other person. Scenario 1 above is an example of two-party negotiation; another is a manager negotiating performance objectives with a subordinate.

2. **Group negotiation** The manager is part of a team or group whose members are negotiating to arrive at a common decision. Scenario 2 is an example of group negotiation; another is a committee that must reach agreement on recommending a new sexual harassment policy.

THE EFFECTIVE MANAGER 13.1

Three Criteria of an Effective Negotiation

CRITERION 1

Quality—The negotiation results offer a "quality" agreement that is wise and truly satisfactory to all sides.

CRITERION 2

Efficiency—The negotiation is "efficient" and no more time consuming or costly than absolutely necessary.

CRITERION 3

Harmony—The negotiation is "harmonious" and fosters rather than inhibits good interpersonal relations.

---

3. **Intergroup negotiation** The manager is part of a group that is negotiating with another group to arrive at a decision regarding a problem or situation affecting both. Scenario 3 is an example of intergroup negotiation; another is negotiation between management groups from two firms to form a joint venture or strategic alliance.

4. **Constituency negotiation** The manager is involved in negotiation with other persons, and each individual party represents a broad constituency. A common example is a team representing "management" negotiating with a team representing "labor" to arrive at a collective bargaining agreement.

Two goals are at stake in any negotiation in any action setting. *Substance goals* are concerned with outcomes relative to the "content" issues at hand, such as the dollar amount of a wage agreement in a collective bargaining situation. *Relationship goals* are concerned with outcomes relating to how well the people involved in the negotiation, as well as any constituencies they may represent, are able to work with one another once the process is concluded. As example is the ability of union members and management representatives to work together effectively after a contract dispute has been settled.

Unfortunately, many negotiations result in a sacrifice of relationships, as parties become preoccupied with self-interests and win–lose outcomes. In contrast, **effective negotiation** occurs when substance issues are resolved *and* working relationships are maintained or even improved. Three criteria for identifying effective negotiation—quality, efficiency, and harmony—are described in The Effective Manager 13.1.[13]

Effective negotiation results in overlapping interests and joint decisions that are "for the better" of all parties. The trick is knowing how to get there. Consider this classic example.

> Two people are alone in the reading room of a library. One wants the window open, and the other wants it shut. They can't agree, become quite angry at each other, and arrive at a negotiating impasse. The observant

librarian intervenes and asks both persons why they want the window open or closed. As it turns out, the person wanting the window open is seeking fresh air; the one wanting it closed wants to avoid a draft. When the librarian suggests that a window in the adjoining room could be opened to provide the fresh air without creating a draft, both parties are satisfied. The negotiated agreement is "for the better" of each.

Different Approaches to Negotiation

Let's use another example to further explore different approaches to negotiation. The simple but intriguing case that follows illustrates an important point.

> **Scenario:** Two sisters want an orange, but only one orange is available. They begin to negotiate over the orange.

For our purposes, the "orange" in this case can represent any scarce organizational resource. It could be money, time, people, facilities, equipment, and so on. Like the two sisters, managers and other workers frequently negotiate with one another over access to scarce organizational resources. In all such cases, the approach taken to the negotiation can have a major influence on its outcomes. In this regard, it is useful to discuss two alternative approaches that differ greatly: distributive negotiation and integrative negotiation.

Distributive Negotiation

In **distributive negotiation,** the focus is on "positions" that the conflicting parties stake out or declare. Each party is trying to "claim" certain portions of the available "pie." Let's return to the orange scenario. If the two sisters adopted distributive bargaining approaches, each would ask the question: "Who is going to get the orange?"

This question, and the way in which it frames or influences subsequent behavior, will have a major impact on the negotiation process and outcomes. Negotiation in such instances usually proceeds along one of two directions. First, "hard" distributive negotiation takes place when each party holds out to get its own way. This approach is highly competitive, with each party seeking dominance over the other while trying to maximize self-interests. Second, "soft" distributive negotiation takes place when one party is willing to make extraordinary concessions to the other just to get things over with. This approach is accommodative or compromising, as one or both parties gives up something of value in order to reach agreement. A common outcome of distributive negotiation is lingering irritation by either the loser, accommodator, or compromiser.

In the case of the two sisters, the hard approach may lead to a win–lose outcome whereby one sister dominates and gains the orange for herself. Or it may lead to an impasse, in which case no one gets the orange. The soft approach may lead to accommodation whereby one sister gets the orange when the other acquiesces. But even in this case there is likely to be at least some latent dissatisfaction on the part of the sister who agrees to give up the orange. The soft approach may also result in the orange being split equally between the sisters. But, here too, dissatisfaction may exist since each sister is still deprived of what she originally wanted—the whole orange.

Integrative Negotiation

In **integrative negotiation,** sometimes called *principled negotiation,* the focus is on the "merits" of the issues. Everyone involved tries to enlarge the available "pie" rather than establish claims to certain portions of it. In the case of the sisters, the integrative approach to negotiation would be prompted by asking the question: "How can the orange best be utilized?" Notice that this is a very different question from the one described for distributive negotiation. It is much less confrontational, and it permits a broader range of alternatives to be explored.

The integrative approach to negotiation has much more of a "win–win" orientation than does the distributive approach; it seeks ways of satisfying the needs and interests of all parties. At one extreme, this may involve selective avoidance, wherein both parties simply realize that there are more important things on which to focus their time and attention. In the case described above, the two sisters might mutually decide to forget about the orange and do other things. Compromise can also play a role in the integrative approach, but it must have an enduring basis. This is most likely to occur when the compromise involves each party giving up something of perceived lesser personal value in order to gain something of greater value. In the case of the sisters, one of them may get the orange this time in return for the other sister getting the orange the next time one becomes available.

Finally, integrative negotiation may involve true collaboration. In this case, the negotiating parties engage in problem solving in order to arrive at a mutual agreement that truly maximizes benefit to each. In the case of the orange, this ideal and integrative approach could lead to the sisters discussing and sharing their reasons for wanting the orange. A possible result is the realization that one sister can get the peel to use for a special jam she is making, while the other can still get the fruit to use for the glass of juice she wants to drink. As you can see, it is almost impossible to realize this win–win solution if the negotiation is approached from a distributive approach—that is, with each sister focused on getting the entire orange for her own use. Only under an integrative approach and the guiding question—"How can the orange best be utilized?"—is such a mutually desirable solution possible.

Anyone committed to integrative negotiation must have both the attitudes and behavioral skills necessary to be successful. The Effective Manager 13.2 offers tips on gaining integrative agreements.

Managerial Issues in Negotiation

Negotiation issues of special relevance to managers include understanding common negotiation pitfalls, communication problems in negotiation, and ethical aspects of negotiation.

THE EFFECTIVE MANAGER 13.2

Gaining Integrative Agreements

ATTITUDINAL FOUNDATIONS

- Each party must be willing to trust the other party.
- Each party must be willing to share information with the other party.
- Each party must be willing to ask concrete questions of the other party.

BEHAVIORAL FOUNDATIONS

- The ability to separate the people from the problem.
- The ability to avoid letting emotional considerations affect the negotiation.
- The ability to focus on interests rather than positions.
- The ability to avoid making premature judgments.
- The ability to use objective standards to evaluate possible agreements.

Negotiation Pitfalls

The negotiation process is admittedly complex, and it is further characterized by all the possible confusions of sometimes volatile interpersonal and group dynamics. Accordingly, individual negotiators need to guard against some common mistakes.[14]

In negotiation it is too easy to stake out your position based on the assumption that, in order to gain your way, something must be "subtracted" from the other party's way. This myth of the "fixed pie" (e.g., the belief that only one sister can get the orange) is a purely distributive approach to negotiation. The whole concept of integrative negotiation is based on the premise that the "pie" can sometimes be expanded or utilized to the maximum advantage of all parties, not just one.

Because parties to negotiations often begin by stating extreme demands, the possibility of escalating commitment is high. That is, once demands have been stated, people become committed to them and are reluctant to back down. As a result, they may be prone to nonrational escalation of conflict. Concerns for "protecting one's ego" and "saving face" may further enhance these tendencies. Self-discipline is needed to spot this tendency in one's own behavior as well as in the behavior of others.

Many negotiators also come to believe that their positions are the only "correct" ones. This stance is characterized by overconfidence and neglect of other's needs. In some cases, negotiators completely fail to see the merits in the other party's position—merits that an outside observer would be sure to spot. Such overconfidence makes it harder to reach a positive common agreement. It may even set the stage for disappointment if the negotiation is turned over to a neutral third party for resolution. In **arbitration,** such as the salary arbitration now common in professional sports, this third party acts as the "judge" and issues a binding decision after listening to the positions advanced by the parties involved in a dispute. Sometimes, a manager may be asked to serve as an arbitrator of disputes between subordinates, ranging from matters as important as the distribution of task assignments to matters as seemingly trivial as access to a photocopy machine.

Communication and Negotiation

It has been said that "negotiation is the process of communicating back and forth for the purpose of reaching a joint decision."[15] When the negotiations cross cultural boundaries, this process is often tested to the limits. In such cases, the parties involved must make special efforts to communicate effectively with one another and to achieve negotiation success.

Two types of communication problems are especially likely to cause difficulties during a negotiation, cross-cultural or otherwise. The first is the *telling problem*. Negotiation sometimes breaks down because the parties don't really "talk" to one another; at least, the parties do not talk to each other in ways that make themselves truly understood. The second is the *hearing problem*. Here negotiation sometimes breaks down because the parties are unable or unwilling to "listen" well enough to understand what each other is saying. As a final reminder, it can be said that positive negotiation occurs only when the communication between the parties can be described as follows.

- Each party frequently asks questions to clarify what the other is saying.
- Each party actively listens to clarify what the other is saying.
- Each party tries to view the situation from the other's perspective.

Ethical Aspects of Negotiation

Because any negotiation involves people with different preferences trying to reach a joint decision, ethical behavior is often an issue. Managers, like anyone else involved in negotiation, should strive for high ethical standards even while participating in compelling negotiations where self-interests are paramount. Indeed, the motivation to behave unethically in negotiations is often a function of[16]

- **Profit motive** The desire of each party to "get more" than the other from the negotiation.
- **Sense of competition** The belief among negotiating parties that there are insufficient resources to satisfy everyone's needs.
- **Concerns for justice** The search by each party for outcomes defined as "fair" only from the narrow perspective of one's self-interests.

When unethical behavior occurs in negotiation, the parties involved often try to rationalize or explain it away. This is indicated by comments such as "It was clearly unavoidable," "Oh, it's harmless," "The results justify the means," or "It's really quite fair." Possible short-run gains from such after-the-fact rationalizations—like the satisfaction of having gotten one's way this time, may be offset by long-run negative consequences—such as not being able to achieve one's wishes again the next time. At the very least, the unethical party may be the target of "revenge" tactics by those who were disadvantaged. Furthermore, once some people have behaved unethically in one situation, they may become entrapped by such behavior and display it again in future circumstances.

In Summary

What is conflict?

- Conflict is a situation in which disagreements create frictions between individuals or groups.
- Conflict can be either substantive—based on work goals—or emotional—based on personal feelings.
- Conflict can be destructive and magnify performance problems; it may also be constructive and act as a stimulus to creativity and improved performance.

How can managers best deal with conflict?

- Conflict management should pursue the goal of conflict resolution, a situation where the underlying reasons for conflict have been eliminated.
- Indirect conflict management approaches include an appeal to common goals, hierarchical referral, and organizational redesign through buffering or the use of linking pins and liaison groups.
- Direct conflict management styles include collaboration and problem solving ("win–win"), direct competition or authoritative command ("win–lose"), and avoidance, smoothing, and compromise ("lose–lose").

What is negotiation?

- Negotiation occurs when two or more people with different preferences must make joint decisions.
- Both substance goals and relationship goals are important in any negotiation.
- Effective negotiation occurs when issues of substance are resolved and working relationships are maintained, or even improved, in the process.

What are the different approaches to negotiation?

- In distributive negotiation, each party stakes out positions in the attempt to claim desired portions of a "fixed pie." This approach to negotiation is similar to win–lose styles of conflict management.
- In integrative negotiation, sometimes called principled negotiation, each party focuses on the merits of the issues and tries to find ways to satisfy everyone's needs. This involves the collaboration and problem solving found in win–win styles of conflict management.

How do good managers deal with negotiation?

- Managers should avoid assuming that for someone to gain someone else must lose, escalating conflict based on bruised egos, and being insensitive to the needs of others.
- Managers should ask questions, listen actively to what others are saying, and try to see things from the other person's perspective.
- Managers should behave according to high ethical standards, even as negotiating parties present different viewpoints and preferences.

14

ORGANIZATIONAL

GOALS AND

STRUCTURES

As you read Chapter 14, keep in mind these study questions:

- What types of goals do organizations have, and what is the basis for these goals?

- What is the formal structure of the organization, and what is meant by the term *division of labor?*

- How does the firm control the actions of its members?

- How is formal authority allocated within the organization?

- What different patterns of horizontal specialization can be used in the organization?

- Which personal and impersonal coordination techniques should the organization use?

T his chapter should provide you with a working knowledge of organizational goals and the division of labor. We devote one major section to the types of goals an organization appears to seek. After a brief overview of the division of labor, we chart how organizations divide managerial duties and control both managers and units. The third major segment of this chapter charts how work is assigned to different parts of the organization and how the efforts in different departments are linked together. Collectively, these three sections provide a basic understanding of what the organization seeks and how it is organized.

Organizational Goals

Organizations, entities with goals,[1] seek to improve themselves over time in many different ways. The goals pursued in this quest for improvement are multifaceted and often conflict with one another. These goals are common to individuals within the organization only to the extent that managers and other members see how individuals' interests can be partially served by the organization. In this section, we examine two types of organizational goals. The firs type centers on how the organization intends to serve society; the second focuses on the organization's survival.

Societal Contributions of Organizations

Through societal contributions organizations may make claims over resources, individuals, markets, and products. When individuals believe that an organization contributes to societal goals they give it broader discretion than other firms. If favorably viewed, a firm may obtain some control at lower costs. A firm may lose this discretion by overemphasizing self-interest, by violating a public trust, or by falling into incompetence.

Just as an individual firm may lose the public's trust and confidence and, consequently, lose legitimacy, so a whole group of firms may also lose legitimacy. For example, in the very near future, the United States will need to obtain electric energy from sources that do not contribute to air pollution. Ideally, U.S. utilities could begin planning to build a new generation of ultra-safe nuclear-powered generating plants for the next century, but they cannot do so because they have lost the public's confidence. Instead, the newest nuclear technology is being planned for Europe and Japan.

Societal Goals and the Organization's Mission Organizations that can effectively translate the character of their societal contribution for their members have an advantage over those that cannot. That is, they have an additional set of motivational tools that are based on a shared sense of noble purpose. In a political party such a sense of purpose may help generate and allocate power for the betterment of all U.S. citizens. Similarly, a church attempts to instill values and to protect the spiritual well-being of all its members. Courts integrate the interests and activities of citizens. Finally, business firms provide economic sustenance and material well-being to society. Specifically, then, **societal goals** reflect an organization's intended contributions to the broader society.[2]

In sum, organizations normally serve a specific societal function or an enduring need of the society.[3] Astute top-level managers build on the organization's professed societal contribution by relating specific organizational tasks and activities to higher purposes.[4] **Mission statements**—written statements of organizational purpose—may incorporate these corporate ideas of service to the society.[5]

Primary Beneficiaries   Although some organizations may provide benefits to the society as a whole, most direct their efforts toward a particular group.[6] In the United States, for example, it is generally expected that the *primary beneficiary* of business firms are the stockholders. Political organizations are to serve the common good, while culturally based organizations, such as churches, may emphasize contributions to their members. In contrast to the internal focus of churches, social service organizations, such as hospitals, are expected to emphasize service to their clients and customers.

Many Japanese firms have a quite different view of organizational goals. Instead of making stockholders the primary beneficiaries, Japanese senior executives place long-time workers at the center of the firm. This approach ensures that those individuals with the proper expertise and the greatest stake in maintaining the company form the core of the organization. This approach is also consistent with the belief among Japanese managers that their role is to develop and expand the business to provide employment security and economic growth for the country. Stockholders are not given the priority of long-term employees. Rather, they are seen as important suppliers of money, just as component suppliers provide a manufacturer with vital raw materials.

Although each organization may have a primary beneficiary, its mission statement may also recognize the interests of many other parties. Thus, business mission statements often include service to customers, the organization's obligations to employees, and its intention to support the community.

Output Goals   Executives in many larger organizations find it useful to state the nature of their business in very careful terms.[7] This statement can form the basis for long-term planning and may help prevent huge organizations from diverting too many resources to peripheral areas. For some corporations, a detailed answer to "What is our business?" may yield a more detailed statement concerning their products and services. These product and service goals provide an important basis for judging the quality of an organization's major contributions to society.

In sum, **output goals** define the type of business an organization is in and provide some substance to the more general aspects of mission statements. Today firms are focusing on a more limited number of related businesses simply because they recognize a new reality: A global market has emerged in many of their industries. Firms find that they can develop world-class competency and compete across the globe by concentrating their efforts on a few product lines. For instance, Data General got into trouble because, as its CEO stated, it "went into 20 different businesses."[8]

Systems Goals and Organizational Survival

Many organizations are facing the immediate problem of just making it through the coming years and do not have the luxury of concentrating on societal contributions or of worrying about who their prime beneficiary should be. For instance, fewer than 10 percent of the businesses founded in a typical year can be expected to survive to their twentieth birthday.[9] The survival rate for public organizations is not much better. Even for organizations where survival is not an immediate problem, one can ask, "What are the types of conditions needed to minimize the risk of demise?" "What types of conditions promote survival?"

To answer these questions, executives may start by developing systems goals for their organizations. **Systems goals** are concerned with the conditions within the organization that are expected to increase the organization's survival potential. The list of systems goals is almost endless, for each manager and researcher links today's conditions to tomorrow's existence in a different way. For many organizations, however, the list includes growth, productivity, stability, harmony, flexibility, prestige, and, of course, human resource maintenance. For some businesses, analysts consider market share and current profitability important systems goals. Other recent studies suggest that innovation and quality also might be considered to be important.[10]

In a practical sense, systems goals represent short-term organizational characteristics that higher level managers wish to promote. Systems goals must often be balanced against one another. For instance, a productivity and efficiency drive may reduce an organization's flexibility. Different parts of the organization may be asked to pursue different types of systems goals. For example, higher level managers may expect to see their production operations strive for efficiency, while pressing for innovation from their R&D lab and promoting stability in their financial affairs.

The relative importance of different systems goals can vary substantially across various types of organizations. Although we might expect a university such as Cal Tech to emphasize prestige and innovation, few would expect businesses such as Siemans or AT&T to emphasize prestige over growth and profitability.

Systems goals are important to firms because they provide a road map that can help link together various units of an organization to assure its survival. Well-defined systems goals are practical and easy to understand; they focus the manager's attention on what needs to be done. Furthermore, accurately stated systems goals offer managers flexibility in devising ways to meet important targets; they can be used to balance the demands, constraints, and opportunities facing the firm; and they can form a basis for dividing the work of the firm into manageable pieces. In short, a firm's systems goals provide a basis for developing a formal structure.

Formal Structures and the Division of Labor

To help accomplish their goals, managers develop a **formal structure** that shows the intended configuration of positions, job duties, and the lines of authority among different parts of the enterprise. Traditionally, the formal structure of the firm has also been called the *division of labor.* Some observers still use this term to separate issues concerning the formal structure of the firm from related questions, such as those concerning the division of markets, the choice of businesses, or the selection of a technology. We emphasize the word "formal" simply because the intentions of organizational designers are never fully realized. Furthermore, no formal structure can provide all the detail needed actually to show the activities within a firm. Yet, the formal structure is still important because it provides the foundations for managerial action. That is, it outlines the job to be done, the person(s) (in terms of position) who will perform specific activities, and the ways in which the total task of the organization will be accomplished. In other words, it is the skeleton of the organization.

Organization charts are diagrams that depict the formal structures of organizations. A typical chart shows the various positions, the position holders, and the lines of authority that link them to one another. Figure 14.1 is a partial organization chart for a large university. The total chart allows university employees to locate their positions in the structure and to identify the lines of authority linking them with others in the organization. For instance, in this figure, the treasurer reports to the vice president of administration, who, in turn, reports to the president of the university.

Vertical Specialization

Most larger organizations make a clear separation of authority and duties by hierarchical rank. This separation represents **vertical specialization,** a hierarchical division of labor that distributes formal authority and establishes where and how critical decisions will be made. This division creates a hierarchy of authority, an arrangement of work positions in order of increasing authority.

In the United States, the distribution of formal authority is evident in the responsibilities typical of managers. Top managers or senior executives plan the overall strategy of the organization and plot its long-term future.[11] They also act as final judges for internal disputes and serve to certify promotions, reorganizations, and the like. Middle managers guide the daily operations of the organization, help formulate policy, and translate top-management decisions into more specific guidelines for action. Lower level managers supervise the actions of subordinates to ensure implementation of the strategies authorized by top management and compliance with the related policies established by middle management.

Managers' responsibilities in Japan are often different from those of managers in the typical U.S. firm. Top Japanese managers do not develop and decide the firm's overall strategy. Rather, they manage a process involving middle managers. The

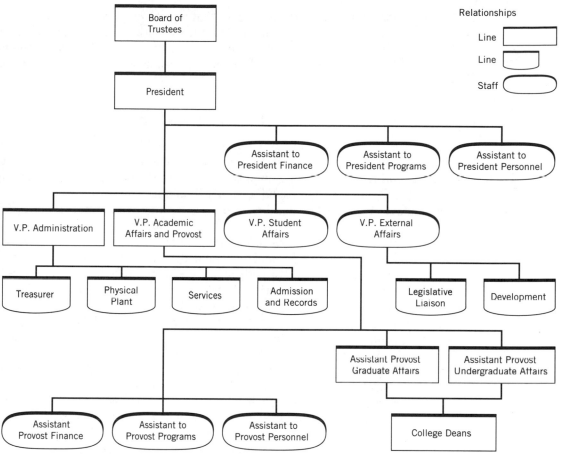

Figure 14.1 A partial organization chart for a state university.

process specifically entails extensive dialogue about actions the firm needs to take. Lower level managers are also expected to act as advocates for the ideas and suggestions of their subordinates. The strategy of the firm therefore emerges from dialogue and discussion, while implementation proceeds according to the ideas and suggestions of lower managers and nonmanagers.

In many European firms, the senior managers are highly trained in the core of their business. For example, it is not unusual for the head of a manufacturing firm to have a Ph.D. in engineering. Thus, many European executives become more centrally involved in plotting the technical future of their firm. In contrast, few U.S. executives have the necessary technical background to tackle this responsibility. Regardless of these differences in managerial responsibilities in Japan, Europe, and North America, all organizations have vertical specialization.

As managers move up the hierarchy, the scope of responsibility expands. Managers become accountable for more individuals, even though they may not directly supervise their activities. Specifying common goals and emphasizing common values are important functions, for they ensure that unseen subordinates will act as if the senior managers were directly supervising their work. As managers move up the hierarchy, they generally gain more discretion as well. We will build on the importance of discretion in our discussions of organizational politics (Chapter 10) and leadership (Chapter 11).

Chain of Command and the Span of Control

Executives, managers, and supervisors are hierarchically connected through the *chain of command.* Individuals are expected to follow their supervisors' decisions in the areas of responsibility outlined in the organization chart. Traditional management theory suggests that each individual should have one boss and that each unit should have one leader. Under the circumstances, there is a *unity of command.* Unity of command is considered necessary to avoid confusion, to assign accountability to specific individuals, and to provide clear channels of communication up and down the organization. Under traditional management with unity of command, the number of individuals a manager can directly supervise is obviously limited. The number of individuals reporting to a supervisor is called the **span of control.** Narrower spans of control are expected when tasks are complex, when subordinates are inexperienced or poorly trained, and when tasks call for team effort. Unfortunately, narrow spans of control yield many organizational levels. The excessive number of levels not only is expensive, but it also makes the organization unresponsive to necessary change. Communications in such firms often become less effective because they are successively screened and modified so that subtle but important changes get ignored. Furthermore, with many levels, managers are removed from the action and become isolated. Only when facing an identifiable, obvious, and direct threat might the firm with many levels be able to react quickly.

In the 1990s, firms have begun to experiment. They are dramatically cutting the number of levels of management, and they are expanding the span of control. In many cases, organizations are modifying the traditional notion of unity of command. Firms are taking a new look at how they use their staffs and are finding new ways of saving money while keeping the necessary skills within the firm.

Line and Staff Units

Line units and personnel conduct the major business that directly affect the organization. The production and marketing functions are two examples. In contrast, **staff units** and personnel assist the line units by providing specialized expertise and services, such as accounting and public relations. For example, in Figure 14.1, the vice president of administration heads a staff unit, as does the vice president of student affairs. All academic departments in the figure are line units because they constitute the basic production function of the university.

A useful distinction that can be made for both line and staff units concerns the amount and types of contacts each maintains with outsiders to the organization. Some units are mainly internal in orientation; others are more external in focus. The following description briefly summarizes the differences between them.

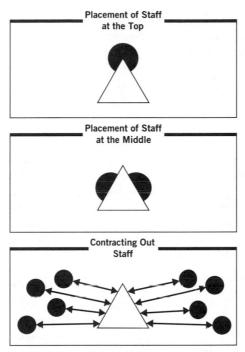

Figure 14.2 How placement of staff changes the look of an organization.

What to Do with the Staff On the surface, it would appear that firms need to handle all potentially useful staff functions. Someone needs to keep the books, hire and train the personnel, deal with the press, and conduct the research and development. In traditional management theory, the question was, How should a firm organize its staff units? In the 1990s, firms are beginning to ask whether certain staff should be a permanent part of the organization at all.

Staff units can be assigned predominantly to senior-, middle-, or lower level managers. When staff is assigned predominantly to senior management, senior management's capability to develop alternatives and make decisions is expanded. When staff is at the top, senior executives can directly develop information and alternatives and check on the implementation of their decisions. Here, the degree of vertical specialization in the firm is comparatively lower because senior managers plan, decide, and control via their centralized staff. In this case, lower level managers and employees often report that formal authority is concentrated at the top.

When staff are removed to the middle of the organization, middle managers see more delegation. They now get the specialized help they need to expand their role.

Figure 14.2 shows how staff placement can change the look of an organization. Unseen are the parallel changes in power as staff can be used to expand the power of middle management.

Many organizations in the 1990s are eliminating some staff units altogether. Manufacturing firms are spinning off much of their accounting, personnel, and public relations activities to small, specialized firms. These manufacturing firms are developing joint research and development agreements with suppliers, distributors, and even potential competitors to concentrate on their core operations. They are finding that, with highly trained managers and employees, middle- and lower level managers can contract out for the necessary staff services.[12]

Figure 14.2 also shows the use of staff via "contracting out." In large part, staff units can be eliminated only when the firm uses another important tool in vertical specialization: managerial techniques.

Managerial Techniques

As we have seen, merely adding staff may not provide the organization with increased efficiency. In fact, one of the foremost trends in modern industry is to streamline operations and reduce staff in order to lower costs and raise productivity.[13] One way to facilitate these actions is to provide line managers with managerial techniques designed to expand on their analytical and decision-making capabilities, thereby eliminating the need for staff "experts." Good examples are the ever increasing role of the computer and associated decision support software in all areas of management.

In one sense, managerial techniques are substitutes for both line and staff managers and staff units.[14] Managerial techniques may be used to detect problems and opportunities, to select among alternative courses of action, and to monitor the progress of implementation. For instance, students of financial management recognize the importance of financial planning models (in detecting problems), financial decision aids, such as capital budgeting models and discounted cash-flow analyses (for selecting among alternatives), and, of course, budgets (to monitor progress and ensure that managers stay within financial limits).

In another sense, managerial techniques are employed to expand the volume and scope of operations a manager can administer.[15] They can allow the manager to handle more sophisticated operations. Decision Support Systems (DSS) combine advances in computer hardware and software with the development of extensive information bases to aid line managers in decision making. More and more "expert systems" are also being created. These sophisticated computer programs can be used to duplicate the judgments of experts in areas calling for considerable skill, experience, intuition, and judgment.

Most organizations use a combination of line and staff units, alliances with specialized providers, as well as managerial techniques to specialize the division of labor vertically (e.g., to distribute formal authority). The most appropriate pattern of vertical specialization depends on the environment of the organization, its size, its technology, and its goals. Generally, as organizations grow, vertical specialization increases. We will return to this theme in the next chapter. For now, let us turn our attention to those issues relating to control of the organization.

Control

Control is the set of mechanisms used to keep action and outputs within predetermined limits. Control deals with setting standards, measuring results versus stan-

---

THE EFFECTIVE MANAGER 14.1

Signs of Too Much Control

Astute managers look for the signs that too much control or inappropriate controls have been placed on their units. They look for:

1. Too much emphasis on one measured goal to the exclusion of all others.
2. Too much emphasis on the quick fix and an unwillingness to look for underlying causes of problems or new opportunities.
3. A tradition of across-the-board cuts rather than reductions linked to demands, constraints, and opportunities.
4. Too many vague and unrealistic expectations that breed defeat.
5. Raising quotas without rewarding employees, particularly after implementing employee suggestions for change.

---

dards, and instituting corrective action. Although controls are needed in all organizations, just a few controls may go a long way. As noted in The Effective Manager 14.1, astute managers need to be aware of the danger of too much control in the organization.

Output Controls

Earlier in this chapter, we suggested that systems goals can be used as a road map to tie together the various units of the organization toward achieving a practical objective. Developing targets or standards, measuring results against these targets, and taking corrective action are all steps involved in developing output controls. **Output controls** focus on desired targets and allow managers to use their own methods for reaching defined targets.

Output controls are popular because they promote flexibility and creativity as well as facilitate dialogue concerning corrective action. Reliance on output controls separates what is to be accomplished from how it is to be accomplished. Thus, the discussion of goals is separated from the dialogue concerning methods. This separation can facilitate the movement of power down the organization, as senior managers are reassured that individuals at all levels will be working toward the goals senior management believes are important.

Process Controls

Few organizations run on outcome controls alone. Once a solution to a problem is found and successfully implemented, managers do not want the problem to recur and so they institute process controls. **Process controls** attempt to specify the manner in which tasks will be accomplished. There are many types of process controls, but three groups have received considerable attention: (1) policies, rules, and procedures, (2) formalization and standardization, and (3) quality management controls.

Policies, Rules, and Procedures Most organizations have a variety of policies, rules, and procedures. These policy controls may be used to help specify the goals of a worker, to indicate the best method for performing a task, to show which aspects of a task are the most important, or to outline how an individual will be rewarded. Usually, we think of a policy as a guideline for action that outlines important objectives and broadly indicates how an activity is to be performed. A policy allows for individual discretion and minor adjustments without direct clearance by a higher level manager. For example, most U.S. firms have a stated policy toward diversity that not only states the firm's goals for increasing the diversity of the workforce but also specifies the procedures to be used in hiring.

Rules and procedures are more specific, rigid, and impersonal than policies. They typically describe in detail how a task or series of tasks are to be performed. They are designed to apply to all individuals, under specified conditions. For example, most car dealers have detailed instruction manuals for repairing a new car under warranty, and they must follow strict procedures in order to obtain reimbursement from the manufacturer for warranty work.

Rules, procedures, and policies are employed as substitutes for direct managerial supervision. Under the guidance of written rules and procedures, the organization can specifically direct the activities of many individuals. It can ensure virtually identical treatment across even distant work locations. Rules, procedures, and policies also allow organizations to practice management by exception. Managers need not concentrate on the routine activities or decisions. They can spend their time on more important, unusual, or unique conditions that may have a more direct impact on performance and satisfaction.

Formalization and Standardization   **Formalization** refers to the written documentation of rules, procedures, and policies to guide behavior and decision making. Beyond substituting for direct management supervision, formalization is often used to simplify jobs. Written instructions allow individuals with less training to perform comparatively sophisticated tasks. Written procedures may also be available to ensure that a proper sequence of tasks is executed, even if this sequence is only performed occasionally.

Most organizations have developed additional methods for dealing with recurring problems or situations. **Standardization** is the degree to which the range of allowable actions in a job or series of jobs is limited. It involves the creation of guidelines so that similar work activities are repeatedly performed in a similar fashion. Such standardized methods may come from years of experience in dealing with typical situations, or they may come from outside training. For instance, managers may be trained to handle crises by setting priorities and dealing with them at all costs. Obviously, such situations call for judgment and cannot be handled by written rules— no written rules could anticipate every possible crisis.

Quality Management   Policies, rules, and procedures, in addition to formalization and standardization, represent the lessons of experience within an organization. That is, managers institute these process controls based on past experience. Another way to institute process controls is to establish a quality management process within the firm.

W. Edwards Deming is the modern-day founder of what is now referred to as the

---

THE EFFECTIVE MANAGER 14.2

W. Edwards Deming's 14 Points for Quality

1. Create a consistency of purpose in the company to
   a. innovate
   b. put resources into research and education
   c. put resources into maintaining equipment and new production aids.
2. Learn a new philosophy of quality to improve every system.
3. Require statistical evidence of process control and eliminate financial controls on production.
4. Require statistical evidence of control in purchasing parts; this will mean dealing with fewer suppliers.
5. Use statistical methods to isolate the sources of trouble.
6. Institute modern on-the-job training.
7. Improve supervision to develop inspired leaders.
8. Drive out fear and instill learning.
9. Break down barriers between departments.
10. Eliminate numerical goals and slogans.
11. Constantly revamp work methods.
12. Institute massive training programs for employees in statistical methods.
13. Retrain people in new skills.
14. Create a structure that will push, every day, on the above 13 points.

---

total quality management movement. The heart of Deming's approach is to institute a process approach to continual improvement based on statistical analyses of the firm's operations. Around this core idea, Deming built a series of 14 points for managers to implement (see The Effective Manager 14.2).[16] As you read the table, note that all levels of management are to be involved in the quality program. Where the properties of the firm's outcomes are well defined, as in most manufacturing operations, Deming's system and emphasis on quality appear to work well. Where the products of the firm and the methods of production are more subjective, successful application of statistical methods is more difficult. Nonetheless, the emphasis on training, learning, and consistency of purpose appears to provide an important lesson that all organizations need to be reminded of constantly.

Allocating Formal Authority

So far, we have examined vertical specialization and control. We have stressed the various uses of output and process controls but have said very little about how the use of controls is matched with vertical specialization. Different firms use very different mixes of vertical specialization, output controls, process controls, and managerial techniques to allocate the authority or discretion to act. In the next chapter, we will outline how different mixes are used by firms of different sizes, with different technologies, and under different competitive conditions. For employees, however, the key to understanding the mix is knowing how they, as individuals, respond to the degree of discretion or freedom to act they are given.

Centralization and Decentralization

The farther up the hierarchy of authority the discretion to spend money, to hire people, and to make similar decisions is moved, the greater the degree of **centralization.** The more such decisions are delegated, or moved down the hierarchy of authority, the greater the degree of **decentralization.** Generally speaking, greater decentralization provides higher subordinate satisfaction and a quicker response to problems. Decentralization also assists in the on-the-job training of subordinates for higher level positions. Decentralization is now a popular approach in many industries.

Closely related to decentralization is the notion of *participation*. Many people want to be involved in making decisions that affect their work. Participation results when a manager delegates some authority for such decision making to subordinates. As we have discussed, employees may want a say in both what the unit objectives should be and how they may be achieved.[17] Especially in recent years and in light of the challenge from the Japanese forms of participation, even conservative firms are experimenting with new ways to decentralize parts of their operations. Throughout this book, we have provided numerous examples of employee empowerment. The foundation of empowerment on the part of the organization is the development of decentralization matched with extensive participation and supported by few managerial levels and few bureaucratically based controls (such as rules and procedures). Firms have found that just cutting the number of organizational levels was insufficient; they also needed to alter their controls toward quality and to stress constant improvement. Furthermore, they needed to change other basic features of the organization, such as the division of work among units or the firm's horizontal specialization.

Horizontal Specialization

Vertical specialization and control are only half the picture. Managers must also divide the total task into separate duties and group similar people and resources together.[18] **Horizontal specialization** is a division of labor that establishes specific work units or groups within an organization; it is often referred to as the *process of departmentation*. Let us examine three basic forms of horizontal specialization: departmentation by function, division, and matrix.

Departmentation by Function

Grouping individuals by skill, knowledge, and action yields a pattern of **functional departmentation.** In business, marketing, finance, production, and personnel are important functions. In many small firms, this functional pattern dominates.

The advantages of the functional pattern include clear task assignments consistent with an individual's training where individuals with similar training are located in one department and can easily learn from one another. Thus, it provides an excellent training ground for new technical managers, and it is easy to explain to others. With all these advantages, it is not surprising that the functional form is extremely popular. It is used in most organizations, particularly toward the bottom of the hierarchy. Of course, functional specialization also has some disadvantages. It may reinforce the narrow training of specialists; it may yield long, complex channels of communication; and instead of looking to serve clients and customers, individuals may concentrate on serving their bosses.

Organizations that rely heavily on functional specialization may expect the following tendencies to emerge over time:

- An emphasis on quality from a technical standpoint.
- Rigidity to change, particularly if change within one functional area is needed to help other functional areas.
- Difficulty in coordinating the actions of different functional areas, particularly if the organization must continually adjust to changing external conditions.

Departmentation by Division

Divisional departmentation groups individuals and resources by products, services, clients, or legal entities. This pattern is often used to meet diverse external threats and opportunities.

Many larger, geographically dispersed organizations that sell to national and international markets use departmentation by geography. The savings in time, effort, and travel can be substantial, and each territory can adjust to regional differences. Organizations that rely on a few major customers may organize their people and resources by client. Here, the idea is to focus attention on the needs of the individual customer. To the extent that customer needs are unique, departmentation by customer can also reduce confusion and increase synergy. Organizations expanding internationally may also divisionalize to meet the demands of complex host-country ownership requirements.

The major advantages of departmentation by division begin with adaptability and flexibility in meeting external demands, particularly as new demands are emerging. It facilitates the integration of specialized personnel even toward the bottom of the firm, and it highlights performance in terms of products, services, clients, or territories. The disadvantages include too much duplication of effort, often by individuals who lack hands-on training in a particular functional area. Division goals can displace organizational objectives, and conflict between divisions often occurs when they are asked to share projects, individuals, and resources. Yet this pattern can help improve customer responsiveness for organizations that operate in many territories, produce quite different products and services, serve a few major customers, or operate internationally.

Organizations that rely heavily on divisional specialization can generally expect the following tendencies to occur over time:

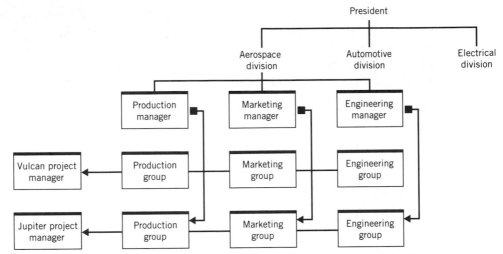

Figure 14.3 A matrix pattern of departmentation in an aerospace division.

- An emphasis on flexibility and adaptability to the needs of important external units.
- A lag in the technical quality of products and services vis-à-vis functionally structured competitors.
- Difficulty in coordination across divisions, particularly where divisions must work closely or sell to each other.

Departmentation by Matrix

From the aerospace industry, a third unique form of departmentation was developed; it is now called **matrix structure.**[19] In aerospace efforts, projects are technically complex, and they involve hundreds of subcontractors located throughout the world. Precise integration and control are needed across many sophisticated functional specialties and corporations. This is often more than a functional or divisional structure can provide. Thus, departmentation by matrix uses both the functional and divisional forms simultaneously. Workers and supervisors in the middle of the matrix have two bosses—one functional and one project. (See Figure 14.3 for an example.)

The major advantage of the matrix form is combining the strengths of both the functional and divisional forms by blending both technical and external emphasis. Thus, over time it provides the organization with managers who are conversant with both technical and marketing concerns. Unfortunately, these advantages come at substantial costs. Not only is the matrix form of departmentation very expensive but also there is a loss of the unity of command since many individuals have more than one boss. The authority and responsibilities of managers overlap, and as a result conflicts and gaps in effort across units often emerge. If you believe it is difficult to envision a matrix, do not feel you are alone. Many employees and managers have difficulty understanding precisely who should be doing specific tasks and who is in charge.

Many organizations use elements of the matrix structure without officially using the term *matrix*. For example, special project teams, coordinating committees, and task forces can be the beginnings of a matrix. Yet, these temporary structures can be used within a predominantly functional or divisional form and without upsetting the unity of command of hiring additional managers.

Mixed Forms of Departmentation

As the matrix concept suggests, it is possible to departmentalize using two different methods at the same time. Actually, organizations often use a mixture of departmentation forms. It is often desirable to divide the effort (group people and resources) by two methods at the same time in order to balance the advantages and disadvantages of each.

A very typical pattern for large organizations is to combine the functional and divisional forms. Division presidents may report to a chief executive officer (CEO). These line units are often treated as strategic business units (SBUs) or quasi-independent firms. Yet the firm may often have a whole series of functionally organized staff units reporting to the office of the CEO. These units might include law, finance, auditing, investor relations, government relations, and the like.

Coordination

Coordination is the set of mechanisms that an organization uses to link the actions of its units into a consistent pattern. Much of the coordination within a unit is handled by its manager. Smaller organizations may rely on their management hierarchy to provide the necessary consistency. As the organization grows, however, managers become overloaded. The organization then needs to develop more efficient and effective ways of linking work units to one another.

Personal Methods of Coordination

Personal methods of coordination produce synergy by promoting dialogue, discussion, innovation, creativity, and learning, both within and across organizational units. Personal methods allow the organization to address the particular needs of distinct units and individuals simultaneously.

There are a wide variety of personal methods of coordination. Perhaps the most popular is direct contact between and among organizational members. The development of an effective informal network of contacts within the organization often underlies an effective executive. In recent years, a number of new technologies have improved the potential for developing and maintaining effective contact networks. For example, many executives use electronic mail and direct computer links to supplement direct personal communication.

Direct personal contact is also associated with the ever present "grapevine." Although the grapevine is notoriously inaccurate in its role as the corporate rumor mill, it is often both quick and accurate enough that managers cannot ignore it. Instead, managers need to work with and supplement the rumor mill with accurate information.

Managers are also often assigned to numerous committees to improve coordination across departments. Even though committees are generally expensive and have a very poor reputation, they can become an effective personal mechanism for mutual adjustment across unit heads. Committees can be effective in communicating complex qualitative information and in helping managers whose units must work together to adjust schedules, work loads, and work assignments to increase productivity.

As more organizations develop flatter structures with greater delegation, they are finding that task forces can be quite useful. Although committees tend to be long lasting, task forces are typically formed with a more limited agenda. Individuals from different parts of the organization are assembled into a task force to identify and solve problems that cut across different departments.

Over a long period of time, individuals within the firm may develop a shared set of values that allow them to predict accurately the responses of others to specific events. Developing a shared set of values is so important to effective management that we will spend a large part of Chapter 16 discussing it.

Impersonal Methods of Coordination

Impersonal coordination methods are often refinements and extensions of process controls, with an emphasis on formalization and standardization. Most larger organizations have written policies and procedures, such as schedules, budgets, and plans, that are designed to mesh the operations of several units into a whole.

The most highly developed form of impersonal coordination comes with the adoption of a matrix form of departmentation. As noted earlier, this form of departmentation is expressly designed to coordinate the efforts of diverse functional units. Few organizations use a matrix structure, however. Today, organizations are more likely to use task forces.

In earlier periods, large organizations developed a whole series of specialized staff units to coordinate the efforts of divisionalized units. For instance, a centralized personnel staff would ensure that all operative divisions used a common set of selection and evaluation criteria. On the one hand, centralized staff units promote consistency and the use of the most modern techniques across all organizational units. On the other hand, centralized staff units are expensive and may enforce consistency where it is not needed. Furthermore, they may block creativity and innovation deeper within the organization.

The final example of impersonal coordination mechanisms is undergoing radical change in many modern organizations. Originally, management information systems were developed and designed so that senior managers could coordinate and control the operations of diverse subordinate units. These systems were intended to be computerized substitutes for schedules, budgets, and the like. In some firms, the management information system still operates as a combined process control and impersonal coordination mechanism. In the hands of astute managers, the management information system becomes an electronic network, linking individuals throughout the organization. Using decentralized communication systems, supplemented with the phone, FAX machine, and electronic mail, a once centrally controlled system becomes a supplement to personal coordination.

In the 1990s, firms are finding that personal coordination mechanisms supplemented with modern communications networks are providing for more effective coordination to meet the ever changing needs of a highly competitive marketplace. Although firms recognize that impersonal methods appear to be cheaper, they are also aware that those methods are less flexible and cannot support the mutual adjustment necessary in today's business.

In Summary

What types of goals do organizations have and what is the basis for these goals?

- Organizations have many types of goals.
- Societal concerns establish the basis for the organization's mission.
- Systems goals (e.g., profit and innovation) establish a basis for its survival and prosperity.

What is the formal structure of the organization and what is meant by the term "division of labor"?

- Formal structures of organizations are typically represented on an organizational chart.
- The formal structure defines the basic division of labor within the organization and identifies the number of management levels in the hierarchy of authority.
- Vertical specialization is the hierarchical division of labor.

How does the firm control the actions of its members?

- Control is a basic management function. It is the set of mechanisms the organization uses to keep action and/or outputs within predetermined levels.
- Output controls focus on desired targets and allow managers to use their own methods for reaching the desired target.
- Process controls attempt to specify the manner in which tasks will be accomplished.

How is formal authority allocated within the organization?

- Centralization/decentralization deal with the discretion to act and the empowerment of this discretion.

What different patterns of horizontal specialization can be used in the organization?

- Horizontal specialization is the division of labor that results in various work units or groups in the firm.
- Three main types of organization structure's "departmentation" are functional, divisional, and matrix departmentation.
- Each of these structures has advantages and disadvantages.

Which personal and impersonal coordination techniques should the organization use?

- Coordination is the set of mechanisms that an organization uses to link the actions of separate units.
- Impersonal methods of control, such as centralized staff units, have traditionally been used in large corporations.
- Firms are learning to use more personal methods of coordination.

15

ORGANIZATIONAL

DESIGN

As you read Chapter 15, keep in mind these study questions:

- Are there basic differences in the organizational design of small and large firms?

- Does the technology of the firm dictate its organizational design?

- What is the relationship between environmental conditions and organizational design?

- What are hybrid designs, and how does the firm balance environmental and technological demands?

- What is strategy, and how are firms combining generic strategies and their own unique competencies?

W e all recognize that the Chrysler auto assembly plant and the musical group Pearl Jam are quite different. Auto assembly plants are organized to emphasize routine, efficient production. In contrast, the musical group is loose, experimental, and organized for artistic expression, even though the logistics of travel, the movement of the equipment, and the sale of the tickets are highly organized. In this chapter, we discuss how managers adjust the basic elements of organizational structure to fit the scale of the operation, the job to be done, the demands of outsiders, and the ways in which senior management intends to compete.

The process of choosing and implementing a structural configuration is referred to as **organizational design.**[1] Our discussion of organizational design will emphasize how executives, like Lee Iacocca, should adjust the structural configuration of their organizations to best meet the challenges faced at any given point in time.

Scale and Organizational Design

Perhaps the most obvious and most easily recognized factor in designing an organization is the firm's scale of operations. Large organizations cannot just be bigger versions of their smaller counterparts. Although there are many reasons for this, we will concentrate on three important differences size makes in the design of the organization.

As the number of individuals in a firm increases arithmetically, the number of possible interconnections among them increases geometrically. In other words, it is impossible to maintain direct interpersonal contact among all members in a large organization. Thus, impersonal coordination techniques must be substituted for direct personal contact. Policies, rules, and procedures are used as substitutes for direct supervision both to save money and to ensure consistency.

One of the competitive strengths of larger organizations can be their efficiency. Economies of scale are possible when an organization can produce products and services efficiently through repetition. Specialization of labor, equipment, and departments is one way of capturing the potential economies of scale. As noted in Chapter 14, increasing specialization calls for increased control and coordination to ensure that action is directed toward common goals and linked together in a meaningful way.

Larger organizations are often more complex than their smaller counterparts in terms of their products, production processes, geographic locations, and the like.

This additional complexity calls for a more sophisticated organizational design. Before discussing these more complex designs, however, it is important to review some basics. First, we examine the structure of a small, comparatively simple organization since simple designs are the basic building blocks. We then examine types of bureaucracies and the conglomerate. Simple designs, bureaucracies, and even the conglomerate are only starting points for analysis, however. Each firm must select its design not only to match scale issues but also to meet the important demands, constraints, and opportunities that arise from its technology, the environment it selects, and the strategy it wishes to pursue.

The Simple Design

The **simple design** is a configuration involving one or two ways of specializing individuals and units. That is, vertical specialization and control typically emphasize levels of supervision without elaborate formal mechanisms (e.g., rule books, policy manuals), and the majority of the control is based in the manager. One or two ways of organizing departments are used, and coordination mechanisms are often personal. The organization visually resembles a pyramid with few staff individuals or units.

The simple design is appropriate for many small firms, such as family businesses, retail stores, and small manufacturing firms.[2] The strengths of the simple design are simplicity, flexibility, and responsiveness to the desires of a central manager—in many cases, the owner. Because a simple design relies heavily on the manager's personal leadership, however, this configuration is only as effective as is the senior manager.

The Bureaucracy

The simple design is a basic building block of all organizations, but as the organization grows, additional layers of management and more specialized departments are added. Line and staff functions are separated, and the organization may begin to expand its territorial scope. In this way, larger organizations become much more structurally complex than small ones.[3] The nature of the organization changes as layers of management increase, as the division of labor and coordination mechanisms become more elaborate, and as formal controls are established. Reliance on a single senior manager is downplayed, and "levels" of management exercise varying degrees of authority.

The famous German sociologist Max Weber suggested that large organizations would thrive if they relied on legal authority, logic, and order.[4] Weber argued that relying on a division of labor, hierarchical control, promotion by merit with career opportunities for employees, and administration by rule were superior to the simple design. To simplify his analysis, Weber created ideal types. Though not found in reality, these "ideal types" highlighted important aspects of organizations. He labeled one ideal type of organization the **bureaucracy.** What we have called the simple design, Weber called a "charismatic" ideal-type organization because its success depends so much on the talents of one individual. For efficiency, Weber pre-

---

THE EFFECTIVE MANAGER 15.1

The Natural Dysfunctional Tendencies of a Bureaucracy

All large organizations must systematically work to minimize the dysfunctional characteristics of the modern bureaucracy. Among these dysfunctions are tendencies to:

1. Overspecialize and neglect to mitigate the resulting conflicts of interest resulting from specialization.
2. Overuse the formal hierarchy and emphasize adherence to official channels rather than problem solving.
3. Reify senior managers as superior performers on all tasks and rulers of a political system rather than as individuals who should help others reach goals.
4. Overemphasize insignificant conformity that limits individual growth.
5. Treat rules as ends in and of themselves rather than as poor mechanisms for control and coordination.

---

ferred the bureaucracy to the simple structure. He hoped that it could also be fairer to employees and provide more freedom for individual expression. Weber correctly predicted that bureaucracy, or some variation of his ideal form, would dominate modern society. Yet, as shown in The Effective Manager 15.1 managers must also avoid some natural dysfunctions of bureaucracy as well.

All the Fortune 500 firms, including Chrysler, GE, IBM, and Texaco, are bureaucracies. Each must work to minimize the dysfunctional tendencies typical of bureaucracies. However, there are subtle but important differences in the way each organization is designed, which builds on the firm's strengths and minimizes its weaknesses. No one design is preferred. The organizational design adopted by a particular firm needs to "fit" a whole series of internal and external realities. Before discussing these contingencies, however, it is important to present some basics of organizational design. We will discuss three popular options: the mechanistic, the organic, and the divisionalized approaches.

Mechanistic Designs and the Machine Bureaucracy   The **mechanistic design** is a highly bureaucratic organization that emphasizes vertical specialization and control. Organizations of this type stress rules, policies, and procedures; specify techniques for decision making; and emphasize developing well-documented control systems backed by a strong middle management and supported by a centralized staff. Henry Mintzberg uses the term **machine bureaucracy**[5] to describe an entire organization that is characterized in this manner. Visually, the machine bureaucracy resembles a tall, thin pyramid with a bulge at the top for the centralized senior staff (see Figure 15.1).

The mechanistic design results in a management emphasis on routine for efficiency. It is quite popular in basic industries with large-scale operations, such as banks, insurance companies, and government offices. When the organization is viewed as too rigid and centralized, however, employees may not like such designs. In a strict hierarchy, where most authority is concentrated at the top, it is also not

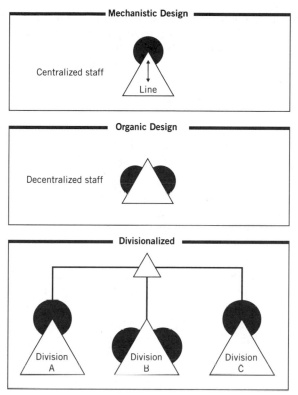

Figure 15.1 Visual depiction of different basic design options.

surprising to find that mechanistic designs can hinder an organization's capacity to adjust to external changes or new technologies. Facing stiff competition from the Japanese, some of the mechanistically designed U.S. auto firms have attempted some dramatic changes, becoming more participative, flexible, and innovative. Both Ford and Chrysler have cut unnecessary rules and procedures, reduced centralized staff, and developed smaller, more autonomous work teams.

Organic Designs and the Professional Bureaucracy The **organic design** is much less vertically oriented than is the mechanistic design. Here, the design strategy emphasizes horizontal specialization. Procedures are minimal, and those that do exist are not as formalized. The organization relies on the judgments of experts and personal means of coordination. When controls are used, they tend to reinforce professional socialization, training, and individual reinforcement. Staff units tend to be placed toward the middle of the organization. (See Figure 15.1.)

What Mintzberg calls a **professional bureaucracy** often relies on organic features in its design.[6] Your university is probably a professional bureaucracy that looks like a broad, flat pyramid with a large bulge in the center for the professional staff. Power in this ideal type rests with knowledge. Moreover, the elaborate staff typically helps the line managers and often has very little formal power. The standardization of professional skills and the adoption of professional routines, standards, and procedures enhance control. Other examples include hospitals, consulting firms, libraries, and social service agencies.

The organic design stresses communication across the organization and focuses attention on customers and technology. Although not as efficient as the mechanistic design, the organic design is better for problem solving and for serving individual customer needs. Because this design emphasizes lateral relations and coordination, centralized direction by senior management is less intense. Thus, this design is good at detecting external changes and adjusting to new technologies, but at the sacrifice of responding to central management direction.[7]

Divisionalized Organizations   Many very large firms find that neither the mechanistic nor the organic designs are suitable for all their operations. Adopting a machine bureaucracy would overload senior management and yield too many levels of management.[8] Yet, adopting an organic design would mean losing control and becoming too inefficient. Some firms find that, although their businesses are related, some businesses call for an organic structure and others for a mechanistic one. The solution is the **divisionalized design,** whereby the firm establishes a separate structure for each business or division (see Figure 15.1). The classic divisional organization was created by Alfred Sloan for General Motors, when he divided GM's operations into divisions for designing and producing Chevys, Olds, Pontiacs, Buicks, and Cadillacs.[9] Each division was treated as a separate business, and each business competed against each other.

In the divisionalized organization, coordination across businesses is provided by a comparatively small centralized staff that offers support, such as financial services and legal expertise. Senior line management provides direction and control over the presumably "autonomous" divisions. In very large organizations, this approach can free top management to establish strategy and concentrate on large, long-term problems. Divisional heads run their own businesses and compete for resources, yet each enjoys the support (financial, personnel, legal, etc.) of the larger parent.

This form is expensive, for redundant staff and support units must be developed for each division. Nonetheless, it allows the firm greater flexibility to respond to different markets and customers. Yet, tension between divisional management and senior management is quite often apparent. It is very difficult for corporate executives and corporate staff to allow the divisions to operate as independent businesses. Over time, senior staff may grow in size and force "assistance" on the divisions. Because they compete for common resources, coordination across divisions is often also quite difficult.

The Conglomerate

In the 1960s, a few organizations began to grow by buying unrelated businesses. On the surface, these firms looked like divisionalized firms, but the various businesses of the divisions were so unrelated that a new term had to be invented. Firms that owned several different unrelated businesses are called **conglomerates.** Pure conglomerates have not done particularly well in the United States mainly because substantive knowledge of the various businesses is often needed for them to be successfully managed.[10]

The line between the divisionalized form and the conglomerate can often be confusing. For our purposes, the key question is whether or not synergy (potential positive linkages) exists among the various businesses owned by the corporation. If there is considerable synergy, we call the firm divisionalized; if there is little synergy, the firm is a conglomerate.

With the wave of mergers and acquisitions in the 1980s, several corporations became conglomerates, as raiders bought and sold various businesses. Here, structure and organizational design, other than cost cutting, were not important; financial manipulation was the key to short-term success. For example, RJR-Nabisco was created through a series of financial maneuvers that brought together a food company and a tobacco firm.

Many state and federal entities are, by necessity, also conglomerates. For instance, a state governor is the chief executive officer of those units concerned with higher education, welfare, prisons, highway construction/maintenance, police, and the like.

Technology and Organizational Design

Thus far, our discussion has suggested that the organization's design will be influenced by its size. On the one hand, a number of scholars argue that the size of an organization is the single most important factor influencing its structure.[11] As size increases, the organization's structure is predicted to become more complicated. On the other hand, a second group argues that a **technological imperative** is involved. That is, successful organizations are said to arrange their internal structures to meet the dictates of their dominant "technologies" or workflows.[12]

Technology

Technology is the combination of resources, knowledge, and techniques that creates a product or service output for an organization. The term is used in various ways in the OB literature. Thus, it will help you to become acquainted with two of the more common classification schemes used by theorists and managers to describe the technologies of organizations.

Thompson's View of Technology James D. Thompson classifies technologies as intensive, mediating, or long-linked. Under *intensive technology,* there is uncertainty as to how to produce desired outcomes.[13] A group of specialists must be brought together to use a variety of techniques to solve problems. There is high interdependence among the members of such teams. Examples are found in a hospital emergency room or a research and development laboratory. It is difficult to develop standard operating procedures for intensive technology, and coordination is achieved by mutual adjustment among those trying to solve the problem.

The *mediating technology* links parties that want to become interdependent. For example, banks link creditors and depositors and store money and information to facilitate such exchanges. Although all depositors and creditors are interdependent, the reliance is pooled through the bank. Thus, if one creditor defaults on a loan, no one depositor is injured. Wholesalers, retailers, and insurance companies are other organizations that use a mediating technology.

The *long-linked technology* is also called mass production or industrial technology. In this case, since the way to produce the desired outcomes is known, the task is broken down into a number of sequential and interdependent steps. A classic example is the automobile assembly line. Traditionally, long-linked technology has been relatively inflexible, with a high output volume required to justify its use. Now, we are entering an era of flexible manufacturing in which mass production can be automated while the organization still maintains some flexibility for the future.

Woodward's View of Technology   Joan Woodward divides technology into three categories: small-batch, mass production, and continuous-process manufacturing.[14]

In units of *small-batch production,* a variety of custom products are tailor made to fit customer specifications, such as tailor-made suits. The machinery and equipment used are generally not very elaborate, but considerable craftsmanship is often needed. In *mass production,* the organization produces one or a few products with an assembly-line type of system. The work of one group is highly dependent on another; the equipment is typically sophisticated; and the workers are given very detailed instructions. Automobiles and refrigerators are produced in this way. Mass production is similar to Thompson's long-linked technology. Organizations using *continuous-process technology* produce a few products with considerable automation. Classic examples are automated chemical plants and oil refineries.

From her studies, Woodward concluded that the combination of structure and technology was critical to the success of the organizations. When technology and organizational design were properly matched, a firm was more successful. Specifically, successful small-batch and continuous-process plants had flexible structures with small work groups at the bottom; more rigidly structured plants were less successful. In contrast, successful mass production operations were rigidly structured and had large work groups at the bottom. This technological imperative has since been supported by various investigations. Yet, today we recognize that technology is just one factor involved in the success of an organization.

Where Technology Dominates: The Adhocracy

More recent work on the role of technology in organizations has taken a much broader perspective. Even though the technology of a firm may favor a particular pattern of specialization, other factors may not. The history of the firm, the attitudes of top management, and a host of economic and political factors may work against organizations that attempt to follow the technological imperative.[15]

The influence of technological considerations is most clearly seen in small organizations and in specific departments within large ones. In some instances, managers and employees simply do not know the appropriate way to service a client or to produce a particular product. This is the extreme of Thompson's intensive type of technology and may be found in some small-batch processes where a team of individuals must develop a unique product for a particular client.

Mintzberg suggests that at these technological extremes, the "adhocracy" may be an appropriate structure.[16] An **adhocracy** is characterized by

- Few rules, policies, and procedures.
- Very decentralized, shared decision making among members.
- Extreme horizontal specialization, as each member of the unit may be a distinct specialist.
- Few levels of management.
- Virtually no formal controls.

The adhocracy is particularly useful when an aspect of the firm's technology presents two sticky problems: (1) the tasks facing the firm vary considerably and provide many exceptions, as in a hospital, and (2) problems are difficult to define and resolve.[17]

The adhocracy places a premium on professionalism and coordination in problem solving. This structure is particularly suited to helping professionals solve technical problems. As such, adhocracies are often used as a supplement to other designs to offset their dysfunctional effects.[18] Firms use temporary task forces, special committees, and even contract consulting firms to provide the creative problem identification and problem solving that the adhocracy promotes. For instance, Lotus Development Corporation creates new autonomous departments to encourage talented employees to develop new software programs. Allied Chemical and 3M also set up quasi-autonomous groups to work through new ideas.

Environment and Organizational Design

If organizational design were merely dictated by size and technological concerns, it would be comparatively easy to specify a configuration for any particular organization. But an effective organizational design reflects powerful external forces as well as the desires of employees and managers. Here, we will focus more on the competitive elements that drive the particular organizational design.

The General and Specific Environments

Organizations, as open systems, need to receive various inputs from the environment and to sell various outputs to their environment. Therefore, we need to be more specific about what the environment is and what elements are likely to be important.[19]

The **general environment** is the set of cultural, economic, legal–political, and educational conditions found in the areas in which the organization operates. The owners, suppliers, distributors, government agencies, and competitors with which an organization must interact in order to grow and survive constitute its **specific environment.**

A firm typically has much more choice over the composition of its specific environment than of its general environment. It can develop policies and strategies to alter the mix of owners, suppliers, distributors, and competitors with which it interacts. For example, the senior managers of the firm may choose to operate in well-developed industries where production techniques are known and where there is a well-developed set of suppliers and distributors. Conversely, the firm may enter the arena of high technology. Some senior managers select a portfolio of related divisions and develop a divisionalized structure. In this case, each divisional design must match the technology and specific environmental conditions facing each division, and the firm may be held together by a small centralized staff.

Although it is often convenient to separate the general and specific environmental influences on the firm, designers need to recognize the combined impact of both. Choosing some businesses, for instance, means entering global competition with advanced technologies. As the Xerox Corporation has found, the nature of the business itself may change with globalization and new technology and require the firm to respond in novel ways.[20]

Environmental Complexity

A basic concern that must be addressed in analyzing the environment of the organization is its complexity. A more complex environment provides an organization with both more opportunities and more problems. **Environmental complexity** is an estimate of the magnitude of the problems and opportunities in the organization's environment, as evidenced by the degree of environmental richness, interdependence, and uncertainty stemming from both the general and specific environment.[21]

Environmental Richness   Overall, the environment is richer when the economy is growing, when individuals are improving their education, and when others the organization relies on are prospering. For businesses, a richer environment means that economic conditions are improving, customers are spending more money, and suppliers (such as banks) are willing to invest in the future of the organization. In a rich environment, more organizations survive, even if they have poorly functioning organizational designs. A richer environment is also filled with more opportunities and dynamism—the potential for change. The organizational design will need the capability to recognize these opportunities and capitalize on them. The opposite of richness is decline. For business firms, a general recession is a good example of a leaner environment. Although corporate reactions vary, it is instructive to examine three typical responses to decline. First, in Japan, core manufacturing firms do not lay off core workers. Instead, they cut the hours of females, move some individuals to long-term suppliers, and initiate training for the remaining workers to prepare for a recovery.

Second, in the United States, firms have traditionally reacted to decline by first issuing layoffs to nonsupervisory workers and then moving up the organizational ladder as the environment became leaner. In the 1980s and 1990s, however, large firms started to alter their organizational designs by cutting staff units and the number of organizational levels in response to more sustained periods of decline. This downsizing is traumatic but can be minimized.

Third, many European firms find it very difficult legally to cut full-time employees when the economy deteriorates. In many cases, firms have turned to national governments for help in sustained periods of decline. Much as in U.S.-based firms, changes in organizational design are viewed as a last but increasingly necessary resort.

Environmental Interdependence   The link between external interdependence and organizational design is often subtle and indirect. The organization may co-opt powerful outsiders by including them. For instance, many large corporations have financial representatives on their boards of directors. The organization may also adjust its overall design strategy to absorb or buffer the demands of a more powerful external element. Perhaps the most common adjustment is the development of a centralized staff department to handle an important external group. For instance, few large U.S. corporations are without some type of governmental relations group at the top. Where service to a few large customers is considered critical, the organization's departmentation is likely to switch from a functional to a divisionalized form.

Increasing internationalization by firms changes not only the number of general environments in which they operate, but also the pattern of interdependencies on others. When environmental interdependence becomes more diffuse, as when Hewlett-Packard successfully internationalized, the design of the firm must become more sophisticated.

Uncertainty and Volatility   Environmental uncertainty and unpredictable volatility can be particularly damaging to large bureaucracies. In times of change, investments quickly become outmoded, and internal operations no longer work as expected. The obvious organizational design response to uncertainty and volatility is to opt for a more organic form. At the extremes, movement toward an adhocracy may be important. However, these pressures may run counter to those that come from large size and technology. It may be too hard or too time consuming for some organizations to make the design adjustments in these cases. Thus, the organization may continue to struggle while adjusting its design just a little bit at a time. Unfortunately, small, unsuccessful attempts at marginal adjustments to the design can often be followed by abrupt and massive changes that may not be sufficient to save the firm.

Hybrid Designs: Balancing Technological and Environmental Demands

As just suggested, technological pressures and environmental conditions can work at cross purposes. The three bureaucratic designs (mechanistic, organic, and divisionalized) may not provide the firm with an appropriate configuration to meet diverse demands and constraints or to capitalize on oppportunities. Here, we discuss two design options. One deals with adjustments to the mechanistic and organic bureaucracies discussed earlier; the other emphasizes the use of alliances.

Bureaucratic Adjustments

As we note in Chapter 17 on planned organizational change, firms often have considerable difficulty changing their design and internal operations. Where possible, firms will attempt to keep their core line operations in tune with technological requirements and to adjust staff units to meet environmental requirements.

An Organic Core with a Mechanistic Shell   Earlier, we suggested that the technology of the organization may call for an organic design to promote flexibility, creativity, and innovation. In reality, there may be organizational limits on the use of a purely organic design. For example, when environmental demands are backed up by powerful external groups, the organization may respond by developing a series of top-level and very mechanistic staff units. This strange design of mechanistic staff units at the top with very organic line units toward the middle and bottom of the organization can externally protect the organization while still allowing responsible internal operations.

A Mechanistic Core with an Organic Shell   Very large organizations with technologies that call for mechanistic designs and economies of scale are vulnerable to environmental uncertainty and volatility. A partial solution to the problem is to wrap these inflexible cores within organic staff units. The staff units have two purposes. First, to the extent possible, they often attempt to change the external conditions by moderating the volatility in the specific environment. Second, they can attempt to absorb or buffer as many changes as possible. This second option is found most often in firms that must balance efficient production with flexible marketing and design operations. Although the assembly line is mechanistically structured, products may be designed by more organically structured teams.

Strategic Alliances

Strategic alliances are announced cooperative agreements or joint ventures between two independent firms. These agreements often involve corporations that are headquartered in different nations.[22] In high-tech areas, such as robotics, semiconductors, advanced materials (ceramics and carbon fibers), and advanced information systems, a single company frequently does not have all the knowledge necessary to bring new products to the market. Often, the firms with the knowledge are not even in the same country. In this case, the organizational design must go beyond the boundaries of the organization into strategic alliances.

   Strategic alliances are quite common in these high-technology industries, as firms not only seek to develop technology but also to make sure that their solutions become standardized across regions of the world. In some cases, the fight for a dominant design pits one nation against another. For instance, Zenith joined forces with AT&T to develop one high-definition television (HDTV) system, while Toshiba,

Sony, and some 30 other Japanese firms formed a strategic network to develop their own system. The U.S. winner will likely get the lion's share of the estimated $20 billion HDTV market in North America. Of course, firms may also develop alliances just to explore potentials for future collaboration.

In more developed industries, strategic alliances are also quite popular, but they are often known by other names. In Europe, for example, they are called informal combines or cartels: Competitors work cooperatively to share the market to decrease uncertainty and improve favorability for all. Except in rare cases, these arrangements are often illegal in the United States.

In Japan, strategic alliances among well-established firms in many industries are quite common. The network of relationships is called a *Keiretsu*. There are two common forms. The first is a bank-centered *Keiretsu*, where firms are linked to each other directly via cross ownership and through historical ties to one bank. The Mitishibi group is a good example. The second type has been called a vertical *Keiretsu*. Here, a key manufacturer is at the hub of a network of supplier firms. The manufacturer typically has both long-term supply contracts with members and cross-ownership ties. These arrangements help isolate Japanese firms from stockholders and provide a mechanism for sharing and developing technology. Toyota is an example of a firm at the center of the vertical *Keiretsu*.

The United States is beginning to see the evolution of the *network organization*. In this organization, the central firm specializes in a core activity, such as design and assembly. The firm works with a comparatively small number of participating suppliers on a long-term basis for both component development and manufacturing efficiency. More extreme variations of this network design are also emerging to meet apparently conflicting environmental, size, and technological demands simultaneously. Firms are spinning off staff functions to reduce their overall size and concentrate their internal design on technological dictates.

Strategy and Organizational Design

Organizational strategy is the process of positioning the organization in its competitive environment and implementing actions to compete successfully.[23] The study of linking strategy, organizational design, and firm performance has a long tradition in organizational analysis. For instance, in the 1960s, Alfred Chandler studied the evolution of major U.S. firms and concluded that structure follows from the strategy established predominantly by senior management. More recent work suggests that a winning strategy is more likely when the firm recognizes both the importance of a singular direction and the unique skills and abilities within the firm.

The strategy process is a two-way street within the organization. On the one hand, senior managers select those systems goals they believe should define corporate success; form these goals into a vision; select a target position within the general and specific environments; and develop a design to accomplish the vision. Senior managers often use so-called generic strategies to help guide their choices. On the other hand, the firm develops specific administrative and technical competencies

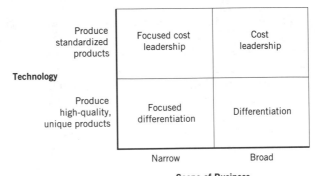

Figure 15.2 Types of generic strategies as affected by the organization's scope of business and technology.

through time. Middle- and lower level managers institute minor modifications and adjustments to solve specific problems and capitalize on specific opportunities. These adjustments are then moved up the organizational ladder. They provide senior managers with the opportunity to adjust, modify, and build on a generic strategy to develop a so-called competency strategy.

Generic Strategies

Four types of generic strategies (as shown in Figure 15.2) are common to many businesses.[24] They are:

1. Focused differentiation.
2. Focused cost leadership.
3. Differentiation.
4. Cost leadership.

These four strategic types are based on some simplified assumptions. The first assumption is that management must decide on the scope of its operations. If the firm is large and selects a broad range of customers and markets, it has breadth; if the choice is narrow, the firm has focus. The second assumption is that management selects technology to produce either comparatively inexpensive, standardized products or more expensive, tailor-made products and services. If the firm competes by providing lower cost, standardized products, it relies on the economies of scale for cost leadership. If it produces higher quality, unique products (even if only in the minds of customers), it differentiates itself.

Matching Generic Strategy and Organizational Design

The Effective Manager 15.2 shows some ideal combinations of size, technology, and design for each of the four strategy types. It essentially summarizes many of the points we have previously made in this chapter. As suggested in the table, no one

THE EFFECTIVE MANAGER 15.2			

Examples of Fit Among Environment, Size, Technology,
Strategy, and Organizational Design

	FOUR STRATEGY TYPES			
	Focused Differentiation	Focused Cost Leadership	Differentiation	Cost Leadership
Environment:				
richness	rich	lean	rich	mixed
interde-pendence	high	high	high	low
volatility	high	stable	stable	mixed
Size	small	medium	large	very large
Technology	intensive	long linked	mediating	mixed intensive
Organization Design	adhocracy	machine	professional bureaucracy	divisionalized bureaucracy
Example	Bio-tech firm:	Steel Mill: Auto Parts Supplier	Prestigious re-search univer-sity: Regional care hospital	Exxon

strategy is always best. Rather, an organization has a better chance of prospering if it can "fit" its strategy and structure to environmental requirements.

Take the example of a small biotechnology firm. In a comparatively new and growing industry, the firm is on the leading edge of technological development. By emphasizing innovation and unique product quality, it can grow and prosper. The strategy is focused differentiation. If the organization is small, and the technical problems are substantial, the organization design need tilts toward the adhocracy. As the organization grows, organic designs based on professionalism, problem solving, and flexibility may be consistent with the need to resolve technical problems, to adjust to specific customer requirements, and to ensure quality.

When faced with growing competition and more customers, some organizations opt for an efficiency strategy and cost leadership. By limiting choices and providing standardized products and services, these organizations can cut production costs and offer lower prices. By capitalizing on economies of scale, for instance, McDonald's and Burger King can produce a standardized hamburger, milkshake, and fries for a fraction of the full-service restaurant's cost. The cost leadership or efficiency strategy places a premium on routinization, standardization, and consistency. Thus, it is little wonder that more mechanistic designs will be preferred.

Competency-based Strategies

Although the list of generic strategies provides a quick overall guide for many senior managers, it is obvious that the firm needs to have the skills and abilities to capitalize on the intended generic strategy; just saying you want your firm to be a technical leader and instituting an adhocracy does not get the job done.

A key to success for most organizations is an appropriate modification of the generic strategy so that the organization builds on and refines its unique experience and competencies. In the process of building on its capabilities, the firm may actually shift generic strategies or combine elements of two generic strategies. In the 1990s, generic strategies are providing the jumping-off point for many corporations, for they must rely on the creativity, innovation, and skills of all their employees.

Kodak, for instance, is on the move, entering into alliances to improve its technical competence in electronic imaging. These moves go beyond personal empowerment or employee participation in implementing the strategy of the firm. Employees and middle managers build a unique strategy based on their skills and abilities. Senior executives at such firms as Ford, AT&T, and Dow are now recognizing that an effective strategy builds on the competence of employees. Technical skills combined with astute management in an organizational design that reinforces employee contribution are fundamental to organizational success in the 1990s and beyond.

In Summary

Are there basic differences in the organizational design of small and large firms?

- Small firms often adopt a simple structure. Larger firms often adopt a bureaucratic form. The bureaucracy is an ideal form based on legal authority, logic, and order.
- Mechanistic designs emphasize focus and work best in stable environments.
- Organic designs stress flexibility and work best in more dynamic settings.
- The divisionalized and conglomerate options involve a mixture of mechanistic and organic units.

Does the technology of the firm dictate its organizational design?

- Technology and organizational design are interrelated.
- Some argue that technology is most important.
- This position is known as the technological imperative.

What is the relationship between environmental conditions and organizational design?

- Environmental and organizational design are interrelated.
- In analyzing environments, both the general (background conditions) and specific (key actors and organizations) environments are important.

- The more complex the environment, the greater the demands on the organization.

What are hybrid designs and how does the firm balance environmental and technological demands?

- When technology and the environment place apparently conflicting demands on the organization, hybrid organizational designs may be used.
- Organizations must respond with more complex designs that often blend mechanistic and organic forms.

What is strategy and how are firms combining generic strategies and their own unique competencies?

- Strategy positions an organization in its competitive environment.
- Four generic strategies pursued by businesses are differentiation, focused differentiation, cost leadership, and focused cost leadership.
- Differentiation strategies are most consistent with organic structures and divisionalization.
- Cost leadership strategies emphasize routinization and efficiency and call for more mechanistic structures.
- Effective managers are able to build upon competency-based strategies to modify and extend the generic strategies

ORGANIZATIONAL

CULTURE

As you read Chapter 16, keep in mind these study questions:

- What is the concept of corporate culture?

- What are the observable aspects of corporate culture?

- What is meant by the phrase *shared values,* and why are these values so important?

- What common assumptions can link individuals together?

- Can the corporate culture be "managed," or are *nurtured* and *guided* more appropriate terms?

- How are ethics and corporate culture tied together?

As we approach the beginning of a new century, many organizations—from the giant auto manufacturers to the small software design firms—are undergoing a transformation. At all levels of operations, people are striving for productivity. Quality, innovation, and value are replacing the drive toward short-term efficiency. Managers are recognizing the need to build viable organizations that stand for something and are rediscovering the critical importance of human resources. The old methods of command and control are being replaced by new methods of participation and involvement. Managers are becoming facilitators, helpers, guides, and coaches. Simply put, today's managers are beginning to change the very essence of what it means to work in the modern organization. In our terminology, they are changing their organization's *culture*. As we will see, a strong and clear culture can be a distinct competitive advantage for an organization.

The Concept of Organizational Culture

In Chapter 3, we examined "culture" as it applies internationally and ethnically to the various nations and peoples of the world. In this chapter, we are concerned with **organizational culture**—the system of shared beliefs and values that develops within an organization and guides the behavior of its members.[1] In the business setting, this system is often called the *corporate culture.* Just as no two individual personalities are the same, no two organizational cultures are perfectly identical. Most significantly, management scholars and consultants increasingly believe that cultural differences can have a major impact on the performance of organizations and the quality of work life experienced by their members. Edger Schein, for example, singles out Digital Equipment Corporation (DEC) as a case in point:[2]

> A strong culture emerged from the entrepreneurial approach of Digital Equipment's founder Ken Olsen. Generations of DEC managers learned Olsen's way of seeing the world—focus on opportunities, not problems— and the role of the firm in that world—solve customer problems and create new opportunities. Wherever you go in DEC, within the United States or in other countries, personnel share common assumptions about how the business should be run. Although this strong culture was an advantage, some critics suggest it has become a liability in the 1990s as

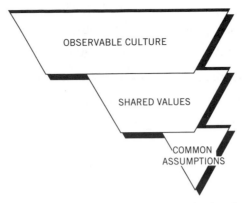

Figure 16.1 Three levels of analysis in studying organizational culture.

DEC is struggling to adjust to a new generation of computers in which the mainframe is no longer king and customers are more diverse.

Levels of Cultural Analysis

Figure 16.1 depicts three important levels of cultural analysis in organizations: observable culture, shared values, and common assumptions. These may be envisioned as layers. The deeper one gets, the more difficult it is to discover the culture.

The first level concerns *observable culture,* or "the way we do things around here."[3] These are the methods that the group has developed and teaches to new members. The observable culture includes the unique stories, ceremonies, and corporate rituals that make up the history of a successful work group.

The second level of analysis recognizes that *shared values* can play a critical part in linking people together and can provide a powerful motivational mechanism for members of the culture. Many consultants suggest that organizations should develop a "dominant and coherent set of shared values."[4] The term *shared* in cultural analysis implies that the group is a whole. Not every member may agree with the shared values, but they have all been exposed to them and have often been told they are important.

At the deepest level of cultural analysis are common assumptions, or the taken-for-granted truths that collections of corporate members share as a result of their joint experience. It is often extremely difficult to isolate these patterns, but doing so helps explain why culture invades every aspect of organizational life. These common assumptions may surface in an organizational crisis.

For instance, to avert bankruptcy, the board of trustees at Mills College in California voted to admit men to the all-women college. They claimed that the changeover to coeducation was an economic necessity. However, when students, alumnae, and administrators demonstrated the educational importance and unique contributions of an all-women's liberal arts college, the board retreated. These often separate constituencies united to develop a new plan to save the tradition and philosophy that they all believed to be fundamental to Mills.

Subcultures and Countercultures

It is often important to recognize distinct groups within a culture. **Subcultures** are groups of individuals with a unique pattern of values and philosophy which is not inconsistent with the organization's dominant values and philosophy.[5] Interestingly, strong subcultures are often found in high-performance task forces, teams, and special project groups in organizations. The culture emerges to bind individuals working intensely together to accomplish a specific task.

In contrast, **countercultures** have a pattern of values and a philosophy that reject the surrounding culture.[6] The anti-apartheid counterculture in South Africa and the Solidarity movement in Poland of the 1980s are two vivid examples of counterculture on a national scale. In the first week of President Clinton's term in 1993, the press was filled with arguments regarding whether or not homosexuals should be allowed to state their sexual preference and still serve in the military. Some argued it was time to be more inclusive, while others were shocked and morally outraged at the idea. Each side of the controversy claimed the other was a minority counterculture.

Within an organization, mergers and acquisitions may produce countercultures. Employers and managers of an acquired firm may hold values and assumptions that are quite inconsistent with those of the acquiring firm. This is known as the "clash of corporate cultures."[7] In the 1980s, Coca-Cola bought Columbia Pictures and began integrating Columbia operations into the Coca-Cola family. Too late, however, the soft-drink company found out that the picture business was quite different from the business of pushing sugar-flavored water. To be successful, Columbia had developed its own culture. Sony has now bought it and is trying to mesh itself with Columbia. Sony might succeed, but the movie subsidiary got off to a very poor start, and many of the senior Columbia managers were terminated.[8]

Imported Subcultures and Cultural Diversity

Every large organization imports potentially important subcultural groupings when it hires employees from the larger society. In the United States, for instance, subcultures and countercultures may naturally form, based on ethnic, racial, gender, generational, or locational similarities. In Japanese organizations, subcultures often form based on the date of graduation from a university, by gender, or by location. In European firms, ethnicity and language play an important part in developing subcultures, as does gender. In many less developed nations, language, education, religion, or family social status are often grounds for forming societally popular subcultures and countercultures.

The difficulty with importing groupings from the larger societies lies in the relevance these subgroups have to the organization as a whole. At the one extreme, senior managers can merely accept these divisions and work within the confines of the larger culture. This approach poses three primary difficulties. First, subordinated groups, such as members of a specific religion or an ethnic group, are likely to form into a counterculture and to work more intensely to change their status than to better the firm.

Second, the firm may find it extremely difficult to cope with broader cultural changes. For instance, in the United States, the expected treatment of women, ethnic minorities, and the disabled has changed dramatically over the last 20 years. Firms that merely accept old customs and prejudices have experienced a greater loss of key personnel and increased communication difficulties and interpersonal conflict than have their more progressive counterparts.

Third, firms that accept and build on natural divisions from the larger culture may find it extremely difficult to develop sound international operations. For example, many Japanese firms have had substantial difficulty adjusting to the equal treatment of women in their U.S. operations.

At the other extreme, managers can work to eradicate all naturally occurring subcultures and countercultures. In the 1990s, firms are groping to develop what Taylor Cox calls the "multicultural organization." The **multicultural organization** is a firm that values diversity but systematically works to block the transfer of societal-based subcultures into the fabric of the organization.[9] Although Cox focuses on some uniquely U.S. problems, his prescription for change appears to apply to organizations located in many different countries as well.

Cox suggests a five-step program for developing the multicultural organization.

1. The organization should develop pluralism with the objective of multibased socialization. To accomplish this objective, members of different, naturally occurring groups need to school one another to increase knowledge and information and to eliminate stereotyping.

2. The firm should fully integrate its structure so that there is no direct relationship between a naturally occurring group and any particular job. For instance, there are no distinct male or female jobs.

3. The firm must integrate the informal networks by eliminating barriers and increasing participation; that is, it must break down existing societally based informal groups.

4. The organization should break the linkage between naturally occurring group identity and that of the firm. In other words, the firm should not be just for the young, old, men, women, and so on.

5. The organization must actively work to eliminate interpersonal conflict based on group identity and the natural backlash of the largest societal-based grouping.

When the society is in turmoil concerning the treatment of societally defined subcultures and groups, it is no wonder that corporations have difficulty coping. Consider the range of sticky issues involved in hiring personnel. Does the firm select on the basis of performance criteria (if it can measure these), or does it attempt to rectify past discrimination? Does the national firm select new managers from all regions where it operates, or should it concentrate on selecting managers from specific schools to ensure that managers share a common underlying culture?

Of course, the key problems associated with fully implementing Cox's program are separating the firm from the larger culture in which it must operate and eliminating some societal-based groupings that are relevant for achieving the firm's goals. For instance, the U.S. military is barred from fully implementing Cox's recommendations simply because it is not currently legal to put women into all combat roles. The issue of generational groupings provides another example. Implementing Cox's recommendations would call for 20 year olds to be represented proportionally in the senior management ranks; but most corporations want and need the judgment honed by experience.

The Functions of Organizational Culture for Its Members

In your first managerial job, you might get lucky. After extensive interviews and some formal training, your new boss will most likely explain what is expected of you. Then, the stark reality will hit, as you perceive the large gap between your education and the actual job at hand. If you are lucky, one of the old hands on the job will sit down with you and explain exactly what is to be done, how it is to be done, and why it is done in a particular way. Experienced individuals know what to do and are aware of all the informal rules surrounding their roles in the firm.

Through their collective experience, members of an organization solve two extremely important survival issues. The first is the question of external adaptation: What precisely needs to be accomplished, and how can it be done? The second issue is that of internal integration: How do members resolve the daily problems associated with living and working together?

External Adaptation

External adaptation issues involve reaching goals and dealing with outsiders. These issues involve the tasks to be accomplished, the methods used to achieve the goals, and the methods of coping with success and failure.

Through their shared experiences, members may develop common views that help guide their day-to-day activities. Organizational members need to know the real mission of the organization, not just the pronouncements to key constituencies, such as stockholders. Members will naturally develop an understanding of how they contribute to the mission via interaction. This view may emphasize the importance of human resources, or it may emphasize the role of employees as cogs in a machine or as a cost to be reduced.

Closely related to the organization's mission and view of contribution are the questions of responsibility, goals, and methods. For instance, in many GM plants, employees believe that following procedures, reaching quantitative outcome targets, and following orders that are consistent with work rules are appropriate responsibilities, goals, and methods.

Each collection of individuals in an organization tends to do the following: (1) separate more important from less important external forces; (2) develop ways to measure their accomplishments; and (3) create explanations for why goals are not always met.

The final issues in external adaptation deal with two important, but often neglected, aspects of coping with external reality. First, individuals need to develop acceptable ways of telling outsiders just how good they are. At 3M, for example, employees talk about the quality of their products and the many new useful products they have brought to the market. At GM, the talk has more often centered on financial ratios. Second, individuals must collectively know when to admit defeat. At 3M, the answer is easy for new projects: At the beginning of the development process, members establish "drop" points at which to quit the development effort and redirect it.

In sum, external adaptation involves answering important instrumental or goal-related questions concerning coping with reality: What is the real mission? How do we contribute? What are our goals? How do we reach our goals? What external forces are important? How do we measure results? What do we do if specific targets are not met? How do we tell others how good we are? When do we quit?

Internal Integration

Although the questions of external adaptation help a collection of individuals cope with a changing environment, the corporate culture also provides answers to the problems of internal integration. **Internal integration** deals with creating a collective identity and with finding ways of matching methods of working and living together.

The process of internal integration often begins by establishing a unique identity; that is, each collection of individuals and each subculture within the organization develops some type of unique definition of itself.

Through dialogue and interaction, members begin to characterize their world. They may see it as malleable or fixed, filled with opportunity or threatening. For instance, real progress toward innovation can begin when group members collectively believe that they can change important parts of the world around them and that what appears to be a threat is actually an opportunity for change.

Three important aspects of working together are (1) deciding who is a member and who is not; (2) developing an informal understanding of acceptable and unacceptable behavior; and (3) separating friends from enemies. For example, effective total quality management holds that subgroups in the organization need to view their immediate supervisor as a member of the group who is expected to represent them to friendly higher managers.

To work together effectively, individuals need to decide collectively how to allocate power, status, and authority. They need to establish a shared understanding of who will get rewards and sanctions for specific types of actions. Too often, managers fail to recognize these important aspects of internal integration. For example, a manager may fail to explain the basis for a promotion and to show why this reward, the status associated with it, and the power given to the newly promoted individual are consistent with commonly shared beliefs.

Collections of individuals need to work out acceptable ways to communicate and to develop guidelines for acceptable friendships. Although these aspects of internal integration may appear esoteric, they are vital. To function effectively as a team, individuals must recognize that some members will be closer than others; friendships are inevitable. However, the basis for friendships can be inappropriately restricted to important divisions outside the firm.

As we mentioned in the discussion of the multicultural organization, managers can work to eliminate bias and watch friendships develop across imported societal divisions. In some firms, managers who are promoted up the ladder are expected to leave their old friends behind. In more progressive firms, this is not the case.

In sum, internal integration involves answers to important questions associated with living together. What is our unique identity? How do we view the world? Who is a member? How do we allocate power, status, and authority? How do we communicate? What is the basis for friendship? Answering these questions is important to organizational members because the organization is more than a place to work; it is a place where individuals spend much of their adult life.

Bringing Executives and Employees Together

We have just seen how the organizational culture helps members by providing answers to important questions of external adaptation and internal integration. There is often an important difference in the answers given to these questions by executives toward the top of the organization and members at the bottom. Senior executives may owe their primary allegiance to their position in the firm. They may identify with the organization as a whole. They may equate organizational and individual success, and they may want all others in the organization to believe much the same. They may believe they are better than mere employees. Naturally, they expect to be handsomely rewarded. Conversely, employees may see themselves as part of a larger, more varied, and complex network of relationships. The job may be just an instrumental mechanism, such as a means of getting the financial rewards necessary to live. The interplay among these various levels of management may establish an overall tone for the firm.[10]

Much of the rest of this chapter is devoted to a discussion of how to bring all organizational members into active participation within the firm on both instrumental and substantive grounds (such as satisfaction of social, competency, and related issues). In the 1990s, more organizations will need to eliminate the separations between executives and employees which have been fostered by traditional bureaucratic hierarchies. For some organizations, merging these apparently disparate groups will call for substantial cultural change on the part of both executives and employees.[11]

Observable Aspects of Organizational Culture

Important parts of an organization's culture emerge from the collective experience of it members. These emergent aspects of the culture help make it unique and may well provide a competitive advantage for the organization. Some of these aspects may be directly observed in day-to-day practices. Others may have to be discovered—for example, by asking members to tell stories of important incidents in the history of the organization. We often learn about the unique aspects of the organizational culture through descriptions of very specific events.[12] By observing employee actions, listening to stories, and asking members to interpret what is going on, we can begin to understand the organization's culture.

Stories, Rites, Rituals, and Symbols

Organizations are rich with stories of winners, losers, successes, and failures. Perhaps one of the most important stories concerns the founding of the organization. *The founding story* often contains the lessons learned from the heroic efforts of an embattled entrepreneur, whose vision may still guide the firm. The story of the founding may be so embellished that it becomes a *saga*—a heroic account of accomplishments.[13] Sagas are important because they are used to tell new members the real mission of the organization, how the organization operates, and how individuals can fit into the company. Rarely is the founding story totally accurate, and it often glosses over some of the more negative aspects of the founders.

If you have job experience, you may well have heard stories concerning the following questions: How will the boss react to a mistake? Can someone move from the bottom to the top of the company? What will get me fired? These are common story topics in many organizations.[14] Often, the stories will provide valuable hidden information about who is more equal than others, whether jobs are secure, and how things are really controlled. In essence, the stories begin to suggest how organizational members view the world and live together.

Some of the most obvious aspects of organizational culture are rites and rituals. **Rites** are standardized and recurring activities that are used at special times to influence the behaviors and understanding of organizational members; **rituals** are systems of rites. Japanese workers and managers, for example, commonly start their workdays together with group exercises and singing of the "company song." Separately, the exercises and song are rites; together, they form part of a ritual. In other settings, such as the Mary Kay Cosmetics Company, scheduled ceremonies reminiscent of the Miss America pageant (a ritual) are used regularly to spotlight positive work achievements and to reinforce high-performance expectations with awards, including gold and diamond pins and fur stoles.

Rituals and rites may be unique to particular groups within the organization. Subcultures often arise from the type of technology deployed by the unit, the specific function being performed, and the specific collection of specialists in the unit. The boundaries of the subculture may well be maintained by a unique language. Often, the language of a subculture, as well as its rituals and rites, emerges from the group as a form of jargon. In some cases, the special language starts to move outside the firm and to enter the larger society.

Of course, no discussion of corporate culture would be complete without mentioning the symbols found in organizations. A **cultural symbol** is any object, act, or event that serves to transmit cultural meaning. Good examples are the corporate uniform worn by UPS and Federal Express delivery personnel. Although many such symbols are quite visible, their importance and meaning may not be.

Shared Meanings

What you see as an outside observer may or may not be what organizational members see. You may see NASA personnel on television filling the tanks of a booster rocket for the space shuttle. If you could ask the workers directly what they are doing, you might be surprised by the answer. They are not just filling booster tanks; they are assisting with an important part of exploring space. Through interaction with one another, and as reinforced by the rest of the organization, the workers have infused a larger shared meaning—or sense of broader purpose—into their tasks. In this sense, organizational culture is a "shared set of meanings and perceptions that are created and learned by organizational members in the course of interactions."[15]

Cultural Rules and Roles

Organizational culture often specifies when various types of actions are appropriate and where individual members stand in the social system. These cultural rules and roles are part of the normative controls of the organization and emerge from its daily routines.[16] For instance, the timing, presentation, and methods of communicating authoritative directives are often quite specific to each organization. In one firm, meetings may be forums for dialogue and discussion, where managers set agendas and then let others offer new ideas, critically examine alternatives, and fully participate. In another firm, the "rules" may be quite different: The manager goes into the meeting with fixed expectations. Any new ideas, critical examinations, and the like are expected to be worked out in private before the meeting takes place. The meeting is a forum for letting others know what is being done and for passing out orders on what to do in the future.

Cultural rules and roles can become deeply ingrained in organizational behavior, as they influence "the way things are done around here." Many times, these rules and roles must be revised in order for the organization as a whole to accomplish planned change.

Values and Organizational Culture

In order to describe more fully the culture of an organization, you must go deeper than the observable aspects. To many researchers and managers, shared common values lie at the very heart of organizational culture. Shared values

- Help turn routine activities into valuable, important actions.

THE EFFECTIVE MANAGER 16.1

Elements of Strong Corporate Cultures

A widely shared philosophy—This philosophy is not an abstract notion of the future but a real understanding of what the firm stands for, often embodied in slogans.

A concern for individuals—This concern often places individual concerns over rules, policies, procedures, and adherence to job duties.

A recognition of heroes—Heroes are individuals whose actions illustrate the shared philosophy and concerns of the company.

A belief in ritual and ceremony—Management understands that rituals and ceremonies are real and important to members and to building a common identity.

A well-understood sense of the informal rules and expectations—Employees understand what is expected of them.

A belief that what employees do is important to others—Networking in order to share information and ideas is encouraged.

- Tie the corporation to the important values of society.
- May provide a distinctive source of competitive advantage.

Linking Actions and Values

Individuals collectively learn (invent, discover, and develop) behaviors and concepts in order to help them deal with their problems. In organizations, what works for one person is often taught to new members as the correct way to think and feel. Important values are then attributed to these solutions to everyday problems. By linking values and actions, the organization taps into some of the strongest and deepest realms of the individual. The tasks a person performs are given not only meaning but also value; what one does is not only workable but also correct, right, and important.

Some successful organizations share some common cultural characteristics. The Effective Manager 16.1 provides a list suggested by two popular consultants—Terrence Deal and Allan Kennedy.[17] As you can see from the table, organizations with "strong cultures" possess a broadly and deeply shared value system. Increasingly, organizations are adopting values statements that express their commitments to such matters as customer service, product and service quality, creativity and innovation, and social responsibility.

A strong culture can be a double-edged sword, however. Unique, shared values can provide a strong corporate identity, enhance collective commitment, provide a stable social system, and reduce the need for formal and bureaucratic controls. Conversely, a strong culture and value system can reinforce a singular view of the organization and its environment. If dramatic changes are needed, it may be very difficult to change the organization. Even though General Motors may have a "strong" culture, for example, the firm faces enormous difficulty in its attempts to adapt its ways in a dynamic and highly competitive environment.

Common Assumptions and Organizational Culture

In many corporate cultures, we find a series of common understanding known to nearly everyone in the corporation: "We are different." "We are better at . . ." "We have unrecognized talents." These shared truths, or common assumptions, often lie dormant until actions violate them.

Common Assumptions and Management Philosophy

Senior managers often share common assumptions, such as the following: "We are good stewards." "We are competent managers." "We are practical innovators." In many firms, broadly shared common assumptions by senior management go even further. The firm may have a well-developed management philosophy.

A **management philosophy** links key goal-related issues with key collaboration issues and comes up with a series of general ways by which the firm will manage its affairs. A well-developed management philosophy is important because

1. It establishes generally understood boundaries on all members of the firm.
2. It provides a consistent way of approaching new and novel situations.
3. It helps hold individuals together by assuring them of a known path toward success.

Elements of the management philosophy may be formally documented in a corporate plan, a statement of business philosophy, or a series of goals. Yet, it is the unstated but well-understood fundamentals these written documents signify that actually form the heart of a well-developed management philosophy.

In many firms, the management philosophy is supported by a series of organizational myths. **Organizational myths** are unproven and often unstated beliefs that are accepted uncritically. For example, in a study of safety in nuclear power plants, senior managers were asked if they felt there was a trade-off between safety and efficiency. The response was clear: A safe plant is an efficient plant. Yet, most of these executives had seen data showing that measures of safety and efficiency were quite independent. To admit there was a trade-off raised the issue of making choices between efficiency and safety. All wanted to believe that to do one was to promote the other.

Although some may scoff at these organizational myths and want to see rational, hard-nosed analysis replace mythology, each firm needs a series of managerial myths. Myths allow executives to redefine impossible problems into more manageable components. Myths facilitate experimentation and creativity, and they allow managers to govern. For instance, senior executives are not just decision makers or rational allocators of resources. All organization members hope these individuals will also be fair, just, and compassionate.

Common Assumptions and National Culture

It is often possible to trace widely held common assumptions to the larger culture of the corporation's host society. For instance, the difference between Sony's corporate emphasis on group achievements and Zenith's emphasis on individual engineering excellence can be traced to the Japanese emphasis on collective action versus the U.S. emphasis on individualism.

National cultural values may also become embedded in the expectations of important organizational constituencies and in generally accepted solutions to problems. When moving across national cultures, managers need to be sensitive to national cultural differences so that their actions do not violate common assumptions in the underlying national culture. For instance, in Japan and Western Europe, executives are expected to work cooperatively with government officials on an informal basis. Informal business/government relations that are perfectly acceptable in these countries would be considered influence peddling in the United States. Although some South American executives expect to pay directly for some government services, in the United States such payments are considered bribes.

In the 1960s, when IBM opened its operations in Japan, newly hired Japanese workers were shocked when an American executive indicated that the goal of the firm was to maximize stockholder wealth. In Japan, stockholders are a less important corporate stakeholder than are core employees. Employees are considered much more important than are mere stockholders because they are expected to dedicate their careers to one firm. Inappropriate actions that violate common assumptions drawn from the national culture can have an important impact on performance and may alienate organizational members, even if managers have the best intentions.

Managing Organizational Culture: Building, Reinforcing, and Changing Culture

In organizations with strong cultures, shared values and beliefs characterize a setting in which people are committed to one another and to an overriding sense of mission. This commitment can be a source of competitive advantage for these organizations over their rivals, as illustrated in The Effective Manager 16.2. It is quite possible that the organization you work for now, or will eventually work for, does not have a strong and resilient culture. Like the conglomerate organizational design discussed in Chapter 15, it may be more a collection of separate units and people who don't seem to share much in common. It is also possible that the organization may have a strong culture but that it is not one that meets the needs of a changing environment. Or the organization may be a mix of subcultures and countercultures. In this case, rivalries and value differences may create harmful conflicts.

For managers—especially top managers—managing organizational culture is a pressing issue. For managers in all organizations, the culture should be considered to be as critical as structure and strategy in establishing the organizational foundations of high performance. Good managers are able to reinforce and support an existing strong culture; they can also help build resilient cultures in situations where they are absent.

THE EFFECTIVE MANAGER 16.2

Using Corporate Culture to Help the Firm Compete

As more firms are moving into volatile industries using advanced technology and con-fronting international competitors, managers will need to help their corporate culture adjust. Here are some pitfalls to avoid and some factors to emphasize when entering and competing in highly volatile, high-tech markets, such as computers, biotechnology, and the like.

1. When entering the market early, do not allow employees to become disen-chanted when facing initial technical barriers and skill development chal-lenges.
2. When entering slowly, do not give competitors too big a lead; keep stressing the necessity of building technical and market skills with all employees.
3. When adding new products to an existing market, make sure that decision making and management of the new product fit new products as well as old ones; challenge old routines.
4. When adjusting to new markets with new products, avoid using "conventional wisdom" and stress the development of new ways to compete.

Managers can modify the visible aspects of culture, such as the language, stories, rites, rituals, and sagas. They can also change the lessons to be drawn from common stories and even encourage individuals to see the reality they see. Because of their positions, senior managers can interpret situations in new ways and can adjust the meanings attached to important corporate events. They can create new rites and rituals. This takes time and enormous energy, but the long-run benefits can also be great.

Top managers in particular can set the tone for a culture and for cultural change. For example, managers at Aetna Life and Casualty Insurance built on its humanistic traditions to provide basic skills to highly motivated but underqualified individuals. Frances Hesselbein of the Girl Scouts stressed the clear mission of helping girls reach their highest potential—in today's world, not yesterday's. Even in the highly cost-competitive steel industry, Chairperson F. Kenneth Iverson of Nucor built on basic entrepreneurial values in the U.S. society to reduce the number of manage-ment levels by half. And, at Procter and Gamble, Richard Nicolosi evoked the shared values for greater participation in decision making dramatically to improve creativity and innovation.

Each of these case examples illustrates how managers can help foster a culture that provides answers to important questions concerning external adaptation and internal integration. Recent work on the linkages among corporate culture and fi-nancial performance reaffirm the importance of an emphasis on helping employees to adjust to the environment. It also suggests that this emphasis alone is not suffi-cient. Nor is an emphasis solely on stockholders or customers associated with long-term economic performance. Instead, managers must work to emphasize all three issues simultaneously. Of course, this emphasis on customers, stockholders, and employees comes at a cost of emphasizing management. Large offices, multimillion-dollar salaries, golden parachutes (protections for executives if the firm is bought by others), as well as the executive plane, dining room, and country club are out.[18]

In these examples, we have witnessed the raw potential of tapping into the shared values of the corporation to build exciting, interesting, and innovative programs. In each case, the visionary manager knew the organization well enough to involve the keepers and holders of the culture and to build on what all the members shared. Sometimes, however, managers attempt to revitalize an organization by dictating major changes rather than by building on shared values. Whereas things may change a bit on the surface, a deeper look often shows whole departments resisting change and many key people unwilling to learn new ways. Such responses may indicate that the responsible managers are insensitive to the effects of their proposed changes on shared values. They fail to ask if the changes are

- Contrary to important values that have emerged from participants within the firm.
- A challenge to historically important corporatewide assumptions.
- Inconsistent with important common assumptions derived from the national culture, outside the firm.

Although reshaping shared values is an executive challenge of the first order, few executives are able to reshape common assumptions or "the take-for-granted truths" in a firm without drastic, radical action. Rodger Smith of General Motors realized this challenge and established a new division to produce the Saturn. At Harley Davidson, a new senior management team had to replace virtually all of the company's middle managers to establish a new, unique, and competitive culture. All too often, however, executives are unable to realize that they too can be captured by the broadly held common assumptions within their firms.

Ethics and Organizational Culture

We have already talked quite a bit about ethics in this book, and we'll continue to do so. For now, we framed the issue in a question: "Do organizations vary in the 'ethical climates' they establish for their members?" The answer to this question is "yes," and it is increasingly clear that the ethical tone or climate of an organization is set at the top. That is, what top managers do, and the culture they establish and reinforce, makes a big difference in the way lower level personnel act and in the way the organization as a whole acts when faced with ethical dilemmas.

The **ethical climate** of an organization is the shared set of understandings about what is correct behavior and how ethical issues will be handled. This climate sets the tone for decision making at all levels and in all circumstances. Many factors may be emphasized in different ethical climates of organizations.[19] The ethical climate can support doing what most individuals believe is the right thing. In other organizations—perhaps too many—concerns for operating efficiency may outweigh social considerations when difficult decisions are faced. Along with other aspects of organizational culture, therefore, the ethical climate will be an important influence on the behavior of individual members and the organization as a whole. When the ethical climate is clear and positive, everyone knows what is expected when the inevitable ethical dilemmas occur. They can then act confidently, knowing full well that they will be supported by top management and the entire organization.

In Summary

What is the concept of corporate culture?

- It is a system of shared beliefs and values that guide and direct the behavior of members.
- Culture can have a strong influence on day-to-day organizational behavior and performance.
- A well-developed culture can assist in responding to both internal and external problems.
- Organizations can also experience the strains of dealing with subcultures among various work units.
- Countercultures can become the source of potentially harmful conflicts.

What are the observable aspects of corporate culture?

- Observable aspects of culture include the stories, rites, rituals, and symbols that are shared by members.
- Cultural rules and roles similarly define expectations for behavior within an organization.

What is meant by the phrase *shared values,* and why are they so important?

- Values are "shared" when individuals are made aware of desired processes and end states whether they agree with them or not.
- Clearly articulated organizational values help guide and direct action.
- When in place and understood, clear and positive values can create a competitive advantage for a firm.
- They can be a unifying force that brings efforts to bear on highly desirable outcomes.

What common assumptions can link individuals together?

- Common assumptions are the taken-for-granted truths that are shared by collections of corporate members.

- Some organizations express these truths in a management philosophy that links key goal-related issues.
- The management philosophy may be supported by a series of corporate myths.

Can the corporate culture be "managed," or are *nurtured* and *guided* more appropriate terms?

- Managing organizational culture is increasingly considered a top-management task.
- It is an extremely difficult task, particularly where no such culture previously existed and/or change is needed to transform existing cultures to become more productive ones.
- To manage organizational culture effectively, the foundations must be established in the management of the culture's observable aspects and in the belief systems.
- Creating shared values among the membership is perhaps the biggest challenge.
- Top management can rarely alter shared meanings.

How are ethics and corporate culture tied together?

- The ethical climate of an organization is the shared set of understandings about what is correct behavior and how ethical issues will be handled.
- When properly established, a positive and clear ethical climate can help all organization members make good choices.
- When the organization is faced with ethical dilemmas, an ethical climate can give them the confidence to act with the understanding that what they are doing is considered correct and will be supported.

17

ORGANIZATIONAL

CHANGE AND

DEVELOPMENT

As you read Chapter 17, keep in mind these study questions:

- What is organizational change?

- What change strategies do managers use?

- Why do people resist change, and what can be done about it?

- How can stress be managed?

- What is organization development?

- How is organization development accomplished?

T he word "turbulence" is frequently used when managers refer to the current environment. Amidst the calls for greater productivity, total quality, and the like, people in the new workplace are being asked to improve performance while dealing with the pressures of continuous change.[1] In the words of Tom Peters, author of *Thriving on Chaos:* "The turbulent marketplace demands that we make innovation a way of life for everyone. We must learn individually and as organizations—to welcome change and innovation as vigorously as we have fought it in the past."[2]

The Nature of Organizational Change

In this chapter, the focus is on **planned change**—change that is deliberate and intentional. Planned change is a direct response to someone's perception of a **performance gap.** This discrepancy between the desired and actual state of affairs indicates the presence of a problem to be solved or an opportunity to be explored. It is useful to think of most planned changes as efforts initiated by managers to resolve performance gaps to the benefit of the organization and its members.

Some planned change may be described as *radical change* or *frame-breaking change.*[3] This is change that results in a major makeover of the organization and its component systems—in other words, massive restructuring. Radical organizational changes are often initiated by a critical event, such as a new CEO, a new ownership brought about by merger or takeover, or a dramatic failure in operating results. Though infrequent, there may be times in an organization's life cycle when its very survival depends on the rigors and demands of radical change.

A more common form of planned organizational change is *incremental change* or *frame-bending change.*[4] This type of change is less traumatic and more a natural part of an organization's evolution. Typical examples are the introduction of new products, technologies, and systems. The capability for continuous improvement through incremental change is an important asset to organizations that are pursuing total quality operations in today's demanding environments.

The success of any planned change in organizations depends, in part, on "change agents" who directly facilitate and support the change processes. A **change agent** is a person or group who takes responsibility for changing the existing pattern of behavior of another person or social system. The change agent role is an important part of every manager's job. It includes being (1) alert to situations or people needing change, (2) open to good ideas, and (3) able to support the implementation of new ideas into actual practice.

Organizational Targets for Change

Working as change agents, managers may direct their attention to a wide variety of organization components, as already discussed in this book. Figure 17.1 depicts

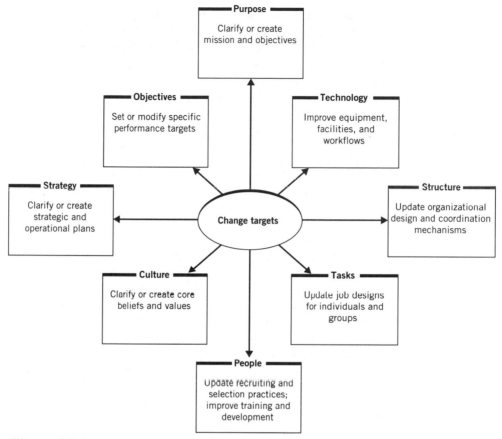

Figure 17.1 Organizational targets for planned change.

possible targets for planned organizational change as purpose, strategy, structure, and people, as well as objectives, culture, tasks, and technology. Good managers, however, recognize that these change targets are highly intertwined. For example, a change in the basic *tasks* performed by an organization—that is, a modification in what it is the organization does—is almost inevitably accompanied by a change in *technology,* a modification in the way in which tasks are accomplished. Changes in tasks and technology usually require alterations in the *structure* of the organization, including changes in the patterns of authority and communication. These technological and structural changes can, in turn, necessitate changes on the part of the organization's *members*—the people who use the resources and make the systems of the organization work. For example, workers may have to acquire additional knowledge and develop new skills in order to perform optimally with the new technology.[5]

Phases of Planned Change

Kurt Lewin, a famous psychologist, recommends that any change be approached as a process consisting of three phases—unfreezing, changing, and refreezing.[6] *Un-*

freezing is the managerial responsibility of preparing a situation for change. It involves disconfirming existing attitudes and behaviors to create a felt need for something new. Unfreezing is facilitated by environmental pressures, declining performance, recognition of a problem, or awareness that someone else has found a better way, among other things.

One of Lewin's basic points is that many changes fail because situations are not properly unfrozen to begin with. Large organizations, in particular, seem susceptible to what is called the "boiled frog phenomenon."[7] A classic physiological experiment demonstrated that a live frog will immediately jump out when placed in a pan of hot water. But when placed in cold water that is then heated very slowly, the frog will stay until boiled to death. Organizations can fall victim to similar circumstances. When managers fail to monitor their environments, recognize the important trends, or sense the need to change, their organizations may slowly suffer and lose their competitive edge.

The *changing* stage involves a managerial responsibility actually to modify a situation—that is, to change people, tasks, structure, or technology. Lewin cautions that many change agents enter this stage prematurely or are too quick to change things. As a result, they often end up creating resistance and slowing the progress of change in situation that is not adequately unfrozen. Given the proper foundations, successful changing requires sustained effort and clear goals to move the process through to a stable and permanent state of affairs.

Refreezing is the final stage of managerial responsibility in planned change. With the goal of maintaining the momentum of a change, refreezing should positively reinforce desired outcomes and provide extra support when difficulties are encountered. Evaluation is a key element in this final step of the change process. It provides data on the costs and benefits of a change, and it offers opportunities to make constructive modifications in the change over time. When refreezing fails or is neglected altogether, even the best intentioned changes are likely to be abandoned or incompletely implemented.

Planned Change Strategies

Managers and change agents use various strategies or ways for mobilizing power, exerting influence over others, and getting people to support planned change efforts. The most common change strategies used by managers are *force-coercion*—the use of force; *rational persuasion*—the use of logic and information; and *shared power*—the use of participation and involvement.[8]

Force-Coercion and Planned Change

Managers pursuing a **force-coercion strategy** use their authority to force others to follow change directives. That is, they act unilaterally to try to "command" change from the legitimate power base of their high-status position in the organization. This may typically include offers of special rewards or threats of punishment. People in lower status positions may respond by doing what the manager wants, but they will do so primarily to gain a reward or avoid a punishment. Such "compliance" with a change agent's directives is usually temporary. It continues only as long as the authority relationship is clear or the possibility exists of being rewarded or punished. The force-coercion strategy may be good for unfreezing a change situation, but it cannot be relied on to deliver long-term results.

Rational Persuasion and Planned Change

Managers who use a **rational persuasion strategy** attempt to bring about change through the communication of special knowledge, empirical support, or logical arguments. This is an information-based strategy for persuading people to accept change directives. It assumes that rational people will be guided by reason and self-interest in deciding whether or not to support a change. Expert power is mobilized to convince others that the cost-benefit value of a proposed change is high—that is, that the change will leave them better off than before. When successful, this strategy results in a longer lasting, more internalized change than does the force-coercion strategy. It is very important to managers and places great value on effective communication skills.

Shared Power and Planned Change

Managers using a **shared power strategy** will actively and sincerely involve other people in planning and making key decisions about any change that will affect them. Sometimes called a *normative-reeducative strategy,* this approach seeks to establish directions and social support for change through the empowerment of others. It builds essential foundations, such as personal values, group norms, and shared goals, so that support for a proposed change emerges naturally. Managers using normative-reeducative approaches emphasize reference power and allow others to participate in planning and implementing the change. Given this high level of involvement, the strategy is likely to result in others having a longer lasting and more internalized commitment to the change.

Resistance to Change

Formally defined, *resistance to change* is any attitude or behavior that reflects a person's unwillingness to make or support a desired change. Such "resistance" is not always bad. Indeed, the very best change agents view resistance to change as a form of feedback they can use to facilitate change objectives.[9] They recognize that when people resist change, they are defending something important—something that is or appears to be threatened by the change.

```
╔══════════════════════════════════════════════════════════════╗
║                  THE EFFECTIVE MANAGER 17.1                    ║
╚══════════════════════════════════════════════════════════════╝
```

How to Minimize Resistance to Change

Type of resistance	Suggested response
Fear of the unknown	Offer information and encouragement.
Need for security	Clarify intentions and methods.
No felt need to change	Demonstrate the problem or opportunity.
Vested interests threatened	Enlist key people in change planning.
Contrasting interpretations	Disseminate valid information and facilitate group sharing.
Poor timing	Delay change and await a better time.
Lack of resources	Provide supporting resources.

Why People Resist Change

Resistance to change is inevitable. The Effective Manager 17.1 summarizes a number of common reasons why people might resist change, and suggests how managers might respond to them. Good managers and change agents understand this advice. They anticipate resistance to change and take steps ahead of time to minimize its adverse consequences.[10]

Consider the case of a manager who wants to introduce advanced personal computers into his work unit. Before proceeding to do so, he might ask: "Why would my subordinates resist this change?" Given reasonable answers to his question, he would then be well prepared to actively plan and successfully implement this change in work unit technology. For example, his workers might resist because they had never before used the computer's operating system (*fear of the unknown*); because they surmised that the manager was introducing the powerful computers just to eventually "get rid" of some of the workers (*need for security*); because they believed they were already doing their jobs very well (*no felt need for change*); because they sensed the manager was pushing the computers onto them without first discussing it with them (*vested interests threatened*); because they heard a rumor that the same type of computers was used elsewhere in the company to get more work out of people with no increase in pay (*contrasting interpretations*); because they were very busy and didn't want to try something new until the work slackened a bit (*poor timing*); or because they believed they wouldn't get good training on the new computer systems (*lack of resources*).

How to Deal with Resistance to Change

All things considered, the sooner resistance to change is recognized and addressed during the change process the better. Once it has been identified, change agents can do a number of things to best deal with resistance to change.[11] *Education and communication* is the use of one-on-one discussions, presentations to groups, memos, reports, or demonstrations to educate people about a change before it is implemented and to help them see the logic of the change. This approach is useful when resistance is based either on a lack of information or on inaccurate information. One problem is that the process of education and communication can be very time consuming if too many people are involved.

Participation and involvement allows others to help design and implement the changes, to contribute ideas and advice, or to serve on task forces and committees to work on the change. This is a good approach when the manager or change agent does not have all the information needed to design the required change. Although this process can be very time consuming, it has one major advantage. People who participate in designing a change tend to be highly committed to its implementation.

In cases where resistance to change is due primarily to adjustment problems, *facilitation and support* is a good response. In such circumstances, people are most likely trying hard to implement the change but are frustrated by external constraints and difficulties. A good manager can help by playing the "supportive" role and trying to make it as easy as possible to continue with the planned change. This can be done by actively listening to problems and complaints, providing training in the new ways, and helping to overcome performance pressures.

The *negotiation and agreement* approach tends to be most useful when someone will clearly lose something as a result of a change. As suggested in the discussion of negotiation in Chapter 13, this may involve offering incentives to actual or potential resistors and working out trade-offs in exchange for assurances that the change will not be blocked. Direct negotiation can sometimes prove a relatively easy way of avoiding or eliminating costly resistance.

The fact is that resistance to change can also be managed through *manipulation and co-optation.* This is the use of covert attempts to influence others. It can be done by selectively providing information and consciously structuring events so that the desired change receives maximum support, or by "paying off" leaders of the resistance to gain their support. Such approaches may be used when other tactics just don't work or are too expensive, but they can easily lead to future problems if people feel manipulated. An even more extreme approach is *explicit or implicit coercion* to force people to accept change. Coercion is often used when speed is critical or when the change agent possesses considerable power. It can be fast and it can overpower resistance. However, it also runs the risk of offending and alienating others. People who experience coercion may become angry at the manager or change agent, and be left without any true commitments to the change or its implementation. As Lewin might say, "Coercion may help unfreeze and change things, but it doesn't do much to refreeze them."

The Dynamics of Stress

Change of any sort in organizations is often accompanied by unintended side effects. One of these is **stress,** a state of tension experienced by individuals facing extraordinary demands, constraints, or opportunities.[12] Someone may experience stress, for example, when faced with an opportunity to make an important presentation; or stress may emerge from a constraint such as the inability to gain a desired promotion.

Stress and Performance

It is easy to get the impression that stress is always bad, but actually stress has two faces—one positive and one negative.[13] **Constructive stress,** or *eustress,* is helpful for an individual or organization. Research in general shows that low to moderate levels of stress act in an energizing way that improves performance. At these levels of intensity, stress can increase effort, stimulate creativity, and encourage work diligence. You may know such stress as the tension that causes you to study hard before exams, pay attention in class, and complete assignments on time. The same positive results of low to moderate stress can be found in the workplace.

Destructive stress, or *distress,* is dysfunctional for an individual or organization. Excessively high levels of stress can overload a person's physical and mental systems. Performance can suffer if illness is brought on by intense stress or if people react to high stress through absenteeism, turnover, errors, accidents, dissatisfaction, reduced performance, or even unethical behavior. One major problem for all of us, of course, is that just exactly what constitutes "high" stress varies from one individual to the next.

Sources of Stress

There are many **stressors,** the things that cause stress, in our environments.[14] One study of stress experienced by executives around the world reports that managers in mature industrialized countries worry about losing their jobs, family and social pressures, lack of autonomy, and poorly trained subordinates.[15] Managers in developing and recently industrialized countries worry about work overloads, interpersonal relations, competition for promotion, and lack of autonomy. Figure 17.2 divides these and other types of stressors into three categories—work, nonwork, and personal factors.

Effective Stress Management

The best first-line strategy for dealing with stress is *stress prevention*—taking action ahead of time to keep stress from reaching destructive levels. Many personal and nonwork stressors should be dealt with in this way to avoid adverse consequences at work.[16] Persons with Type A orientations may exercise self-discipline, for example, while supervisors of Type A workers may model behavior of a more relaxed personal style. Family problems might be relieved by a new work schedule; a supervisor who acts in a caring and understanding way may also help reduce stress originating in anxiety over family affairs.

One of the best preventative measures for dealing with workplace stress is good ongoing communication between supervisors and subordinates. This can help avoid very common forms of work stress caused by role ambiguities, conflicts, and overloads. Some additional organization and management strategies for controlling stress are presented in The Effective Manager 17.2.

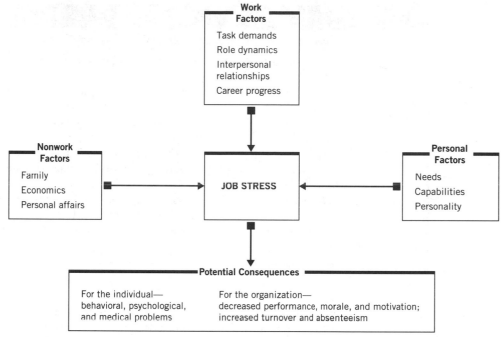

Figure 17.2 Potential consequences of work, nonwork, and personal stressors for individuals and organizations.

The term *personal wellness* is often used to describe the pursuit of one's physical and mental potential through a health promotion program.[17] It involves the acceptance of personal responsibility for enhancing and maintaining wellness through a disciplined approach to one's physical and mental health. The key targets of such discipline include smoking, weight, diet, alcohol use, and general physical fitness. The essence of personal wellness is pursuit of a life-style that reflects a true commitment to good health. More and more employers are finding ways to encourage such personal wellness. A survey of more than 600 businesses found that 76 percent had attempted to help manage employee health through comprehensive wellness programs. Among the documented advantages claimed by those who are finding the programs cost effective are reduced health care claims, lowered absenteeism, and improved employee retention.[18]

Organization Development

Organizations and their managers must work hard to adapt and innovate with the times. The challenge is clear: The best organizations and their managers engage in

> ## THE EFFECTIVE MANAGER 17.2
> ### Management and Organizational Strategies for Controlling Stress
>
> - *Empowerment and participation*—Allowing workers to have more say in decisions affecting them and their work.
> - *Job redesign*—Creating "enriched" jobs that make work more interesting and responsible for individuals and groups.
> - *Goal setting*—Making sure that every worker understands job expectations and has challenging, but achievable, performance goals.
> - *Communication*—Providing everyone with continuous information about performance accomplishments—by themselves, their work groups, and the organization as a whole.
> - *Selection, placement, and training*—Emphasizing a proper "person–job" match when filling jobs; moving people as appropriate to new jobs; and giving everyone the chance to continually update and expand their skills through training and development.

an ongoing process of self-assessment and planned change. This "continuous improvement" is necessary to stay abreast of problems and opportunities in a complex and demanding environment. One useful resource in this regard is **organization development (OD)**—a comprehensive approach to planned change that is designed to improve the overall effectiveness of organizations. Formally defined, OD is the application of behavioral science knowledge in a long-range effort to improve an organization's ability to cope with change in its external environment and to improve its internal problem-solving capabilities.[19]

Goals of Organization Development

Organization development pursues two main goals in planned change. The *process goals* of OD focus on how well people work together. They include achieving improvements in such areas as communication, interaction, and decision making among an organization's members. The *outcome goals* of OD focus on what is actually accomplished through individual and group efforts. They include achieving improvements in task performance.

OD is a process of planned change, but it is also something more. Think of it as "planned change *plus*," if you'd like. That "plus" is the goal of creating change in such a way that organization members develop a capacity for continual self-renewal by learning how to implement similar diagnosis–intervention–reinforcement cycles in the future. True OD, therefore, seeks more than just the successful accomplishment of one planned change. Rather, it seeks to achieve change in such a way that the organization's members become more active and confident in taking similar steps to maintain longer run organization effectiveness. In so doing, OD tries to help organizations and their members by[20]

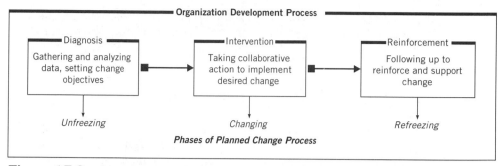

Figure 17.3 Organization development and planned change. *Source:* Adapted from John R. Schermerhorn, Jr., *Management for Productivity,* 4th ed. (New York: John Wiley & Sons, 1993), p. 672. Used by permission.

- Creating an open problem-solving climate throughout an organization.
- Supplementing formal authority with that of knowledge and competence.
- Moving decision making to points where relevant information is available.
- Building trust and maximizing collaboration among individuals and groups.
- Increasing the sense of organizational "ownership" among members.
- Allowing people to exercise self-direction and self-control at work.

The Process of Organization Development

A general model of OD and planned change is shown in Figure 17.3. Organization development begins with *diagnosis*—a stage of gathering and analyzing data to assess a situation and set appropriate change objectives. A good diagnosis helps to unfreeze an existing situation and to pinpoint appropriate action directions. Next, OD enters the stage of *active intervention* during which change objectives are pursued through a variety of specific action interventions. This stage parallels the changing phase of the planned-change process. The last stage of organization development is one of *reinforcement.* Here, changes are monitored, reinforced, and evaluated. Refreezing should occur and the foundations for future use of similar diagnosis–intervention–reinforcement cycles should be set. For one business firm, these stages evolved as follows:

Diagnosis Management perceived a performance gap and hired a consultant. The consultant interviewed key people and planned a workshop where managers could analyze the interview results in a problem-solving format.

Intervention The workshop was held. Participants were coached on how to analyze the data and how to determine appropriate action directions; they also received advice on the effectiveness of the group process.

Reinforcement The consultant continued to meet periodically with the group to review its progress; additional help was given when things got "bogged down"; problem-solving workshops became annual events for the firm.

Organization Development Interventions

The implementation phase of organization development depends heavily for its success on the proper choice and use of **OD interventions.** These are activities that are initiated by the consultant or manager to facilitate planned change and to assist the client system in developing its own problem-solving capabilities.[21]

Organizationwide Interventions

An effective organization is one that achieves its major performance objectives while maintaining a high quality of work life for its members. With this definition in mind, OD interventions designed for systemwide application include the following.

Survey feedback is a popular intervention that begins with the collection of data via questionnaire responses from organization members, or a representative sample of such responses. The data are then presented to the members or "fed back" to them. They subsequently engage in a collaborative process to interpret the data and to develop action plans in response. The role of the OD practitioner is to collect the data and manage the feedback sessions; the role of the client system is to assume responsibility for collaboratively analyzing the data and taking constructive action to improve organizational effectiveness based on the data's implications.

The *confrontation meeting* intervention was refined by Richard Beckhard and is designed to help quickly determine how an organization might be improved and to take initial actions to improve matters.[22] The intervention involves a one-day meeting conducted by an OD facilitator for a representative sample of organizational members, including top management. In a structured format, the consultant asks participants to make individual lists of what they feel could be done to improve things. Then, through a series of small-group work sessions and sharing of results, these ideas are refined into a tentative set of actions that top management then endorses for immediate implementation.

Structural redesign involves realigning the structure of the organization or major subsystems in order to improve performance. As suggested in Chapter 15, this includes examining the best "fit" between structure, technology, and environment. In today's highly dynamic environments, and in light of the increasing involvement of organizations in international operations, a structure can easily grow out of date. Thus, structural redesign is an important OD intervention that can be used to help maintain the best fit between organizational structures and situational demands.

It is sometimes difficult for organizations with intense day-to-day performance pressures to accomplish creative problem solving. The *collateral organization* is designed to make this possible by pulling a representative set of members out of the formal organization structure to engage in periodic small-group problem-solving sessions.[23] These collateral, or "parallel," structures are temporary and exist only to supplement the activities of the formal structure. This OD intervention allows the formal structure to continue to work with maximum efficiency while also experiencing the benefit of periodic and creative support from members working in the collateral structure.

Management by objectives (MBO) can be used as a systemwide OD intervention. In this case, a joint goal-setting process between managers and subordinates is formalized throughout an organization and across all hierarchical levels. The intention is to try to link the activities of all individuals and subunits into meaningful means–end chains that will ensure the accomplishment of major organizational performance objectives.

Group and Intergroup Interventions

OD interventions at the group level are designed to improve group effectiveness. As defined in Chapter 8, group effectiveness involves enhancing both task performance and human resource maintenance within a group. The major interventions at this level include the following.

As described in Chapter 9, *team building* involves a manager or consultant engaging the members of a group in a series of activities designed to help them examine how the group functions and decide what to do to make it function better. Like survey feedback at the organizational level, team building uses data collection and feedback to establish a framework for collaborative problem solving by all group members. Team building is often done at "retreats" or "off-site" meetings, where group members spend two to three days working intensely together on this reflection–analysis–planning process.

Process consultation is related to team building in that it involves structured activities that are facilitated by the OD practitioner and is designed to improve group functioning. Process consultation has a more specific focus than does team building, however; its attention is directed toward the key "processes" through which members of a group work with one another. As discussed in Chapters 8 and 9 on group dynamics, the process consultant is concerned with helping a group function better in such areas as norms, cohesiveness, decision-making methods, communication, conflict, and task and maintenance activities.

Intergroup team building is a special form of team building designed to help two or more groups improve their working relationships with one another and, hopefully, to experience improved group effectiveness as a result. Here, the OD practitioner engages the groups or their representatives in activities that increase awareness of how each group perceives the other and is perceived by the other in return. Given this understanding, collaborative problem solving can take place to improve coordination between the groups and to encourage more mutual support of one another as important components in the total organization.

Individual Interventions

Task performance and job satisfaction are important concerns in respect to improving individual effectiveness in the workplace. OD interventions at this level of attention range from those that address personal issues to those that deal more with specific job and career considerations. Individual-level OD interventions include the following.

Sensitivity training is designed to increase the self-awareness of individuals and their "sensitivity" toward others. It typically involves a number of persons—usually strangers—working together with a professional trainer in a small group called a T-group or training group. In this setting, T-group participants are encouraged to share feelings and concerns and to listen to those expressed by others. Because the opportunity exists for people to get very personal—both in exposing their emotions are in responding to others—this is a controversial type of intervention. It must be exercised only under the guidance of a highly skilled group facilitator.

A most common and useful individual intervention is *management training*. This activity can take place as formal "classroom" style training or as less formal training that occurs on the job. In all cases, the goal is to improve people's management skills and thereby improve their effectiveness. Management training is important, in part, because managers exert an important influence on the performance and satisfaction of other workers. Thus, improvements in management skills can exert an extended positive impact throughout an organization. Management training covers all the topics presented in this book and is an extremely useful professional development activity.

Role negotiation is a way of clarifying what individuals expect to give and receive of one another in their working relationships. Because roles change over time and as personnel changes, role negotiation can be an important means for maintaining task understandings among individuals in an organization. This kind of understanding is quite easily accomplished by helping people who work together clarify what they need from one another in order to do their jobs well.

In Chapter 7, we discussed various approaches to job design and emphasized the importance of achieving a good "fit" between task demands and individual capabilities. As an OD intervention, *job redesign* is the process of adjusting task demands to achieve and maintain this fit. A good example is the Hackman et al. diagnostic approach to job enrichment which involves (1) analyzing the core characteristics of a job or a group of jobs; (2) analyzing the needs and capabilities of workers in those jobs; and (3) taking action to adjust the core job characteristics either to enrich or to simplify the jobs to best match individual preferences.[24]

Organization Development and Career Planning

Career planning is an important way of achieving long-term congruence between individual goals and organizational career opportunities. The best career planning takes the form of structured opportunities for individuals to work with their managers and staff experts from the personnel or human resources department on career issues. Together they may "map" career goals, "assess" personal development needs, and actively "plan" possible short-term and longer term moves.[25]

In the new workplace, thoughts about careers take on a special relevance.[26] We live and work at a time when the implications of constant change pressure us to continually review and reassess our career progress.[27] The old notions of a career based within a single organization that takes responsibility for one's career development are increasingly obsolete. The new notions about careers are dramatically different.

In his book *The Age of Unreason,* British scholar and consultant Charles Handy argues forcefully that each of us must take charge of our own careers.[28] He says we must prepare for inevitable uncertainties and changes by building a "portfolio" of skills. This portfolio of personal skills and competencies should keep you marketable and always make you attractive to many possible employers at any given point in time. As Handy says: "Executives will begin to think of their careers as a sequence of jobs that may or may not be in the same organization."[29] This portfolio must also be subject to continuous development; each new job assignment must be well selected and rigorously pursued as a learning opportunity. And according to Handy, all of this is entirely a *personal* responsibility. He states: "The new executive must look out for himself or herself . . . the future is not guaranteed . . . education in those circumstances becomes an investment, wide experience is an asset provided that it is wide and not shallow."[30] *World Executive's Digest* considers Stephanie Ho "a good example of Handy's professional career person."

> As new director of institutional business—electronic equipment rental and integrated TV systems—for Hong Kong based Thorn/EMI, Stephanie Ho came to the post with a broad mix of business experience and skills. While working with the Hong Kong Tourist Association she completed an MBA part-time at the Chinese University of Hong Kong. Then Stephanie joined the advertising agency Ogilvy & Mather in what she calls a "strategic and opportunistic move." Another move followed to Citicorp; then she was "headhunted" into Hong Kong Bank where she moved into a variety of management posts. Upon hearing that the bank was entering the international card business, she asked to be assigned to the project. She visited every branch location, including Saudi Arabia where she was the first female executive ever to visit from the bank. Says Ho: "I had to go around escorted by a male employee of the bank and wear a long black cloak. But it wasn't too difficult . . ." With six years of Hong Kong Bank behind her, Stephanie took a job with Rothman's as general manager of the tobacco firm's China operations. Within a year she was headhunted again—this time by Thorn/EMI. Stephanie Ho's promising and still emerging executive career is now well supported by industry experience in tourism, advertising, banking, and tobacco. She also has functional experience in media, public relations, business development, and marketing.[31]

Having now completed the chapters of this book, you have been exposed to the major OB concepts, theories, and applications that can help you master the challenges of change. As you look ahead to this exciting future, remember these final career commandments.

1. **Perform** The basic foundation of success is high performance. It will show your value to the organization, earn you respect from higher levels as well as

from your peers and subordinates, and call attention to yourself as a person of high career potiential.

2. **Learn** Life-long learning is an undeniable personal responsibility. It is your primary resource for dealing with ever present change. Only those managers who continuously fail to learn and develop their skills and competencies will not succeed in the long term.

3. **Change** Do not get locked into a job that you have already mastered or a work situation that is narrow or limited in the growth opportunities it offers. Opt for a mix of broadening assignments, including lateral moves as well as promotions.

4. **Learn** Maintain the "yearn to learn." Make a real commitment to your continued personal and professional development. Don't expect others to do this for you. Build and maintain a portfolio of skills that makes you "valuable" to many possible employers.

5. **Communicate** Let others know you are working hard, are dedicated to organizational values and objectives, and are delivering results. Do this in a professional manner and without becoming known as a braggart.

6. **Learn** Learn as much as you can from others. Stay in contact with "mentors" who act as role models, provide advice, and get you the right jobs. "Network" with peers and others who can support your hard work, both now and in the future.

7. **Manage** Accept your personal responsibility for your career; be relentless and diligent in actively managing it. Take charge of your career and *stay* in charge. Remember what Charles Handy says: "The future is not guaranteed."[32]

In Summary

What is organizational change?

- Planned change in organizations is radical or incremental change that takes place because people make it happen.
- Change agents are managers and other persons who actively try to bring about changes in people and/or systems.
- Organizational targets for planned change include purpose, strategy, culture, structure, people, tasks, and technology.
- The three phases of planned change identified by Lewin are unfreezing, changing, and refreezing.

What change strategies are used by managers?

- Change strategies are the means used by change agents to implement desired change.

- Force-coercion strategies utilize a manager's position power to try to "command" that change will take place as directed; temporary compliance is a likely outcome.

- Rational-persuasion strategies use logical arguments and appeals to knowledge and facts to convince people to support change; this can increase commitment to change.

- Shared-power strategies actively involve other persons in planning and implementing change; this creates more long-lasting commitments to the change.

Why do people resist change and what can be done about it?

- Resistance to change is to be expected and it offers "feedback" that can be used by a change agent to increase the effectiveness of a change effort.

- People sometimes resist change because they do not find value or believe in the change.

- They sometimes resist change because they find the change strategy offensive or inappropriate.

- They sometimes resist change because they do not like or identify positively with the change agent as a person.

- Good change agents respond to resistance in ways that create a better "fit" among the change, the situation, and the people involved.

What is stress and how can it be managed?

- Stress is a state of tension caused by extraordinary demands, constraints, and/or opportunities in work or personal situations.

- Moderate levels of stress can be constructive and facilitate performance; too much stress can be destructive and inhibit performance.

- Stress can adversely impact a person's mental and physical health.

- Stress can be managed through both stress prevention and personal wellness strategies.

What is organization development?

- Organization development (OD) is a special application of behavioral science knowledge to create a comprehensive effort to improve organizational effectiveness.

- OD has both outcome goals, involving improved task accomplishments, and process goals, involving improvements in the way organization members work together.

- The process of OD involves the stages of diagnosis, intervention, and reinforcement.

How is organization development accomplished?

- OD interventions, activities designed to bring about planned change, can be applied to improve effectiveness at the individual, group, or total organization levels.

- Very often, more than one intervention is used in building-block fashion and with ongoing identification of the problems to be resolved.

- Organization-level, or system-wide interventions, include survey-feedback, management by objectives, confrontation meetings, collateral organization, and structural redesign.

- Group-level interventions include team building, process consultation, and intergroup team building.

- Individual-level interventions include sensitivity training, role negotiation, job redesign, management training, and career planning.

N O T E S

CHAPTER 1

[1] Quote from John Huey, "Managing in the Midst of Chaos," *Fortune* (April 5, 1993), pp. 38–48. See also Tom Peters, *Thriving on Chaos* (New York: Knopf, 1991).

[2] Ibid.

[3] See John P. Fernandez, *Managing a Diverse Workforce* (Lexington, Mass.: D. C. Heath, 1991); and Julie O'Mara, *Managing Workplace 2000* (San Francisco: Jossey-Bass, 1991).

[4] See Philip B. Crosby, *Quality Is Free* (New York: McGraw-Hill, 1979); Philip B. Crosby, *The Eternally Successful Organization* (New York: McGraw-Hill 1989); Joseph M. Juran, *Quality Control Handbook,* 3rd ed. (New York: McGraw-Hill, 1987); and W. Edwards Deming, *The Deming Guide to Quality and Competitive Advantage* (Englewood Cliffs, N.J.: Prentice-Hall, 1987).

[5] See Walter Kiechel III, "How We Will Work in the Year 2000," *Fortune* (May 17, 1993), pp. 38–52.

[6] For a good overview of the OB discipline, see Jay W. Lorsch, ed., *Handbook of Organizational Behavior* (Englewood Cliffs, N.J.: Prentice-Hall, 1987).

[7] Ibid.

[8] Geert Hofstede, "Cultural Constraints in Management Theories," *Academy of Management Executive* 7 (1993), pp. 81–94. See also Geert Hofstede, *Culture's Consequences* (Beverly Hills, Calif.: Sage, 1980).

[9] See Uma Sekaran, *Research Methods for Managers,* 2nd ed, (New York: John Wiley, 1992).

[10] Tom Peters, "Managing in a World Gone Bonkers," *World Executive Digest* (February 1993), pp. 26–29. See also Tom Peters, *Liberation Management* (New York: Knopf, 1992).

[11] Developed from the *Outcome Measurement Project of the Accreditation Research Committee, Phase II: An Interim Report* (St. Louis: American Assembly of Collegiate Schools of Business, 1984), pp. 15–18.

[12] Information from *The Columbus Dispatch* (March 22, 1990), p. 2C.

[13] Abridged and adapted from p. 30 of *The Nature of Managerial Work* by Henry Mintzberg (New York: Harper & Row, 1973), p. 30. Copyright © 1973 by Henry Mintzberg. Reprinted by permission of Harper & Row Publishers, Inc.

[14] Developed from Mintzberg, op. cit.; Morgan W. McCall, Jr., Ann M. Morrison, and Robert L. Hannan, *Studies of Managerial Work: Results and Methods,* Technical Report No. 9 (Greensboro, N.C.: Center for Creative Leadership, 1978; John P. Kotter, *The General Managers* (New York: Free Press, 1982a); Robert E. Kaplan, *The Warp and Woof of the General Manager's Job,* Technical Report No. 27 (Greensboro, N.C.: Center for Creative Leadership, 1986). See also Fred Luthans, Richard M. Hodgetts, and Stuart A. Rosenkrantz, *Real Managers* (New York: HarperCollins, 1988); Fred Luthans, Stuart Rosenkrantz, and Harry Hennessey, "What Do Successful Managers Really Do?" *The Journal of Applied Behavioral Science* 21, No. 2 (1985), pp. 255–270; Fred Luthans, "Successful versus Effective Real Managers," *Academy of Management Executive* 2, No. 2 (1988), pp. 127–132. See also Fred Luthans, "Fifty Years Later: What Do We Really Know about Managing and What Managers Do?" *Academy of Management Newsletter* 10 (1986), pp. 3, 9–10.

[15] Mintzberg, op. cit.

[16] Adapted from ibid., p. 46.

[17] Allen I. Kraut, Patricia R. Pedigo, D. Douglas McKenna, and Marvin D. Dunnette, "The Role of the Manager: What's Really Important in Different Management Jobs," *Academy of Management Executive* 3, No. 4 (1989), pp. 286–293.

[18] John P. Kotter, *The General Managers* (New York: Free Press, 1982); John P. Kotter, "What Effective General Managers Really Do," *Harvard Business Review* 60 (November–December 1982), p. 161. See also Robert E. Kaplan, "Trade Routes: The Manager's Network of Relationships," *Organizational Dynamics* 12 (Spring 1984), pp. 37–52.

[19] Robert L. Katz, "Skills of an Effective Administrator," *Harvard Business Review* 52 (September–October 1974), p. 94. See also Richard E. Boyatzis,

The Competent Manager: A Model for Effective Performance (New York: John Wiley, 1982).

CHAPTER 2

[1] Quotes from Andrew Grove, *High Output Management* (New York: Random House, 1983; and Henry Mintzberg, *The Nature of Managerial Work* (New York: Harper & Row, 1973).

[2] See Alvin Toffler, *Powershift: Knowledge, Wealth, and Violence at the Edge of the 21st Century* (New York: Bantam Books, 1990).

[3] See, for example, John Naisbitt, and Patricia Aburdene, *Megatrends 2000: Ten New Directions for the 1990s* (New York: William Morrow, 1990); and Toffler, op. cit.

[4] Keniche Ohmae, *The Borderless World* (New York: Harper, 1989).

[5] Michael Hammer and James Champy, *Reengineering the Corporation* (New York: HarperCollins, 1993). See also Michael Hammer and James Champy, "The Promise of Reengineering," *Fortune* (May 3, 1993), pp. 94–97.

[6] Shoshana Zuboff, *In the Age of the Smart Machine* (New York: Basic Books, 1988).

[7] See, for example, David L. Bradford and Allan R. Cohen, *Managing for Excellence* (New York: John Wiley, 1984); Peter M. Senge, *The Fifth Discipline* (New York: Doubleday, 1990); Marvin A. Weisbrod, *Productive Workplaces: Organizing and Managing for Dignity, Meaning, and Community* (San Francisco: Jossey-Bass, 1987).

[8] Charles Handy, *The Age of Unreason* (Boston: Harvard Business School Press, 1990).

[9] William H. Davidow and Michael S. Malone, *The Virtual Corporation: Structuring and Revitalizing the Corporation of the 21st Century* (New York: Harper Business, 1993).

[10] See Edward E. Lawler III, *Organizing for the Future* (San Francisco: Jossey-Bass, 1993).

[11] See Philip B. Crosby, *Quality Is Free* (New York: McGraw-Hill, 1979); Philip B. Crosby, *The Eternally Successful Organization* (New York: McGraw-Hill, 1989); Joseph M. Juran, *Quality Control Handbook*, 3rd ed. (New York: McGraw-Hill, 1987); W. Edwards Deming, *The Deming Guide to Quality and Competitive Advantage* (Englewood Cliffs, N.J.: Prentice-Hall, 1987); and Rafael Aguayo, *Dr. Dem-*

ing: The American Who Taught the Japanese about Quality (New York: Fireside, 1990).

[12] Edward E. Lawler III, "Total Quality Management and Employee Involvement: Are they Compatible?" *Academy of Management Executive* 8 (February 1994), pp. 68–78.

[13] Quote from *Fortune,* special advertising supplement (September 24, 1990).

[14] Regina Key Brough, "Total Quality Management in State Government: The Eight Rules for Producing Results," *The Journal of State Government* (1992), pp. 4–8.

[15] See John P. Fernandez, *Managing a Diverse Workforce* (Lexington, Mass.: D. C. Heath, 1991); and, Julie O'Mara, *Managing Workplace 2000* (San Francisco: Jossey-Bass, 1991).

[16] *Workforce 2000: Work and Workers for the 21st Century* (Indianapolis: Towers Perrin/Hudson Institute, 1987).

[17] Ibid. See also *Workforce 2000: Competing in a Seller's Market: Is Corporate America Prepared?* (Indianapolis: Towers-Perrin/Hudson Institute, 1990).

[18] This concept is further discussed in Chapter 3. See Nancy J. Adler, *International Dimensions of Organizational Behavior,* 2nd ed. (Boston: PWS-Kent, 1991).

[19] *Workforce 2000: Work and Workers for the 21st Century,* 1987.

[20] See the discussion by R. Roosevelt Thomas, Jr., "From Affirmative Action to Affirming Diversity," *Harvard Business Review* (March–April 1990), pp. 107–117.

[21] Blair Sheppard, Roy J. Lewicki, and John Minton, *Organizational Justice: The Search for Fairness in the Workplace* (New York: Lexington Books, 1992).

[22] See Steven N. Brenner and Earl A. Mollander, "Is the Ethics of Business Changing," *Harvard Business Review* 55 (January–February 1977), pp. 50–57; Saul W. Gellerman, "Why 'Good' Managers Make Bad Ethical Choices," *Harvard Business Review* 64 (July–August 1986), pp. 85–90; Barbara Ley Toffler, *Tough Choices: Managers Talk Ethics* (New York: John Wiley, 1986); Justin G. Longnecker, Joseph A. McKinney, and Carlos W. Moore, "The Generation Gap in Business Ethics," *Business Horizons* 32 (September–October 1989), pp. 9–14; John B. Cullen, Vart Victor, and Carroll Stephens,

"An Ethical Weather Report: Assessing the Organization's Ethical Climate," *Organizational Dynamics* (Winter 1990), pp. 50–62.

[23] Developed in part from Alan L. Otten, "Ethics on the Job: Companies Alert Employees to Potential Dilemmas," *The Wall Street Journal* (July 14, 1986), p. 17. See also the discussion in John R. Schermerhorn, Jr., *Management for Productivity,* 4th ed. (New York: John Wiley, 1993), Chapter 3.

[24] Based on Saul W. Gellerman, "Why 'Good' Managers Make Bad Ethical Choices," *Harvard Business Review* 64 (July 1986), pp. 85–97.

[25] C. Welles, "What Led Beech-Nut Down the Road to Disgrace," *Business Week* (February 22, 1988), pp. 124–128.

[26] Charles J. Cranny, Patricia C. Smith, and Eugene F. Stone, *Job Satisfaction: How People Feel About Their Jobs, and How It Affects Their Performance* (New York: Lexington Books, 1992).

[27] These items are from the Job Descriptive Index (JDI), available from Dr. Patricia C. Smith, Department of Psychology, Bowling Green State University.

[28] See David A. Nadler and Edward E. Lawler III, "Quality of Work Life: Perspectives and Directions," *Organizational Dynamics* 11 (1983), pp. 22–36; the discussion of QWL in Thomas G. Cummings and Edgar F. Huse, *Organization Development and Change* (St. Paul, Minn.: West, 1990).

CHAPTER 3

[1] Michael Porter, *The Competitive Advantage of Nations* (New York: Free Press, 1990).

[2] Shawn Tully, "The Hunt for the Global Manager," *Fortune* (May 21, 1990), pp. 140–144; and Robert T. Moran and John R. Riesenberger, *Making Globalization Work: Solutions for Implementation* (New York: McGraw-Hill, 1993). See also Nancy J. Adler and Susan Bartholomew, "Managing Globally Competent People," *Academy of Management Executive* 6 (August 1992), pp. 52–65; and John L. Daniels and Dr. N. Caroline Daniels, *Global Vision: Building New Models for the Corporation of the Future* (New York: McGraw-Hill, 1993).

[3] These terms are used in Nancy J. Adler, *International Dimensions of Organizational Behavior,* 2nd ed. (Boston: PWS-Kent, 1991), p. 14.

[4] *Workforce 2000* (Indianapolis: Hudson Institute, 1987); and, *Workforce 2000: Competing in a Seller's Market: Is Corporate America Prepared?* (Indianapolis: Towers/Perrin-Hudson Institute, 1990). See Gilbert Fuchberg, "Many Businesses Responding Too Slowly to Rapid Work Force Shifts, Study Says," *The Wall Street Journal* (July 20, 1990), pp. 31, 33.

[5] Geert Hofstede, *Culture's Consequences: International Differences in Work-Related Values,* abridged edition (Beverly Hills, Calif.: Sage, 1984). For an historical perspective, see A. L. Kroeber and F. Kluckhohn, *Culture: A Critical Review of Concepts and Definitions, Peabody Museum Papers,* Vol. 47 (Cambridge, Mass.: Harvard University Press, 1952).

[6] A classic work here is Benjamin Lee Whorf, *Language, Thought and Reality* (New York: John Wiley, 1956).

[7] The classic work here and the source of our examples is Edward T. Hall, *The Silent Language* (New York: Anchor Books, 1959).

[8] Edward T. Hall's book *The Hidden Dimension* (New York: Anchor Books, 1969 and Magnolia, Miss.: Peter Smith, 1990) is a classic reference and the source of our examples. See also Edward T. Hall, *Hidden Differences* (New York: Doubleday, 1990).

[9] The classic work is Max Weber, *The Protestant Ethic and the Spirit of Capitalism* (New York: Scribner, 1930).

[10] Hofstede, op. cit., 1984.

[11] Geert Hofstede and Michael H. Bond, "The Confucius Connection: From Culture Roots to Economic Growth," *Organizational Dynamics* 16 (1988), pp. 4–21.

[12] Geert Hofstede, "Cultural Constraints in Management Theories," *Academy of Management Executive* 7 (February 1993), pp. 81–94.

[13] Hofstede uses the terms *masculine* and *feminine* to anchor this dimension. We do not suggest any connection between these attributes and males or females today.

[14] Hofstede, 1984 and 1993, op. cit.; Hofstede and Bond, op. cit.

[15] Adler, op. cit., 1991.

[16] Ibid.

[17] Ibid.

[18] Alvin Toffler, *The Third Wave* (New York: William Morrow, 1980), p. 320.

[19] See Hofstede, op. cit., 1984 and 1993; and Adler, op. cit., 1991; Daniels and Daniels, op. cit.

[20] Adler, op. cit.

[21] See, for example, Rosalie Tung, "Expatriate Assignments: Enhancing Success and Minimizing Failure," *Academy of Management Executive* (May 1987), pp. 117–126; and Adler, op. cit., 1991.

[22] Developed from Robert T. Moran, "Making Globalization Work," *World Executive Digest* (January 1993), pp. 16–18.

[23] See Geert Hofstede, "Motivation, Leadership and Organization: Do American Theories Apply Abroad?" *Organizational Dynamics* (Summer 1980), pp. 42–63; Adler, op. cit., 1991, pp. 123–148.

[24] See the discussion in Adler, op. cit., 1991, pp. 128–141.

[25] R. Roosevelt Thomas, Jr., "From Affirmative Action to Affirming Diversity," *Harvard Business Review* (March–April 1990), pp. 107–117.

[26] Quoted in Ibid., p. 132.

[27] Based on Adler, op. cit., 1991.

[28] Hofstede, op. cit., 1980.

[29] For a good discussion of translation problems in international business, see David A. Ricks, *Blunders in International Business* (Cambridge, Mass.: Blackwell Publishers, 1993).

[30] Hall, op. cit., 1959.

[31] William Ouchi, *Theory Z: How American Businesses Can Meet the Japanese Challenge* (Reading, Mass.: Addison-Wesley, 1981); Richard Tanner and Anthony Athos, *The Art of Japanese Management* (New York: Simon & Schuster, 1981).

[32] Jerry Sullivan and Richard B. Peterson, "Japanese Management Theories: A Research Agenda," pp. 255–275, in Benjamin A. Prasad, *Advances in International Comparative Management* 4 (Greenwich, Conn.: JAI Press, 1989).

[33] James R. Lincoln, "Employee Work Attitudes and Management Practice in the U.S. and Japan: Evidence from a Large Comparative Survey," *California Management Review* 20 (Fall 1989), pp. 89–106.

CHAPTER 4

[1] See John P. Fernandez, *Managing Diverse Work Force* (Lexington, Mass.: Lexington Books, 1991).

[2] See George T. Milkovich and John Bondreau, *Human Resource Management* (Sixth Ed.), (Homewood, Ill.: Irwin, 1991).

[3] Fernandez, op. cit.

[4] See G. N. Powell, *Women and Men in Management* (Beverly Hills, Calif.: Sage Publications, 1988), based on Gary N. Powell, "One More Time: Do Female and Male Managers Differ?" *Academy of Management Executive* 4, No. 3 (1990), p. 74.

[5] Reported in W. B. Johnston *Workforce 2000: Work and Workers for the 21st Century* (Indianapolis: Hudson Institute, 1987).

[6] Johnston, ibid.

[7] Paul Mayrand, "Older Workers: A Problem or the Solution?", *AARP Textbook Authors Conference Presentation* (October 1992), p. 29; G. M. McEvoy and W. F. Cascio "Cumulative Evidence of the Relationship Between Employee Age and Job Performance," *Journal of Applied Psychology* (February 1989), pp. 11–17.

[8] Fernandez, op. cit.

[9] See Taylor H. Cox and Stacy Blake, "Managing Cultural Diversity: Implications for Organizational Competitiveness," *Academy of Management Executive* 5, No. 3 (1991), p. 45.

[10] Literature covering this topic is reviewed in Stephen P. Robbins, *Organizational Behavior,* 6th Ed., Englewood Cliffs, NJ: Prentice-Hall, 1993, Ch. 4.

[11] Larry L. Cummings and Donald P. Schwab, *Performance in Organizations: Determinants and Appraisal* (Glenview, Ill.: Scott, Foresman, 1973), p. 8.

[12] See Geert Hofstede, *Culture's Consequences: International Differences in Work-Related Values,* abridged edition (Beverly Hills: Sage, 1984).

[13] See Brody, N. *Personality: In Search of Individuality* (San Diego, Calif.: Academic Press, 1988), pp. 68–101; Holden, C., "The Genetics of Personality," *Science* (August 7, 1987), pp. 598–601.

[14] Chris Argyris, *Personality and Organization* (New York: Harper & Row, 1957).

[15] Daniel J. Levinson, *The Seasons of a Man's Life* (New York: Alfred A. Knopf, 1978).

16 See David A. Whetten and Kim S. Cameron, *Developing Management Skills,* 2nd ed. (New York: HarperCollins), pp. 66.

17 Raymond G. Hunt, Frank J. Krzystofiak, James R. Meindl, and Abdalla M. Yousry, "Cognitive Style and Decision Making," in *Organizational Behavior and Human Decision Processes* 44, No. 3 (1989), pp. 436–453; Ferdinand A. Gul, "The Joint and Moderating Role of Personality and Cognitive Style on Decision Making," *The Accounting Review* (April 1984), pp. 264–77; Brian H. Kleiner, "The Interrelationship of Jungian Modes of Mental Functioning with Organizational Factors: Implications for Management Development," *Human Relations* (November 1983), pp. 997–1012; James L. McKenney and Peter G. W. Keen, "How Managers' Minds Work," *Harvard Business Review* (May–June 1974), pp. 79–90.

18 J. B. Rotter, "Generalized Expectancies for Internal versus External Control of Reinforcement," *Psychological Monographs* 80 (1966), pp. 1–28.

19 Don Hellriegel, John W. Slocum, Jr., and Richard W. Woodman, *Organizational Behavior,* 5th ed. (St. Paul: West, 1989), p. 46.

20 Niccolo Machiavelli, *The Prince,* George Bull, trans. (Middlesex: Penguin, 1961).

21 Richard Christie and Florence L. Geis, *Studies in Machiavellianism* (New York: Academic Press, 1970).

22 See M. Snyder, *Public Appearances/Private Realities: The Psychology of Self-Monitoring* (New York: W. H. Freeman, 1987).

23 Ibid.

24 See Meyer Friedman and Ray Roseman, *Type A Behavior and Your Heart* (New York: Alfred A. Knopf, 1974). For another view, see Walter Kiechel III, "Attack of the Obsessive Managers," *Fortune* (February 16, 1987), pp. 127–128.

25 See P. E. Jacob, J. J. Flink, and H. L. Schuchman, "Values and Their Function in Decisionmaking," *American Behavioral Scientist* 5, 1962 (Supplement 9), pp. 6–38.

26 See M. Rokeach and S. J. Ball Rokeach, "Stability and Change in American Value Priorities, 1968–1981," *American Psychologist* (May 1989), pp. 775–784.

27 Milton Rokeach, *The Nature of Human Values* (New York: Free Press, 1973).

28 Gordon Allport, Philip E. Vernon, and Gardner Lindzey, *Study of Values* (Boston: Houghton Mifflin, 1931).

29 Bruce M. Meglino, Elizabeth C. Ravlin, and Cheryl L. Adkins, "Value Congruence and Satisfaction with a Leader: An Examination of the Role of Interaction," unpublished manuscript (1990), University of South Carolina, pp. 8–9.

30 See Martin Fishbein and Icek Ajzen, *Belief, Attitude, Intention and Behavior: An Introduction to Theory and Research* (Reading, Mass.: Addison-Wesley, 1975).

31 Leon Festinger, *A Theory of Cognitive Dissonance* (Palo Alto, Calif.: Stanford University Press, 1957).

32 Ibid.

33 Dewitt C. Dearborn and Herbert A. Simon, "Selective Perception: A Note on the Departmental Identification of Executives," *Sociometry* 21 (1958), pp. 140–144.

34 J. Sterling Livingston, "Pygmalion in Management," *Harvard Business Review* 47 (July–August 1969).

35 See H. H. Kelley, "Attribution in Social Interaction," in E. Jones et al. (Eds.), *Attribution: Perceiving the Causes of Behavior* (Morristown, NJ: General Learning Press, 1972).

36 See Terence R. Mitchell, S. G. Green, and R. E. Wood, "An Attribution Model of Leadership and the Poor Performing Subordinate," pp. 197–234, in Barry Staw and Larry L. Cummings, eds., *Research in Organizational Behavior* (New York: JAI Press, 1981); John H. Harvey and Gifford Weary, "Current Issues in Attribution Theory and Research," *Annual Review of Psychology* 35 (1984), pp. 427–459.

37 Data reported in John R. Schermerhorn, Jr., "Team Development for High Performance Management," *Training & Development Journal* 40 (November 1986), pp. 38–41.

CHAPTER 5

1 See John P. Campbell, Marvin D. Dunnette, Edward E. Lawler III, and Karl E. Weick, Jr., *Managerial Behavior Performance and Effectiveness* (New York: McGraw-Hill, 1970), Chapter 15.

2 Lyman W. Porter, "Job Attitudes in Management:

II. Perceived Importance of Needs as a Function of Job Level," *Journal of Applied Psychology* 47 (April 1963), pp. 141–148.

³Douglas T. Hall and Khalil E. Nougaim, "An Examination of Maslow's Need Hierarchy in an Organizational Setting," *Organizational Behavior and Human Performance* 3 (1968), pp. 12–35.

⁴Lyman W. Porter, "Job Attitudes in Management: IV. Perceived Deficiencies in Need Fulfillment as a Function of Size of Company," *Journal of Applied Psychology* 47 (December 1963), pp. 386–397.

⁵John M. Ivancevich, "Perceived Need Satisfactions of Domestic Versus Overseas Managers" 54 (August 1969), pp. 274–278.

⁶See Nancy J. Adler, *International Dimensions of Organizational Behavior* 2 (Boston: PWS-Kent, 1991). Richard M. Hodgetts and Fred Luthans, *International Management* (New York: McGraw-Hill, 1991), Chapter 11.

⁷See Clayton P. Alderfer, "An Empirical Test of a New Theory of Human Needs," *Organizational Behavior and Human Performance* 4 (1969), pp. 142–175; Clayton P. Alderfer, *Existence, Relatedness, and Growth* (New York: Free Press, 1972); Benjamin Schneider and Clayton P. Alderfer, "Three Studies of Need Satisfaction in Organization," *Administrative Science Quarterly* 18 (1973), pp. 489–505.

⁸Sources pertinent to this discussion are David C. McClelland, *The Achieving Society* (New York: Van Nostrand, 1961); David C. McClelland, "Business, Drive and National Achievement," *Harvard Business Review* 40 (July–August 1962), pp. 99–112; David C. McClelland, "That Urge to Achieve," *Think* (November–December 1966), pp. 19–32; G. H. Litwin and R. A. Stringer, *Motivation and Organizational Climate* (Boston: Division of Research, Harvard Business School, 1966); pp. 18–25.

⁹David C. McClelland and David H. Burnham, "Power Is the Great Motivator," *Harvard Business Review* 54 (March–April 1976), pp. 100–110; David C. McClelland and Richard E. Boyatzis, "Leadership Motive Pattern and Long-Term Success in Management," *Journal of Applied Psychology* 67 (1982), pp. 737–743.

¹⁰Charles M. Kleey, "The Interrelationship of Ethics and Power in Today's Organizations," *Organiza-tional Dynamics* 5 (Summer 1987); Christopher Farrell, "Gutfreund Gives Salmon's Young Lions More Power," *Business Week* 32 (October 20, 1986); Jolie Solomon, "Heirs Apparent to Chief Executives Often Trip Over Prospect of Power," *The Wall Street Journal* 29 (March 24, 1987).

¹¹The complete two-factor theory is well explained by Herzberg and his associates in Frederick Herzberg, Bernard Mausner and Barbara Bloch Synderman, *The Motivation to Work,* 2nd ed. (New York: John Wiley, 1967); and Frederick Herzberg, "One More Time: How Do You Motivate Employees?" *Harvard Business Review* 46 (January–February 1968), pp. 53–62.

¹²Dual-Factor Theory of Job Satisfaction and Motivation: A Review of the Evidence and a Criticism," *Personnel Psychology* 20 (Winter 1967), pp. 369–389; and Steven Kerr, Anne Harlan, and Ralph Stogdill, "Preference for Motivator and Hygiene Factors in a Hypothetical Interview Situation," *Personnel Psychology* 27 (Winter 1974), pp. 109–124.

¹³See, for example, J. Stacy Adams, "Toward an Understanding of Inequality," *Journal of Abnormal and Social Psychology* 67 (1963), pp. 422–436; and J. Stacy Adams, "Inequity in Social Exchange," in L. Berkowitz, ed., *Advances in Experimental Social Psychology* 2 (New York: Academic Press, 1965), pp. 267–300.

¹⁴For an excellent review, see Richard T. Mowday, "Equity Theory Predictions of Behavior in Organizations," in Richard M. Steers and Lyman W. Porter, eds., *Motivation and Work Behavior,* 4th ed. (New York: McGraw-Hill, 1987), pp. 89–110.

¹⁵Victor H. Vroom, *Work and Motivation* (New York: John Wiley, 1964).

¹⁶See Nancy J. Adler, *International Dimensions of Organizational Behavior* (1991), p. 159.

¹⁷Lyman W. Porter and Edward E. Lawler III, *Managerial Attitudes and Performance* (Homewood, Ill.: Richard D. Irwin, 1968).

¹⁸This integrated model is not based only on the Porter and Lawler model but is consistent with the kind of comprehensive approach suggested by Evans in a recent review. See Martin G. Evans, "Organizational Behavior: The Central Role of Motivation" in J. G. Hunt and J. D. Blair, eds., *1986 Yearly*

Review of Management of the Journal of Management 12 (1986), pp. 203–222.

CHAPTER 6

[1] For some of B. F. Skinner's work, see *Walden Two* (New York: Macmillan, 1948), *Science and Human Behavior* (New York: Macmillan, 1953), and *Contingencies of Reinforcement* (New York: Appleton-Century-Crofts, 1969).

[2] See M. E. Gist, "Self Efficacy: Implications in Organizational Behavior and Human Resource Management," *Academy of Management Review* 12 (1987), pp. 472–485; A. Bandura, "Self Efficacy Mechanism in Human Agency," *American Psychologist* 37 (1987), pp. 122–147.

[3] E. L. Thorndike, *Animal Intelligence* (New York: Macmillan, 1911), p. 244.

[4] Both laws are stated in Keith L. Miller, *Principles of Everyday Behavior Analysis* (Monterey, Calif.: Brooks/Cole, 1975), p. 122.

[5] Developed in part from Hamner, "Using Reinforcement Theory in Organizational Settings," in Henry L. Tosi and W. Clay Hamner, eds.; *Organizational Behavior and Management: A Contingency Approach* (Chicago: St. Clair Press, 1977), pp. 388–395. Based on an example in Luthans and Kreitner op. cit. (1975), pp. 125–126.

[6] Charles C. Manz and Henry P. Sims, Jr., *Superleadership* (New York: Berkley, 1990).

[7] See H. L. Angle, C. C. Manz, and A. H. Van de Ven, "Integrating Human Resource Management and Corporate Strategy: A Preview of the 3M Story," *Human Resource Management* 24 (1985), pp. 51–68.

[8] See Edward E. Lawler, *Pay and Organization Development* (Reading, Mass.: Addison-Wesley, 1981).

[9] See Jone L. Pearce, "Why Merit Pay Doesn't Work: Implications from Organization Theory," in David B. Balkin and Luis R. Gomez-Mejia, eds., *New Perspectives on Compensation* (Englewood Cliffs, N.J.: Prentice-Hall, 1987), pp. 169–178; Jerry M. Newman, "Selecting Incentive Plans to Complement Organizational Strategy," in David R. Balkin and Luis R. Gomez-Mejia, eds., *New Perspectives on Compensation* (Englewood Cliffs, N.J.: Prentice-Hall, 1987), pp. 214–224; Edward E. Lawler III, "Pay for Performance: Making It Work," *Compensation and Benefits Review* 21, 1 (1989), pp. 55–60.

CHAPTER 7

[1] See H. L. Tosi, John R. Rizzo and Stephen J. Carroll, *Managing Organizational Behavior,* 2nd ed. (New York: Harper & Row, 1990), Chapter 8; Ramon J. Aldag and Arthur P. Brief, "The Intrinsic–Extrinsic Dichotomy: Toward Conceptual Clarity," *Academy of Management Review* 2 (1977), pp. 497–98.

[2] See F. K. Foulkes and J. L. Hirsch (1984), "People Make Robots Work," *Harvard Business Review* 62, 1 (1984), pp. 94–102.

[3] Frederick Herzberg, "One More Time: How Do You Motivate Employees?", *Harvard Business Review* 46 (January–February 1968), pp. 53–62.

[4] For a complete description and review of the research, see J. Richard Hackman and Greg R. Oldham, *Work Redesign* (Reading, Mass.: Addison-Wesley, 1980).

[5] J. C. Latack and L. W. Foster, "Implementation of Compressed Work Schedules: Participation and Job Redesign as Critical Factors for Employee Acceptance," *Personnel Psychology* 38 (1985), pp. 75–92.

[6] Jon L. Pierce and John W. Newstrom, "Toward a Conceptual Clarification of Employee Responses to Flexible Working Hours: A Work Adjustment Approach," *Journal of Management* 6 (1980), pp. 117–134.

[7] M. Creger, "Flextime Continues to Edge Upwards," *Management World* (July–August 1988), p. 15.

[8] Getsy M. Selirio, "Job Sharing Gains Favor as Corporations Embrace Alternative Work Schedule," *Lubbock Avalanche-Journal* (December 13, 1992), p. 2E.

[9] See Daniel C. Feldman and Helen I. Doerpinghaus, "Missing Persons No Longer: Managing Part-Time Workers in the '90s," *Organizational Dynamics* (Summer 1992), pp. 59–72.

[10] Randall S. Schuler, *Personnel and Human Resource Management,* 3rd ed. (St. Paul, Minn.: West, 1987), p. 464.

[11] *Women in Business* (July–August 1992), p. 10.

[12] P. Latham, "Goal Setting and Task Performance: 1969–1980," *Psychological Bulletin* 90 (July–November 1981, pp. 125–52). See also Gary P. Latham

and Edwin A. Locke, "Goal Setting—A Motivational Technique That Works," *Organizational Dynamics* 8 (Autumn 1979), pp. 68–80; Gary P. Latham and Timothy Steele, "The Motivational Effects of Participation versus Goal-Setting on Performance," *Academy of Management Journal* 26 (1983), pp. 406–17; Miriam Erez and Frederick H. Kanfer, "The Role of Goal Acceptance in Goal Setting and Task Performance," *Academy of Management Review* 8 (1983), pp. 454–63.

[13] See Edwin A. Locke and Gary P. Latham, "Work Motivation and Satisfaction: Light at the End of the Tunnel," *Psychological Science* 1, 4 (July 1990), pp. 240–46.

[14] Ibid.

[15] For a good review of MBO, see Anthony P. Raia, *Managing by Objectives* (Glenview, Ill.: Scott, Foresman, 1974); Steven Kerr summarizes the criticisms well in "Overcoming the Dysfunctions of MBO," *Management by Objectives* 5, 1 (1976).

[16] Fred Luthans, *Organizational Behavior,* 5th ed. (New York: McGraw-Hill, 1989), p. 282.

[17] We especially thank Dr. Lawrence Peters, Texas Christian University, for his fine critique of an earlier version of this material and the many useful suggestions provided.

[18] Charles J. Fombrun and Robert L. Laud, "Strategic Issues in Performance Appraisal, Theory and Practice," *Personnel* 60 (November–December 1983), p. 24.

[19] See G. P. Latham and K. N. Wexley, *Increasing Productivity Through Performance Appraisal* (Reading, Mass.: Addison-Wesley, 1981), p. 80.

[20] See Herbert H. Meyer, "A Solution to the Performance Appraisal Feedback Enigma, *Academy of Management Executive* 5 (February 1991), pp. 68–76.

[21] See David L. Devries, Ann M. Morrison, Sandra L. Shullman, and Michael L. Gerlach, *Performance Appraisal on the Line* (Greensboro, NC: Center for Creative Leadership, 1986), Chapters 3 and 6.

[22] For more detail, see Latham and Wexley, op. cit.; Stephen J. Carroll and Craig E. Schneier, *Performance Appraisal and Review Systems* (Glenview, Ill.: Scott, Foresman, 1982).

CHAPTER 8

[1] For a good discussion of recent thinking, see Jon R. Katzenbach and Douglas K. Smith, *The Wisdom of Teams: Creating the High-Performance Organization* (Boston: Harvard Business School Press, 1993a).

[2] For a good discussion and review, see Alvin Zander, *The Purpose of Groups and Organizations* (San Francisco: Jossey-Bass, 1985).

[3] For a good discussion of task forces, see James Ware, "Managing a Task Force," Note 478-002, Harvard Business School, 1977.

[4] This definition is adapted from Jon R. Katzenbach and Douglas K. Smith, "The Discipline of Teams," *Harvard Business Review* (March–April 1993b), pp. 111–120; see also Katzenbach and Smith, op. cit.

[5] Ibid.

[6] Rensis Likert, *New Patterns of Management* (New York: McGraw-Hill, 1961).

[7] Harold J. Leavitt, "Suppose We Took Groups Seriously," in Eugene L. Cass and Frederick G. Zimmer, eds., *Man and Work in Society* (New York: Van Nostrand Reinhold, 1975), pp. 67–77.

[8] See, for example, Edward E. Lawler III, *High-Involvement Management* (San Francisco: Jossey-Bass, 1986) and Marvin E. Shaw, *Group Dynamics: The Psychology of Small Group Behavior,* 2nd ed. (New York: McGraw-Hill, 1976).

[9] For a recent discussion, see W. Jack Duncan, "Why Some People Loaf in Groups While Others Loaf Alone," *Academy of Management Executive* 8 (1991), pp. 79–80. See also Bib Latane, Kipling Williams, and Stephen Harkins, "Many Hands Make Light the Work: The Causes and Consequences of Social Loafing," *Journal of Personality and Social Psychology* 37 (1978), pp. 822–832; E. Weldon and G. M. Gargano, "Cognitive Effort in Additive Task Groups: The Effects of Shared Responsibility on the Quality of Multiattribute Judgments," *Organizational Behavior and Human Decision Processes* 36 (1985), pp. 348–361.

[10] Developed from Rensis Likert, *New Patterns of Management* (New York: McGraw-Hill, 1961), pp. 166–169.

[11] See Paul S. Goodman, ed., *Designing Effective Work Groups* (San Francisco: Jossey-Bass, 1986).

[12] George C. Homans, *The Human Group* (New York: Harcourt Brace, 1950).

[13] Example from "Time to Toss Tradition?" *Enterprise* (Fall 1989), pp. 35–39.

[14] See Kenichi Ohmae, "Quality Control Circles: They Work and Don't Work," *The Wall Street Journal,* March 29, 1982, p. 16; Robert P. Steel, Anthony J. Mento, Benjamin L. Dilla, Nestor K. Ovalle, and Russell F. Lloyd, "Factors Influencing the Success and Failure of Two Quality Circles Programs," *Journal of Management* 11, No. 1 (1985), pp. 99–119; Edward E. Lawler III and Susan A. Mohrman, "Quality Circles: After the Honeymoon," *Organizational Dynamics* 15, No. 4 (1987), pp. 42–54.

[15] Richard S. Wellings, William C. Byhnam, and Jeanned M. Wilson, *Empowered Teams: Creating Self-Directed Work Groups that Improve Quality, Productivity, and Participation* (San Francisco: Jossey-Bass, 1991).

[16] "Saturn," *Business Week* (August 17, 1992), pp. 86–91.

[17] Information from Vanaja Dhanan and Cecille Austria, "Where Workers Manage Themselves," *World Executive's Digest* (October 1992), pp. 14–16.

[18] Developed in part from Richard S. Wellins, William C. Byham, and Jeanne M. Wilson, "Proactive Teams Achieve Inspiring Results," *World Executive's Digest* (October 1992), pp. 18–24.

[19] Katzenbach and Smith, op. cit., 1993b, p. 116.

[20] For a good discussion of team building, see William D. Dyer, *Team Building,* 2nd ed. (Reading, Mass.: Addison-Wesley, 1987).

[21] Based in part on Katzenbach and Smith, op. cit., 1993a, p. 113.

CHAPTER 9

[1] Information from *Fortune* (May 7, 1990), pp. 52–60.

[2] This approach is based on J. Steven Heinen and Eugene Jacobson, "A Model of Task Group Development in Complex Organization and a Strategy of Implementation," *Academy of Management Review* 1 (October 1976), pp. 98–111; Bruce W. Tuckman, "Developmental Sequence in Small Groups," *Psychological Bulletin* 63 (1965), pp. 384–399; and Bruce W. Tuckman and Mary Ann C. Jensen, "Stages of Small Group Development Revisited," *Group & Organization Studies* 2 (1977), pp. 419–427.

[3] See Daniel C. Feldman, "The Development and Enforcement of Group Norms," *Academy of Management Review* 9 (1984), pp. 47–53.

[4] Developed from Robert F. Allen and Saul Pilnick, "Confronting the Shadow Organization: How to Detect and Defeat Negative Norms," *Organizational Dynamics* (Spring 1973), pp. 6–10.

[5] Ibid. See also Alvin Zander, *Making Groups Effective* (San Francisco: Jossey-Bass, 1982), Chapter 4; and, Feldman, op. cit.

[6] For a good summary of research on group cohesiveness, see Marvin E. Shaw, *Group Dynamics* (New York: McGraw-Hill, 1971), pp. 110–112, 192.

[7] For a review see B. Mullen and C. Copper, "The Relation Between Group Cohesiveness and Performance: An Integration," *Psychological Bulletin* 11 (1994), pp. 210–227.

[8] Robert F. Bales, "Task Roles and Social Roles in Problem-Solving Groups," in Eleanor E. Maccoby, Theodore M. Newcomb, and E. L. Hartley, eds., *Readings in Social Psychology* (New York: Holt, Rinehart & Winston, 1958).

[9] For a good description of task and maintenance functions, see John J. Gabarro and Anne Harlan, "Note on Process Observation," Note 9-477-029, Harvard Business School, 1976.

[10] Ibid.

[11] This discussion is developed from Edgar H. Schein, *Process Consultation,* vol. 1, 2nd ed. (Reading, Mass.: Addison-Wesley, 1988), pp. 49–53; Rensis Likert, *New Patterns of Management* (New York: McGraw-Hill, 1961), pp. 166–169. The concept of interacting, coacting, and counteracting groups is presented in Fred E. Fiedler, *A Theory of Leadership Productivity* (New York: McGraw-Hill, 1967).

[12] Alex Bavelas, "Communication Patterns in Task-Oriented Groups," *Journal of the Accoustical Society of America* 22 (1950), pp. 725–730. See also "Research on Communication Networks," as summarized in Shaw, op. cit., pp. 137–153.

[13] Bavelas, op. cit.; Shaw, op. cit.

[14] This discussion is developed from Schein, op. cit., pp. 69–75.

[15] Ibid., p. 73.

[16] Developed from the classic article by Norman R. F. Maier, "Assets and Liabilities in Group Problem Solving," *Psychological Review* 74 (1967), pp. 239–249.

[17] Jerry Harvey, "Managing Agreement in Organizations: The Abilene Paradox," *Organizational Dynamics* (Summer 1974), pp. 63–80.

[18] Irving L. Janis, "Groupthink," *Psychology Today* (November 1971), pp. 43–46; Irving L. Janis, *Groupthink,* 2nd ed. (Boston: Houghton Mifflin, 1982). See also J. Longley and D. G. Pruitt, "Groupthink: A Critique of Janis' Theory," in L. Wheeler, ed., *Review of Personality and Social Psychology* (Beverly Hills, Calif.: Sage, 1980); Carrie R. Leana, "A Partial Test of Janis's Groupthink Model: The Effects of Group Cohesiveness and Leader Behavior on Decision Processes," *Journal of Management* 11 No. 1 (1985), pp. 5–18.

[19] Developed from Schein, ibid.

[20] Developed from ibid.

CHAPTER 10

[1] Rosabeth Moss Kanter, "Power Failure in Management Circuit," *Harvard Business Review* (July–August 1979), pp. 65–75.

[2] John R. P. French and Bertram Raven, "The Bases of Social Power," in Dorwin Cartwright, ed., *Group Dynamics: Research and Theory* (Evanston, Ill.: Row, Peterson, 1962), pp. 607–623.

[3] See ibid.

[4] Stanley Milgram, "Behavioral Study of Obedience," in Dennis W. Organ, ed., *The Applied Psychology of Work Behavior* (Dallas: Business Publications, Inc., 1978), pp. 384–398. Also see Stanley Milgram, "Behavioral Study of Obedience," *Journal of Abnormal and Social Psychology* 67 (1963), pp. 371–378; Stanley Milgram, "Group Pressure and Action Against a Person," *Journal of Abnormal and Social Psychology* 69 (1964), pp. 137–143; "Some Conditions of Obedience and Disobedience to Authority," *Human Relations* 1 (1965), pp. 57–76; *Obedience to Authority* (New York: Harper & Row, 1974).

[5] Chester Barnard, *The Functions of the Executive* (Cambridge, Mass.: Harvard University Press, 1938).

[6] Ibid.

[7] John P. Kotter, "Power, Success, and Organizational Effectiveness," *Organizational Dynamics* 6 (Winter 1978), p. 27.

[8] David A. Whetten and Kim S. Cameron, *Developing Managerial Skills* (Glenview, Ill.: Scott, Foresman, 1984), pp. 250–259.

[9] Ibid., pp. 260–266.

[10] David Kipinis, Stuart M. Schmidt, Chris Swaffin-Smith, and Ian Wilkinson, "Patterns of Managerial Influence: Shotgun Managers, Tacticians, and Bystanders," *Organizational Dynamics* 12 (Winter 1984), pp. 60, 61.

[11] Ibid., pp. 58–67; David Kipinis, Stuart M. Schmidt, and Ian Wilkinson, "Intraorganizational Influence Tactics: Explorations in Getting One's Way," *Journal of Applied Psychology* 65 (1980), pp. 440–452.

[12] Warren K. Schilit and Edwin A. Locke, "A Study of Upward Influence in Organizations," *Administrative Science Quarterly* 27 (1982), pp. 304–316.

[13] Ibid.

[14] New Ways to Exercise Power," *Fortune* (November 6, 1989), pp. 52–64.

[15] Although the work on organizational politics is not extensive, useful reviews include a chapter in Robert H. Miles, *Macro Organizational Behavior* (Santa Monica, Calif.: Goodyear, 1980); Bronston T. Mayes and Robert W. Allen, "Toward a Definition of Organizational Politics," *Academy of Management Review* 2 (1977), pp. 672–677; Gerald F. Cavanagh, Denis J. Moberg, and Manuel Velasquez, "The Ethics of Organizational Politics," *Academy of Management Review* 6 (July 1981), pp. 363–374; Dan Farrell and James C. Petersen, "Patterns of Political Behavior in Organizations," *Academy of Management Review* 7 (July 1982), pp. 403–412; D. L. Madison, R. W. Allen, L. W. Porter, and B. T. Mayes, "Organizational Politics: An Exploration of Managers' Perceptions," *Human Relations* 33 (1980), pp. 92–107.

[16] Mayes and Allen, op. cit., p. 675.

[17] Jeffrey Pfeffer, *Power in Organizations* (Marshfield, Mass.: Pitman, 1981), p. 7.

[18] B. E. Ashforth and R. T. Lee, "Defensive Behavior in Organizations: A Preliminary Model," *Human*

Relations (July 1990), pp. 621–648; personal communication with Blake Ashforth, December 1992.

[19] Developed from James L. Hall and Joel L. Leldecker, "A Review of Vertical and Lateral Relations: A New Perspective for Managers," pp. 138–146 in Patrick Connor, ed., *Dimensions in Modern Management,* 3rd ed. (Boston: Houghton Mifflin, 1982), which was based in part on Leonard Sayles, *Managerial Behavior* (New York: McGraw-Hill, 1964).

[20] See Jeffrey Pfeffer, *Organizations and Organization Theory* (Boston: Pitman, 1983); Jeffrey Pfeffer and Gerald R. Salancik, *The External Control of Organizations* (Englewood Cliffs, N.J.: Prentice-Hall, 1978).

[21] Ibid.

[22] James D. Thompson, *Organizations in Action* (New York: McGraw-Hill, 1967).

[23] R. N. Osborn and D. H. Jackson, "Leaders, Riverboat Gamblers, or Purposeful Unintended Consequences in Management of Complex Technologies," *Academy of Management Journal* 31 (1988), pp. 924–947; M. Hector, "When Actors Comply: Monitoring Costs and the Production of Social Order," *Acta Sociologica* 27 (1984), pp. 161–183; T. Mitchell and W. G. Scott, "Leadership Failures, the Distrusting Public and Prospects for the Administrative State," *Public Administration Review* 47 (1987), pp. 445–452.

[24] Adapted from Cavanagh, Moberg, and Velasquez, "The Ethics of Organizational Politics," pp. 363–374.

[25] These criteria are developed from ibid.

[26] Saul W. Gellerman, "Why 'Good' Managers Make Bad Ethical Choices," *Harvard Business Review* 64 (July 1986), pp. 85–97.

[27] Ibid.

CHAPTER 11

[1] See Alan Bryman, *Charisma and Leadership in Organizations* (London: Sage, 1992), Chapter 5.

[2] See Bernard M. Bass, *Bass and Stogdill's Handbook of Leadership,* 3rd ed. (New York: Free Press, 1990).

[3] Bass, op. cit.

[4] Rensis Likert, *New Patterns of Management* (New York: McGraw-Hill, 1961).

[5] Bass, op. cit., Chapter 24.

[6] Robert R. Blake and Jane S. Mouton, *The New Managerial Grid* (Houston: Gulf, 1978).

[7] See M. F. Peterson, "PM Theory in Japan and China: What's in It for the United States?" *Organizational Dynamics* (Spring 1988), pp. 22–39; J. Misumi and M. F. Peterson, "The Performance-Maintenance Theory of Leadership: Review of a Japanese Research Program," *Administrative Science Quarterly* 30 (1985), pp. 198–223; P. B. Smith, J. Misumi, M. Tayeb, M. F. Peterson and M. Bond, "On the Generality of Leadership Style Measures Across Cultures," paper presented at the International Congress of Applied Psychology, Jerusalem, July 1986.

[8] See Henry P. Sims, Jr., "The Leader as a Manager of Reinforcement Contingencies: An Empirical Example and a Model," in J. G. Hunt and L. L. Larson, eds., *Leadership Frontiers* (Kent, Ohio: Comparative Administration Research Institute, Kent State University, 1977); P. M. Podsakoff, W. D. Toder, R. A. Grover, and V. L. Huber, "Situational and Personality Moderators of Leader Reward and Punishment Behaviors: Fact or Fiction?" *Organizational Behavior and Human Performance* 34 (1984), pp. 810–821.

[9] A. R. Korukonda and James G. Hunt, "Pat on the Back versus Kick in the Pants: An Application of Cognitive Inference to the Study of Leader Reward and Punishment Behaviors," *Group and Organization Studies* 14, No. 3 (1989), pp. 299–324.

[10] This section is based on Fred E. Fiedler and Martin M. Chemers, *The Leader Match Concept,* 2nd ed. (New York: John Wiley, 1984).

[11] This section is based on Fred E. Fiedler and Joseph E. Garcia, *New Approaches to Effective Leadership* (New York: John Wiley, 1987).

[12] This section is based on Robert J. House and Terence R. Mitchell, "Path-Goal Theory of Leadership," *Journal of Contemporary Business* (Autumn 1977), pp. 81–97.

[13] See the discussion of this approach in Paul Hersey and Kenneth H. Blanchard, *Management of Organizational Behavior* (Englewood Cliffs, N.J.: Prentice-Hall, 1988).

[14] The discussion in this section is based on Steven Kerr and John Jermier, "Substitutes for Leadership: Their Meaning and Measurement," *Organizational Behavior and Human Performance* 22 (1978), pp. 375–403. Jon P. Howell, David E. Bowen, Peter W.

Dorfman, Steven Kerr, and Philip M. Podsakoff, "Substitutes for Leadership: Effective Alternatives to Ineffective Leadership," *Organizational Dynamics* (Summer 1990), pp. 21–38.

[15] See T. R. Mitchell, S. G. Green, and R. E. Wood, "An Attributional Model of Leadership and the Poor Performing Subordinate: Development and Validation." In L. L. Cummings and B. M. Staw, eds., *Research in Organizational Behavior* 3 (Greenwich, Conn.: JAI Press, 1981), pp. 197–234.

[16] See James G. Hunt, *Leadership: A New Synthesis* (Newbury Park, Calif.: Sage, 1991), Chapter 7.

[17] James G. Hunt, Kimberly B. Boal, and Ritch L. Sorenson, "Top Management Leadership: Inside the Black Box," *The Leadership Quarterly* 1, 1990, pp. 41–65.

[18] Based on Geert Hofstede, "Cultures Consequences: International Differences in Work Related Values" (Beverly Hills, Calif.: Sage, 1984).

[19] Hunt, Boal, and Sorenson, op. cit.

[20] See J. Pfeffer, "Management as Symbolic Action: *The Creation and Maintenance of Organizational Paradigms.*" In L. L. Cummings and B. M. Staw, eds., *Research in Organizational Behavior* 3 (Greenwich, Conn.: JAI Press, 1981), pp. 1–52.

[21] James R. Meindl, "On Leadership: An Alternative to the Conventional Wisdom," in B. M. Staw and L. L. Cummings, eds., *Research in Organizational Behavior* 12 (JAI Press, 1990), pp. 159–203.

[22] Bass, op. cit., 1990, Chapter 12.

[23] Jay A. Conger and R. N. Kanungo, eds., *Charismatic Leadership: The Elusive Factor in Organizational Effectiveness* (San Francisco: Jossey-Bass, 1988).

[24] See B. M. Bass, *Leadership and Performance Beyond Expectations* (New York: Free Press, 1985); Bryman, op. cit., pp. 98–99.

CHAPTER 12

[1] D. Nadler and M. Tushman, *Strategic Organizational Design* (Glenview, Ill.: Scott, Foresman, 1988).

[2] Richard V. Farace, Peter R. Monge, and Hamish M. Russell, *Communicating and Organizing* (Reading, Mass.: Addison-Wesley, 1977), pp. 97–98.

[3] This research is reviewed by John C. Athanassiades, "The Distortion of Upward Communication in Hierarchical Organizations," *Academy of Management Journal* 16 (June 1973), pp. 207–226.

[4] See M. P. Rowe and M. Baker, "Are You Hearing Enough Employee Concerns?" *Harvard Business Review* 62 (May–June 1984), pp. 127–135.

[5] This discussion is based on Carl R. Rogers and Richard E. Farson, "Active Listening" (Chicago: Relations Center of the University of Chicago).

[6] Adapted from John Anderson, "Giving and Receiving Feedback," in Paul R. Lawrence, Louis B. Barnes, and Jay W. Lorsch, eds., *Organizational Behavior and Administration,* 3rd ed. (Homewood, Ill.: Irwin, 1976), p. 109. See also John F. Kiloski and Joseph A. Litterer, "Effective Communication in the Performance Appraisal Interview," *Public Personnel Management* 9 (Spring 1983), pp. 33–42.

[7] See Robert L. Kahn, Donald M. Wolfe, Robert F. Quinn, and J. Diedrick Snoek, *Organizational Stress: Studies in Role Conflict and Ambiguity* (New York: John Wiley, 1964); Daniel Katz and Robert L. Kahn, *The Social Psychology of Organizations,* 2nd ed. (New York: John Wiley, 1978).

[8] For an excellent overview, see George P. Huber, *Managerial Decision Making* (Glenview, Ill.: Scott, Foresman, 1980).

[9] Subsequent discussion is adapted with permission from John R. Schermerhorn, Jr., *Management for Productivity* (New York: John Wiley, 1989), pp. 70–71. Copyright © 1989 John Wiley & Sons. Reprinted by permission of John Wiley & Sons, Inc.

[10] This discussion is based on James G. March and Herbert A. Simon, *Organizations* (New York: John Wiley, 1958), pp. 137–142.

[11] Ibid. See also Herbert A. Simon, *Administrative Behavior* (New York: Free Press, 1947).

[12] Weston H. Agor, *Intuition in Organizations* (Newbury Park, Calif.: Sage, 1989).

[13] Henry Mintzberg, "Planning on the Left Side and Managing on the Right," *Harvard Business Review* 54 (July–August 1976), pp. 51–63.

[14] The classic work in this area is found in a series of articles by D. Kahneman and A. Tversky: "Subjective Probability: A Judgment of Representativeness," *Cognitive Psychology* 3 (1972), pp. 430–454; "On the Psychology of Prediction," *Psychological Review* 80 (1973), pp. 237–251; "Prospect Theory:

An Analysis of Decision Under Risk," *Econometrica* 47 (1979), pp. 263–291; "Psychology of Preferences," *Scientific American* (1982), pp. 161–173; "Choices, Values, Frames," *American Psychologist* 39 (1984), pp. 341–350.

[15] Definition and subsequent discussion based on Max H. Bazerman, *Judgment in Managerial Decision Making,* 2nd ed. (New York: John Wiley, 1990), pp. 11–39.

[16] Barry M. Staw, "The Escalation of Commitment to a Course of Action," *Academy of Management Review* 6 (1981), pp. 577–587; Barry M. Staw and Jerry Ross, "Knowing When to Pull the Plug," *Harvard Business Review* 65 (March–April 1987), pp. 68–74. See also Glen Whyte, "Escalating Commitment to a Course of Action: A Reinterpretation," *Academy of Management Review* 11 (1986), pp. 311–321.

[17] Bazerman, op. cit., pp. 79–83.

[18] Wallas, G., *The Art of Thought* (New York: Harcourt, 1926). Cited in Bazerman, op. cit.

[19] James A. F. Stoner, *Management,* 2nd ed. (Englewood Cliffs, NJ: Prentice Hall, 1982), pp. 167–168.

[20] See Victor H. Vroom and Philip W. Yetton, *Leadership and Decision Making* (Pittsburgh: University of Pittsburgh Press, 1973); Victor H. Vroom and Arthur G. Jago, *The New Leadership* (Englewood Cliffs, NJ: Prentice Hall, 1988).

[21] George Huber, "Organizational Learning: The Contributing Process and the Literature," *Organization Science* 2, No. 1 (1991), pp. 88–115.

[22] J. W. Myer and B. Rowan, "Institutionalized Organizations: Formal Structure as Myth and Ceremony," *American Journal of Sociology* 83 (1977), pp. 340–363.

[23] March and Levin.

[24] Osborn and Jackson, 1988.

[25] Cohen, 1991; Sinchcomb, 1990.

[26] Ibid.

[27] Osborn and Jackson, op. cit.

[28] O. P. Walsch and G. R. Ungson, "Organization Memory," *The Academy of Management Review* 16, No. 1 (1991), pp. 57–91.

[29] Marcus et al., 1992.

[30] Ibid.

CHAPTER 13

[1] See Henry Mintzberg, *The Nature of Managerial Work* (New York: Harper & Row, 1973); and John R. P. Kotter, *The General Managers* (New York: Free Press, 1982).

[2] Richard E. Walton, *Interpersonal Peacemaking: Confrontations and Third-Party Consultation* (Reading, Mass.: Addison-Wesley, 1969).

[3] Kenneth W. Thomas and Warren H. Schmidt, "A Survey of Managerial Interests with Respect to Conflict," *Academy of Management Journal* 19 (1976), pp. 315–318.

[4] These two types are discussed in Walton, op. cit.

[5] See Jay Galbraith, *Designing Complex Organizations* (Reading, Mass.: Addison-Wesley, 1973).

[6] Rensis Likert and Jane B. Likert, *New Ways of Managing Conflict* (New York: McGraw-Hill, 1976).

[7] David Nadler and Michael Tushman, *Strategic Organizational Design* (Glenview, Ill.: Scott, Foresman, 1988).

[8] See Alan C. Filley, *Interpersonal Conflict Resolution* (Glenview, Ill.: Scott, Foresman, 1975); and L. David Brown, *Managing Conflict at Organizational Interfaces* (Reading, Mass.: Addison-Wesley, 1983).

[9] Robert R. Blake and Jane Strygley Mouton, "The Fifth Achievement," *Journal of Applied Behavioral Science* 6 (1970), pp. 413–427.

[10] Kenneth Thomas, "Conflict and Conflict Management," in M. D. Dunnett, ed., *Handbook of Industrial and Organizational Behavior* (Chicago: Rand McNally, 1976), pp. 889–935.

[11] Filley, op. cit., pp. 27, 29.

[12] For an excellent overview, see Roger Fisher and William Ury, *Getting to Yes: Negotiating Agreement Without Giving In* (New York: Penguin, 1983). See also James A. Wall, Jr., *Negotiation: Theory and Practice* (Glenview, Ill.: Scott, Foresman, 1985).

[13] Wall, op. cit., pp. 4–7.

[14] See Max H. Bazerman, *Judgment in Managerial Decision Making,* 3rd ed. (New York: John Wiley, 1994).

[15] Fisher and Ury, op. cit., p. 33.

[16] Roy J. Lewicki and Joseph A. Litterer, *Negotiation* (Homewood, Ill.: Irwin, 1985), pp. 315–319.

CHAPTER 14

[1] See Richard M. Cyert and James G. March, *A Behavioral Theory of the Firm* (Englewood Cliffs, NJ: Prentice Hall, 1963). A good discussion of organizational goals is also found in Charles Perrow, *Organizational Analysis: A Sociological View* (Belmont, CA: Wadsworth, 1970) and in Richard H. Hall, "Organizational Behavior: A Sociological Perspective," in Jay W. Lorsch, ed., *Handbook of Organizational Behavior* (Englewood Cliffs, NJ: Prentice Hall, 1987), pp. 84–95.

[2] See Richard N. Osborn, James G. Hunt, and Lawrence R. Jauch, *Organization Theory: Integrated Text and Cases* (Melbourne, Fla.: Krieger, 1985).

[3] H. Talcott Parsons, *Structure and Processes in Modern Societies* (New York: Free Press, 1960).

[4] See, for instance, Thomas J. Peters and Richard Waterman, Jr., *In Search of Excellence: Lessons from America's Best-Run Companies* (New York: Harper & Row, 1982).

[5] Adapted from Terri Lammers, "The Effective and Indispensable Mission Statement," *Inc.* (August 1992).

[6] See, for instance, I. C. MacMillan and A. Meshulack, "Replacement versus Expansion: Dilemma for Mature U.S. Businesses," *Academy of Management Journal* 26 (1983), pp. 708–726.

[7] William H. Starbuck and Paul C. Nystrom, "Designing and Understanding Organizations," in P. C. Nystrom and W. H. Starbuck, eds., *Handbook of Organizational Design: Adapting Organizations to Their Environments* (New York: Oxford University Press, 1981).

[8] Laura Didio, "How Data General is Turning Itself Around," *LAN Times* (January 6, 1992), pp. 26–29.

[9] See Osborn, Hunt, and Jauch, 1986, op. cit.

[10] See Paul R. Lawrence and Jay W. Lorsch, *Organization and Environment* (Homewood, Ill.: Irwin, 1969).

[11] For a review, see Osborn, Hunt, and Jauch, 1985, op. cit.

[12] James B. Quinn, *Intelligent Enterprise: A Knowledge and Service Based Paradigm for Industry* (New York: The Free Press, 1992).

[13] See Osborn, Hunt, and Jauch, 1985, op. cit.

[14] For further discussion, see J. Ivancevich, J. Donnelley, and J. Gibson, *Managing for Performance* (Plano, TX: Business Publications, 1986); Herbert Simon, "Making Management Decisions, The Role of Intuition and Emotion." *Academy of Management Executive* 1 (1987), pp. 57–64.

[15] William G. Ouchi and M. A. McGuire, "Organization Control: Two Functions," *Administrative Science Quarterly* 20 (1977), pp. 559–569.

[16] Adapted from W. Edwards Deming, "Improvement of Quality and Productivity Through Action by Management," *Productivity Review* (Winter 1982), pp. 12–22; and W. Edwards Deming, *Quality, Productivity and Competitive Position* (Cambridge, Mass.: MIT Center for Advanced Engineering, 1982).

[17] Ibid.

[18] This section is based on Osborn, Hunt, Jauch, *Organization Theory,* pp. 273–303.

[19] For a good discussion of Matrix Structures, see Stanley Davis, Paul Lawrence, Harvey Kolodny, and Michael Beer, *Matrix* (Reading, Mass.: Addison-Wesley, 1977).

CHAPTER 15

[1] R. N. Osborn, J. G. Hunt, and L. Jauch, *Organization Theory: Integrated Text and Cases* (Melbourne, Fla.: Krieger, 1984), pp. 123–215.

[2] See Henry Mintzberg, *Structure in Fives: Designing Effective Organizations* (Englewood Cliffs, NJ: Prentice Hall, 1983).

[3] For a comprehensive review, see W. Richard Scott, *Organizations: Rational, Natural, and Open Systems,* Second Edition (Englewood Cliffs, NJ: Prentice Hall, 1987).

[4] Max Weber, *The Theory of Social and Economic Organization,* translated by A. M. Henderson and H. T. Parsons (New York: Free Press, 1947).

[5] Mintzberg, 1983, op. cit.

[6] Mintzberg, 1983, op. cit.

[7] See Osborn et al. 1984, op. cit., for an extended discussion.

[8] See Peter Clark and Ken Starkey, *Organization Transitions and Innovation-Design* (London: Pinter Publications, 1988).

[9] Osborn, 1984, op cit.

[10] Ibid.

[11] See Peter M. Blau and Richard A. Schoenner, *The Structure of Organizations* (New York: Basic Books, 1971).

[12] Joan Woodward, *Industrial Organization: Theory and Practice* (London: Oxford University Press, 1965).

[13] James D. Thompson, *Organization in Action* (New York: McGraw-Hill, 1967).

[14] Woodward, 1965, op. cit.

[15] For reviews, see Osborn et al., 1980, op. cit., and Louis Fry, "Technology-Structure Research: Three Critical Issues," *Academy of Management Journal* 25 (1982), pp. 532–552.

[16] Mintzberg, 1983, op. cit.

[17] Charles Perrow, *Complex Organizations: A Critical Essay,* 3rd ed. (New York: Random House, 1986).

[18] Osborn, 1984, op. cit.

[19] This section is based on R. N. Osborn and J. G. Hunt, "The Environment and Organization Effectiveness," *Administrative Science Quarterly* 19 (1974), pp. 231–246, and Osborn et al., 1984, op. cit.

[20] Brian Dumaine and James A. Anderson, "The Bureaucracy Busters," *Fortune* (June 17, 1991), pp. 16–17, 38–50.

[21] See R. N. Osborn and C. C. Baughn, "New Patterns in the Formation of U.S./Japanese Cooperative Ventures," *Columbia Journal of World Business* 22 (1988), pp. 57–65.

[22] See John Ettlie, "Technology Drives a Marriage," *The Journal of Commerce* (Friday, March 16, 1990), p. 6.

[23] L. R. Jauch and R. N. Osborn, "Toward an Integrated Theory of Strategy," *Academy of Management Review* 6 (1981), 491–498; Alfred D. Chandler, *The Visible Hand: The Managerial Revolution in America* (Cambridge, Mass.: Bellknap, 1977); Karen Bantel and R. N. Osborn, "The Influence of Performance, Environment, and Size on Firm Strategic Clarity," working paper, Department of Management, Wayne State University, 1990.

[24] Adapted from Robert Quinn, *Beyond Rational Management* (New York: Jossey-Bass, 1988). Used with permission.

CHAPTER 16

[1] E. Schein, "Organizational Culture," *American Psychologist* 45 (1990), pp. 109–119.

[2] These examples were reported in an interview with Edgar Schein, "Corporate Culture is the Real Key to Creativity," *Business Month* (May 1989), pp. 73–74.

[3] T. Deal and A. Kennedy, *Corporate Culture* (Reading, Mass.: Addison-Wesley, 1982).

[4] T. Peters and R. Waterman, *In Search of Excellence* (New York: Harper & Row, 1982).

[5] G. Hofstede and M. H. Bond, "The Confucius Connection: From Cultural Roots to Economic Growth," *Organizational Dynamics* 16(4), pp. 4–21.

[6] R. A. Cooke and D. M. Rousseau, "Behavioral Norms and Expectations: A Quantitative Approach to the Assessment of Organizational Culture," *Group and Organizational Studies* 13 (1988), pp. 245–273.

[7] J. Martin and C. Siehl, "Organization Culture and Counterculture," *Organizational Dynamics* 12 (1983), pp. 52–64.

[8] "Is Sony Finally Getting the Hang of Hollywood?" *Business Week* (September 7, 1992), p. 76.

[9] Taylor Cox, Jr., "The Multicultural Organization," *The Academy of Management Executive* 2, No. 2 (May 1991), pp. 34–47.

[10] Based on work by Jeffrey Sonnenfeld, as reported by Carol Hymowitz, "Which Corporate Culture Fits You?" *The Wall Street Journal* (July 17, 1989), p. B1.

[11] A. C. Cooper and C. G. Smith, "How Established Firms Respond to Threatening Technologies," *Academy of Management Executive* 6, No. 2 (1992), pp. 56–69.

[12] E. Schein, "Organizational Culture," *American Psychologist* 45, No. 2 (1990), pp. 109–119; and E. Schein, *Organizational Culture and Leadership* (San Francisco: Jossey-Bass, 1985), pp. 52–57.

[13] C. Gertz, *The Interpretation of Culture* (New York: Basic Books, 1973).

[14] J. M. Byer and H. M. Trice, "How an Organization's Rites Reveal Its Culture," *Organizational Dynamics* (Spring 1987), pp. 27–41.

[15] J. Martin, M. S. Feldman, M. J. Hatch, and S. B. Stikin, "The Uniqueness Paradox in Organizational

Stories," *Administrative Science Quarterly* 28 (1983), pp. 438–453.

[16] H. M. Trice and J. M. Beyer, "Studying Organizational Cultures Through Rites and Ceremonials," *Academy of Management Review* 3 (1984), pp. 633–669.

[17] Developed from Terrence Deal and Allan Kennedy, *Corporate Cultures: The Rites and Rituals of Corporate Life* (Reading, Mass.: Addison-Wesley, 1982).

[18] J. Kotter and J. Heskett, *Corporate Culture and Performance* (New York: The Free Press, 1992).

[19] See J. G. Hunt, *Toward a Leadership Paradigm Change* (Newbury Park, Calif.: Sage, in press).

CHAPTER 17

[1] See Peter F. Drucker, *Managing for the Future: The 1990s and Beyond* (New York: Truman Talley Books/Dutton, 1992).

[2] Tom Peters, *Thriving on Chaos* (New York: Knopf, 1988).

[3] Described in Jeremy Main, "How to Steal the Best Ideas Around," *Fortune* (October 19, 1992), pp. 102–106.

[4] Ibid.

[5] Robert A. Cooke, "Managing Change in Organizations," in Gerald Zaltman, ed., *Management Principles for Nonprofit Organizations* (New York: American Management Association, 1979). See also David A. Nadler, "The Effective Management of Organizational Change," pp. 358–369 in Jay W. Lorsch, ed., *Handbook of Organizational Behavior* (Englewood Cliffs, N.J.: Prentice-Hall, 1987).

[6] Kurt Lewin, "Group Decision and Social Change," in G. E. Swanson, T. M. Newcomb, and E. L. Hartley, eds., *Readings in Social Psychology* (New York: Holt, Rinehart & Winston, 1952), pp. 459–473.

[7] This phenomenon is described in Noel M. Tichy and Mary Anne Devanna, *The Transformational Leader* (New York: John Wiley, 1986).

[8] The classic work in this area is still Robert Chin and Kenneth D. Benne, "General Strategies for Effecting Changes in Human Systems," in Warren G. Bennis, Kenneth D. Benne, Robert Chin, and Kenneth E. Corey, eds., *The Planning of Change,* 3rd ed. (New York: Holt, Rinehart & Winston, 1969), pp. 22–45.

[9] Donald Klein, "Some Notes on the Dynamics of Resistance to Change: The Defender Role," in Bennis et al., eds., *The Planning of Change,* pp. 117–124.

[10] Rosabeth Moss Kanter, *The Change Masters* (New York: Simon & Schuster, 1983).

[11] John P. Kotter and Leonard A. Schlesinger, "Choosing Strategies for Change," *Harvard Business Review* 57 (March–April 1979), pp. 109–112.

[12] Arthur P. Brief, Randall S. Schuler, and Mary Van Sell, *Managing Job Stress* (Boston: Little, Brown & Co., 1981), pp. 6–7.

[13] For a classic work, see H. Selye, *The Stress of Life,* rev. ed. (New York: McGraw-Hill, 1976).

[14] See Orlando Behling and Arthur L. Darrow, *Managing Work-Related Stress* (Chicago: Science Research Associates, 1984).

[15] Cary L. Cooper, "Executive Stress Around the World," *University of Wales Review of Business and Economics* (Winter 1987), pp. 3–8.

[16] See John M. Ivancevich and Michael T. Matteson, "Optimizing Human Resources: A Case for Preventive Health and Stress Management," *Organizational Dynamics* 9 (Autumn 1980), pp. 6–8; Matteson and Ivancevich, *Controlling Work Stress: Effective Human Resource and Management Strategies* (San Francisco: Jossey-Bass, 1987).

[17] See Robert Kreitner, "Personal Wellness: It's Just Good Business," *Business Horizons* 25 (May–June 1982), pp. 28–35.

[18] Julie Cohen Mason, "Healthy Equals Happy Plus Productive," *Management Review* (July 1992).

[19] W. Warner Burke, *Organization Development* (Reading, Mass.: Addison-Wesley, 1987); Wendell L. French and Cecil H. Bell, Jr., *Organization Development,* 4th ed. (Englewood Cliffs, N.J.: Prentice-Hall, 1990); Edgar F. Huse and Thomas G. Cummings, *Organization Development and Change,* 4th ed. (St. Paul, Minn.: West, 1989).

[20] Warren Bennis, "Using Our Knowledge of Organizational Behavior," pp. 29–49 in Lorsch, op. cit.

[21] Excellent overviews are found in ibid.; and French and Bell, op. cit.

[22] Richard Beckhard, "The Confrontation Meeting," *Harvard Business Review* 45 (March–April 1967), pp. 149–155.

[23] See Dale Zand, "Collateral Organization: A New Change Strategy," *Journal of Applied Behavioral Science* 10 (1974), pp. 63–89; Barry A. Stein and Rosabeth Moss Kanter, "Building the Parallel Organization," *Journal of Applied Behavioral Science* 16 (1980), pp. 371–386.

[24] J. Richard Hackman and Greg R. Oldham, *Work Redesign* (Reading, Mass.: Addison-Wesley, 1980).

[25] See Frederick G. Harmon, *The Executive Odyssey: Secrets of a Career without Limits* (New York: John Wiley, 1989).

[26] For a research review, see Daniel C. Feldman, "Careers in Organizations: Recent Trends and Future Directions," *Yearly Review of Management* 15 (June 1989), pp. 135–156.

[27] Walter Kiechel, III, "How We Will Work in the Year 2000," *Fortune* (May 17, 1993), pp. 38–52.

[28] Charles Handy, *The Age of Unreason* (Boston: Harvard Business School Press, 1991).

[29] Quote from "The New Professionals," *World Executive's Digest* (May 1993), p. 14.

[30] Ibid.

[31] "The New Professionals," *World Executive's Digest* (May 1993), pp. 14–16.

[32] Handy, op. cit.

G L O·S S A R Y

The parenthetical numbers following the definition indicate the chapter(s) in which the term is defined.

A

Ability is the capacity to perform the various tasks needed for a given job. (4)

Absenteeism is the failure of people to attend work on a given day. (5)

Achievement-oriented leadership is leadership behavior that emphasizes setting challenging goals, stressing excellence in performance, and showing confidence in the group members' ability to achieve high standards of performance. (11)

Active listening is communication by the receiver that helps the source of a message articulate what he or she really means. (12)

Active management by exception involves watching for deviations from rules and standards and taking corrective action. (11)

Adhocracy is an organizational structure that emphasizes shared, decentralized decision making, extreme horizontal specialization, few levels of management, the virtual absence of formal controls, and few rules, policies, and procedures. (15)

Affective components of an attitude are the specific feelings regarding the personal impact of the antecedents. (4)

Anchoring and adjustment heuristic is the means of assessing an event by beginning with an initial value taken from an historical precedent or other outside source and then making subsequent assessments based only on incremental adjustments to that value. (12)

Aptitude is the capability to learn something. (4)

Arbitration is where a neutral third party acts as judge and issues a binding decision affecting parties at a negotiation impasse. (13)

Attitudes are predispositions to respond in a positive or negative way to someone or something in one's environment. (4)

Attribution theory is the attempt to understand the cause of an event, assess responsibility for outcomes of the event, and assess the personal qualities of people involved. (4)

Authoritarianism is a personality trait that focuses on the rigidity of a person's beliefs. (4)

Automation is a job design that allows machines to do work previously accomplished by human effort. (7)

Availability heuristic is the means of assessing an event based on instances of occurrences of that event that are easily available in one's memory. (12)

B

Behavioral components of an attitude are the intentions to behave in a certain way based on a person's specific feelings or attitude. (4)

Behavioral decision theory is the idea that people act only in terms of what they perceive about a given situation. (12)

Bureaucracy is an ideal form of organization whose characteristics were defined by the German sociologist Max Weber. (15)

C

Central tendency error occurs when managers lump everyone together around the average, or middle, category. (7)

Centralization is the degree to which the authority to make decisions is restricted to higher levels of management. (14)

Centralized communication networks are group communication networks in which all communication flows through a central person who serves as the "hub" of the network. (9)

Certain environments are decision environments in which information is sufficient to predict the results of each alternative in advance of implementation. (12)

Channels are the media through which the message may be delivered. (12)

Charisma is a dimension of leadership that provides vision and a sense of mission and instills pride, respect, and trust. (11)

Charismatic leaders are those leaders who, by force of their personal abilities, are capable of having a profound and extraordinary effect on followers. (11)

Classical conditioning is a form of learning through association that involves the manipulation of stimuli to influence behavior. (6)

Classical decision theory is a theory that views the manager as acting in a world of complete certainty. (12)

Coercive power is the extent to which a manager can deny desired rewards or administer punishments to control other people. (10)

Cognitive components of an attitude are the beliefs, opinions, knowledge, or information a person possesses. (4)

Cognitive dissonance is a state of perceived inconsistency between a person's expressed attitudes and actual behavior. (5)

Cognitive learning is a form of learning achieved by thinking about the perceived relationship between events and individual goals and expectations. (6)

Cohesiveness is the degree to which members are attracted to and motivated to remain a part of a group. (9)

Compressed work week is any work schedule that gives employees daily choices in the timing between work and nonwork activities. (7)

Conceptual skill is the ability to view the situation as a whole and solve problems for the benefit of everyone concerned. (1)

Conflict is a situation in which two or more people disagree over issues of organizational substance and/or experience some emotional antagonism with one another. (13)

Conflict resolution occurs when the reasons for a conflict are eliminated. (13)

Conglomerates are firms that own several different unrelated businesses. (15)

Constructive conflict is conflict that results in positive benefits to the group. (13)

Constructive stress (eustress) is stress that

acts in a positive way for the individual and/or the organization. (17)

Consultative decisions are decisions made by an individual after seeking input from or consulting with members of a group. (12)

Content theories offer ways to profile or analyze individuals to identify the needs that motivate their behaviors. (5)

Contingent rewards are rewards that are given in exchange for mutually agreed upon goal accomplishments. (11)

Continuous improvement is the belief that anything and everything done in the workplace should be continually evaluated to see if it can be done better. (2)

Control is the set of mechanisms used to keep actions and outputs within predetermined limits. (14)

Controlling is the process of monitoring performance, comparing actual results to objectives, and taking corrective action as necessary. (1)

Coordination is the set of mechanisms used in an organization to link the actions of its subunits into a consistent pattern. (14)

Corporate culture is the system of shared beliefs and values that develops within a business setting and guides the behavior of the members. (14)

Corporate social responsibility is the obligation of organizations to behave in ethical and moral ways. (2)

Countercultures are the patterns of values and philosophies that outwardly reject those of the larger organization or social system. (16)

Crafted decisions are decisions created to deal specifically with a situation at hand. (12)

Creativity is the development of unique and novel responses to problems and opportunities of the moment. (17)

Critical incident diaries is a method of performance appraisal whereby supervisors record incidents of each subordinate's behavior that led either to unusual success or failure in a given performance aspect. (7)

Cultural symbol is any object, act, or event that serves to transmit cultural meaning. (16)

D

Decentralization is the degree to which the authority to make decisions is given to lower levels in an organization's hierarchy. (14)

Decentralized communication networks are group communication networks in which all members communicate directly with one another. (9)

Decoding is the interpretation of the symbols sent from the sender to the receiver. (12)

Deficit cycle is a pattern of deteriorating performance that is followed by even further deterioration. (12)

Destructive conflict is conflict that works to the group's or organization's disadvantage. (13)

Destructive stress (distress) is stress that acts in a dysfunctional way for the individual and/or the organization. (17)

Directive leadership is leadership behavior that spells out the what and how of subordinates' tasks. (11)

Disruptive behavior is any behavior that harms the group process. (9)

Distributive justice is the degree to which all people are treated the same under a policy, regardless of race, ethnicity, gender, age, or any other demographic characteristics. (2)

Divisional departmentation is the grouping of individuals and resources by product, service, client, or legal entity. (14)

Divisionalized design is an organization that establishes a separate structure for each business or division. (15)

Dogmatism is a personality trait that regards legitimate authority as absolute and accepts or rejects others based on their acceptance of authority. (4)

E

Effective groups are groups that achieve high levels of both task performance and human resource maintenance. (8)

Effective manager is a manager whose work unit achieves high levels of both task performance and human resource maintenance. (1)

Effective negotiation occurs when issues of substance are resolved without any harm to the working relationships among the parties involved. (13)

Efficient communication is communication at minimum cost in terms of resources expended. (12)

Employee involvement groups are groups of workers who meet regularly outside of their normal work units for the purpose of collectively addressing important workplace issues. (8)

Empowerment is allowing individuals or groups to make decisions that affect them or their work. (10)

Encoding is the process of translating an idea or thought into meaningful symbols. (12)

Environmental complexity is the magnitude of the problems and opportunities in the organization's environment as evidenced by the degree of richness, interdependence, and uncertainty. (15)

Equity theory is based on the phenomenon of social comparison and posits that as people gauge the fairness of their work outcomes compared to others, felt inequity is a motivating state of mind. (5)

ERG theory categorizes needs into existence, relatedness, and growth needs. (5)

Escalating commitment is the tendency to continue with a previously chosen course of action even when feedback suggests that it is failing. (12)

Ethical climate is the shared set of understandings in an organization about what is correct behavior and how ethical issues will be handled. (16)

Ethical dilemma is a situation in which a person must decide whether or not to do something that—although benefitting oneself or the organization or both—may be considered unethical and perhaps illegal.

Ethnocentrism is the tendency to consider one's culture and its values superior to others. (3,12)

Existence needs are desires for physiological and material well-being. (5)

Expatriate is a person who takes employment and lives in a foreign country. (3)

Expectancy is the probability assigned by an individual that work effort will be followed by a given level of achieved task performance. (4,5)

Expectancy theory argues that work motivation is determined by individual beliefs regarding effort-performance relationships and the desirabilities of work outcomes that are associated with different performance levels. (5)

Expert power   is the ability to control another's behavior due to the possession of knowledge, experience, or judgment that the other person does not have but needs. (10)

External adaptation   is the process of reaching goals and dealing with outsiders. (16)

Externals   are persons with an external locus of control, who believe that what happens to them is beyond their control. (4)

Extinction   is the withdrawal of the reinforcing consequences for a given behavior. (6)

Extrinsic rewards   are positively valued work outcomes that are given to the individual by some other person in the work setting. (5,6)

F

Feedback   is the process of telling someone else how one feels about something the person did or said or about the situation in general. (12)

Felt negative inequity   exists when individuals feel that they have received relatively less than others have in proportion to work goals. (5)

Felt positive inequity   exists when individuals feel that they have received relatively more than others have. (5)

Flexible benefits plans   are pay systems that allow workers to select benefits according to their individual needs. (6)

Flexible working hours   is any work schedule that gives employees daily choices in the timing between work and nonwork activities. (7)

Force-coercion strategy   tries to "command" change through the formal authority of legitimacy, rewards, and punishments. (17)

Forced distribution   is a method of performance appraisal that uses a small number of performance categories such as "very good," "good," "adequate," "poor," and "very poor." (7)

Formal authority   is legitimate power, or the right of command vested in a managerial position. (10)

Formal communication channels   are communication channels that follow the chain of command established by the organization's hierarchy. (12)

Formal structure   is the intended configuration of positions, job duties, and lines of authority among the component parts of an organization. (14)

Formalization   is the written documentation of work rules, policies, and procedures. (13)

Functional departmentation   is the grouping of individuals and resources by skill, knowledge, and action. (14)

Fundamental attribution error   is the tendency to underestimate the influence of situational factors and to overestimate the influence of personal factors in evaluating someone else's behavior. (4)

G

Gain sharing   is a pay system that links pay and performance by giving workers the opportunity to share in productivity gains through increased earnings. (6)

General environment   is the set of cultural, economic, educational, and legal-political forces common to organizations operating within a given geographical area. (15)

Global geographic structure   is a structure whereby a firm engaged in extensive international business uses a geographic breakdown for operations in foreign countries. (3)

Global product structure   is a structure whereby a firm engaged in extensive international business uses a product breakdown for operations in foreign countries. (3)

Goal setting   is the process of developing, negotiating, and formalizing the targets or objectives that an employee is responsible for accomplishing. (7)

Graphic rating scale   lists a variety of dimensions that are thought to be related to high-performance outcomes in a given job and that the individual is expected to exhibit. (7)

Group decisions   are decisions made by all members of the group, ideally with consensus being achieved. (12)

Group dynamics   are the forces operating in groups that affect group performance and member satisfaction. (8)

Group processes   are the forces operating in groups that affect task performance and human resource maintenance. (8)

Groups   are collections of two or more people

who work with one another regularly to achieve one or more common goals. (8)

Groupthink is the tendency for highly cohesive groups to lose their critical evaluative capabilities. (9)

Growth needs are desires for continuous personal growth and development. (5)

H

Halo effect occurs when one attribute of a person or situation is used to develop an overall impression of the person or situation. (4)

Halo error results when one person rates another person on several different dimensions and gives a similar rating for each dimension. (7)

Heuristics are simplifying strategies or "rules of thumb" that people use when making decisions. (12)

Higher-order needs are esteem and self-actualization needs in Maslow's hierarchy. (5)

Hindsight trap is a biased situation in which the manager overestimates the degree to which he or she really could have predicted an event that has already taken place. (12)

Horizontal loading involves increasing the breadth of a job by adding to the variety of tasks performed by the worker. (7)

Horizontal specialization is a division of labor through the formation of work units or groups within an organization. (14)

Human resources are the individuals and groups whose performance contributions make it possible for the organization to serve a particular purpose. (1)

Human resource maintenance is the attraction and continuation of a viable workforce. (1)

Human skill is the ability to work well in cooperation with other persons. (1)

Hygienes (hygiene factors) are dissatisfiers that are associated with aspects of a person's work setting. (5)

I

Individual decisions are decisions made by one individual on behalf of the group. (12)

Individualized consideration is a leadership dimension whereby the leader provides personal attention, treats each employee individually, and coaches and advises subordinates. (11)

Influence is a behavioral response to the exercise of power. (10)

Informal communication channels are communication channels that do not adhere to the organization's hierarchy. (12)

Informal groups are groups that emerge unofficially and are not formally designed as parts of the organization. (8)

Inspiration is the communication of high expectations, the use of symbols to focus efforts, and the expression of important purposes in simple ways. (11)

Instrumental values are values that reflect a person's beliefs about the means for achieving desired ends. (4)

Instrumentality is the probability assigned by the individual that a given level of achieved task performance will lead to various work outcomes. (5)

Integrative negotiation is negotiation in which the focus is on the merits of the issues, and the parties involved try to enlarge the available "pie" rather than stake claims to certain portions of it. (13)

Intellectual stimulation promotes intelligence, rationality, and careful problem solving. (11)

Internal integration is the creation of a collective identity and the means of matching methods of working and living together. (16)

Internals are people with an internal locus of control, who believe that they control their own fate or destiny. (4)

International management is management that involves the conduct of business activities in more than one country. (3)

International organizational behavior is the study of individuals and groups in organizations operating in an international setting. (3)

Intrinsic motivation is a desire to work hard solely for the pleasant experience of task accomplishment. (7)

Intrinsic rewards are positive value work outcomes that are received by the individual directly as a result of task performance. (5,7)

J

Job characteristics theory identifies five core job characteristics (skill variety, task identity, task significance, autonomy, and job feedback) as having special importance to job designs. (7)

Job context are factors related to a person's work setting. (5)

Job design is the planning and specification of job tasks and the work setting in which they are to be accomplished. (7)

Job Diagnostic Survey (JDS) is a questionnaire used to examine each of the dimensions of the job characteristics model. (8)

Job enlargement involves increasing task variety by combining into one job tasks that were previously assigned to separate workers. (7)

Job enrichment is the practice of building motivating factors into job content. (7)

Job rotation involves increasing task variety by periodically shifting workers among jobs involving different tasks. (7)

Job satisfaction is the degree to which individuals feel positively or negatively about their jobs. (5)

Job sharing is the assignment of one full-time job to two or more persons who divide the work according to agreements made between themselves and the employer. (7)

Job simplification is standardizing work procedures and employing people in very clearly defined and specialized tasks. (7)

Jobs are one or more tasks that an individual performs in direct support of an organization's production purpose. (7)

L

Laissez faire is a leadership style that involves abdicating responsibilities and avoiding decisions. (11)

Law of contingent reinforcement is the view that for a reward to have a maximum reinforcing value, it must be delivered only if the desired behavior is exhibited. (6)

Law of effect is Thorndike's observation that behavior that results in a pleasing outcome will be likely to be repeated; behavior that results in an unpleasant outcome is not likely to be repeated. (6)

Law of immediate reinforcement states that the more immediate the delivery of a reward after the occurrence of a desirable behavior, the greater the reinforcing effect on behavior. (6)

Leadership is a special case of interpersonal influence that gets an individual or group to do what the leader wants done. (11)

Leading is the process of directing and coordinating the work efforts of other people to help them to accomplish important tasks. (1)

Learning is a relatively permanent change in behavior that occurs as a result of experience. (6)

Least preferred coworker (LPC) scale is a measure of a person's leadership style based on a description of the person with whom respondents have been able to work least well. (11)

Legitimate power is the extent to which a manager can use the internalized values of a subordinate that the "boss" has a "right of command" to control other people. (10)

Leniency error is the tendency to give relatively high ratings to virtually everyone. (7)

Line units are work groups that conduct the major business of the organization. (14)

Locus of control is the internal–external orientation; that is, the extent to which people feel able to affect their lives. (4)

Lose–lose conflict occurs when nobody really gets what he or she wants. (13)

Lower-order needs are physiological, safety, and social needs in Maslow's hierarchy. (5)

Lump-sum pay increase is a pay system in which people elect to receive their annual wage or salary increase in one or more "lump-sum" payments. (6)

M

Machiavellians are people who view and manipulate others for purely personal gain. (4)

Machine bureaucracy is an entire organization characterized by the mechanistic design. (15)

Maintenance activities are activities that support the emotional life of the group as an ongoing social system. (9)

Maladaptive specialization is extensive experience with and/or knowledge of a competitively inferior process, procedure, technology, or business. (12)

Management philosophy is a philosophy that links key goal-related issues with key collaboration issues to come up with general ways by which the firm will manage its affairs. (16)

Management process involves planning, organizing, leading, and controlling the use of organizational resources to achieve high performance results. (1)

Managerial script is a series of well-known routines for problem identification and alternative generation and analysis common to managers within a firm. (12)

Managers are people in organizations who are responsible for the performance of one or more others. (1)

Matrix structure is a combination of functional and divisional patterns wherein an individual is assigned to more than one type of unit. (14)

Mechanistic design is a highly bureaucratic organization that emphasizes vertical specialization and control, an extensive use of managerial techniques, impersonal coordination and control, and a heavy reliance on rules, policies, and procedures. (15)

Merit pay is a compensation system that bases an individual's salary or wage increase on a measure of the person's performance accomplishments during a specified time period. (6)

Mimicry is the copying of successful practices of others. (12)

Mission statements are written statements of organizational purpose. (13)

Mixed messages are messages that appear mixed when a person's words communicate one message while the individual's actions or nonverbal language communicate another. (12)

Monochronic culture is a culture in which people tend to do one thing at a time. (3)

Motivators (motivator factors) are satisfiers that are associated with what people actually do in their work. (5)

Motivator–hygiene theory distinguishes between sources of work dissatisfaction (hygiene fac-

tors) and satisfaction (motivators); it is also known as the two-factor theory. (5)

Multiculturalism is the presence in the same work setting of people from more than one cultural background. (2)

Multicultural organization is a firm that values diversity but systematically works to block the transfer of societal-based subcultures into the fabric of the organization. (15)

Multinational corporation (MNC) is a business firm that has extensive international operations in more than one foreign country. (3)

N

Need for achievement (nAch) is the desire to do something better, solve problems, or master complex tasks. (5)

Need for affiliation (nAff) is the desire to establish and maintain friendly and warm relations with others. (5)

Need for power (nPower) is the desire to control others, influence their behavior, and be responsible for them. (5)

Negative reinforcement is the withdrawal of negative consequences that tend to increase the likelihood of repeating the behavior in similar settings; it is also known as avoidance. (6)

Negotiation is the process of making joint decisions when the parties involved have different preferences. (13)

Noise is anything that interferes with the effectiveness of the communication attempt. (12)

Nonverbal communication is communication that takes place through facial expressions, body, eye contact, and other physical gestures. (12)

O

OD interventions are activities initiated in support of an OD program and designed to improve the work effectiveness of individuals, groups, or the organization as a whole. (17)

Open systems transform human and physical resources received from their environments into goods and services that are then returned to the environment. (1)

Operant conditioning is the process of controlling behavior by manipulating its consequences. (6)

Organic design is an organizational structure that emphasizes horizontal specialization, an extensive use of personal coordination, and loose rules, policies, and procedures. (15)

Organization charts are diagrams that depict the formal structures of organizations. (14)

Organization development (OD) is the application of behavioral science knowledge in a long-range effort to improve an organization's ability to cope with change in its external environment and increase its problem-solving capabilities. (17)

Organizational behavior is the study of individuals and groups in organizations. (1)

Organizational behavior modification (OB Mod) is the systematic reinforcement of desirable work behavior and the nonreinforcement or punishment of unwanted work behavior. (6)

Organizational communication is the process by which entities exchange information and establish a common understanding. (12)

Organizational culture is the system of shared beliefs and values that develops within an organization or within its subunits and that guides the behavior of its members. (16)

Organizational design is the process of choosing and implementing a structural configuration for an organization. (15)

Organizational learning is the process of knowledge acquisition, information distribution, information interpretation, and organizational retention. (12)

Organizational myth is a commonly held cause-effect relationship or assertion that cannot be empirically supported. (12, 16)

Organizational strategy is the process of positioning the organization in the competitive environment and implementing actions to compete successfully. (15)

Organizations are collections of people working together, in divisions of labor, to achieve a common purpose. (1)

Organizing is the process of dividing up the work to be done and then coordinating results to achieve a desired purpose. (1)

Output controls are controls that focus on desired targets and allow managers to use their own methods for reaching defined targets. (14)

Output goals are the goals that define the type of business an organization is in. (14)

P

Paired comparison is a comparative method of performance appraisal whereby each person is directly compared with every other person being rated. (7)

Parochialism is the tendency to assume that the ways of one's culture are the only ways of doing things. (3)

Participative leadership is a leadership style that focuses on consulting with subordinates and seeking and taking their suggestions into account before making decisions. (11)

Passive management by exception involves intervening with subordinates only if standards are not met. (16)

Performance appraisal is a process of systematically evaluating performance and providing feedback on which performance adjustments can be made. (7)

Performance effectiveness is a measure of whether or not important task goals are being attained. (1)

Performance efficiency is a measure of how well resources are being utilized. (1)

Performance gap is a discrepancy between an actual and a desired state of affairs. (17)

Permanent part-time work is a situation in which a worker is considered permanent but works fewer hours than the standard work week. (7)

Personal bias error occurs when a rater allows specific biases (e.g., racial, age, gender) to enter into performance appraisals. (7)

Planned change is change that happens as a result of specific efforts on its behalf by a change agent. (17)

Planning is the process of setting performance objectives and identifying the actions needed to accomplish them. (1)

Polychronic culture is a culture in which people tend to do more than one thing at a time. (3)

Positive reinforcement is the administration of

positive consequences that tend to increase the likelihood of repeating the behavior in similar settings. (6)

Power is the ability to get someone else to do something you want done, or the ability to make things happen or get things done the way you want. (10)

Power-oriented behavior is behavior directed primarily at developing or using relationships in which other people are to some degree willing to defer to one's wishes. (10)

Primary beneficiaries are particular groups expected to benefit from the efforts of specific organizations. (12)

Procedural justice is the degree to which the rules and procedures specified by policies are properly followed in all cases under which the policies are applied. (2)

Process controls are controls that attempt to specify the manner in which tasks will be accomplished. (14)

Process theories seek to understand the thought processes that take place in the minds of people and that act to motivate their behavior. (5)

Productivity is a summary measure of the quantity and quality of work. (1)

Professional bureaucracy is an organization that relies on organic features in its design. (15)

Programmed decisions are decisions that implement specific solutions determined by past experience as appropriate for the problems at hand. (12)

Projection is the assignment of personal attributes to other individuals. (4)

Punishment is the administration of negative consequences that tend to reduce the likelihood of repeating the behavior in similar settings. (6)

Q

Quality circles are groups of workers who meet periodically to discuss and develop solutions for production problems relating to quality, productivity, or cost. (2)

Quality means that the customer's needs are being met and that all tasks are done right the first time. (2)

Quality of work life is a term used to indicate the overall quality of human experiences in the workplace. (2)

Quasiformal channels are planned communications connections between holders of the various positions within the organization. (12)

R

Ranking is a comparative technique of performance appraisal that involves rank ordering each individual from best to worst on each performance dimension being considered. (7)

Rational persuasion strategy is an attempt to bring about a change through communication of special knowledge, empirical support, or logical arguments. (17)

Receivers are the individuals or groups of individuals that hear the message. (12)

Recency error is a biased rating that develops by allowing the individual's most recent behavior speak for his or her overall performance on a particular dimension. (7)

Referent power is the ability to control another's behavior because of the individual's wanting to identify with the power source. (10)

Relatedness needs are desires for satisfying interpersonal relationships. (5)

Representativeness heuristic is a means of assessing the likelihood of an event occurring based on the similarity of that event to one's stereotypes of similar occurrences. (12)

Reward power is the extent to which a manager can use extrinsic and intrinsic rewards to control other people. (10)

Risk environment is a decision environment involving a lack of complete certainty but one that includes an awareness of probabilities associated with the possible outcomes of various courses of action. (12)

Rites are standardized and recurring activities used at special times to influence the behaviors and understanding of organizational members. (16)

Rituals are systems of rites. (16)

Role is a set of expectations for the behavior of a person holding a particular office or position. (12)

Role ambiguity is the uncertainty of a person

about what other group members expect of him or her. (12)

Role conflict is the inability of a person in a role to respond to the expectations of one or more members of the role set. (12)

Role overload is a situation in which there are simply too many role expectations being communicated to a person at a given point in time. (12)

Role set is the various people who hold expectations regarding the behavior of someone in a role. (12)

S

Satisficing is choosing the first satisfactory rather than the optimal decision alternative. (12)

Scanning is looking outside the firm and bringing back useful solutions to problems. (12)

Selective perception is the tendency to single out for attention those aspects of a situation or person that reinforce or emerge and are consistent with existing beliefs, values, and needs. (4)

Self-managing teams are small groups of people empowered to manage themselves and the work they do on a day-to-day basis. (8)

Self-monitoring reflects a person's ability to adjust his or her behavior to external, situational (environmental) factors. (4)

Self schemas contain information about one's own appearance, behavior, and personality. (5)

Self-serving bias is the tendency to deny personal responsibility for performance problems but to accept personal responsibility for performance success. (4)

Shamrock organizations are organizations characterized by three "leaves" representing (1) a core group of workers made up of permanent, full-time employees; (2) outside operators engaged on contracts by the core group; and (3) part-timers. (2)

Shaping is the creation of a new behavior by the positive reinforcement of successive approximations to the desired behavior. (6)

Shared power strategy (normative-reeducative strategy) attempts to bring about change by identifying or establishing values and assumptions such that support of the change naturally emerges. (17)

Simple design is a configuration involving one or two ways of specializing individuals and units. (15)

Situational control is the extent to which leaders can determine what their group is going to do and what the outcomes of their actions and decisions are going to be. (11)

Skill-based pay is a pay system that rewards people for acquiring and developing job-relevant skills in a number and variety relevant to organizational needs. (6)

Social learning is learning that is achieved through the reciprocal interaction between people and their environments. (6)

Societal goals are goals reflecting the intended contributions of an organization to the broader society. (14)

Span of control is the number of individuals reporting to a supervisor. (14)

Specific environment is the set of suppliers, distributors, competitors, and government agencies with which a particular organization must interact to survive and grow. (15)

Staff units are groups that assist the line units by performing specialized services to the organization. (14)

Standardization is the degree to which the range of actions in a job or series of jobs is limited. (14)

Stimulus is something that incites action. (6)

Strategic alliances, or joint ventures, are announced cooperative agreements or joint ventures between two independent firms. (15)

Stressors are things that cause stress (e.g., work, nonwork, and personal factors). (17)

Strictness error occurs when a rater tends to give everyone a low rating. (7)

Subcultures are unique patterns of values and philosophies within a group that are not consistent with the dominant culture of the larger organization or social system. (16)

Supportive leadership is a leadership style that focuses on subordinate needs and well-being, and promoting a friendly work climate; it is similar to consideration. (11)

Synergy is the creation of a whole that is greater than the sum of its parts. (1)

Systems goals are goals concerned with conditions within the organization that are expected to increase its survival potential. (14)

T

Task activities are the various things members do that directly contribute to the performance of important group tasks. (9)

Task performance is the quality and quantity of work produced. (1)

Team building is a sequence of planned action steps designed to gather and analyze data on the functioning of a group and to implement changes to increase its operating effectiveness. (8)

Teams are small groups of people with complementary skills who work together to achieve a common purpose for which they hold themselves collectively responsible. (8)

Teamwork is when members of a team work together in such a way that certain core values that promote the utilization of skills to accomplish certain goals are represented. (8)

Technical skill is the ability to use a special proficiency or expertise relating to a method, process, or procedure. (1)

Technological imperative is the idea that if an organization does not adjust its internal structure to the requirements of the technology, it will not be successful. (15)

Technology is the combination of resources, knowledge, and techniques that creates a product or service output for an organization. (15)

Telecommuting is work done at home using a computer and/or facsimile ("fax") machine as links to the central office or other places of employment. (7)

Temporary part-time work is a situation in which an employee is classified as temporary and works less than the standard 40-hour work week. (7)

Total quality management (TQM) is management that ensures an organization and all its members operate with commitment to continuous improvement and to meeting customer needs completely. (1)

Transactional leadership is a leadership style whereby the leader exerts influence during daily leader–subordinate exchanges without much emotion. (11)

Transformational leadership is a leadership style whereby the followers' goals are broadened and elevated and whereby confidence is gained to go beyond expectations. (11)

Type A orientation is an orientation characterized by impatience, desire for achievement, and perfectionism. (4)

Type B orientation is an orientation characterized by being easygoing and less competitive in daily life. (4)

U

Uncertain environments are decision environments in which managers are unable to assign probabilities to the possible outcomes of various courses of action. (12)

Upside-down pyramid is a perspective of organizations that reflects the emerging view of managers as "helpers," "coaches," and "supporters." (2)

V

Valence is the values attached by the individual to various work outcomes. (5)

Value congruence occurs when individuals express positive feelings upon encountering others who exhibit values similar to their own. (4)

Vertical loading involves increasing job depth by adding responsibilities, like planning and controlling, previously done by supervisors. (7)

Vertical specialization is a hierarchical division of labor that distributes formal authority and establishes how critical decisions will be made. (14)

Virtual corporation is an organization that exists only as a temporary network or alliance of otherwise independent companies who are jointly pursuing a particular business interest. (2)

W

Whistleblower is someone who exposes organizational wrongdoing in order to preserve ethical standards and protect against wasteful, harmful, or illegal acts. (2)

Win–lose conflict occurs when one party achieves its desires at the expense and to the exclusion of the other party's desires. (13)

Win–win conflict is achieved by collaboration to address the real issues in a conflict situation and the use of problem solving to reconcile differences. (13)

Work teams or units are task-oriented groups that include a manager and his or her direct reports. (1)

Workforce diversity is a workforce consisting of a broad mix of workers from different racial and ethnic backgrounds, of different ages and genders, and of different domestic and national cultures. (2)

Z

Zone of indifference is the range of authoritative requests to which a subordinate is willing to respond without subjecting the directives to critical evaluation or judgment, hence to which the subordinate is indifferent. (10)

SUGGESTED READING

Part I: The New Work Environment

CHAPTER 1

Boyatzis, Richard E. *The Competent Manager.* New York: John Wiley, 1982.

Bradford, David L., and Allan R. Cohen. *Managing for Excellence.* New York: John Wiley, 1984.

Drucker, Peter F. *The New Realities.* New York: HarperCollins, 1989.

Kotter, John P. *The General Managers.* New York: Free Press, 1982.

Luthans, Fred, Richard M. Hodgetts, and Stuart A. Rosenkrantz. *Real Managers.* New York: HarperCollins, 1988.

CHAPTER 2

Cranny, Charles J., Patricia C. Smith, and Eugene F. Stone. *Job Satisfaction: How People Feel about Their Jobs, and How It Affects Their Performance.* New York: Lexington Books, 1992.

Gentile, Mary C. (ed.), *Differences That Work: Organizational Excellence Through Diversity.* Boston: Harvard Business School Press, 1994.

Hoffman, Gerald M. *The Technology Payoff: How to Profit with Empowered Workers in an Information Age.* Burr Ridge, Ill.: Irwin, 1994.

Lawler, Edward E. III. *Employee Involvement and Total Quality Management.* San Francisco: Jossey-Bass, 1990.

Senge, Peter M. *The Fifth Discipline.* New York: Doubleday, 1990.

CHAPTER 3

Austin, James A. *Managing in Developing Countries.* New York: Free Press, 1990.

Gannon, Martin J. and Associates. *Understanding Global Cultures: Metaphorical Journeys Through 17 Countries.* Thousand Oaks, Calif.: Sage, 1994.

Ohmae, Kenichi. *Borderless World.* New York: HarperCollins, 1990.

Redding, Gordon. *The Spirit of Chinese Capitalism.* London: Walter de Gruyter & Co., 1990.

Rehfeld, John E. *Alchemy of a Leader: Combining Western and Japanese Management Skills to Transform Your Company.* New York, John Wiley, 1994.

Part II: Individuals in Organizations

CHAPTER 4

Fernandez, John P. *Managing a Diverse Workforce.* Lexington, Mass.: Lexington Books, 1991.

Eden, Dov. *Pygmalion in Management: Productivity as a Self-Fulfilling Prophesy.* Lexington, Mass.: Lexington Books, 1990.

Jamieson, David, and Julie O'Mara. *Managing Workforce 2000.* San Francisco: Jossey-Bass, 1991.

Naisbitt, John, and Patricia Aburdene. *Megatrends 2000.* New York: Avon Books, 1990.

Newstrom, John W., and Jon L. Pierce. *Windows into Organizations.* New York: AMACOM, 1990.

Raelin, Joseph A. *Clash of Cultures: Managers and Professionals.* Cambridge, Mass.: Harvard University Press, 1986.

Wanous, John P. *Organizational Entry: Recruitment, Selection and Socialization of Newcomers.* Reading, Mass.: Addison-Wesley, 1980.

CHAPTER 5

Drucker, Peter. *Management: Tasks, Responsibilities, and Practices.* New York: HarperCollins, 1973.

Maslow, Abraham. *Motivation and Personality.* 2nd ed. New York: HarperCollins, 1970.

McGregor, Douglas. *The Human Side of Enterprise.* New York: McGraw-Hill, 1960.

Newstrom, John W., and Jon F. Pierce, *Windows into Organizations.* New York: AMACOM, 1990.

CHAPTER 6

Lawler, Edward E. III. *Strategic Pay: Aligning Organizational Strategies and Pay Systems.* San Francisco: Jossey-Bass, 1990.

Luthans, Fred, and Robert Kreitner. *Organizational Behavior Modification and Beyond.* Glenview, Ill.: Scott, Foresman, 1985.

Milkovich, George T., and A. K. Wigdor, eds. *Pay for Performance: Evaluating Performance Appraisal and Merit Pay.* Washington, D.C.: National Academy Press, 1991.

Newstrom, John W., and Jon L. Pierce. *Windows into Organizations.* New York: AMACOM, 1990.

CHAPTER 7

Cohen, Allan R., and Herman Gadon. *Alternative Work Schedules: Integrating Individual and Organizational Needs.* Reading, Mass.: Addison-Wesley, 1978.

Griffin, Ricky W. *Task Design: An Integrative Approach.* Glenville, Ill.: Scott, Foresman, 1982.

Locke, Edwin A., and Gary P. Latham. *A Theory of Goal Setting and Task Performance.* Englewood Cliffs, N.J.: Prentice-Hall, 1990.

Newstrom, John W., and Jon L. Pierce. *Windows into Organizations.* New York: AMACOM, 1990.

Schor, Juliet. *The Overworked American: The Unexpected Decline of Leisure.* New York: Basic Books, 1991.

Part III: Groups in Organizations

CHAPTER 8

Larson, Carl E., and Frank M. J. LaFasto. *Teamwork: What Must Go Right/What Can Go Wrong.* San Francisco: Jossey-Bass, 1989.

Parker, Glenn M. *Team Players and Teamwork: The New Competitive Strategy.* San Francisco: Jossey-Bass, 1990.

Tjosovold, Dean W. *Teamwork for Customers.* San Francisco: Jossey-Bass, 1992.

Tjosovold, Dean W., and Mary M. Tjosovold. *Leading the Team Organization: How to Create Enduring Competitive Advantage.* New York: Lexington Books, 1992.

CHAPTER 9

Burleson, Clyde W. *Effective Meetings: The Complete Guide.* New York: John Wiley, 1990.

Dyer, William G. *Team Building: Issues and Alternatives.* 2nd ed. Reading, Mass.: Addison-Wesley, 1987.

Harvey, Jerry B. *The Abilene Paradox and Other Meditations on Management.* Lexington, Mass.: Lexington Books, 1988.

Ketchum, Lyman D., and Eric Trist. *All Teams Are Not Created Equal: How Employee Empowerment Works.* Thousand Oaks, Calif.: Sage, 1992.

Phillips, Nicola. *Managing International Teams.* Burr Ridge, Ill.: Irwin, 1994.

Part IV: Processes in Organizations

CHAPTER 10

Block, Peter. *The Empowerment Manager.* San Francisco: Jossey-Bass, 1987.

Boulding, Kenneth E. *Three Faces of Power.* Newbury Park, Calif.: Sage, 1989.

Cohen, Allan R., and David L. Bradford. *Influence Without Authority.* New York: John Wiley, 1990.

Korda, Michael. *Power: How to Get It, How to Use It.* New York: Random House, 1975.

Kotter, John P. *A Force for Change: How Leadership Differs from Management.* New York: Free Press, 1990.

CHAPTER 11

Bass, Bernard M. *Bass & Stogdill's Handbook of Leadership.* New York: Free Press, 1990.

Bryman, Alan. *Charisma & Leadership in Organizations.* London: Sage, 1992.

DuPree, Max. *Leadership Is an Art.* East Lansing: Michigan State University Press, 1987.

Gardner, John W. *On Leadership.* New York: Free Press, 1989.

Kouzes, James M., and Barry Z. Posner. *The Lead-*

ership Challenge. San Francisco: Jossey-Bass, 1989.

Locke, Edwin A., and Associates. *The Essence of Leadership.* New York: Lexington/Macmillan, 1991.

CHAPTER 12

Agor, Weston H. *Intuition in Organizations.* Newbury Park, Calif.: Sage, 1989.

Bazerman, Max H. *Judgment in Managerial Decision Making,* 2nd ed. New York: John Wiley, 1990.

Huber, George. "Organizational Learning: The Contributing Process and the Literature," *Organization Science,* 2 (1): 88–115, 1991.

Nutt, Paul. *Making Tough Decisions.* San Francisco: Jossey-Bass, 1989.

CHAPTER 13

Bazerman, Max H., and Margaret A. Neale. *Negotiating Rationally.* New York: Free Press, 1991.

Hall, Lavinia, ed. *Negotiation: Strategies for Mutual Gain.* Thousand Oaks, Calif.: Sage, 1992.

Herrick, Neal Q. *Joint Management and Employee Participation: Labor and Management at the Crossroads.* San Francisco: Jossey-Bass, 1990.

Johnson, Ralph A. *Negotiation Basics: Concepts, Skills, and Exercises.* Thousand Oaks, Calif.: Sage, 1993.

Kolb, Deborah M., and Jean Bartunek, eds. *Hidden Conflict in Organizations: Uncovering Behind the Scenes Disputes.* Thousand Oaks, Calif.: Sage, 1992.

Part V: Organizations

CHAPTER 14

Chandler, Alfred D. Jr. *Strategy and Structure: Chapters in the History of American Industrial Enterprise.* Cambridge, Mass.: MIT Press, 1962.

Davis, Stanley M., Paul R. Lawrence, Harvey Kolodny, and Michael Beer. *Matrix.* Reading, Mass.: Addison-Wesley, 1977.

Mintzberg, Henry. *The Structuring of Organizations.* Englewood Cliffs, N.J.: Prentice-Hall, 1986.

Morgan, Gareth. *Images of Organizations.* Newbury Park, Calif.: Sage, 1986.

Quinn, James B. *Intelligent Enterprise: A Knowledge and Service Based Paradigm for Industry.* New York: The Free Press, 1982.

CHAPTER 15

Osborn, R. N., J. G. Hunt, and L. R. Jauch. *Organization Theory.* New York: John Wiley, 1980.

Weber, Max. *The Theory of Social and Economic Organization,* trans. A. M. Henderson and H. T. Parsons. New York: The Free Press, 1957.

CHAPTER 16

Schein, Edgar H. *Organizational Culture and Leadership.* San Francisco: Jossey-Bass, 1985.

Trace, Harrison M., and Janice M. Beyer. *The Cultures of Work Organizations.* Englewood Cliffs, N.J.: Prentice-Hall, 1993.

CHAPTER 17

Coates, Joseph F., Jennifer Jarratt, and John B. Mahaffie. *Future Work: Seven Critical Forces Reshaping Work and the Work Force in North America.* San Francisco: Jossey-Bass, 1990.

Davenport, Thomas H. *Process Innovation: Reengineering Work Through Information Technology.* Boston: Harvard Business School Press, 1992.

Kanter, Rosabeth Moss, Barry Stein, and Todd D. Jick. *The Challenges of Organizational Change: How Companies Experience It and How Leaders Guide It.* New York: Free Press, 1992.

Peters, Tom. *Liberation Management.* New York: Knopf, 1992.

Strebel, Paul. *Breakpoints: How Managers Exploit Radical Business Change.* Boston: Harvard Business School Press, 1992.

I N D E X